END OF A WAR

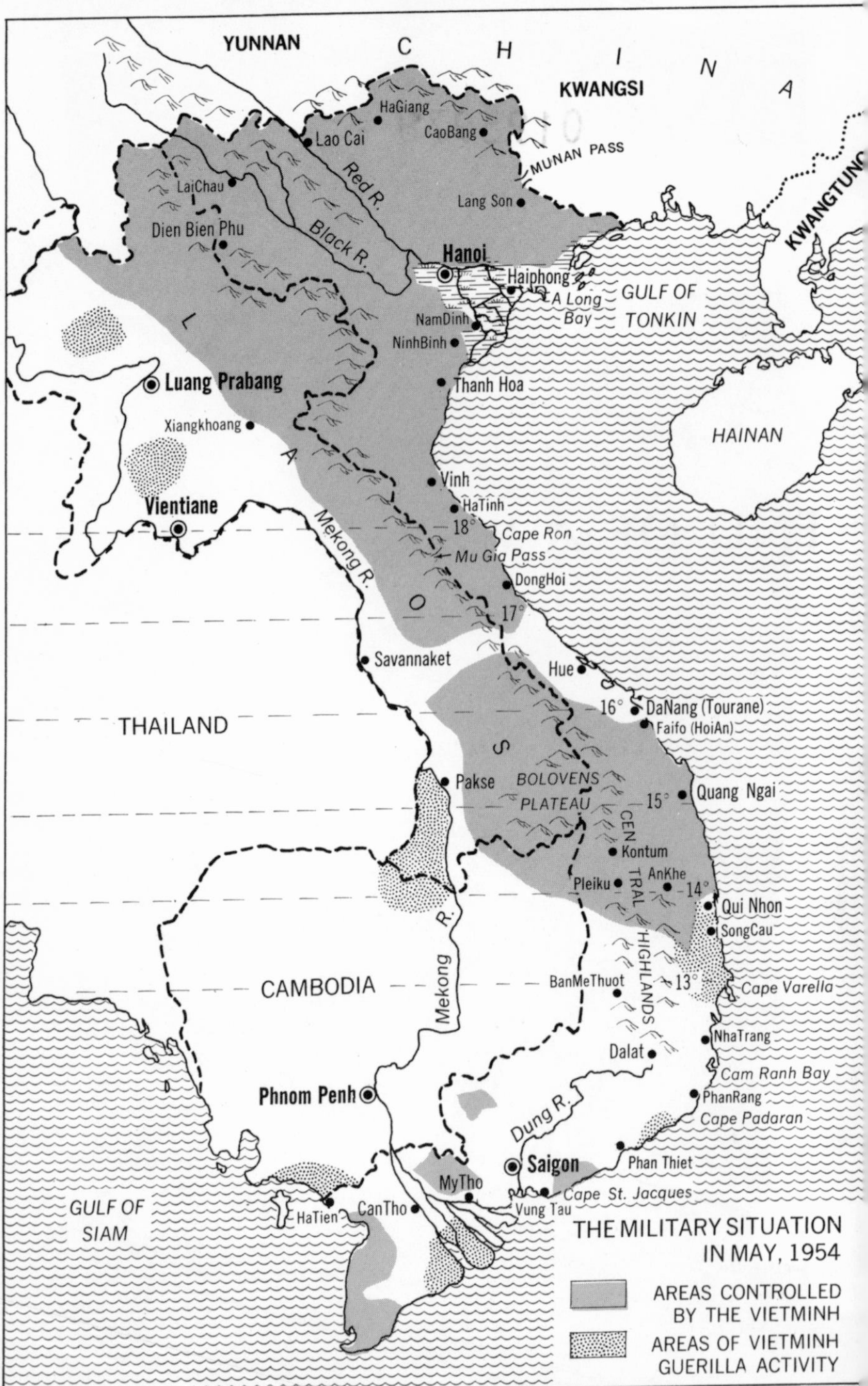

YUNNAN
C H I N A
KWANGSI
KWANGTUNG
HaGiang
Lao Cai
CaoBang
MUNAN PASS
LaiChau
Red R.
Lang Son
Dien Bien Phu
Black R.
Hanoi
Haiphong
A Long Bay
GULF OF TONKIN
NamDinh
NinhBinh
Luang Prabang
Thanh Hoa
L A O S
Xiangkhoang
HAINAN
Vinh
Vientiane
HaTinh
18°
Cape Ron
Mekong R.
Mu Gia Pass
DongHoi
17°
Savannaket
Hue
16°
DaNang (Tourane)
THAILAND
Faifo (HoiAn)
Pakse
BOLOVENS PLATEAU
15°
Quang Ngai
CENTRAL HIGHLANDS
Kontum
Pleiku
AnKhe
14°
Qui Nhon
SongCau
CAMBODIA
BanMeThuot
13°
Cape Varella
Mekong R.
NhaTrang
Dalat
Cam Ranh Bay
Phnom Penh
PhanRang
Dung R.
Cape Padaran
Saigon
Phan Thiet
MyTho
Cape St. Jacques
Vung Tau
GULF OF SIAM
HaTien
CanTho
THE MILITARY SITUATION IN MAY, 1954
AREAS CONTROLLED BY THE VIETMINH
AREAS OF VIETMINH GUERILLA ACTIVITY

END OF A WAR

Indochina, 1954

Philippe Devillers

AND

Jean Lacouture

PM

PALL MALL PRESS
London

Published in Great Britain in 1969 by
The Pall Mall Press Limited
5, Cromwell Place, London, S.W.7

Translated by Alexander Lieven and Adam Roberts

SBN 269 67173 0

Printed in the United States of America

FOREWORD

This book was written in 1959, and published in France in the beginning of 1960, before the creation of the National Liberation Front, while Ngo Dinh Diem's regime was countering sporadic guerrilla attacks with the discreet assistance of the United States. No serious observer thought that the situation was stabilized, but the war between revolutionary Vietnamese nationalism and French colonialism had come to an end, and a whole phase of history had ended with it. The book was entitled *End of a War: Indochina 1954*, because the authors wanted to describe the procedure by which a war is terminated and the first, tentative possibilities of coexistence are created.

Nine years later, this book is being published in English, while the United States, in its turn, attempts to disengage itself from its own counterrevolutionary crusade in Vietnam. However, there are considerable differences between the French edition and this English version. Part I, describing how their battlefield reverses and their diplomatic isolation forced the French to negotiate, and Part II, describing the talks at Geneva between April and July, 1954, have been translated without substantive changes.

Part III is entirely new. In the French edition, this section (entitled "The Harvest of the Truce") described the changing situation in Laos, Cambodia, and the two zones of Vietnam between 1954 and 1960. In the present edition, Philippe Devillers explains how France's Asian responsibilities were transferred to the United States between July, 1954, and January, 1955. What he describes is in fact a transition in the war; this operation, which began discreetly at a technical level, demonstrates a continuity whose pattern and components are more easily seen today.

The original title has been retained, because it suited a book that was intended to describe history, not to forecast it. But if we were to write a book today about the Geneva negotiations, we would certainly give it a less definitive title. It is now clear that, although the torch actually passed from Paris to Washington during the period described in Part III, this process had begun much earlier, and the transfer of responsibilities had been in progress for many a long year.

The Geneva conference did not end a war in 1954. It merely marked the abandonment of the fight by one of the contenders—France. For the others, especially the Vietnamese and the Americans, it only provided a pause, a breathing space. Instead of using this intermission to work for the peaceful reunification of Vietnam in accordance with the Geneva agreements, the South Vietnamese and their American allies chose to resume the anti-Communist crusade which had just brought defeat to Bao Dai and his French allies. The war was to start again or, rather, flare up after the truce.

A French general and a Vietminh political commissar signed the military cease-fire agreements at Geneva on July 20, 1954. The Indochina war—"the French war"—was over, but the Vietnam war—"the American war"—had actually been in progress for more than four years.

In 1944–45, at the dawn of the Vietnamese national revolution, the anticolonialism of the Roosevelt era led some of General Wedemeyer's units to collaborate for several months with the rising Vietminh movement, first against the Japanese and later against the French forces in Indochina. But thereafter, the United States gradually changed sides.

In September, 1945, less than six months after Roosevelt's death, the State Department informed the French Government that it would do nothing to jeopardize French sovereignty in Indochina. It took America four more years to move from this uneasy neutrality to an attitude of active sympathy. The actual change of policy, in 1949, stemmed primarily from Dean Acheson's determination to cement France more firmly into the Atlantic alliance, but some of his colleagues also wanted to strengthen Western resistance to the Chinese revolution.

A year later, the vicissitudes of the Korean War made these concerns more pressing, and during his visit to Washington in September, 1952, General de Lattre used them as the basis for urging a coherent strategy: the joint crusade against Asian Communism.

The Vietnamese revolutionaries denounced American intervention without waiting for such public indications of it; they feared it more than the actions of a nation as weakened as France. As early as March 19, 1950, crowds in Saigon demonstrated against American intervention in answer to a call from a group of Leftist leaders: among them was Nguyen Huu Tho, now Chairman of the National Liberation Front. In February, 1951, three years before Geneva, Ho Chi Minh stated that the Americans were the real enemies of the Vietnamese revolution and the French were no more than their mercenaries. And, indeed, the war was financed by Washington during the three years that followed.

Thus, it was not surprising that, when Dien Bien Phu was threatened in April, 1954, the French Government asked its American ally for direct intervention in the form of an air attack against the Vietminh positions by several hundred U.S. bombers. The American Government, heeding warnings from London and from a majority of the U.S. Senate, twice refused to accept the risks inherent in Operation Vulture, as this proposed attack was called. John Foster Dulles worked out an alternative strategy: his imperiled French allies, now somewhat of an embarrassment to him, would be left to their own devices, forced to halt the Communist onslaught as best they could. The anti-Communist counterattack could then be prepared and launched from that part of South Vietnam that was salvaged by the West in the cease-fire agreements. Dulles made this point on June 3, six weeks before the agreements were concluded . . . but now we are back within the framework of the present book.

Certainly the two conflicts cannot be treated as though they were completely identical. But with every passing day, the underlying continuity has become more evident. France fought to retain its influence in Vietnam through a ruling class tied to its interests; the United States launched its expeditionary force to secure victory for counterrevolution and to show the whole Third World that opting for the Marxist road to progress draws the vengeance of the Lord. A single thread of history links the two campaigns.

America's position in the world in 1968 has little in common with that of France in 1954; Dean Rusk's view of the world certainly differs from Bidault's, and General Abrams's war maps bear little resemblance to those of General Navarre. Nevertheless, the similarities between the two conflicts are stronger than the differences:

1. In both cases, the Western power tried in vain to convert the Vietnamese people to the regime, the leadership, and the way of progress it had chosen for them.
2. In both cases, the Western power ignored the profound, fundamental, and biological unity of the Vietnamese people and persisted in maintaining geographic and ideological frontiers which the Vietnamese themselves rejected.
3. In both cases, the Westerners claimed they were fighting a Communist invasion fomented by Moscow or Peking, and refused to recognize the essentially Vietnamese nature of the opposing Vietminh or Vietcong cause.
4. In both cases, the Western expeditionary corps (though certainly better supported by local allies in 1968 than in 1954) was patently alien to the country and was opposed by the great majority of the people and all the forces of nature—jungles, monsoons, swamps, malaria, and even the rhythm of life.

Will a similar war end in a similar peace settlement? There are great differences between the two powers that have intervened in Vietnam, just as there are differences between the Vietminh of 1954 and the Hanoi-NLF partnership of 1968. But the similarities between the two conflicts—or, better, the two phases of the conflict—seem to open the way to similar methods of settlement. That is why we believe that, now, our book has more than a purely historical interest. That is also why we feel as responsible now, as Frenchmen, as we did when we wrote it in 1959: for this war that refuses to end is still the war that French forces started more than twenty years ago and that French diplomats failed to end in 1946 and 1954.

May this book serve as a reminder that, if there can be no secure peace without a respect for treaties, neither can there be a war without an end.

JEAN LACOUTURE

Paris
January, 1969

Chapters 1-7, 9-12, 14, and 24-29 are by Philippe Devillers; chapters 8, 13, and 15-23 are by Jean Lacouture.

CONTENTS

Foreword v

PART I: FROM COLONIAL EXPEDITION TO WORLD CONFLICT

1 *Seven Years of Blindness* 3
2 *Light at the End of the Tunnel* 22
3 *The Road to Negotiation* 47
4 *The Pleven Mission* 60
5 *Operation Vulture* 71
6 *On the Brink* 90
7 *Between the Unattainable and the Unacceptable* 100

PART II: THE GENEVA CONFERENCE

8 *A Lakeside Rendezvous* 121
9 *The Two of Clubs and the Three of Diamonds* 132
10 *Bidault and Dong Lay Down Their Cards* 151

11 *Military Moves in Indochina* 171
12 *Bidault's Trump Card* 186
13 *Toward Partition* 200
14 *Washington Backs Out* 210
15 *Bidault Leaves the Game* 225
16 *Vietminh and Chinese Initiatives* 232
17 *Mendès-France: One Month To Make Peace* 243
18 *A Disappointing Tête-à-Tête with the Vietminh* 259
19 *Bringing the English and the Americans into France's Game* 266
20 *Scaling the Parallels* 275
21 *One Hundred and Sixty Hours To Go* 284
22 *The Clocks of the Palais des Nations* 295
23 *The Compromise* 301

PART III: AMERICA TAKES OVER

24 *The Manila Pact* 317
25 *France's Associate* 329
26 *The Sainteny Mission* 352
27 *Transfers of Power* 361
28 *The Creation of a Dictator* 382
29 *Full Circle* 394

Bibliography 399
Index 405

I

FROM COLONIAL EXPEDITION TO WORLD CONFLICT

1

SEVEN YEARS OF BLINDNESS

On February 18, 1954, in snow-covered Berlin, the sixth Four Power conference ended. For four weeks, France, Britain, America, and Russia had tried in vain to find a solution to the problem of German reunification and disarmament. For Europe, it was stalemate once again, but the Four Powers had moved to break their deadlock in Asia. This was not because they had arranged to meet at Geneva on April 26 "with a view to attaining a peaceful settlement of the Korean question," but because they had decided to examine "the problem of re-establishing peace in Indochina" as well.

For the first time, the war in Indochina was to be the subject of high-level talks. Both sides had shown a desire to negotiate, and it seemed that there was some chance of a solution at last.

Eight years earlier, on March 18, 1946, General Leclerc had entered Hanoi and re-established the French presence in Tonkin—but only after the signature of an agreement with the Vietnamese government of national union (led by Ho Chi Minh) guaranteeing the freedom of the Democratic Republic of Vietnam (D.R.V.) within the French Union. A clever negotiation, coupled with a military threat, had led to this achievement that was hailed by Asia and the world as a triumph of French wisdom. France, then, won credit as the first of the Western powers to acknowledge the trend of political and social developments in Asia.

But only nine months later, however, the war broke out again, and from then on it raged for nearly eight years. By February, 1954, French troops had been forced onto the defensive throughout Indochina by the Vietnamese People's Army (VPA), led by Vo Nguyen Giap. The equivalent of a whole division was surrounded at Dien Bien Phu, and the VPA had invaded several provinces in neighboring Laos. Because of what it was costing France in men and money, and because of the symbolic character it had assumed, the Indochina war had become France's most pressing problem, and its solution took precedence over everything else.

But however deep its political and psychological significance, the war was far from clearly understood even at late as the beginning of 1954.[1] France's war aims were expressed only in vague terms of "We cannot let . . ." Admittedly there were many variations on the theme: "We cannot let these natives govern themselves, they are not capable of it. We have a civilizing mission. . . ." "We cannot let the empire built up by Gallieni and Doumer be torn apart. . . ." "We cannot let these lovable people fall under the domination of convicts and terrorists, or [a little later] Communists in the pay of Moscow, or [later still] the satellites of China. . . ." "We cannot let Southeast Asia be cut off from the Free World: there are Catholic minorities living there, and besides, it supplies the West with tin, rubber, and much of its rice." This defensive, paternalistic, and negative mythology could arouse no trust or enthu-

[1] In a lecture in March, 1957, General Navarre, the penultimate French commander in chief in Indochina, stated unequivocally: "We had no policy at all. . . . After seven years of war we were in a complete imbroglio, and no one, from private to commander in chief, knew just why we were fighting.

"Was it to maintain French positions? If so, which ones? Was it simply to participate, under the American umbrella, in the 'containment' of Communism in Southeast Asia? Then why did we continue to make such an effort when our interest had practically ceased to exist?

"This uncertainty about our political aims kept us from having a continuing and coherent military policy in Indochina. . . . This rift between policy and strategy dominated the entire Indochina war."

siasm—except perhaps in a handful of military officers when, for a few months, General de Lattre de Tassigny, as commander in chief and high commissioner, gave it a certain style. What was needed was a clear understanding of the situation.

The "troubles" had begun in 1945. On the evening of March 9, the Japanese forces in Indochina, after being warned by a somewhat noisy anti-Japanese resistance movement, suddenly crushed the French administration with which they had coexisted since 1940. Two days later, the Japanese had the Vietnamese emperor Bao Dai proclaim the independence of Vietnam, and on March 12 the young King Norodom Sihanouk similarly declared the independence of neighboring Cambodia.

An independence granted by Japan under the pressure of wartime circumstances did not appeal to those who realized that the fall of the Third Reich would inevitably be followed by the defeat of Japan. But the word "independence" stirred so many memories, obliterated so many humiliations, and embodied so many of the hopes of the Vietnamese nationalists who had been struggling for two generations, that even the tainted pledge of the Japanese acted as a powerful catalyst. Inflamed by forceful propaganda, Vietnam's youth rose up, determined to fight, even after the defeat of Japan, for the independence that had just been returned to their country by an accident of history.

Within four months, the first Vietnamese government, headed by Tran Trong Kim, had succeeded in obtaining from the Japanese the transfer of most of the French administrative services; the dissolution of the Gouvernement Général, which had administered all of French Indochina, was secured in July; and Vietnam was reunited at the beginning of August when the Japanese permitted the return of Cochin China to Vietnam. The architect of this success was the Minister of Foreign Affairs, Tran Van Chuong; nine years later, we shall encounter him in the government of Ngo Dinh Diem. The leaders of the youth movement were Phan Anh, Ta Quang Buu, and Dr. Pham Ngoc Thach; they too will reappear later, but on the side of Ho Chi Minh's Vietminh.

When Japan surrendered on August 15, 1945, the Vietnamese

nationalist movement was well under way, and the wind had by now blown up into a tempest. On August 20, Bao Dai, though scarcely renowned as an innovator, expressed the feelings of his countrymen with unforgettable clarity in a message to General de Gaulle:

> You have suffered enough for four disastrous years to understand that the people of Vietnam, with twenty centuries of glorious history behind them, no longer want, and can no longer tolerate, any foreign domination or administration.
>
> You would understand better if you could see what is happening here, if you could feel the desire for independence which burns in every heart, and which no human force can now extinguish. Even if you should manage to re-establish a French administration here, it would no longer be obeyed: each village would be a nest of resistance, each former collaborator an enemy, and your officials and colonials themselves would beg to be freed from this asphyxiating atmosphere.
>
> I beg you to understand that the only way to safeguard French interests and the spiritual influence of France in Indochina is to recognize openly the independence of Vietnam and to renounce all ideas of re-establishing French sovereignty or any form of French administration. We could so easily understand each other and become friends, if you would drop this claim to be our masters once again.
>
> We appeal to the well-known idealism of the French people and the great wisdom of their leader, and hope that peace and joy, which are the prerogative of all the nations of the world, will be assured for all the inhabitants of Indochina, natives and foreigners alike.[2]

Riding the tidal wave of nationalist enthusiasm, a new and little-known political force, claiming it had the support of the conquering Allies, seized power. On August 19, only four days after the Japanese surrender, this force seized control in Hanoi; on August 23, it won the support of Emperor Bao Dai in Hue; and on September 2, it proclaimed the independence of the Democratic Republic of

[2] *Viet-Nam Tan Bao* (Hue), August 20, 1945, quoted in Philippe Devillers, *Histoire du Viêt-Nam de 1940 à 1952* (Paris, 1952), p. 138. De Gaulle was then President of the French Government.

Vietnam (D.R.V.). This new force was called the Vietminh, or the Vietnam Liberation Front, and it was dominated and controlled by Communists—a fact that was bound to influence later events.[3]

To most of those who lived through the Vietminh's "August Revolution" of 1945, or who had been able to follow events closely, it was clear that what had just happened was irreversible; the old French regime could never be brought back. But did anyone in France understand this? On March 24, 1945, believing that it was making a generous gesture, and completely ignoring the independence just granted by Japan, General de Gaulle's government had published a charter promising the whole of Indochina a vague political and economic autonomy within a federal framework. It was as bearers of this irrelevant text that French officials arrived in Saigon in September to "liberate" Indochina from a Japanese occupation of which it was already relieved.

Inevitably, the returning colonial power had to resort to armed force. France and the French had been humiliated, insulted, and ridiculed in Vietnam since March 9—by a mob, and in sight of everybody there. The French felt they had to make a dazzling show of strength, to prove that France was still a great power, that it had the resources to take action if necessary, and above all that it would protect those under its jurisdiction. In these circumstances, the landing of an armored force and seasoned units in Saigon during September and October, 1945, was considered a necessity.

But some people looked beyond this flurry of activity. This first contact with armed Vietnamese nationalism proved to some intelligent French officers that their show of strength had to lead to something new, that in itself it was meaningless. After four months of fighting in Cochin China and South Annam, and four months of analyzing the Vietnamese forces which were taking shape in the north, the more far-sighted military leaders saw that they could not hope to re-create the pre-war regime or even to establish the autonomous Vietnamese government implied in the French Gov-

[3] Devillers, *op. cit.*, p. 135. At least seven of the ten members of the Vietnamese People's Liberation Committee were Communists. And of the fifteen members of the provisional government formed on August 29, 1945, at least ten were Communists.

ernment's charter of March 24. Events were moving in a quite different direction. For political as well as military reasons—the weakness of his forces, the risk of a massacre of the French in Tonkin, the vital necessity of preventing a Sino-Vietnamese collaboration—General Philippe Leclerc, commander of the French forces in Indochina, and his staff wanted to sign an agreement with the Ho Chi Minh government *before* the planned landing of French forces at Haiphong. It was not simply a question of a short-term expedient. He needed a basis for lasting cooperation with responsible Vietnamese authorities who were known to the populace, who would be strong enough not to have to rule by demagoguery, and who would be capable of checking extremism and keeping a pledge to associate a free Vietnam with a renovated French "community"—the word was already being used, even in the Vietminh press. An agreement with the Vietminh was needed, and it was reached.

The Franco-Vietnamese agreement of March 6, 1946—coming one week after a convention providing for the rapid evacuation of the Chinese troops which had been occupying Vietnam north of the 16th Parallel—was thus signed in Hanoi on the very day of the French landing at Haiphong by Jean Sainteny, French Commissioner for Northern Indochina, and by the President and Vice-President of the Government of the Democratic Republic of Vietnam, the Communist Ho Chi Minh and the nationalist Vu Hong Khanh. Under the terms of this agreement, Vietnam would be a free state, a member of both an Indochinese federation and the French Union. It would have its own government, its own parliament, its own army, and its own finances. A referendum would be held to determine whether Cochin China would be part of the new state.

One month later, on April 3, the political agreement was complemented by a Franco-Vietnamese military pact, signed by General Salan of France and the Vietnamese Defense Minister, Vo Nguyen Giap. Under its terms, the Vietnamese army was to receive aid from France for its training, its leadership program, and its matériel. For five years, the French Army would occupy bases, mainly on the Chinese frontier, together with Vietnamese units.

At the end of the five years, when the Vietnamese were prepared to relieve them, the French would evacuate Vietnam.

Thus, the outlines of a political settlement had been defined less than six months after the return of the first French units to Saigon, without much bloodshed and without much effort on the part of the French. It was the army that had opened the way to a liberal policy it considered both just and profitable. In a now-famous report dated March 27, 1946, General Leclerc stated that the March 6 agreement was the best that could be hoped for in the circumstances. He urged his government to take advantage of the favorable atmosphere to define the terms of a permanent relationship—even if they had to mention the word "independence." It was necessary not only to persuade Vietnam to give its allegiance to a new community, but also to relieve the French Army as soon as possible. After five years of war and occupation, said General Leclerc, France had better things to do than to bog down its army 7,500 miles away from home in rice fields and jungles. A country must tailor its policies to fit its means, and France must concentrate on building a modern army that would enable it to recover its place in Europe.

But the army, during this period, was once again the silent partner within the French Government. General Leclerc was branded as an appeaser by some supporters of the "policy of grandeur"; his mission ended, he made way for the politicians. He had put France in a position to work with the forces of Asian nationalism toward common goals. In Vietnam, he had made French technology, commerce, and civilization acceptable to a movement that had all too many reasons for turning to China, the Soviet Union, or the United States.[4]

It rapidly became clear that Leclerc, Sainteny, and their advisers —Colonel Repiton-Preneuf and Léon Pignon—had not been lis-

[4] A secret Vietminh order, dated March 7, 1946, said in part: "We must renounce forthwith systematic hostility toward France. Our nation's struggle now runs parallel with that of France, just as before it ran parallel with China's. . . . Our only enemy is the French party of *reaction*." Quoted by Devillers, *op. cit.*, p. 231.

tened to in Paris. Even though one-third of the French Government was Communist (and, naturally, opposed to conflict with Ho Chi Minh), France still had not accepted the idea of a confederation of sovereign nations, equal in law, with itself as the head, guide, and "eldest nation." The delegates of the Hanoi government were forced to recognize this fact during the Franco-Vietnamese talks at Dalat (April, 1946) and Fontainebleau (August). They were aware that almost all their opposite numbers could think of Vietnam only as a satellite within an Indochinese federation, whose services would be entirely controlled from Paris and whose ruler would be the French high commissioner. Not only would this federation be responsible at the local level for the currency, customs, defense, and economic development (all essential attributes of sovereignty), but, at a higher level, it would be absorbed into a French Union, directed at the summit according to a constitution drawn up and passed unilaterally by the parliament of the one and only République Française.[5] The liberty that Paris was proposing was clearly a restricted one, and none of the Vietnamese could misunderstand that. After the first elation had subsided, Ho Chi Minh and his colleagues realized that the French objective was not to implement the terms of the Hanoi agreement of March 6, but rather to take back, step by step, some of the concessions made in it.

Thus, in Paris, the three-party government blocked the way to a possible reconciliation between the two nations and frustrated the beginnings of cooperation. At the same time, in Saigon, the French administration under the aegis of Admiral Thierry d'Argenlieu sponsored the autonomous "Republic of Cochin China" in obvious rivalry with Ho Chi Minh's Democratic Republic of Vietnam in the north, and in direct violation of the spirit of the March 6 agreement. At the request of Marius Moutet, socialist Minister for Overseas Territories,[6] the administration also gave the

[5] General Navarre was to put it even more frankly in March, 1957, when he said: "We went back after the war to re-establish if not the colonial regime, at least something like it—the French Union formula of 1946."

[6] Dispatches of March 11 and 14, 1946.

go-ahead for the military occupation of the central highlands.[7]

Thus, the French view of Franco-Vietnamese relations became narrow and short-sighted, and the way in which policies were executed in Saigon seemed increasingly like a clear and direct sabotage of the agreements: The summer of 1946 was to see the ruination of all the hopes which the spring had awakened.

One result of this policy was to weaken the position of those leaders of the Democratic Republic of Vietnam who had decided to go along with France (Communists like Ho Chi Minh and Pham Van Dong, nationalists like Hoang Minh Giam, Phan Anh, and Trinh Van Binh), and to confirm the fears of "leftist" radicals such as Hoang Quoc Viet, Tran Huy Lieu, and Dang Xuan Khu. The latter all thought that it was useless and even dangerous to negotiate with France, because they knew that sooner or later the former colonizers would try to take back by force what they had yielded under pressure of necessity.

Unfortunately, events in Indochina after the beginning of August, 1946, appeared to justify these fears: French troops occupied public buildings; customs controls were progressively tightened; federal institutions were established without consultation; and, finally, in November, incidents in Haiphong brought down the terrible naval bombardment of November 23, carried out by order of the new Commander in Chief, General Valluy, to "teach the Vietminh a good lesson."[8]

December 19, 1946, saw the end of the period in which some form of working relationship between France and the young Democratic Republic of Vietnam nationalists had seemed possible. Spurred on by the extremists, the Vietnamese Tu Ve (militia) in Hanoi attacked French districts and seized French civilians to serve as hostages during the new crisis. The following day, French troops relieved the attacked districts and drove the Vietnamese government to take refuge a few miles to the west, near Hadong.

Was this a major incident or a final breakdown? The first theory

[7] This vast area covers two-thirds of Vietnam south of the 17th Parallel. It is also known as the Montagnard Plateaus, and as the Moi Plateaus, after the Moi people, who number more than 1 million and inhabit these regions.

[8] Telegram to Colonel Dèbes, November 22, 1946.

is worth examining if one is to judge the behavior of the Ho Chi Minh government in the two months that followed, its repeated offers of negotiation, and the contacts it made with French officials. The truth is that the French local authorities wanted to hear no more of this man, who was disqualified as a negotiator, as far as they were concerned, by the actions of December 19.[9]

The French opponents of the March 6 agreement were triumphant. They put forward an argument which from then on was to serve as an explanation and justification of errors already committed and still to be committed: France could concede nothing whatsoever to a Communist-controlled Vietnamese government. The whole structure of the French Union would be undermined, the worm would be in the apple, accredited representatives of a foreign (not to say hostile) power would participate in secret debates in the Elysée Palace. This was an unthinkable prospect, it was later said.[10]

But this argument ignored the fact that every French government during that period (whether that of Gouin, Bidault, or Ramadier) contained many Communists. It also ignored the fact that the Vietnamese government which signed the agreement of March 6, 1946, although headed by the Communist Ho Chi Minh, contained a strong minority of non-Communist nationalists, who could have challenged the Marxists if given the chance to prove that a policy of entente with France was possible and profitable.

Quite the opposite happened. In the elation of the first months of collaboration, the French army had in fact helped the Vietminh under General Giap to crush its opponents, the pro-American nationalists, whose leaders had been forced to take refuge in China. The French then stood by and watched the gradual transformation of the Democratic Republic of Vietnam into a totalitarian regime. Yet, because of France's refusal to fulfill Vietnamese nationalist aspirations, the nationalists remained allied to

[9] An interview with Admiral d'Argenlieu in *France-Soir* (Paris), January 2, 1947, and Directive No. 9 of January 4, 1947, by Léon Pignon, Political Adviser to Admiral Thierry d'Argenlieu.

[10] Conversation with Maurice Schumann, April 1, 1959.

the Communists in a battle in which patriotic considerations were uppermost.

Clearly, the French misunderstood the unique character of the Vietminh. No other party in the recent history of the international Communist movement had been prepared to sacrifice "its own interests to those of the race" and had voluntarily dissolved itself. But this is just what the Indochinese Communist Party did on November 11, 1945—thereby laying itself open to accusations of deviationism from foreign Communist movements for years thereafter.

The Communist-led Vietnamese government was swept away on December 20, 1946, by the renewed hostilities which it had, in part, provoked. If the dialogue had been taken further, a fresh start might have been made, with new participants. In fairness to Admiral d'Argenlieu, it must be said that he wanted to try this new experiment, either with a nationalist such as Ngo Dinh Diem or with the ex-emperor Bao Dai. He was not to blame for the murkiness of French policy at that time.[11]

By refusing, right up until 1936, to allow any nationalist activity within the colonial framework, the Third French Republic had prevented the Vietnamese from establishing open and legal organizations and had thereby helped to embed revolutionary Communism firmly within the heart of the Vietnamese nationalism.

The only way of preventing the irrevocable identification of Communism with patriotism, which had been developing over fifteen years, was to solve the national problem. This became clear to General Leclerc during a later mission to Indochina in January, 1947. He confided to Colonel Repiton-Preneuf: "Anti-Communism will be a lever without a fulcrum so long as the national problem remains unresolved."

[11] Marius Moutet, Minister for Overseas Territories, refused to negotiate with Ho Chi Minh or to capture him. In a note dated February 12, 1947, Admiral d'Argenlieu divulged the exact spot where the members of the Vietminh government were hiding; it was a canyon near Ha Dong. A parachute operation, closing up the two ends of the hiding place, would have permitted the capture of Ho Chi Minh and his colleagues. But Moutet would not give his consent. The French Government, he replied, would not behave like bandits and gangsters.

In his opinion, the solution had to be found quickly. In spite of what certain people seemed to think,[12] time was not on France's side.

Future historians will be astounded that this fundamental aspect of the Indochinese question was apparently not understood by any of the governments from 1947 to 1953, from the departure of Léon Blum to the inauguration of Joseph Laniel.

When the responsibility for Indochinese policy passed from the SFIO[13] to the MRP[14] in November, 1947, and the French Government, after various maneuverings, was free to deal with a Vietnamese "national" government (that is, with leaders who did not owe their allegiance to Communism), it became obvious that it had not been Ho Chi Minh's Marxism as such that had prevented Paris from making the essential concessions at the right time. Nationalism was the problem.

On the two basic themes of unity and independence, Bao Dai immediately confronted France with the same claims as Ho Chi Minh: the restoration of Cochin China and the central highlands to Vietnamese rule, a separate army and diplomatic corps, and the lifting of federal controls and arrangements such as customs unions.

A realistic policy would undoubtedly have been based on an assessment of all the material and psychological advantages of a rapid and generous settlement giving satisfaction to the Viet-

[12] In his press conference of November 17, 1948, General de Gaulle, President of the RPF (Rassemblement du Peuple Français, founded the year before), said: "The rule to follow in Indochina at present is not to do anything rash. We must take our time. We must stick it out. Why should we be in such a hurry? Some day the French solution will be adopted—the solution which I myself put forward as early as March, 1945: to talk, when possible, with all who are truly representative of Indochina, provided that they are not enemies of France." Frédéric-Dupont, however, wrote somewhat later that, "In an insurrection, time is always on the side of the insurgents." Edouard Frédéric-Dupont, *Mission de la France en Asie* (Paris, 1956), p. 197.

[13] SFIO: Section Française de l'International Ouvrière—a union of socialists brought together in 1905 through the mediation of the Second International; known generally as the Socialist Party.

[14] MRP: Mouvement Républicain Populaire—a progressive Catholic Party born out of the pre–World War II Popular Democrats.

namese. This would have restored their confidence in France, and permitted the establishment of a Vietnamese state of international standing which might have been able to separate its patriotic prestige from the political and military actions of the Vietminh.

But when the MRP, taking over the reins in Indochina, barred the Vietminh from any negotiations and persuaded the French Government to adopt the "Bao Dai solution," what followed was simply a long, tragic, and disappointing attempt to reconcile the irreconcilable.

In a secret protocol which Bollaert managed to get Bao Dai to sign on December 7, 1947, at a meeting on the Bay of Along, it was clearly stated that France would recognize the independence of Vietnam and that it was up to the Vietnamese to unify their country. But this concession was balanced by numerous limitations imposed on Vietnam in the military, diplomatic, economic, and financial sectors. The nationalists grouped around Ngo Dinh Diem were quite justified in calling it a "gimcrack independence," and even Bao Dai had to go back on his acceptance of this document. But France went on trying to impose such limitations on Bao Dai for years. The French did not realize that in so doing they were destroying the remaining prestige of the very man they wanted to use to oppose the Vietminh.

It was not until May 20, 1948, that a provisional central government for all of Vietnam was formed under French auspices as a counterweight to the Democratic Republic of Vietnam. And not until April, 1949, did France agree to transfer Cochin China to Baodaist Vietnam officially (after the semblance of referendum). Only then did the signing of a mediocre agreement at the Elysée Palace oblige Bao Dai to return at last to Vietnam and take over the direction of the state.

Meanwhile, the Vietminh used France's reticence, tricks, and delays to convince the people that it alone struggled for true independence, while the others were mere puppets of the French. Far from having "promoted" a non-Communist nationalism in Vietnam, the leaders of the MRP had in fact ruined many nationalists and forced others to take a stand against the French in order to hold the attention of the masses.

It should be realized that Bao Dai was accepted by the French, given the trappings of power, and protected only insofar as he presided over a palace regime; furthermore, Bao Dai was a man whose material needs made him easy to manipulate. The "ruler" was thus tied to the protective authority—hence, his obstinate refusal to consider any reform that might give the regime a popular, even representative, foundation, in the absence of elections. As power was held only through Bao Dai, no Vietnamese prime minister could enforce his own ideas.

At the same time, the French political parties were waging a relentless battle for control, through intermediaries, of the Vietnamese rulers. This was the only real cause of the famous "affair of the generals" over the Revers report.[15]

What France now had as a partner was not an "entirely separate" state, but a satellite. And everything was vitiated by this basic political mistake. Satellites are never good investments. France had set up Bao Dai against Ho Chi Minh to counter the Communists. But it failed to give him the trump cards necessary for success: independence, an army, and international standing.

In such circumstances it was unrealistic to make Vietnam enter the war on the French side. The stigma of collaboration doomed the Bao Dai regime to failure. And, compared with the battle for independence and liberty being waged by the Vietminh, the future offered by Bao Dai looked unalluring.

As a result of the incredible maneuvers and disconcerting delays of the years from 1947 to 1950, thousands of men who were not attracted to Communism joined or remained with the Vietminh. France had well and truly "put Vietnam into the war"—but in resistance to France's policy, not in support of it.

[15] The Revers report was prepared by General Revers, Chief of the General Staff, after an inspection tour in Indochina in 1949. A copy of the secret report, which contained some controversial criticisms and recommendations for French withdrawal from isolated garrisons, reached the Vietminh. When they broadcast its contents, a vast scandal broke out, involving French generals and financial interests. The French administration was also implicated.

The solution of the military problem was not, as we have said before, a preliminary to a political solution. In fact, the reverse was true.

With their armor, their aircraft, their parachute troops, and their overwhelming superiority of resources, the French command had long thought that they would be able to enforce a solution. In September, 1947, General Valluy firmly believed that he could crush all organized resistance in three months.

However, the completely new character of this revolutionary war gradually impressed itself on the military chiefs. They already knew how elusive the enemy was when he mingled with the people, enjoyed their complicity and their more or less voluntary protection, and took advantage of this fact to build up an intelligence system enabling him to surround his enemies with guerrillas, engendering an atmosphere of constant insecurity. Without actually conquering, the Vietminh could make everything rotten, insecure, and unproductive. It could destroy opposing policies with a word. Having innumerable fighters, since virtually the whole population was ready to do battle for the cause of national resistance, the D.R.V.'s main problem was finding enough weapons.

Faced for the first time with the methods of modern revolutionary warfare, France started off on the wrong foot. The military problem, closely linked with the political one, was a question of "submergence." If France were to conquer, to render the enemy powerless, it would have to submerge the whole country and then set up within it an administration, a militia, an army. It would have to place at its head a political authority that was incontestable, both morally and materially (a basic condition that was never satisfied), and create a government and a military general staff capable of attracting, training, and galvanizing the best of the nation's youth. How could this be done? The Vietnamese would have to be offered plans for the building of a united, independent, and truly democratic Vietnam. The key to the military problem would have been a strong, popular Vietnamese political force which, by "national" methods, might have been able—village by village, hamlet by hamlet—to identify, isolate, and neutralize (or win over) the "lost sheep."

This was the only way to "victory." But because it was also the way to Vietnamese independence, Paris and its representatives refused to adopt it and initiated instead a succession of half-baked solutions that came to nothing.

This war, which the government seemed to be so ashamed of that they would not give it its true name, was officially a pacification operation. Neither the defense minister nor the General Staff was responsible for it. It was the minister for overseas territories[16] who acted as the delegate of the Prime Minister[17] in supervising the management of troops in Indochina.[18] He did this according to government directives, drawn up by the National Defense Committee. But the government, continually divided as it was, and lacking any real understanding of the Vietnamese situation, had such difficulty drawing up and defining a policy that the minister, in fact, had virtually complete autonomy. Under his authority, two officials had important powers, although they did not always agree: the high commissioner, a civilian as a rule, representing France in Indochina; and the commander in chief of the army, his assistant. In Indochina, as elsewhere, the army could be no more than the instrument of a policy. "Military operations," as Marshal Juin would say one day, "have always been subordinated to political directives."

Most serious was the complete absence of a clear policy. In Paris, all was compromise and confusion; advocates and opponents

16 In the course of 1949 and 1950, under a series of treaties and conventions, France recognized the independence of the three countries—Vietnam, Laos, and Cambodia—that had formed the Indochinese Federation. The independence granted under these agreements was strictly qualified, and the three states all remained within the French Union. Under this new arrangement the three states were known as the Associated States. Hence, from 1950, the minister for overseas territories was also the minister for associated states.

17 Not one prime minister (whose ultimate responsibility it was) set foot in Indochina during these eight years. Admittedly the almost daily harassment to which he was subjected in the National Assembly made such a journey difficult.

18 Decree 50–1506 of December 4, 1950. The defense minister was simply the supplier of matériel and personnel, according to a policy in which he had equal "observation rights" with his colleagues on the National Defense Committee.

of Vietnamese independence canceled each other out. Some mistrusted Bao Dai; others simply wanted to remove him. One group thought that France should concentrate on holding the south; another believed that Tonkin was the key to Southeast Asia; and so on. Paris, the nerve center of the French Union, radiated an uncertainty and ambiguity that was hardly conducive to effective action. In fact, the war was not directed at all. Because the government was divided and its plans were confused, the war was fought without a goal.[19]

The government made the war, but it seemed reluctant to provide the means of winning it. Operational plans drawn up and proposed by the local command were emasculated in Paris: they demanded too great and too far-sighted an effort on the part of the government, and they might have had dangerous effects on domestic policies. As this was officially no more than a colonial pacification, it was understood from the beginning that only volunteers could be sent to Indochina; but the government must have realized very soon what problems were created by this policy.

In January, 1947, General Leclerc had predicted that it would take a force of 500,000 men to suppress the "insurrection" quickly. Appalled, the ministers of state turned to more mundane problems. Several months later, General Valluy believed he could enforce a peace with 130,000 men. But, after his offensive had failed, it became clear that the war could not be carried on with French metropolitan volunteers alone. Despite the bounty given for enlistments, the number of volunteers remained inadequate.

From the start, the French units had been supplemented with Vietnamese recruits. This would have been effective if it had been a step toward the creation of an authentically Vietnamese army and an apportioning of tasks that would gradually bring

[19] One of the leaders of the right-wing opposition, Michel Debré, said at the end of 1953: "The French people feel that this war is out of their control and in the hands of destiny. . . . They have the impression . . . that France does not know what she wants and that we are fighting aimlessly, without a clear objective. What is painful is not so much the fact of fighting and accepting sacrifices; it is that we are apparently fighting without any goal." *Journal officiel, Débats parlementaires, Conseil de la République*, 1953, p. 1741.

the battle against the guerrillas under Vietnamese command, leaving the task of seeking out the regular Vietminh Army to the French Expeditionary Force. This was never the case, and, until 1953, the Vietnamese units were considered as auxiliary to the French forces and enjoyed hardly any autonomy. Providing officers for them also created considerable problems; the French were obliged to reduce the number of officers in the metropolitan, central African, and North African units, and to set up a sort of conveyor-belt for officers and NCO's throughout the French Union.

How could the French inspire those Vietnamese who came to fight at their side? They were a strange mixture: members of politico-religious sects, Catholic partisans, victims of Communism, and simple peasants from the rice paddies, attracted by short-sighted propaganda. Except for the feudal troops (Caodaists, the Hoa-Hao, Binh Xuyen, and such), these "yellow" units were all under French command, with French officers and NCO's. Since they were fighting according to plans set down by the French General Staff, using tactics unsuited to the country, it is little wonder that they were tormented by a sense of inferiority when faced with the Vietminh.

It is not surprising that, in this warped and ambiguous situation, the French Expeditionary Force failed to achieve decisive results. Its efforts were fruitless. The French had no overall strategy based on a firm policy, no plan of operations, and no cause worthy of the struggle. After 1947, they limited themselves to a series of fragmentary and murderous operations. "Hit-and-run," "mopping up," "raking over," commando raids—all these could never bring victory: on the contrary, by sowing more and more ruin and hatred and by constantly increasing the burden of the war upon the people, such actions turned the peasant masses against the French and greatly simplified the psychological and material tasks of the enemy.

Because the political leaders had shirked their responsibilities, confusion and ambiguity were rife. In this demoralizing and Sisyphean war, which seemed ever to be starting afresh, the feeling inevitably grew that the sacrifices being made were futile and absurd. And with this feeling came bitterness and revolt. Did the Fourth Republic suspect that by letting the confidence and morale of its army disintegrate like this, it was digging its own grave?

2

LIGHT AT THE END OF THE TUNNEL

The civil war which broke out in China in 1947 had already taken a decisive turn by 1948. The worm-eaten façade of the Kuomintang regime was collapsing under the persistent hammering of the People's Army. In January, 1949, Mao Tse-tung captured Peking, the old imperial capital. Five months later, Nanking and Shanghai fell in their turn.

It might take anything from a hundred days to two years before Mao subdued the whole of China; but it was clear, from that moment on, that the prospect of his complete victory, resulting in a junction between Ho Chi Minh's redoubt and the forces of international Communism, would entirely upset the military and political terms of the war in Vietnam. The threat appeared to be so serious and the French position so vulnerable that General Revers, Chief of the General Staff, recommended that France should no longer cling to the Chinese frontier, where its forces were too thinly stretched and liable to be overwhelmed, but should concentrate its effort in the Red River delta.

In December, 1949, the Chinese Communists took up positions along the border of Indochina. They immediately started a series of political and military talks with the Vietminh leaders, in Nanning. On January 14, 1950, Ho Chi Minh granted recognition to the Chinese People's Republic, though not without having previously offered to establish diplomatic relations with all the countries of the world. Liu Shao-chi,[1] the Chinese Acting Head of State, took advantage of a visit to Moscow by Mao Tse-tung and arranged for the recognition of the D.R.V. by Peking on January 18. The Kremlin followed suit a few days later. What had been a more or less concealed colonial war now suddenly became a "front" in the great world-wide confrontation.

The gravity of the resulting situation was very quickly appreciated in Paris. The effects of the war in Vietnam were already making themselves harshly felt in France. Massive transfers of officers and NCO's to Indochina had cut back metropolitan army cadres to about 80 per cent of the level of manning considered safe. And the French forces in North Africa had been run down to such an extent that some authorities feared for the security of the area. If metropolitan France could not provide normal replacements for the Expeditionary Corps in 1950–51, it might not be possible to continue the policy followed until then. And what would happen if China decided to give massive support to Ho Chi Minh?

In March, 1950, the Chiefs of Staff Committee stated that military policy in Indochina must be revised without delay, in the light of the threat that now hung over the frontier to the north and taking into account the emergence of an anti-Communist national Vietnamese government. Basically it was a matter of: (1) organizing the Vietnamese National Army so that it could relieve the French forces of their pacification and police duties

[1] Liu Shao-chi, who later followed Mao Tse-tung as President of the Chinese People's Republic, could be regarded during that period as the leader of the extremist or leftist group in Peking. On November 16, 1949, he made a speech in Peking advocating the extension of the armed struggle to all semi-colonial territories in Southeast Asia. In North Korea, in 1950, it was the "Chinese" group (the Yenan Koreans and the military cadres returning from China) that drew the "Russian" group (led by Kim Il Sung) into the war against South Korea. Philippe Devillers, "L'URSS, la Chine, et les origines de la guerre de Corée," *Revue Française de Science Politique* (Paris, December, 1964), pp. 1185–87.

and (2) regrouping the French forces in step with the deployment of the Vietnamese Army, so that, with their improved mobility, they could better defend the territory against the external threat —by basing themselves, for example, in the vital areas of the Red River delta. Such a regrouping would remove the risk of a military catastrophe—a very real risk at that time—if the outside threat suddenly materialized.

These recommendations were implemented only half-heartedly. The French Government, for reasons that are by no means clear, even refused to order the evacuation of the most exposed posts near the Chinese frontier, such as that at Cao Bang. There was a rude awakening in store, and events were about to show who was clear-sighted and nimble.

Vo Nguyen Giap, the commander of the Vietminh Army, had been announcing for three years past that he would soon switch to "a general counteroffensive." (By this time, Vietminh propaganda simply referred to this attack as the GCO.) The Vietminh forces, armed and re-equipped by China, were now in a position to take the offensive. Profiting from the French delay in evacuating the post at Cao Bang, they annihilated two important French columns in October, 1950. In the course of two months, they blasted the few remaining French barriers, particularly that at Lang Son, which until then had prevented Chinese aid from flooding in unhindered. Five Vietminh divisions, the first such major units, were spotted coming into the Red River delta, which was already alive with partisans and guerrilla units and was now virtually besieged. A full-scale war had begun. The tragedy had assumed its true proportions.

French public opinion could not fail to react to this blow. After a long silence, Pierre Mendès-France, a former minister in General de Gaulle's government and a Radical deputy, struck: on November 19 and 22, 1950, in two speeches that mark a chapter in the history of the war, he denounced the incoherence of government policy and stressed the need to make a choice:

> It is the overall conception of our action in Indochina that is false, because it relies both on a military effort that is too thin and weak

> to provide a solution through strength, and on a political effort that is too thin and weak to secure for us the allegiance of the population. . . . This cannot be on.
>
> There are only two solutions. The first would be to fulfil our objectives in Indochina by force of arms. If we choose it, let us now give up illusions and pious falsehoods. In order to achieve decisive military successes rapidly, we will need three times as many forces on the ground and three times as many funds, and we will need them very quickly. . . . The military solution involves a new and massive effort, massive enough and quick enough to overtake the already considerable development of the forces that oppose us.[2]

Mendès-France stressed the price that would have to be paid: new taxes, a slowing down of economic growth through a reduction in investments, austerity measures and restrictions on the standard of living, inability to provide an adequate defense for French interests in Europe and Africa, and inability in such circumstances to oppose the rearmament of West Germany advocated by the United States. He continued:

> The other solution is to seek a political agreement, an agreement, obviously, with those who oppose us. . . . An agreement means concessions, wide concessions—certainly more important concessions than those which would once have been sufficient.[3]
>
> One can reject this solution. It is difficult to implement. It would cause painful sacrifices and bitter disappointments. . . . But otherwise the country will have to be told the truth. It will have to be informed of the price to be paid if the alternative solution is to be achieved.
>
> A choice must be made. . . . Apart from the military solution, the solution of force, there is only one possibility—negotiation. . . .

[2] *Journal officiel, Débats parlementaires, Assemblée nationale,* 1950, pp. 7002–3.

[3] On November 22, Mendès-France listed the conditions for a settlement: recognition of Vietnamese independence; free and genuine elections without delay, under the supervision of bilateral or neutral commissions; a pledge to refrain from reprisals; evacuation of French forces within time-limits fixed by negotiation. Vietnam could be given the status of a neutral state on the Swiss model (cf. Ho Chi Minh's statement to Sol Sanders in December, 1949) and would sign an economic and cultural agreement with France.

> Have we the means of escaping this outcome when we ourselves have made it unavoidable by our failures and our mistakes?[4]

Given the nature of the government's parliamentary majority and the international climate during that period, the second choice, that of negotiating with the enemy, seemed out of the question for the time being. Whatever some of his public statements in 1949 may have suggested, Ho Chi Minh was, without a shadow of a doubt, a Communist. The French Government was a member of the Atlantic alliance, it was fighting in Korea side by side with the United States against a Communist power defined as an aggressor state by the United Nations, and it was therefore neither politically nor psychologically prepared for negotiations with another Kremlin satellite. It could hardly renounce its commitments and give up its efforts so abruptly and completely after it had cut off all attempts at a *rapprochement* between Bao Dai and Ho Chi Minh only one year before, and based its policy on the emergence of a "national" Vietnam, for which it had with great difficulty secured recognition from its reluctant NATO allies. But even if these transitory considerations are given due weight, it must still be said that, by clinging unyieldingly and blindly to its policy, the French Government only helped to move Ho Chi Minh closer to Moscow and Peking.

Indeed, the arrival of the Chinese Communists on the frontier meant the end of the "National Front" period for the Vietminh. As the price of their support, the Chinese insisted that there should be an end to pretense: Marxism must no longer disguise itself in the Democratic Republic of Vietnam. The Indochinese Communist Party, dissolved in 1945, must be reconstructed, and its leading role must be asserted. All aspects of political life, which until then preserved the appearance of an independent national-

[4] General Navarre later stated the choice in almost identical terms:

"Victorious Chinese Communism reached the frontiers of Tonkin in 1949. . . . A great political decision faced us: either to win the war by investing the necessary resources before Chinese aid to the Vietminh assumed massive proportions, or to end it quickly by a political agreement. There was no intermediate solution." Henri Navarre, *Agonie de l'Indochine* (Paris, 1956), p. 19, and lecture of March, 1957.

ism, albeit left-wing, must be brought into line. This policy resulted in the creation of the Communist Lao Dong (Workers' Party), the great purge of 1950–51, the gradual transformation of the Democratic Republic of Vietnam into a People's Democracy, and finally the launching of a great land-reform program on the Chinese model. The hopes of those who expected that the Vietminh would evolve on the pattern set by the Yugoslav Communists were thus soon whittled away. Peking was even more chary than Moscow of taking risks with its satellites, especially since factions continued to exist within the Vietminh. (The accession of the notoriously pro-Chinese Truong Chinh as Secretary-General of the Lao Dong Party for instance, did not necessarily mean the eclipse of Vo Nguyen Giap, the Vietminh's Commander in Chief, who was believed to lean toward a more "national" form of Communism.)

And so, because the Vietminh, like the North Koreans, had been brought into step by the hard-line extremists in Peking, the struggle was the same in Tonkin as in Korea. But we must also acknowledge that once French policy had blocked every other way out, Ho Chi Minh had no choice between annihilation and alignment with Peking.

The military reverses caused an awakening and a stiffening in France. General Jean de Lattre de Tassigny, a military leader with a great reputation, was appointed both High Commissioner and Commander in Chief. Within a few weeks, he checked the downward slide toward catastrophe, re-established morale, and, with the slender means at his disposal, managed to stop the rush of Vietminh units toward Hanoi in February, 1951, at Vinh Yen. A little later, he succeeded in securing the entire perimeter of the Red River delta from Mao Khe to Ninh Binh against enemy assault.

But to *reverse* the situation, the new commander in chief needed reinforcements, and very large ones at that. His request for such aid aroused great uneasiness in political and military circles in Paris.

While the Chiefs of Staff Committee recommended a concentration of effort in southern Indochina, where the chief French interests lay, de Lattre maintained—and secured government support for his views—that the loss of Tonkin would lead to the West's loss of Indochina and Southeast Asia. Here was the bolt to the door, he claimed, and he added that a serious setback in the north might well cause the Vietnamese government simply to fade away. Having thus linked the fates of Indochina and Tonkin, he demanded absolute priority for this theater of war and the immediate dispatch of large reinforcements.

Where could these be found? The General Staff argued that there were already insufficient volunteers to provide replacements for 1951. It stressed that, to satisfy General de Lattre, complete units would have to be drafted to the Far East and that these units would have to be taken from metropolitan France or from West Germany. As a result, the whole of that year's conscript draft would have to be sent to Indochina, and military service would have to be increased to two years in order not to weaken the defense plan (the so-called Ten Division Plan) provided for in the NATO agreements. The alternative was to diminish France's contribution to the defense of Europe and to undermine the resources of Western strategy. Would the Allies agree to this? Would this not encourage the United States to push even more strongly for the rapid rearmament of West Germany?

A refusal to provide the reinforcements requested and to accept the consequences of the situation outlined above, the Chiefs of Staff argued, would force General de Lattre to adjust his policy and tactics to fit the limited resources available to him, and his role would be reduced to that of making the best possible use of these resources. The Chiefs of Staff considered that, under these circumstances, he should have complete freedom of action in Tonkin, even in Indochina as a whole, with his basic assignment being to avoid the destruction of the Expeditionary Corps under any circumstances.[5]

Several ministers countered these arguments by stressing the need to hold on in Indochina without cramping or delaying the

[5] According to the Chiefs of Staff, the minimal limitations upon this freedom of action included the retention of a bridgehead at Haiphong and provision for the defense of southern Indochina on a line roughly coinciding with the 16th Parallel.

Western rearmament plan, and they maintained that the needed additional resources could be found in Africa. The military leaders retorted that both these objectives could not be met without sending some of the conscripts to Indochina and extending the term of military service to two years: drawing on resources in Africa involved serious risks in that area and only worsened the difficulties caused by the shortage of officers and NCO's and the resulting dislocation of units and supporting services.

Yet this is what the government was preparing to do. The Premier, Henri Queuille, thought that Tonkin could be held even if the dispatch of the conscripts was deferred. On March 20, 1951, he granted General de Lattre the reinforcements he had asked for, and the requisite cadres were obtained by disbanding several army units in North Africa.[6] In theory, these reinforcements were to be sent home by July 1, 1952. Thus, the government still evaded the issue. It adopted in principle an operation that it knew to be dangerous but that it regarded as a temporary measure to gain time until the results of the "military stabilization" of the Government of Vietnam could be assessed. It thereby implicitly renounced the military solution Mendès-France had formulated five months earlier.[7]

In fact, the decision of March 20, 1951, merely compounded the military and political mistakes piled up so far. Hindsight makes it easier for us to see these things clearly. But the consequences for France of sending North African (particularly Moroccan and Algerian) and Black African units to Indochina, of bringing Africans into contact with an anticolonial revolution, could

[6] The units disbanded included eleven infantry battalions, three armored regiments, four artillery groups, two engineer battalions, and one communications battalion. Only two battalions were sent back from Indochina in 1952.

[7] The terms of this military solution were later confirmed by General Navarre and Marshal Juin. The latter wrote in November, 1954: "The situation could only have been rectified by the total involvement of France in a war which was too far away and for which she was neither morally nor materially prepared." In any case, it seems that the government had long ceased to believe in the possibility of a military victory. (Interviews with René Pleven, February 17, 1957, and February 5, 1959, and statements of Jean Letourneau, Minister of Associated States, on December 29, 1951.)

have been foreseen even then. It has become a commonplace to ask how many of the cadres of the North African independence struggles had served in these units which had been so rashly involved in Indochina and had thus been given a deep knowledge of the methods, organization, and results of armed resistance. And while young Africans received this education in subversion, French Africa was drained of troops. The vacuum that the General Staff had warned against was effectively created. It made possible the fellagha agitation in Tunisia as early as 1952, then the Moroccan insurrection movement from 1953 on and finally rising in the Aurès mountains in 1954, which marked the beginning of the Algerian War.[8]

Once the Paris government had decided not to give the commander in chief the resources that might have enabled him to administer a lasting check to the Vietminh, it had to look for ways to disengage itself discreetly. There were two possible alternatives: American aid and the development of a Vietnamese army that might one day make it possible to cut back the Expeditionary Corps to a strength compatible with Western rearmament plans.

France had thus given up the hope of long-term victory. De Lattre knew even better than the government that it was now impossible. True, he had obtained from the Americans a substantial increase in aid, and he had given the go-ahead to the formation of the Vietnamese Army, which was at last being taken seriously, but he realized that sooner or later the conflict would have to be transferred to the political arena. To negotiate from a position of strength, he had to inflict painful lessons on the Vietminh, while encouraging the growth of a viable, nationalist Vietnamese army and government. And so it was that de Lattre, the soldier, extracted from Paris political concessions and transfers of power that had been hanging fire for months.

But his massive military drive brought about no lasting or de-

[8] This may be the place to recall the terrifying remark of Pham Ngoc Thach, Vietminh Secretary of State for Information, in 1946: "It is on the battlefields of Vietnam that the French Union will disintegrate."

cisive military improvement. Pushed for political reasons into a risky operation at Hoa Binh intended to smash the Vietminh fighting force, de Lattre found himself having to fight a hard and costly battle. The enemy took advantage of this running sore to infiltrate new forces into the Red River delta, already massively infected by the Vietminh. From that moment on, France completely lost the initiative and went over to the defensive.

In the meantime, armistice negotiations had started in Korea in July, 1951, and the intensity of the fighting there had abated. The French Government was deeply uneasy: it dreaded the possibility that China would turn toward the southern theater of operations and increase its aid to the Vietminh so heavily as to enable them to win the war. Since the government no longer hoped to gain the upper hand, it decided that a compromise must be reached while the balance of power was still in France's favor.

From the beginning of 1952, the language used by the politicians became highly charged with hints of compromise. "If an armistice were to come about in Korea," Jean Letourneau, Minister for the Associated States, said on February 25, "the Government would be in favor of calling an international conference aimed at achieving a political settlement of the conflict." He even added: "France will not refuse to talk with the Vietminh, but she will not take the first step." In April, he admitted:

> We have no chance of being able to provide a greater effort in terms of manpower in Indochina, unless the military circumstances there undergo a complete transformation. . . . At present, the only thing for France to do is to hold on, because we lack the means of doing anything else. . . . We must hold on while doing everything that is essential, so that our effort can gradually be supplemented by the national forces of the Associated States.

But the burden of Indochina was becoming heavier and heavier, and North Africa, from Tunis to Casablanca, was beginning to smolder. General de Lattre had provided no more than a breathing space. By the end of 1952, the Vietminh was scoring again. With the dual aim of dispersing the French forces and bypassing their fortresses in the Red River delta, it dislocated their Black River front at Nghia Lo, invaded the Thai area, and penetrated upper Laos, which it was to invade openly during the following spring with a drive toward the royal capital of Luang Prabang.

The chances of righting the situation were becoming more doubtful with each passing month. The government must have been convinced by then that the need for negotiations was becoming ever more urgent, yet it took no real steps to initiate the talks it claimed to want. Letourneau did indeed meet Nguyen Van Chi, the semi-official representative of the Vietminh in Paris. But in January, 1953, he broke off the contact which Raphäel-Leygues and Buu Hoi had established with the Vietminh in Rangoon on Antoine Pinay's authority.

No direct negotiations, perhaps. But what benefits could be expected from an international conference? It seemed that the government was trying to link the solution of the Indochinese problem with that of the Korean conflict, so that China could not use an armistice in Korea to give unlimited aid to the Vietminh. It was hoped that China would, rather, abandon its interest in Vietnam in return for some concessions like those offered in 1946. This would pave the way for a compromise between Bao Dai and Ho Chi Minh which would confirm the victory of the former or, as a major concession, acknowledge the full control of the latter over certain areas. There appeared to be no inkling in high places that any renewed discussion with the Chinese about the future of Vietnam would deeply offend the strong nationalist feelings of the Vietnamese.

But there was not the slightest sign from the opposite camp of any wish to negotiate. All the talk was of "total victory over the colonialists"—everything for the front, everything for victory. And the intransigence of the Chinese at Panmunjom indicated clearly the source of the Vietminh's attitude.

Was it, then, merely a matter of holding on for the present, and standing firm until a way out appeared at the end of the long tunnel? The French Government might well have reversed the deteriorating situation if it had boldly played the card of Vietnamese independence, combining it with the offer of a cease-fire and thereby regaining the psychological advantage.

Meanwhile, after March, 1953, the war overflowed from Vietnam into the whole of Indochina. By moving on Luang Prabang and pushing his forces beyond Samneua up to the Plain of Jars, Giap showed that Tonkin was no longer "the bolt to the door to Southeast Asia" and that it could be bypassed. It seemed that the Mekong was becoming one of his major objectives, along with the Red River delta.

It was clear that the French fortunes were entering a critical phase. The latest campaign had proved that the Vietminh's advantage was increasing. To oppose the Vietminh's fighting force of more than six divisions, the French could muster the equivalent of only three divisions—seven Groupes Mobiles and eight parachute battalions. Of the 500,000 men finally committed to Indochina, 350,000 were tied down in static assignments, such as guard posts and pacification teams, or in noncombatant supply, maintenance, and office work. The future, for the French, looked foreboding indeed.

In order to create a military situation in which it would be possible to seek "an honorable solution,"[9] it was essential to reconstruct, with the least possible delay, a fighting force more powerful than that of the Vietminh, and no less mobile. That, at any rate, was the conclusion reached in the spring of 1953 by General Salan, the Commander in Chief. To build this striking force, he planned to uproot the static elements of the Expeditionary Corps and make them mobile again. This, in turn, required an increase in the armies of the Associated States, so that they could take over the essential task of pacification from the French.

Both these methods involved a sizeable increase in armaments, and this in turn required American aid. The French Government supported its requests for credits and equipment by informing the United States of the main outlines of Salan's plan. It obtained a

[9] General Navarre has confirmed that this was, in his opinion, the aim of the René Mayer cabinet. See Navarre, *op. cit.*, p. 3. (On these points, see also pp. 46–47 and 75.)

promise that the United States would provide the resources needed to implement the plan, with particular emphasis on the equipment for the armies of the Associated States.[10]

To launch this vigorous new policy, a change of team was thought necessary. On May 8, 1953, the French Government appointed as Commander in Chief General Henri Navarre, aged 55, until then Chief of Staff to Marshal Juin, Commander in Chief of Allied Forces in Central Europe, and regarded as one of the most brilliant strategists in the French Army. The General took up his command in Saigon on May 20, a day before the Mayer government was brought down in Paris by a miscellaneous combination of Communists, Socialists, and former members of the RPF.[11]

This government crisis was expressive of the inability of the French parliament to formulate an Indochina policy, but, equally, of its genuine desire to put an end to the war. The international climate was beginning to look more propitious. The *détente* that had set in after Stalin's death in March became more pronounced with every passing month. Even the Chinese at Panmunjom be-

[10] American agreement seems to have been obtained "on condition that the French Government would adopt a program capable, in every aspect, of ensuring military success in Indochina." (Memorandum of April 26, para. 5, sub-para. C, quoted in *Le Monde* (Paris), July 26, 1953.) The creation of the Vietnamese Army had been more or less marking time for two years. General de Lattre and Bao Dai had decided on a phased build-up of eight divisions. These were to be equipped and armed with United States matériel. In March, 1952, Bao Dai appointed Nghiem Van Tri Minister of National Defense, and set up a General Staff under the direction of General Nguyen Van Hinh, the son of Premier Tam. The regular arrival of American supplies at the rate of 8,000 tons a month, and the ease with which recruits were obtained at that time, gave grounds for hope that the large units planned could soon be formed. But finding officers and NCO's presented a very grave problem. They were in short supply, and time was needed to train those who were available. From the beginning of 1953, Tri's plan for a regular Vietnamese Army, armed to match the Vietminh and stiffened by French cadres for as long as necessary, lost ground to General Hinh's proposal for the more rapid creation of light battalions with purely Vietnamese cadres, to deal with pacification duties while the Expeditionary Corps faced the Vietminh's main force. More than 50 light battalions were to be formed in 1953. The choice of this plan led to the resignation of Nghiem Van Tri in February, 1953.

[11] The Gaullist RPF was disbanded in 1953.

gan to relax the unyielding position they had held since December, 1951. It seemed more and more likely that a Korean armistice was not far off and that its conclusion would lead to a conference of the Big Four. On May 11, Sir Winston Churchill expressed the hope that a meeting would take place "on the highest level."[12]

Some seemed to think that in the context of "a general settlement in Asia" it would also be possible to put an end to the conflict in Indochina—by negotiating with China. A number of political figures who had been asked to form a government—Paul Reynaud, Georges Bidault, and André Marie among them—hinted at the possibility in their declarations of policy. But at this very moment the Indochinese crisis suddenly flared up again, and this time it was France's Indochinese allies rather than the Vietminh who provided the spark. Vietnam (which had been deeply offended by the way in which the devaluation of the piastre was carried out) and Cambodia almost simultaneously demanded full sovereignty and independence. To highlight his demands, the King of Cambodia even went into exile in Bangkok.

A new government was finally formed in Paris on June 28 with Joseph Laniel as Premier and with the participation of the "ex-Gaullists." It tackled the problem of Indochina immediately, and in a more realistic and down-to-earth way than its predecessors.

From the first, this government set out to find a solution to the "national problem." Reynaud, the new Vice-Premier, who had taken a close interest in Asian affairs for many years and had recently visited Indochina, provided the driving force. He was determined to carry out the policy of turning the Associated States into independent states. "This war," as he put it, "must stop being a French war supported by Vietnam and become a Vietnamese war supported by France."[13] In a statement dated July 3, drafted by Reynaud, the French Government declared its determination to "perfect the independence of the Associated States," and invited the governments in Saigon, Phnom Penh, and Vientiane to

[12] *Hansard* (London), May 11, 1953, col. 897.
[13] *Le Monde* (Paris), June 27, 1953.

fresh talks, which it hoped would prove decisive. The statement was favorably received.

The Cambodian crisis was essentially resolved in the fall when the French forces evacuated the right bank of the Mekong and transferred responsibility for military affairs in Cambodia to the Khmer High Command.

The negotiations with Vietnam, which opened in August, proved more difficult. Bao Dai gave the impression to some that at heart he did not care for genuine independence which, as he foresaw, would put him at the mercy of true nationalists as soon as his French protectors were gone.[14] Moreover, while ministers such as Reynaud, Pleven, and Faure took a very liberal view of Vietnamese aspirations, a cabinet faction led by Bidault opposed the granting of independence unless it was accompanied by a solemn pledge of Vietnamese allegiance to the French Union, including the restrictions on sovereignty embodied in the French Constitution of 1946.

Nevertheless the "national problem" was moving toward a solution, and it was now a question of achieving a political settlement of the conflict. Such a settlement, though still obscure and difficult to forecast in detail, was to be sought simultaneously on two levels: the diplomatic, where it was a matter of trying to induce China to cease its aid to the Vietminh (to have any chance of success, such an approach required that the military situation be stable and that the French suffer no military setbacks), and the military. On the military level, the mission of the commander in chief was, as General Navarre admitted, "to create the military conditions for an honorable political solution which would be adopted when the time was ripe."[15]

General Navarre, who had returned to Paris to brief the government, had adopted the framework of the Salan Plan. Navarre's version called for a strong and mobile battle force, unhampered by

[14] Conversation of the authors with Paul Reynaud, June 15, 1959.

[15] Navarre, *op. cit.*, p. 72. The General added: "I never hoped for more or promised more, and I was never asked for more." However, when he was pressed by Reynaud on July 24, 1953, the General was more sanguine.

local security tasks, with which the High Command would regain the initiative from the fall of 1954 onward. This military pressure, it was hoped, would force the Vietminh to negotiate, particularly if China had been persuaded to end its support. General Navarre knew that he had no hope of strong reinforcements from metropolitan France, and he banked on the rapid development of the Vietnamese Army. But his Franco-Vietnamese fighting force would need several months to become operational, and he had to deal with the threat of a decisive enemy offensive in the meantime.

The Commander in Chief therefore stated that throughout the 1953–54 campaign he would adopt a strictly defensive strategy north of the 18th Parallel, where he faced Giap's divisions. He would try to avoid a general engagement in these areas. South of the 18th Parallel, however, he would attempt to clear the zones still held by the Vietminh, particularly in Central Annam and in Cochin China, during the spring or summer of 1954. As soon as he had tilted the balance in his favor, which he hoped to do by the fall of 1954, he would launch a general offensive north of the 18th Parallel "with the object of creating a military situation which would make a political solution of the conflict possible."

Until the Vietnamese Army could take on a significant proportion of the pacification work, temporary reinforcements would have to be supplied from metropolitan France. General Navarre therefore requested the dispatch, by December 1, 1953, of twelve battalions of infantry, one battalion of engineers, and one artillery group, as well as a considerable increase in bomber and transport aircraft strength and the provision of a naval supply force.

Navarre's plan provoked the same misgivings in Parisian military circles as had that of General de Lattre three years before. "The manning of the forces at present in Indochina," wrote one of the Chiefs of Staff, "taxes the resources of the regular army to the limit. Any increased effort requires the use of new resources: conscripts and the reserves." No further units could be disbanded in Europe and North Africa without calling on these additional sources of manpower. Failure to utilize these replacements would not only lower the margin of safety in Europe and Africa, but also imperil the results achieved in the field of rearmament during the previous four years.[16]

On July 24, after long deliberations, the ministers of the National Defense Committee finally decided to grant General Navarre eight infantry battalions, one engineer battalion, one artillery group, and naval and air reinforcements. But the cadres the General had requested could not be supplied in full. In view of these shortages, he was asked to restrict his operations in accordance with the means being made available to him.

In reply, Navarre argued that, with the limited resources at his disposal, he might not be able to stand and fight wherever it was essential to do so. The General Staff, for its part, thought the Navarre Plan might be defeated if the Vietminh launched an offensive against Laos in October. It urged that Navarre not allow himself to be outmaneuvered if the Laos offensive materialized.[17] In the opinion of the General Staff, the defense of Vietnam was the goal of the French operations, and the main defense effort should therefore cover the Red River delta, central Vietnam, and Cochin China. The Thai area and Laos should be only lightly defended, and if necessary the main line of defense could be pulled back to a line running roughly along the 18th Parallel, from Pak Sane in Laos to the Porte d'Annam on the coast of Vietnam. But this recommendation does not seem to have been endorsed by the French Government, and in practice it gave a free hand to General Navarre.[18]

The orders of the new commander in chief for the defensive stage of his operations were to seize the initiative everywhere, to harass the enemy, and to disrupt his plans. The daring raids on July 11, against Lang Son, where Giap received supplies from

[16] General Navarre considered that there was no serious threat of war in Europe at that time and recommended a "finesse" in that theater so that two or three complete divisions could be sent to Indochina. Navarre, *op. cit.*, p. 79.

[17] An Agence France Presse dispatch from Saigon (quoted by *Le Monde* [Paris], May 15, 1953) already stated that: "It is quite out of the question that, with the resources at its disposal, the High Command in Indochina should make a stand at the same time both in northern Laos and in the Red River delta."

[18] See General Georges Catroux, *Deux actes du drame indochinois* (Paris, 1959), pp. 147–48, 168.

China; the successful evacuation of the fort at Na San in the Thai area in August;[19] and Operation Mouette in September–October, which destroyed the bases for the offensive that the Vietminh was preparing to launch against the southern part of the Red River delta—these all showed that, as far as the French were concerned, a defensive posture did not mean passivity.

The Navarre Plan, then, got off to a good start, and once again Frenchmen began to hope for victory (provided, of course, that China did not stage a massive intervention). Meanwhile, what was Peking doing? On July 27, 1953, an armistice—the result of prolonged pressure on Peking from Moscow—was signed in Korea. A political conference was to follow within ninety days. The Quai d'Orsay immediately tried to hitch the "Indochinese wagon" to it. It suggested in a memorandum addressed to London and Washington that an attempt should be made "to let the Chinese understand . . . that their good will could not remain limited to areas lying north of the 38th Parallel and that they would be taking an obvious risk by limiting their peaceful intentions in this way." Peking should not be allowed to assume that it had secured anything in Korea until tangible signs of Chinese good will had been given in Southeast Asia.

Paris believed that it could count on the good will of Washington in this matter. The new Republican Administration—in particular, Secretary of State John Foster Dulles and the new Chairman of the Joint Chiefs of Staff, Admiral Arthur Radford—favored a firm policy toward China,[20] while trying to end all existing conflicts.

[19] Where General Salan succeeded in averting a disaster forshadowing that of Dien Bien Phu.

[20] In his book, *Vietnam, A Diplomatic Tragedy* (New York, 1965), p. xii, Victor Bator writes:

> In 1953, General Eisenhower became President. The majority of the American people voted for the Republicans after twenty years of government by the Democratic Party. The new President interpreted the vote *not* as authority for the continuation of the external policy preceding his administration but as a clear mandate for change. Thus he selected for his administration's highest cabinet post, for Secretary of State, John Foster Dulles, a man who had the self-confidence, talent, and intellectual courage to bring the change in operation. Dulles had the ambition to leave his personal mark on world affairs. The Republican Party platform drafted by him marked out the changed course. . . . The Eisenhower platform promised the abandonment of what was referred to as the "Asia Last"

In this context, the dynamism of the French Commander in Chief made it possible to revive negotiations with the United States. Navarre's plan of operations and his proposals for the development of the Vietnamese Army had caught the imagination of the responsible officials in America. An American military mission had been established in Saigon as early as June, and in September, Washington was to provide $400 million toward the equipment of the armies of the Associated States.

But there was a danger of being caught in a vicious circle. The Navarre Plan, conceived as a means of making negotiations easier, required American aid. If France received this aid for a clearly stated purpose, would it retain the freedom of political action it needed? Would the United States, which was paying for two-thirds of the cost of the war, permit France to conduct serious *unilateral* negotiations with the Communist world?

The Communist world did, indeed, show signs that it might be willing to negotiate. Soviet Premier Georgi Malenkov was a vigorous advocate of the policy of *détente*. Despite the elimination of his ally Beria on July 11 (following the revolt in East Berlin), he seemed to have carried the day once more against those Soviet leaders who were arguing for extreme caution or a continuation of the Cold War.[21] Since the Korean armistice, Chinese as well as Soviet radio stations had been broadcasting statements favoring a peaceful solution in Indochina.[22] And in June, Chinese officials in

---

policy, it promised the end of neglect of the Far East and of its sacrifice to gain time for the West, and thereby, the strengthening of the morale of the peoples of the Far East. It promised the end of the defensive containment of Communism and asserted a firm will to defeat it and roll back Communist Russia into its prewar orbit. It held out the promise of depriving International Communism of the political and military initiative. See also Dulles's article, "A Policy of Boldness," *Life*, May 19, 1952.

[21] The explosion of its first hydrogen bomb in August proved that Russia's initiatives for peace could not be interpreted as signs of weakness.

[22] On August 3, *Krasnaya Zvezda* (Moscow), organ of the Red Army, wrote that the Korean armistice should be an inducement to end the war in Indochina. On September 5, the *Far Eastern Economic Review* (Hong Kong) felt able to say that Moscow was seeking means of achieving a truce in Indochina. It hinted that the Vietminh were far from united on this subject. Between September 8 and 14, Kunming, Peking, and Pyongyang Radios all mentioned the possibility of a Korean-style armistice in Indochina.

Peking discussed Indochina with a French businessman, Bernard de Plas, head of the first Western economic mission to Communist China, telling him that a solution in Indochina, while respecting the independence of the peoples of the peninsula, must above all safeguard the friendship between France and China.[23]

In France, the pressure of public and parliamentary hopes for a political settlement was increasing. To a growing number of ordinary citizens, political leaders, and even military men, the war in Indochina now seemed to be a bottomless pit, a pointless adventure, and an absurd sacrifice. In September, 1953, political events in Indochina reinforced this bleak prognosis.

Bao Dai had encouraged the convocation of a congress in Saigon to support his negotiations in Paris. He believed he had this meeting well under control and thought that it would, if suitably manipulated, produce "constructive" demands. Instead, the congress demanded complete independence and withdrawal from the French Union and then attempted to assume the status of a national congress charged with supervision of the imperial government. Bao Dai was asked by Paris to explain his actions, to disavow the congress, and to state clearly whether or not he accepted the French Union. He managed to evade the issue and left it to his Premier, Nguyen Van Tam, to reply—that is, to compromise or discredit himself.[24]

But the mask had fallen at last. Everyone in France now knew what had been clear enough from the start: even if France won the war, it would have to leave Indochina. Everywhere there was bitterness and anger at having been blind for so long, and a hunt for a villain began. Most of all, though, it became clear that the ruinous undertaking in Indochina must be brought to an end as soon as possible.

The mood in the National Assembly was changing rapidly. The idea spread that France was no longer fighting for her national interests, that the "independence" promised to the Baodaists

[23] Interviews with Bernard de Plas, May 8, 1954, and April 9, 1959. The Chinese even hinted that they saw no objection to Vietnam remaining in the French Union.

[24] On this Saigon Congress, see Donald Lancaster, *The Emancipation of French Indo-China* (London, 1961), pp. 274–78.

would not turn into a restoration or reassertion of French influence, but that it would simply bring to power a number of ultranationalists as determined as the Vietminh to eliminate France from Vietnamese life. Seen in this light, the burden of the war appeared unbearable. Even American aid, though it had relieved the financial burdens of the war and provided a highly useful supply of hard currency, no longer could make public opinion accept the role of "the Free World's foot soldier" in which the United States seemed to have cast France in Southeast Asia. Finally, the alarming turn of events in North Africa—the Sultan deposed in Morocco, the guerrilla war spreading in Tunisia—forced those in charge to look quickly for an end to the Indochinese conflict.

An important debate took place in the National Assembly at the end of October, 1953. The Laniel government, attacked by the opposition particularly on its Indochina policy, carried the debate on October 28 with a three-point motion recommending that:

1. The armies of the Associated States should be developed.
2. Everything should be done to achieve the general pacification of Southeast Asia by means of negotiation.
3. The independence of the Associated States within the French Union should be completed.

Even more important—for it shows how the idea of negotiation had gained ground even within Indochina—was Laniel's statement that France, in agreement with the Associated States, "would study every constructive proposal" emanating from the Vietminh and would "not refuse to negotiate an armistice."[25]

Some days later, on November 12, the Premier made it clear that "there need not necessarily be a military solution. . . . We do not demand an unconditional surrender from the enemy before negotiating with him, any more than the Americans did in Korea." And, Laniel added, "If an honorable settlement were in sight, on either the local or the international level, France . . . would be happy to accept a diplomatic solution to the conflict."[26]

[25] *Journal officiel, Débats parlementaires, Assemblée Nationale,* 1953, pp. 4603–6.

[26] *Journal officiel, Débats parlementaires, Conseil de la République,* 1953, p. 1748.

It seemed, from then on, as though the debate was between those who opted with Mendès-France for direct negotiations with the enemy after a cease-fire had been agreed,[27] and those who considered this solution impossible for reasons of prestige and who therefore sought an international meeting at which the great powers could act as conciliators, and possibly bring some pressure to bear on the enemy. It was the latter course that appeared to be favored in government circles in Paris. During the October debates, the majority spokesmen, particularly those of the MRP and the independents, argued as though the possibility of direct talks with Ho Chi Minh were definitely excluded.

However, the government did not appear to have made up its mind. On November 13, the Committee for National Defense met and, after having discussed General Navarre's demands for reinforcements, decided not to fulfill them. Instead, it asked the Commander in Chief to "adjust his plans to the means at his disposal" and confirmed to him that "the objective of our action in Indochina (is) to make the enemy realize that it (is) impossible for him to win a military decision." But the problem was to know whether the military situation would continue to improve as it had since summer—whether, in brief, it was preferable to delay negotiations for a few months more, or to negotiate without delay. Pleven, in particular, wanted to know as soon as possible where and when France could admit that it had reached the limits of military effort. He thought that Navarre's recent successes had put France "in a position that we may never regain." He also wished to ask Navarre what he thought the present balance of forces was, if he thought it better to negotiate at once or later, and if, once the negotiations began, France should make haste to conclude them.

To get clear answers to all these questions, Rear Admiral Cabanier of the permanent secretariat general of national defense was sent on a secret mission to Saigon. In the presence of President Auriol and Pleven, Laniel gave the admiral verbal instructions[28] to "ask

[27] Mendès-France repeated his preference for this solution in an interview granted to *L'Express* (Paris), May 16, 1953. Albert Sarraut had also adopted this point of view in the same publication.

[28] Nothing whatsoever was put in writing. See Joseph Laniel, *Le drame indochinois* (Paris, 1957), p. 37.

the Commander in Chief whether he does not think that the time has come—in view of the improvement in the military situation that he has thus far secured, and of the signing of the armistice in Korea—to make a strong effort to open cease-fire negotiations."[29] Leaving Paris on the 17th of November and arriving in Saigon on the 19th, Cabanier did not see Navarre (who had thus far been in the North) until the 20th. Navarre stated that he did not think that the time had come to start negotiations. The military situation, he said, would be better in the spring and summer, and would enable discussions to take place in circumstances that certainly would be more favorable. This was the answer that Admiral Cabanier took back to Paris on November 25.[30]

Meanwhile, military events rushed ahead in Vietnam. Operation Mouette had crushed the preparations of the Vietminh 320th Division to launch an offensive at the southern part of the Red River delta, but, suddenly, Giap seemed to be radically changing his plan of operations. His 316th Division left its bases in Thanh Hoa province on October 27 and moved northwest toward the highlands along Provincial Route 41. Other units moved after it in the same direction. A new attack on Laos was clearly taking shape.

General Navarre had maintained in July that he lacked the means to defend Laos. But, in November, he and the High Commissioner, Maurice Dejean, felt morally obliged to do so, as the treaty promulgating the independence of Laos and its adherence to the French Union had just been signed on October 22. To blunt the threat presented to Laos by the Vietminh 316th Division, the Commander in Chief launched Operation Castor on November 20: six paratroop battalions occupied the bowl-shaped depression of Dien Bien Phu, nearly 200 miles northwest of Hanoi.[31]

Then the bombshell burst. On November 29, the Swedish daily

[29] *Ibid.*, p. 41.

[30] On the Cabanier mission, see Pierre Rocolle, *Pourquoi Dien Bien Phu?* (Paris, 1968), pp. 215–17; Jules Roy, *La bataille de Dien Bien Phu* (Paris, 1963), pp. 56–58, 76; and Paul Ely, *L'Indochine dans la tourmente*, (Paris, 1964), p. 34.

[31] On the decision to occupy Dien Bien Phu, see Rocolle, *op. cit.*, pp. 173–91.

Expressen published the reply it had just received from Ho Chi Minh to a series of questions put (from Paris) by the paper's correspondent in the French capital, Sven Löfgren.[32] The Vietminh leader stated that the Democratic Republic of Vietnam was ready to study every proposal for a cease-fire if France wished to put an end to the conflict.

Five days later, General Navarre, who had argued previously that the Vietminh main force could not be engaged with any chance of success before the fall of 1954, issued his general directive. He decided to accept battle in the northwest *by centering his defense on the base of Dien Bien Phu,* which must *be held at all costs.*[33]

Naturally, he had no knowledge of what the other side had just decided; that did not become known until much later. The fact that both the Russians and the Chinese were leaning toward global negotiations had driven the leaders of the D.R.V. to inten-

32 Ho's reply, dated November 20, said in part: "If, having drawn the lessons of these years of war, the French Government wishes to conclude an armistice and solve the question of Vietnam by means of negotiations, the people and government of the Democratic Republic of Vietnam (D.R.V.) are ready to examine the French proposals. . . . The basis of an armistice is that the government of France should really respect the independence of Vietnam. . . . The negotiation of an armistice is essentially a matter for the government of France and that of Vietnam." Ho Chi Minh, *Selected Works* (Hanoi, 1962) II, 409–11. As he left the Palais Bourbon on the evening of the last debate in October, Sven Löfgren had the idea of checking whether (as the spokesmen of the majority maintained) any direct conversation with Ho Chi Minh was out of the question. With the help of the Swedish embassy in Peking, and through the representative of the D.R.V. in China, he put this series of questions to Ho himself.

33 See Joseph Laniel, *Le drame indochinois* (Paris, 1957), p. 38. One must recognize, as General Catroux has done *(op. cit.),* that when the commander in chief issued his directive of December 3, he probably did not imagine that the Vietminh would commit almost the whole of their fighting force at Dien Bien Phu and that the greatest battle of the war would take place there. Navarre thought (see his instruction of December 7) that central Vietnam, where he intended to take the offensive, would become the main theater of operations in the course of the next six months. In any case, when General Navarre issued his order of December 3 directing the defense of Dien Bien Phu, he did not yet know whether or not the government had decided to defend Laos. For the full text of Navarre's directive, see Roy, *op. cit.,* pp. 422–3.

sive preparations for a decisive effort. On September 2, during the celebration of the eighth anniversary of independence, all the talk was of "total victory." At the end of September, the Politburo of the Lao Dong party met under Ho's chairmanship, and examined Giap's operational plans for the winter of 1953–54. From November 19 to 23, the central military committee worked out its plan of operations with the senior commanders in the light of the political bureau's instructions.

During this conference, Ho replied to Löfgren's questions. Following the lead of Moscow and Peking, he was conciliatory, and seemed ready to negotiate (on the basis of the independence of Vietnam); but all the while he was preparing to make a decisive improvement in his military position. On December 6, Giap issued an order mobilizing the population, calling upon it to do everything in its power to keep the French from reoccupying the northwest and exhorting it to seize victory on that front.[34]

In the course of one week, the fate of the war had been sealed.

[34] The text of Giap's mobilization order is in Roy, *op. cit.*, p. 426. On the meetings and decisions of Vietminh leaders, see *Etudes Vietnamiennes* (Hanoi) No. 3, pp. 30–41, pp. 143–47; and Roy, *op. cit.*, p. 179.

3

THE ROAD TO NEGOTIATION

Ho Chi Minh's statements to *Expressen* created a new situation. Before their appearance, the motions and resolutions offered by political parties and personalities favoring direct negotiations had raised no more than pious hopes. For months, even years, ever since Giap launched his counteroffensive in the fall of 1950, nothing had suggested that the Vietminh might agree to negotiations or compromises of any sort.

Now, everything was different—even though a Quai d'Orsay spokesman informed Löfgren that "policy is not made in the classified ads"—and Marc Jacquet, Secretary of State for the Associated States, realized it immediately. The Vietminh had responded to the French overtures and showed themselves willing to consider proposals. It was now a matter of establishing who would take the first step, for each side had hinted that it expected the other to make the first move.

The French generally thought that they could take the initiative only in agreement with the Associated States (especially Vietnam), the United States, and even, perhaps, Great Britain. But Ho Chi Minh's statement, which the Vietminh radio confirmed in broadcasts on several successive days,[1] divided the government. A majority still wanted international negotiations, but some, including Reynaud, began to favor an initial contact with China or even the Vietminh.

The international discussions, so ardently desired, now seemed at hand in any case. On November 27, 1953, the Kremlin had accepted the Western offer of a Four Power conference and suggested that it be held in Berlin.

London and Washington had both been cool toward the idea, but at the Bermuda Conference in December, Eisenhower and Churchill gave in to requests by Laniel and Bidault and agreed that the conference should take place. They felt this was necessary to strengthen the Laniel government on the home front and help to free it of some encumbrances which were hampering its freedom of action: the growing opposition in France to the European Defense Communtiy (EDC) was causing concern in Washington.

Yet was it not also advisable to grasp the lifeline held out by Ho Chi Minh? In the French parliament, a trend of opinion inspired by Mendès-France favored direct negotiations with Ho Chi Minh as being the most promising possibility. After all, it was in the mutual interest of France and the Vietminh to reach an understanding without resorting to mediation by the great powers, which would certainly exact a price for their help.

In any event, the government was no longer in a position to evade negotiations. Though political circles were preoccupied with the impending Congress of Versailles, called to elect a successor to Vincent Auriol as President of the Republic, they were shaken nonetheless by recently published revelations[2] about the way in which the Ramadier government had suppressed D.R.V. peace offers in 1947. In these circumstances, Minister of National Defense René Pleven, whose problems in Indochina were constantly increasing, suggested to a Socialist deputy, Alain Savary, that he

[1] Ho confirmed the statement himself on December 18, in his speech commemorating the seventh anniversary of National Resistance. *The New York Times*, December 18, 1953.

[2] See *L'Express* (Paris), December 19, 1953, "La paix trahie en Indochine" (an article with supporting documents by Philippe Devillers).

make contact with the D.R.V. to sound out its real intentions. Savary said that he would do so, but only with the formal approval of the government. Laniel told him that the government had requested him to make this contact, but when the Minister of Foreign Affairs was consulted, he vetoed the project.[3]

Unfortunately, political and military events were very soon to belie General Navarre's optimism. In the political sphere, the crisis that had been smoldering in Vietnam for two months now burst into the open. When Bao Dai returned to Vietnam, he was subjected to growing pressure from nationalist circles. Ho Chi Minh's interview had alerted them to the threat of possible talks between France and the D.R.V.; now they demanded the speedy realization of independence and the formation of a genuinely nationalist government, and asked for the dismissal of Premier Nguyen Van Tam. On December 17, Bao Dai threw Tam to the wolves and gave the post to his own cousin, Prince Buu Loc, until then Vietnamese High Commissioner in France.

Everybody felt that the confrontation with the Vietminh was at hand, and bidding for the mantle of nationalism was obviously rising to a climax. To many Vietnamese, it was less a matter of achieving genuine independence than of displaying an unbroken record of resistance. Under the double impact of a sweeping psychological offensive by the Vietminh and the struggles of many Vietnamese to put themselves in the clear before they were left in the lurch by France, political life now degenerated rapidly.

This was the logical outcome of the process so often described since 1946: by the very force and nature of things, Vietnamese "nationalism," which had been encouraged only as a counter to Communist "rebellion," now also demanded total independence. Until this moment, it had been possible to contain it, but from now on, France could neither evade the issue nor equivocate.

[3] As a result, the matter dragged on for three months. Bidault did not receive Savary until the beginning of March and then only to tell him: "Ho Chi Minh is on the point of capitulating, we are going to beat him. Don't support him by a contact of this kind." "You are taking a terrible responsibility," Savary replied. Laniel and Pleven urged Bidault to agree, but by the time they succeeded in persuading him, the inevitable had begun to happen at Dien Bien Phu, and Savary's journey ended in Moscow in April.

After eight years of war, the subtlest political minds were compelled to realize that the French army was fighting only for the sort of victory that would bring a request to leave the day after it had been won. Then the safeguarding of French interests—whether economic, political, or cultural—would depend entirely on the good will and interests of the leaders in Saigon, just as in Baghdad, Cairo, or Addis Ababa.

Forthright assurances by France might, even at this late date, have been able to arrest this degeneration of Vietnamese political life. But military events too contributed to the new sense of urgency.

Contrary to the assessment made in November, 1953, the developing Vietminh threat was not focused on upper Laos. The units sent by Giap toward Laos from the Red River delta, which were to have been blocked by the occupation of Dien Bien Phu, had shown few signs of life. But suddenly, on December 20, the Vietminh General Staff struck. The Vietminh 325th Division emerged from the forests of the Annamite mountains near Na Phao (just inside Laos, near the Mu Gia pass), broke through the exceedingly slender screen of French posts in that area, and infiltrated the whole territory between the mountains and the Mekong, under cover of bad weather which limited air observation. The possibility of such an offensive had been included among others in General Navarre's assessment,[4] but the Vietminh forces were driving both west *and* south. Confusion gripped some of the French units, and the Vietminh troops reached the Mekong at several points after a series of forced marches. On December 26, they occupied the Laotian town of Thakhek, which the French had hastily evacuated. A few days later, a powerful French counterattack was launched from the combined air and land base at Seno: it flushed the Vietminh units from Thakhek on January 20, 1954, and threw them back to the Mahaxay Plateau. Finding the way to the Mekong barred, the enemy swung south. He moved through the thick jungles of the interior toward Colonial Route 9 (RC9), the

[4] See General Staff Meeting of February 9, 1954, in Saigon.

road from Dong Ha on the coast of Annam to Savannakhet in Laos. Fighting broke out near sensitive points such as Tchepone, Muong Phine, and Muong Phalane.

The French position was re-established, but the enemy had opened a new front and forced the French to disperse their forces, although the object of the Navarre Plan was to concentrate them. Another danger now arose, that of a linkup between the Vietminh forces in northern Annam and those in the Vietminh's Intersector V.[5] Meanwhile, an enemy push beyond the Bolovens Plateau toward Pakse and Cambodia threatened to cut off Laos from the French bases. The war map had been brutally altered in only two weeks.

As for the bolt General Navarre had sought to place at Dien Bien Phu to bar the door of northern Laos against invasion, it had lost much of its value. The bowl-shaped valley, transformed into a formidable fort by unrelenting toil, was quickly invested. By January 1, 1954, it was surrounded by a screen of battle-hardened Vietminh troops strong enough to imperil any French patrol that dared venture more than half a mile beyond the camp's outer defenses. The camp was now well and truly encircled. Its garrison could no longer gain elbow room, and the enemy easily bypassed it in order to resume his advance to northern Laos. Dien Bien Phu had become a trap.

Yet Giap's intentions were still by no means clear. Was he preparing to attack the fortified camp or to drive on Luang Prabang or Vientiane? Whatever his plans, he was obviously launching a major effort. Chinese aid had greatly increased of late, and most of it was funneling to the highlands. The Vietminh had mobilized tens of thousands of coolies to build a road network linking Lang Son and Tuyen Quang to the Thai country, thus making it possible to send a great deal of equipment to both northern Laos and their base at Tuan Giao, close to Dien Bien Phu. The military outlook was changing rapidly, and General Navarre indicated, in a report dated January 1, that he could no longer be confident about

[5] Intersector V (or Lien Khu V) was the Vietminh zone in central Vietnam reaching from south of Tourane (Da Nang) down to the Tuy Hoa area.

the outcome of a Vietminh assault on the fortified camp; yet at that time Dien Bien Phu still might have been successfully evacuated.

General Navarre had multiplied the number of combined air and land bases—Dien Bien Phu, Muong Soi, Luang Prabang, the Plain of Jars, Seno—in order to contain Vietminh drives which were now ranging in so many different directions that they seemed to be turning into a general offensive.

This "hedgehog" strategy, which had cost the Germans dear during World War II, unfortunately required a level of air power that France did not possess. Since General Navarre asserted that these resources were essential for success, they had to be obtained from the United States. Transport aircraft—C-47 Dakotas and the larger C-119's—were urgently needed, as were B-26 medium bombers. Their imminent dispatch was announced from Washington. But France was now caught on a terrible rack, because there were not enough trained personnel available to fly or maintain these aircraft. Authorities in Saigon tried to recruit American civilian crews for the twelve promised C-119's. An interministerial committee in Paris decided on January 16, 1954, to ask the United States for 400 specialists (mechanics, etc.) to maintain the B-26 and C-47 aircraft already in Indochina, and enough ground crews for the promised C-119's and B-26's. For political reasons, however, the government decided not to ask for these American flying personnel after all. And Saigon was instructed not to employ American aircrews on missions "involving the overflying of operational zones or dissident zones" under any circumstances.

On January 30, 1954, the U.S. Government announced that it would send 200 mechanics to Indochina immediately, along with some of the B-26 aircraft requested. The remainder would follow when the necessary French personnel were available.[6]

In the United States, these continual French requests were causing lively concern in the government and the press. People began

[6] Training of these personnel was undertaken in France as a matter of urgency.

to realize that France was nearing exhaustion in Indochina and that the Navarre Plan had so far failed to achieve the expected improvement. The latest Vietminh successes gave rise to a wave of serious misgivings.[7] Influential military men led by Admiral Radford (Chairman of the Joint Chiefs of Staff), the "China Lobby," and the entire right wing of the Republican Party led by Vice President Nixon, stressed the gravity of the situation and made no secret of the fact that the United States would probably be forced to intervene if it did not wish to see the Communists overrun Southeast Asia.

The possibility that American forces might have to fight in Indochina, which Nixon mentioned in November, now came to the fore again. Democratic Senator Mike Mansfield put the question simply and clearly in the Senate on February 8 when he asked whether the sending of American technicians to Indochina meant that "if the French and the Associated States forces become harder pressed, we will send in naval and air support? Does it mean that if the situation warrants it, American combat troops will be sent to Indochina?"[8]

Public opinion in the United States strongly opposed the idea of direct American involvement in Indochina, and on February 9, Secretary of Defense Charles E. Wilson tried to reassure the public that a military victory of the Franco-Vietnamese forces in Indochina remained "both possible and probable." He added that victory would "be delayed and get to be a little different problem" should the Chinese communists intervene.[9] But Wilson thought that there was no need to increase American aid above the existing level.

On February 9, while American newspapers with nationalist and isolationist leanings were denouncing "the intrigues of the Pentagon" aimed at "pushing the United States into the war," Demo-

[7] The dispatch of technicians intensified these misgivings, especially because Congress felt that its hand had been forced, since the relevant committees were informed and consulted only after the technicians were already on their way.

[8] *Congressional Record, Senate,* February 8, 1954, p. 1504.

[9] *The New York Times,* February 10, 1954.

cratic Senator John Stennis expressed the fear that the dispatch of American technicians to Indochina would involve the United States in a third world war. Alarm was mounting to such an extent that at a news conference on February 10, President Eisenhower gave the following clarification in reply to questions from journalists about Stennis's statement: "No one could be more bitterly opposed to ever getting involved in a hot war in that region than I am."[10] Nothing could be more tragic for the United States than to be dragged into a general war in Indochina or elsewhere in Southeast Asia, he said.

That was why the American Government was doing all it could to eliminate such a possibility while supporting the Vietnamese and the French, for whom the struggle was a matter of liberty and defense against Communist expansion. The President firmly repeated his assurances that the United States would not be drawn into the war in Indochina without prior consultation of Congress, in accordance with the Constitution.

While the White House was opting for caution, the East-West encounter that France had wanted was already in progress.

The start of the Four Power conference had been delayed for three weeks to allow for the election in Versailles of a new President of the French Republic. The conference opened on January 25, 1954, in the American Sector of Berlin, in the interallied building on the Potsdamerstrasse, where General Sokolovsky's walk-out had put an end to Four Power rule in Berlin six years earlier. Georges Bidault and Vyacheslav Molotov, who had been negotiating with each other for the past ten years, found themselves together again, in company with Anthony Eden and John Foster Dulles.

Germany occupied first place on the agenda. The U.S.S.R. wished to raise the questions of European security, German reunification, and alliances, for the treaty creating the European Defense Community was coming up for ratification.

[10] Dwight D. Eisenhower, *Public Papers of the Presidents of the United States: 1954* (Washington), p. 250.

At the very first session, Molotov demanded the convocation of a five-power conference, including Communist China, in May or June; such a conference had been a main theme of Soviet propaganda ever since the Russians had first demanded it in Berlin in 1951. The Soviet minister knew the Four Power conference had stemmed from France's wish to settle the problem of Indochina, and he probably believed he could bargain his hopes for a convocation of a five-power conference against the prospect of satisfying the hopes of the French.

In fact, Dulles lost no time in barring the way, and he did so bluntly. Time and again, he said that the United States would not take part in any five-power conference, for it refused to discuss the problem of world peace with unrepentant aggressors.[11]

Molotov refused to be put off. He stressed the part that China, "a great power," could play in consolidating peace, and requested again that a meeting be held in May or June. It seemed then (although Moscow quickly rectified any such impression) as if he were suggesting that a five-power conference should confine itself to the issues of Korea and Indochina.

This time Bidault replied. As he saw it, the Big Four must seek to re-establish peace in Asia and put an end to the fighting under conditions acceptable to all concerned. Nothing required or justified the urgent convocation of a five-power conference. (This was by no means the opinion of Reynaud, in Paris.) The Chinese People's Republic, said Bidault, ought first to give a token of good will, since "it has persisted in contributing to the equipment and training of the Vietminh troops." The French minister repeated, however, that his government was ready to grasp any opportunity for peace in Indochina, in full agreement with the Associated States.

Molotov remained evasive and suggested that committees of experts be set up to study these questions. It looked now as though

11 "It is one thing to recognize evil as a fact: it is another thing to take evil to one's breast and call it good," as the Secretary of State was to put it on March 29 at a meeting at the Overseas Press Club of America (*The New York Times*, March 30, 1954).

the proposal for a conference on Indochina would go up in smoke. This possibility alarmed Paris, and Bidault, whose prejudices against negotiations over Indochina were well known, was instructed to display greater flexibility.[12] The search for a way to solve the Indochina problem was for France, after all, the prime objective of the Berlin conference. So that useful discussions could continue, Bidault then proposed that the Four Powers hold closed sessions, and this was accepted in principle by the three other powers.

Meanwhile, the Laniel government was working to get the American and British governments to agree in principle that a solution in Indochina should be sought by way of Moscow and Peking, and these efforts were beginning to bear fruit. On February 5, Dulles took some American journalists into his confidence and spoke to them of the conditions under which he might be willing to discuss Korea and Indochina with Communist China.

In fact, the Berlin conference gradually bogged down over the German question. On February 6, deadlock was reached on this point of the agenda, and negotiations in closed session, concerning Asia, began in earnest. The Four Powers devoted no less than five whole sessions to Far Eastern problems and finally agreed on a future conference to work out solutions for them.

The three Western powers made their basic position clear from the start. They rejected, and went on rejecting, any suggestion that the future conference should involve five powers. In no circumstances could China be treated on an equal footing with the Big Four. One after the other, every Soviet attempt to circumvent this position was defeated.

At the very first closed session, on February 8, Dulles expounded on the thesis he had so often expounded before, explaining that it would be impossible for any American government to agree to a meeting that might set up a "Big Five" that included the Chinese People's Republic. The five powers involved had no special mandate to decide the fate of the world. On the other hand, his government acknowledged the de facto situation created by the existence of Communist China, and he was prepared to negotiate

[12] Conversation of the authors with Maurice Schumann, April 1, 1959.

with it on particular problems whenever this might serve the cause of peace.

Dulles accepted the principle of a Korean conference to which the Four Powers would invite South Korea, the countries that had supplied troops to the United Nations Command, North Korea, and the Chinese People's Republic, although he made it clear that neither the invitation to the conference nor the fact that it was held was to be construed as giving diplomatic recognition except where this already existed. As soon as Communist China's behavior, at the conference and in Southeast Asia, gave proof of its peaceful intentions, the Four Powers would determine the conditions for calling a conference aimed at securing peace in Indochina.

First Dulles and then Bidault heavily emphasized this "absolute necessity" of obtaining tokens of Peking's will for peace. As Bidault saw it, the basic reason for the prolongation of the war in Indochina was Communist China's aid to the Vietminh. Therefore, if China wished to take its place with the others at the conference table, it must first demonstrate its willingness to end this war. France would be very willing to reconsider the Chinese problem when China had reconsidered the problem of Indochina.

Molotov replied that China had nothing to do with Indochinese events, which had begun long before the establishment of the Chinese People's Republic. It was unthinkable that the Peking government should accept an invitation which in effect condemned it as an aggressor state and threw doubts on its will for peace. If the Five Powers were to consider the problems of Korea and Indochina, they could only do so on the basis of formulas acceptable to all of them. For its part, the Soviet Union was prepared to agree that a Five Power conference should deal only with these two problems at first.

On February 11, Bidault suggested that a Korean conference be held in Geneva on April 15. As soon as it showed "favorable prospects," and provided that the same situation prevailed in Indochina, the possibility of a conference aimed at restoring peace in Indochina could then be examined.

Molotov asked why the Indochinese conference should be made

to depend on the success of a Korean conference, which was by no means assured. Bidault thought he detected a note of pleading in the Soviet minister's words and believed there was now less cause for haste than ever. The U.S.S.R. had at last revealed its concern for a settlement in Indochina; on February 12, Molotov accepted April 15 and Geneva for the date and location of the Korean conference. Bidault therefore stated that, in his opinion, an examination of the problem of Indochina did not in the least depend on a solution of the Korean problem but that both depended on China's will for peace.

It was Anthony Eden who found the necessary compromise. The British plan no longer discriminated between great and small powers, between hosts and guests. It simply listed the countries concerned more or less in alphabetical order, but retained the idea of "favorable prospects," in other words the subordination of the Indochinese conference to the Korean conference. Finally, a meeting of experts, called at the Soviet Union's suggestion, drafted a text to which the Four Powers agreed on February 18. The U.S.S.R. agreed that the holding of a conference should not imply recognition of Peking. The Western powers, for their part, agreed that the problem of restoring peace in Indochina should be examined "equally" at the Korean conference, which would open on April 26 in Geneva. It was specified that representatives of the United States, France, Great Britain, the Soviet Union, China, and the other states concerned would be invited to this conference.

Bidault suggested a way of evading the delicate problem of invitations to the Korean conference. The U.S.S.R. would invite China and North Korea; the United States would invite South Korea and the other countries that had fought under the United Nations Command.

And so a decision was reached to hold an international conference on Indochina—the fulfillment of the French Government's earnest hopes of many months.

One would like to think that the French Government, before it made the proposal, had given due thought to all the dangers attendant upon it—in particular, the danger that the enemy might intensify his offensive in order to show the conference a panoply of victories, thereby taking the "crisis" to its climax.[13]

[13] General Navarre was apparently not consulted about the timeliness of this diplomatic action. Nevertheless, it seems clear that he was duty-bound to warn the government of this danger (especially since the Cabanier mission had alerted him to the government's exact intentions) as soon as the press mentioned negotiations about Asia. Up to the present, we have no evidence that he did so.

4

THE PLEVEN MISSION

In Paris, pressure in favor of a peaceful solution to the Indochinese problem was mounting, but in Indochina itself, the stakes were again being raised.

General Navarre had just launched a new offensive, although his forces were dangerously dispersed and the situation in Laos was highly fluid. Fearing a Vietminh offensive from Intersector V against French positions on the plateaus and in southern Laos, he committed twenty battalions to Operation Atlante. A landing at Tuy Hoa on January 20, 1954, began the operation which, Navarre hoped, would make it possible to start pacification of the entire area south of the 18th Parallel.

Taken in isolation, there was something to be said for this move. Besides, the French Government had known about the plan since January 1 or even earlier and had raised no objections. But it is possible to ask whether there was not undue risk involved, in view of the amount of troops and resources already committed elsewhere. Once again, it was a matter of believing that everything could be done at once.

Now that the "*grande négociation*" was within reach, it was essential that French military and political leaders have an exact, full, and up-to-date picture of the war. Jacquet went to Indochina in January and carried out a thorough analysis of the political situation there. The Secretary of State for the Armed Forces (War), de Chevigné, the Chief of Staff of the Land Forces, General Blanc, and the Chief of Staff of the Air Force, General Fay, went to inspect the various fronts in Indochina and to get a close look at the military situation in late January and early February.

In addition, the government announced on January 26 that René Pleven, Minister of National Defense, would also make an inspection tour of Indochina at the beginning of February; it was stated that the purpose of his visit would be mainly military. In reality, the Minister (who had never been to Indochina) had asked Laniel to let him study at first hand not only the overall military situation—in other words, the prospects—but also the development of the armies of the Associated States and the conditions under which allied aid was being supplied. Basically, he wanted to know whether time was on the side of France or the Vietminh. Was France waging an endless war? Or could a trained and battle-hardened Vietnamese army relieve France's military burden by intervening massively on the battlefield?

On January 27, the enemy began to move again. The 308th Division, grouped in the Dien Bien Phu–Tuan Giao area, suddenly marched west. There could now be no mistake about it: the offensive against Luang Prabang had started.

Immediately, two messages sped from Paris to Saigon. Navarre and Dejean both put the same question: was Laos to be defended? Some ministers had maintained a few months earlier that if the Vietminh mounted a powerful offensive in Laos, it would be best to withdraw the line of defense farther south, toward Pak Sane. It seemed to Dejean that such a solution had serious political drawbacks. He felt that Laos should be defended in front of its historical capital. "One does not defend France at Orléans."

The National Defense Committee met on February 6 to study the problem. Pleven asked whether it was still the policy of the government to defend Laos. He wanted to know because he would be on the spot in the midst of a Vietminh offensive against Luang

Prabang: how should he reply if General Navarre asked him whether or not to evacuate the city in case of a Vietminh attack? After discussing the matter, the Committee empowered Pleven, should the need arise, to give instructions to the commander in chief about the evacuation of upper Laos, bearing in mind that the safety of the Expeditionary Corps remained the first priority.

Pleven landed at Saigon on February 9, accompanied by General Ely, Chairman of the Chiefs of Staff Committee, and held an important meeting with the chief military leaders on the same day. At the outset, he spoke of his and the government's misgivings about the "hedgehog" strategy which, he feared, created "game preserves" for the Vietminh. General Navarre told him that the French strong points were laid out as combined air and land bases provided with all the resources needed to withstand Vietminh attacks, and that each of them could be reinforced by air. As for Dien Bien Phu, the strength of the forces encircling it was still not fully known. The enemy had intended to attack it but now seemed to have abandoned the idea because the position appeared too strong. Navarre added that the existence of Dien Bien Phu had delayed the offensive in Laos, which might otherwise have started two months earlier.

General Fay inquired whether the landing strip at Dien Bien Phu might not become unusable after three weeks of rain. "This weakness has never been pointed out to me," answered General Navarre; but, he said, he would check this point. The commander in chief then stressed the great importance he attached to Operation Atlante, which he had just launched. This aggressive movement in central Vietnam plainly showed that the French were not content to leave the initiative to the enemy. It would improve the war map by subduing an important area south of the 18th Parallel, which the enemy was preparing to use as a base for a number of offensives, and by denying the Vietminh command the use of a large number of troops. Above all, it would give the Vietnamese Government an opportunity of displaying its effectiveness.

Next, Pleven investigated every aspect of the problem of the Vietnamese army, both with the French and Vietnamese authorities in Saigon and with Bao Dai at Dalat. He then visited the various war fronts, beginning with Tonkin, where he studied the situation in the Red River delta with General Cogny. (He visited Operation Atlante on his way there.) On February 19, he went to Dien Bien Phu with de Chevigné and General Ely and found the fort's garrison full of an extraordinary confidence. Everyone, from Colonel de Castries to the last gunner, was looking forward to the Vietminh assault and seemed to fear nothing except the possibility that the enemy might abandon the attempt. The garrison's optimism, and its firm belief that it could break the Vietminh fighting force, impressed the visitors, but the sight of the circle of hills which dominated the position filled them with foreboding.

The minister went next to Luang Prabang, directly threatened by Giap's offensive (the Vietminh's forward elements were now only thirty miles away). The city was preparing for the coming attack, and the Royal Laotian Government let it be known that it intended to remain there. But would the French defend the city?

On February 24, the Vietminh forces suddenly halted. Two days later, they began a "withdrawal" toward Dien Bien Phu—a "disengagement" that some immediately connected with the publication of the Berlin communiqué.

Pleven returned to Saigon on February 25. There, he received a hint that the Vietminh wished to make contact with him, as it had succeeded in doing very fleetingly a month earlier with Jacquet, and he therefore retired for three days to Cap Saint-Jacques, where an approach could be made more easily, on the pretext of drafting his report. But the Vietminh gave no sign of life, and on February 28, Pleven and his party left for Paris, where they arrived on March 1.

There was no delay in informing the French Government of all the conclusions reached by the Minister and the Secretary of State for Armed Forces during their parallel tours of inspection. Pleven reported to Laniel on the very day of his return, then addressed interministerial committees and restricted cabinet meetings, and spoke before the National Defense Committee. To avoid leaks, no written report was prepared and no formal statement was submitted to the Council of Ministers.

Two sets of conclusions emerged from the visit: one from the military leaders who had preceded Pleven or had accompanied him, the other from Pleven himself. The first, contained in reports of the three generals, Ely, Blanc, and Fay, was that no military solution could be achieved, in spite of the scale of air, ground, and sea forces at General Navarre's disposal. Not even heavy reinforcement of the Expeditionary Corps could influence the outcome in any way. Moreover, France had already reached the limits of its military effort. The most it could now hope to achieve was the optimum military conditions for a political settlement.

General Blanc was the most outspoken of the three generals. In his opinion, the Indochinese conflict had to be settled *that year*. France could no longer tolerate the demands it made on its material resources and morale, nor could it stand the increasingly heavy casualties, particularly among officers and NCO's. Blanc considered that it would be a crime against the French forces and the noncombatant population to continue the struggle in the Red River delta, which had become a graveyard for the French. The French, he thought, should pull out of the "Tonkinese wasp's nest" and bring their full weight to bear in Laos and the Vietnamese territories south of the Savannakhet–Dong Ha road, which could then be pacified completely. Blanc believed that such a solution could be negotiated without violating any existing French obligations, that it could be done with the agreement and cooperation of Vietnam, and that French military prestige could be preserved in the process.[1]

In the opinion of the three generals, the only factor that might alter the outcome of both the struggle and the negotiations during the coming months and years was the Vietnamese Army. The formation of this army should be France's principal military and political concern in Indochina, for the determination and unity of such a force could well be a major influence for the country's well-being: if this army could master its role within eighteen months, France would be able to reduce its casualties to a bearable level, even if it could not cut back significantly.

[1] This foreshadowed the agreements made in Geneva five months later, after the fall of Dien Bien Phu.

This was possible only if Vietnam really began to participate in the war and if an effective and responsible Vietnamese administration fully supported a government capable of imparting faith and spirit to the country. Unless these conditions were met, the generals said, there could be no outcome to the war.

Pleven's conclusions were very similar.

It seemed to him that the existing military situation made it impossible for the Vietminh to inflict decisive defeats on the French[2] but that the status quo was precarious. The French were unlikely to get into major difficulties so long as China did not intervene directly and so long as the Vietminh lacked air power. But the facts were inescapable: the balance of forces could be maintained only by means of increasingly murderous operations, and the French held their positions only at the price of increasingly heavy casualties.[3] The resources and morale of the Expeditionary Corps were being worn down at a dangerous and accelerating rate.

Pleven pointed out that Chinese aid to the Vietminh was increasing every day and the enemy's state of training was improving. Backed by an inexhaustible Chinese reserve, the Vietminh would draw the French into a tougher and tougher struggle, demanding ever greater efforts from them. Even if the Navarre Plan succeeded, it would at best slow down the Vietminh, but it could not force it to make peace.

Pleven noted that on January 1, 1954, the Vietnamese Army had reached a strength of 210,000 men, most of whom were in the ranks of 160 infantry battalions, and that an ambitious plan existed to enlarge it to nearly 400,000 men by the beginning of 1956. He praised "the Vietnamese soldier, born of the country-

[2] Pleven, however, expressed doubts about Dien Bien Phu. In describing the eagerness with which the garrison looked forward to the attack, he wrote, "Personally, I do not look forward to it." But evacuation had long since become impossible anyway.

[3] The casualties were as follows:

December,	1952:	1,261	(including 51 officers)
December,	1953:	1,789	(including 83 officers)
February,	1953:	479	(including 28 officers)
February,	1954:	1,840	(including 83 officers)

side," but stressed that he would become fully effective only when his imagination had been fired, when he had acquired faith in the Vietnamese fatherland, and when he knew that he went into battle to defend it and not merely to serve French interests.

But no real progress had been made in the political area, and Pleven did not conceal his misgivings about this failure. The Vietminh may not have been loved, but it was feared and respected, and time was on its side. The new Vietnamese government had an honest reputation and was animated by a genuine desire to do well, but it was still too newly established, it had not yet won popular support, and it lacked the resources to accomplish the double task of building an army and an administrative service. Unfortunately, there could be no doubt that throughout the country the number of villages under effective Baodaist control was tending to diminish rather than increase. As the Vietminh's control spread, the French forces would no longer obtain that minimum of cooperation without which no army can survive on foreign soil.

Pleven therefore urged that a general military convention be negotiated as quickly as possible with the Vietnamese authorities. This agreement should specify the stages and timing of the formation of an army that could eventually engage in full-scale war and take over the tasks of the Expeditionary Corps. If Vietnam would not accept these obligations, France would be forced to reconsider its position.

Bearing all these factors in mind, the Minister of Defense made his formal recommendation: every possibility raised at the Geneva conference must be explored to find an acceptable solution to the conflict in Indochina. Since any direct negotiations with the Vietminh would be regarded as a betrayal by the Baodaist authorities the Geneva conference provided the only honorable means of bringing the war to an end.

The conclusions reached by the Minister and the military leaders convinced the government that there was no time to lose. France had to demonstrate its willingness to end the war without further delay. On February 22, Nehru's proposal for a cease-fire in Indochina gave the government an opportunity to state its position.

In the National Assembly, the opposition seized upon the problem; it would undoubtedly heckle the government. The Socialist Party, which had called for a truce a few months before, now renewed its demand.

What reply should be given? The General Staff had already given its opinion. It warned against a repetition of what had happened in 1946, saying that a cease-fire should be the result, not the beginning, of any negotiations capable of providing the Expeditionary Corps with the requisite safeguards.

After a briefing by Pleven, who passed on the advice of the General Staff, the Premier went before the National Assembly on March 5 to state the conditions under which France would be willing to conclude a cease-fire:

1. Evacuation of Cambodia and Laos by the Vietminh forces.
2. Establishment of a "no man's land" around the Red River delta and the evacuation of the delta by regular Vietminh forces.
3. Regrouping of Vietminh forces in central Vietnam within an area to be determined.[4]

This declaration found an echo. On March 10, five days after a conciliatory speech by Chen Yun in Peking, the D.R.V. announced that it was prepared to receive the French proposals.

The war, altered both by the rising level of Chinese aid and by the approaching conference in Geneva (the two factors were probably not unconnected) was reaching the turning point. Every effort had to be made to avoid a military collapse or serious reverses before the conference. From now on, the war had to be guided carefully every step of the way. Deploring the errors of the past, Pleven suggested on March 11 that a select War Committee be created which would meet at frequent intervals and make whatever decisions the situation required. This committee, whose very existence would be kept from the public, should include the Premier, the minister of foreign affairs, the minister of national defense, and the military secretaries of state. Its decisions would

[4] *Journal officiel, Débats parlementaires Assemblée nationale, 1954*, p. 714. Pleven personally considered these conditions a little too restrictive.

be implemented by the secretary of state for the Associated States, to whom the commander in chief would continue to report.

In its preparations for the Geneva conference, the government had to consider not only its own interests and those of its Vietnamese allies, but also the interests of the United States, which still seemed to believe in the possibility of a military victory.

At a crucial meeting of the Council of Ministers on March 11, Pleven suggested that General Ely be sent to Washington (he already had an invitation to come from Admiral Radford). He would be able to explain the true state of the military situation to the American leaders, so that they would not go into the Geneva conference believing the war could still be won.

Pleven was also worried about the effect of any Chinese intervention in the air. A few MIG-15's over Indochina would radically alter the entire situation in a week, so dependent were the French on air transport at that time.[5] He was uneasy; he could find no evidence of a written assurance that the United States would respond to such an eventuality. Should not the United States be asked for a guarantee of extremely rapid intervention in such a case? Bidault admitted that there was no written commitment from the United States, only a verbal promise that the problem would be reconsidered if direct Chinese air intervention occurred. But he was sure that the American Government would be honor-bound to intervene in such a case. Pleven persisted, stressing that an assurance of immediate intervention must be obtained, since France was taking disproportionate risks in Indochina as a direct result of American policy toward China.

Pleven's view prevailed, and it was decided that General Ely would ask Washington for an assurance of immediate intervention by the U.S. Air Force against any air force that might be brought into action by the enemy. He would also inquire more generally into the American reactions to any possible further increase in Chinese aid to the Vietminh.

On March 13, two days after this memorable meeting of the

[5] The increasing strength and accuracy of Vietminh antiaircraft fire was already threatening French air supremacy.

Council of Ministers, the Vietminh launched the expected full-scale attack against Dien Bien Phu.

This furious assault was preceded by a tremendous artillery preparation, which revealed for the first time the modern equipment and hitherto unsuspected firepower of Giap's new army. The number and caliber of the guns[6] and the abundance of ammunition came as a complete surprise.

Surprise was so complete, in fact, that three of the support positions covering the northern complex of Dien Bien Phu—Beatrice, Gabrielle, and Anne-Marie—fell during the first hours of the attack. One of the first shells of the Vietminh barrage entered a loophole of Gabrielle's command post, killing Colonel Gaucher, the commander of the Foreign Legion's 13th Half-Brigade, and three of his assistants. This caused great confusion, and the Thai troops holding the forward positions, unable to stand the hail of fire, broke and ran. The support positions were soon overwhelmed by waves of attacking Vietminh infantry.

The French artillery reacted. It attempted to silence the enemy guns, but the Vietminh had hidden them in underground bunkers (as had the Chinese in Korea), and their exact sites could not be located. The French fired blindly and achieved no apparent result.

The counterattacks launched by Colonel de Castries to recapture the supporting positions only succeeded in recovering part of Anne-Marie. Beatrice and Gabrielle were gone for good. This was tragic, because their crossing fields of fire dominated the landing strip—as vital to the submerged camp's garrison as oxygen to a diver. The bowl of Dien Bien Phu was already dominated, and the enemy found it easy to direct his artillery fire from the surrounding heights. The power of the Vietminh artillery—105-mm. howitzers, 120-mm. heavy mortars, and the deadly Russian 37-mm. antiaircraft guns—played its full part in tightening the steel vise that was closing on the twelve battalions of the garrison.

Navarre, Dejean, and the general staffs in Hanoi and Saigon knew in their heart of hearts, from the morning of March 15 on-

[6] Yet Lucien Bodard, the correspondent of *France-Soir*, had reported as early as January 4 that the Vietminh were concentrating 105-mm. guns around the fortified camp.

ward, that the battle was lost. Without a powerful intervention from outside (and where could such a force be found?) Dien Bien Phu was under sentence of death.

The prospect of a major defeat was now beginning to take shape. Seven years of mistakes, followed by four months of optimism and overconfidence, had led to this tragic result at the very moment when France was on the eve of negotiations it longed for, when it most needed a position of strength and an impressive war map. General Navarre had lost his bet and, in so doing, was likely to ruin the efforts—or perhaps one should say the improvisations—of his diplomatic colleagues.

5

OPERATION VULTURE

The violence of the Vietminh attack on Dien Bien Phu, the abundance of enemy resources, the shock of his artillery—all caused such painful surprise in Hanoi and Saigon that there was unconcealed anxiety about the outcome of the siege. The recent large increase in Chinese aid to the Vietminh had changed the whole nature of the operation. Navarre's staff saw more clearly with each passing day that only a rapid intensification of air support could avert disaster.

By now it was less a matter of flying in troops than of supplying more equipment, ammunition, and food. Dien Bien Phu was a trap, and to reinforce it meant losing, or risking, even more men. General Navarre wrote on March 29 that "the fate of Dien Bien Phu depends upon our ability to parachute supplies and evacuate men." Strategic and tactical support must also be given to the garrison by attacking the enemy's rear, harassing his supply lines, cutting his communications, destroying his stores, neutralizing his artillery batteries, pinning his infantry to the ground, and drawing a ring of death around the fortified camp with napalm. This was the only alternative to disaster, the only way to avoid negotiating for peace under the shadow of defeat. It was also the only way of keeping the price within bounds.

Dejean lost no time in approaching the United States embassy and the American military mission in Saigon for the top-priority dispatch of the aircraft already requested—B-26 bombers, F8F fighters, and C-47 transports. He also asked for American authorization to use the borrowed C-119's—with French crews—"for the massive use of napalm." He sent an urgent plea to Paris for additional air support; so did General Navarre. General Ely, the French Chief of Staff, was about to leave for Washington and would thus be able to press directly for accelerated shipments of supplies to Indochina.

General Ely arrived in Washington on March 20. The American capital was uneasy about the fate of Dien Bien Phu. Would the fort hold out? General Ely was optimistic. Dien Bien Phu would indeed hold out, particularly if the supplies requested were delivered quickly so that the enemy could be hit hard. The climate of opinion was extremely favorable to the French requests. General Ely found that officials in the American Government were very optimistic and confident about the outcome of the war. He was received on the morning of March 22 by President Eisenhower in the presence of Admiral Radford. The President told the Admiral that General Navarre's requests should be fulfilled at once and that special priority should be given to everything that might contribute to the success of the current battle. And, indeed, French requirements—in particular those for B-26 bombers—were met during the following weeks from bases in the Philippines, Formosa, and Japan. Dulles, whom Ely saw on March 23, said that he could see no reason for abandoning the Navarre Plan, which forecast successes or even victory during the next campaign, in other words during the following year.[1]

But what Ely had to say to these American policy-makers helped

[1] A part of the memorandum Dulles sent to the President after his talk with Ely was published by Eisenhower in his memoirs; Dulles did not seem prepared to engage America's prestige in a doubtful enterprise. Dwight D. Eisenhower, *Mandate for Change* (New York, 1963), p. 345.

to dissipate their mood of optimism and to replace it by lively misgivings. The government and the administration suddenly awoke to the danger: France had reached a point at which it was ready to negotiate, even under the worst conditions, unless it received massive aid. It became increasingly clear to the American leaders that they would have to commit the United States more deeply to the struggle.

In fact, American policy was changing rapidly. A deep and thorough examination of the situation in Southeast Asia had taken place at the highest level, and the National Security Council had recommended, at its meeting on March 6, that the United States should take all possible measures to prevent the Communists from gaining control over this area, the loss of which would have incalculable consequences for the "Free World." More than 600 million Asians had already been drawn into Moscow's orbit. No more should be allowed to go the same way. Southeast Asia supplied the Free World with a number of vital commodities. It also represented a first-class trading partner for Japan, and, if it fell, the Japanese Government might find it difficult to maintain its alliance with the United States. Southeast Asia must be held at all costs, and Indochina was the key to the whole area.[2]

It was against this evolving background that General Ely's talks in Washington took place. They covered three essential points, apart from the urgent need for aircraft to assist Dien Bien Phu. Two of these points were more or less long-term; the third was short-term, but its implications were immense.

The first dealt with the means of enabling Vietnam to resist the Communist drive *by itself*. The Americans strongly criticized the French method of forming and training the Vietnamese Army —a subject about which they felt they had a right to speak, since they supplied most of the funds and equipment for the purpose. A special mission under General John O'Daniel was ready to go to Vietnam as soon as the French and Americans had agreed on a new training program for the Vietnamese. General Ely discussed

[2] Hence Eisenhower's March 24 declaration on the importance of Indochina. Dwight D. Eisenhower, *Public Papers of the Presidents of the United States: 1954* (Washington), p. 250.

this subject very frankly with Admiral Radford, particularly on March 24. Clearly, the Americans were sticking to their conviction that a large, well-equipped, and well-trained Vietnamese Army (along the lines of the South Korean Army) could put a stop to Communist plans.

The second point—the main object of Ely's mission—covered the guarantee of American action in case of Chinese air intervention. It was the massive increase in Chinese aid that had enabled the Vietminh to place the French in such a precarious position in Indochina, and the Chinese continued to display an aggressive spirit (denounced by Dulles in his press conference on March 23). The approaching Geneva conference might well force them to give the Vietminh the means to score a decisive success. Any Chinese miscalculations before the opening of the conference must therefore be discouraged; China must be persuaded there and then that the Free World would intervene rather than allow the situation in Indochina to deteriorate any further as a result of its aid to the Vietminh. A clear warning to China was essential, but the National Security Council suggested that resistance to Communism in Southeast Asia should not be the responsibility of the United States alone.

General Ely could therefore take very satisfactory answers back to Paris: the urgent requests for aircraft would be met; the United States would do more to help with the formation of the Vietnamese Army; and, without giving a formal guarantee in connection with possible Chinese intervention, they would issue fresh warnings to Peking. General Ely prepared to leave for Paris on March 25 as arranged.

At the last moment, his departure was delayed by twenty-four hours. On that extra day, a conversation of major significance with Admiral Radford opened up new and important prospects.

In the light of President Eisenhower's instructions to do everything to help the French in the battle for Dien Bien Phu, the Chairman of the Joint Chiefs of Staff felt that—given the unforeseen increase in Chinese supplies of artillery and antiaircraft equipment—American assistance to the Expeditionary Corps could be taken a little further, perhaps as far as limited and temporary tactical air support. Radford suggested to Ely that such support could be given in the absence of any Chinese provocation, solely to help and perhaps save the defenders of the besieged camp. It would not in any sense bring America into the war or herald its intervention.

Admiral Radford's proposal was that some sixty B-29 heavy bombers should carry out several night raids on Dien Bien Phu from their base at Clark Field, near Manila. They would drop 450 tons of bombs on each raid. They would be escorted by 150 fighters from the aircraft carriers of the U.S. Seventh Fleet. This saturation bombing would shatter the besieger's ring around the camp and destroy much of the Vietminh equipment. Admiral Radford did not hide the fact that such an operation represented the extreme limit of American assistance to France in its struggle in Indochina and that its political implications would have to be considered carefully by both governments. All preparations would be made, in advance, to avoid any delay in launching the operation, but the signal for it could only be given when government approval was received (it was understood that the French government would have to request assistance). Approval must therefore be obtained as quickly as possible, and the two Chiefs of Staff should now make this their chief concern.[3]

As soon as he returned to Paris on March 27, General Ely informed Pleven of the results of his mission and especially of Admiral Radford's extraordinary proposal. A War Committee[4] met in closed session on March 29 to discuss the political, diplomatic, and strategic implications of what thereafter became known as Operation Vulture.

All those present thought that such an operation by the United States Air Force would be interpreted as the first act of direct U.S. intervention in the war in Indochina and might well result in a

[3] Ely describes this talk in his book, but appears inclined to minimize its importance. Paul Ely, *L'Indochine dans la tourmente* (Paris, 1964), pp. 76–77, 82–83.

[4] Participating in this meeting were: Laniel, Reynaud, Bidault, Pleven, de Chevigné, Gavini, Christiaens, and Jacquet; Generals Ely, Blanc, Fay, and Crépin; and Admiral Nomy.

violent Chinese reaction. But this was not considered to be a very serious threat, and it was decided that on the whole it was a risk worth taking. It was decided to send an officer of General Ely's staff to Indochina immediately to obtain General Navarre's opinion as to the probable effectiveness of such a raid.

Colonel Brohon, the officer chosen for this assignment (who had gone to Washington with Ely), arrived in Saigon on April 1 and left immediately for Hanoi, where he met with Navarre and Dejean on April 2. He explained that General Ely wished to know whether Navarre thought that Operation Vulture, which he described in broad outline, could save Dien Bien Phu. If General Navarre approved the operation, the French Government would endorse it and the project would be put to the American Government.

General Navarre's reply was clear-cut. He said that such an intervention by the U.S. Air Force would destroy the enemy's artillery and antiaircraft batteries and thus allow the situation at the camp to be stabilized.

In fact, the situation at Dien Bien Phu had seriously deteriorated during the past three days. The Vietminh launched a new attack on March 30 and made dangerous progress along the eastern side of the French position. The landing strip was under fire from the captured outposts. The wounded could no longer be evacuated—the last aircraft had left on March 26—and the garrison could now only be supplied by parachute drops. Vietminh antiaircraft fire made these drops increasingly inaccurate as the days went by.

Colonel Brohon left for Paris on the same day. Another closed session of the War Committee was called on his return, on the evening of Sunday, April 4.[5] This time, a decision had to be made. The government felt that it had no right to refuse anything that might save the garrison at Dien Bien Phu. Even the ministers best placed to assess the danger of "international complications"

[5] Participating in this meeting were: Laniel, Reynaud, Bidault, Schumann, Pleven, de Chevigné, Gavini, Jacquet; Generals Ely and Crépin; and Admiral Nomy. There is very little information about these meetings, at which, on the specific instructions of Laniel, no minutes were taken. The ministers and generals present were also instructed not to take notes.

felt unable to resist the proposed request to the United States if there were no other way of saving the besieged garrison. Everybody believed—rashly, perhaps—that this "limited operation" would not lead to an extension of the war. Apparently all those present agreed that the operation had some chance of lifting the siege or at least of significantly helping its garrison. Echoing General Navarre's words, they stressed that all that mattered was that the intervention be both massive and immediate.

As soon as there was agreement, the meeting broke off to enable Maurice Schumann to summon American ambassador Douglas Dillon to the Hotel Matignon at 11:30 that night. He was received by Laniel in the presence of Bidault. On behalf of the French Government, the Premier asked the Ambassador to request the American Government to intervene with heavy bombers capable of delivering 2-ton bombs or heavier, in order to save the garrison of Dien Bien Phu. Ambassador Dillon first said that in his opinion Congress would have to be consulted, but he promised to transmit the request to his government without delay.[6]

The reply came quickly enough. The next day Dillon handed Bidault a telegram he had just received from Dulles. It said that the Secretary of State had explained to General Ely, in the presence of Admiral Radford, that the United States could not undertake warlike acts in Indochina until it had a political understanding with France and other countries and the approval of Congress as well. After consultations at the highest level, he must now confirm this attitude. The United States would do everything in its power, within constitutional limitations, to facilitate concerted action in Indochina. Such action, however, was impossible so long as a coalition involving the active cooperation of the British Commonwealth had not been formed. In the meantime, Dulles concluded, everything possible would be done, short of war.

[6] Officially, the reason for this unusual summons was to obtain some clarification about the delivery of B-26 aircraft. Schumann stated that the Ambassador's reply "was considered to be satisfactory." The true story was first given in the American press and was later confirmed by Laniel. See his lecture of June 24, 1955, at Caen, and Joseph Laniel, *Le drame indochinois* (Paris, 1957), p. 85.

Thus, the American Government rejected the French request, and the idea of a raid on Dien Bien Phu was set aside, at any rate for the time being.

What had happened? Quite simply, Admiral Radford in Washington did not have the same success in persuading his government as General Ely had had in Paris. Radford and Dulles had studied the political and military implications of the proposed operation, both were clearly aware of the need to do something to prevent a French defeat before the Geneva conference and to restore the French Government's determination and sense of confidence, but they had no illusions about America's unwillingness to get involved in the Indochina war. Congress and American public opinion were more than reluctant in this respect and would undoubtedly interpret the proposed air strike at Dien Bien Phu as the first step toward a major American commitment in Indochina. It was therefore necessary to prepare public opinion and Congress in advance, before any action could be taken—and this in election year! Also, the agreed warning would have to be sent to China. All this would take time, and although Radford considered speed essential for military reasons, Dulles insisted on securing political cover.

The Secretary of State opened his campaign with a speech at the Overseas Press Club in New York on the evening of March 29, 1954. He denounced the assistance given by the Communist bloc to the Vietminh; he dwelt on the supply of Czech guns and ammunition to the Vietminh and on the presence in the Vietminh army of "2,000 Chinese Communists" who functioned "in staff sections of the high command, at the division level, and in specialized units such as signals, engineering, artillery, and transportation." He recalled the warning to China on September 7, 1953, by the sixteen powers that had fought in Korea, stating that any new Chinese act of aggression would provoke a reaction which would not necessarily be confined to Korea.

> It seems desirable [the Secretary of State continued] to clarify further the United States position. Under the conditions of today, the imposition on Southeast Asia of the political system of Communist

> Russia and its Chinese Communist ally, by whatever means, would be a grave threat to the whole free community.
>
> The United States feels that that possibility should not be passively accepted, but should be met by united action. This might have serious risks, but these risks are far less than would face us a few years from now if we dare not be resolute today.[7]

Dulles's speech caused a major uproar in political and diplomatic circles in Washington. Ambassadors inquired about its real significance. Congressmen were worried, and administration officials had to reassure them. The State Department explained that before it was delivered, the speech had been read by congressional leaders of both parties, and the passage referring to concerted action had been communicated to the British and French governments. Nobody had raised any objections.

The incident was significant. On the following day (March 30), Jean Daridan, minister counselor at the French embassy, asked a senior official in the State Department how the speech should be interpreted; he was told that the American Government was contemplating direct intervention in Indochina which would stop short of relieving the French troops on the ground.

This was the heart of the matter. Dulles wanted to persuade American public opinion that intervention, which he thought would have to be decided upon quickly, was the only way of preventing Indochina from falling into Communist hands. As the American leaders saw it, this would involve air and naval operations but not any ground forces. The administration hoped that the war could be won or at least a compromise obtained without sending American troops to Indochina. Intimidation and the threat of direct intervention would, it was hoped, induce China to abandon its expansionist policy. However, President Eisenhower blunted the edge of the Secretary of State's declaration by saying, at his press conference on March 31, that he could not imagine anything more to the disadvantage of the United States than the employment of its land forces, or indeed any other forces, in distant operations.

7 *The New York Times*, March 30, 1954.

Meanwhile, Dulles and Radford had already warned congressional leaders of what was at stake in the struggle. The Admiral thought that the administration should seek congressional authority for the measures necessary to prevent a Communist victory in Southeast Asia, with special reference to the possibility of a serious deterioration in the situation in Indochina. President Eisenhower was opposed to this suggestion, while Dulles thought that such a request would be rejected. In any case, congressional leaders had to be sounded out first and given the opportunity of hearing the assessment of the Joint Chiefs of Staff.

On April 3, Dulles arranged a two-hour meeting at the State Department with Admiral Radford and eight leading congressmen —three Republicans and five Democrats.[8] The Admiral revealed the true military situation in Indochina and the very real danger of a French collapse and a Vietminh take-over if the French were not given the support they needed so urgently. He explained that massive Chinese aid to Ho Chi Minh had altered the strategic terms of the conflict and that the United States must take appropriate action immediately if it wished to avoid a very costly commitment at a later date.

The Chairman of the Joint Chiefs of Staff and the Secretary of State asked the representatives whether the time was ripe to seek a congressional resolution empowering the President to employ air power. They got a negative answer. Congress, they were told, was not inclined to let the Executive embark on a course of action that could lead the United States into another conflict of the Korean type.

The congressmen asked Admiral Radford whether the Chiefs of Staff considered that Congress should give the President such authority as a matter of urgency. The Admiral replied that the Chiefs of Staff had made no assessment and that he spoke only

[8] Present at this meeting were: Dulles, Radford, Under Secretary of Defense Roger Keyes, Navy Secretary Robert B. Anderson, Senators William F. Knowland, Eugene D. Millikin, Lyndon B. Johnson, Richard B. Russell, and Earle C. Clements, and Representatives Joseph P. Martin, John McCormack, and J. Percy Priest. Chalmers M. Roberts, "The Day We Didn't Go to War," *The Reporter* (New York), September 14, 1954.

for himself. He admitted that the Chiefs of Staff did not agree with him about the possible value of a raid on the area around Dien Bien Phu. Both Dulles and Radford stressed that they were not speaking on behalf of the President or trying to rush Congress into a decision.

In the end, the congressional leaders declared that the first step in formulating an American policy was to establish which countries would be willing to join the United States in taking "concerted action." Under no circumstances could the United States act alone in this matter. British cooperation, in particular, seemed necessary. Dulles said that this was also his view.[9]

And so Admiral Radford's plan was stalled. The proposed raid on Dien Bien Phu was regarded in leading political circles, not as an extreme form of help to France and Vietnam in dealing with a rebellion (which was technically not a matter of belligerence), but as a plain act of war. When Admiral Radford was asked whether all types of American forces, including infantry, might have to be committed as a consequence of such a raid, he replied that he could not entirely exclude this possibility. The congressional leaders had been frightened off.

Their reactions were nonetheless disconcerting. Republican Senator William Knowland, Majority Leader, said on leaving the meeting that the question as to whether Indochina would remain on this side of the Iron Curtain or not would be decided in the coming months. After all, he remarked, the Free World had several means of reacting without resorting to the dispatch of American land forces—for example, the bombing of Chinese territory, a naval blockade of China, an unleashing of the Nationalist forces in Formosa, or joint action by the free nations of Asia.[10]

[9] The main source on this April 3 meeting is Chalmers M. Roberts, *op. cit.* See also Senator Mike Mansfield in the *Congressional Record* (Washington), July 9, 1954, p. 1037; John R. Beal, *John Foster Dulles* (New York, 1957), p. 207; Representative John McCormack, *The New York Times,* January 23, 1956; and Melvin Gurtov, *The First Vietnam Crisis* (New York, 1967), pp. 94–96. On the way Dulles defeated the Radford-Ely plan on April 3 and rallied the congressmen to his own, see Victor Bator, *Vietnam, a Diplomatic Tragedy* (New York, 1965), pp. 38–40.

[10] *L'Information* (Paris), April 6, 1954.

Operation Vulture had been blocked from the start because of the congressional leaders' anguished caution and their absolute refusal to consider it. But they had provided themselves with a foreign alibi that later enabled them to point to Great Britain as the scapegoat.

After this meeting, at which the proposal to intervene had been categorically rejected, Dulles spent an hour with the French ambassador, Henri Bonnet, and explained what he meant by "concerted action."

As the Secretary of State saw it, peace in Indochina could, in present circumstances, only be negotiated at France's expense. Peace talks could only lead to an arrangement that would more or less successfully conceal a French defeat. To reverse this situation, it was necessary to convince the Communists that, despite their present successes, they had no chance whatsoever of final victory. For this purpose, a coalition capable of stopping the advance of Communism in Southeast Asia by joint and concerted action must be formed without delay.

According to Dulles, Great Britain, Australia, New Zealand, Thailand, and the Philippines could join France and the United States to form such a coalition. The agreement uniting them could be based on the United Nations Charter, but any attempt to stop Communism in Indochina through U.N. action meant endless discussions without any certainty of a practical result, and speed was all-important.

Dulles actually hoped for a decision about the coalition before the Geneva conference, so that the Communists would not be left in any doubt about the practical considerations underlying the negotiations. Faced by concerted determination across the conference table, they would doubtless abandon their plans and resign themselves to the need for major concessions, Dulles believed. This concerted determination could be embodied in a joint declaration, which would also serve as a solemn warning to China.

The Secretary of State added that such an agreement, whatever the form it took, would need the approval of Congress, since it would give the President the power to take actions that could result in war. He then asked Bonnet to submit this proposal to his government, as he wished to obtain its reaction, at least in principle, as soon as possible.

On the afternoon of April 4, after meeting with Dulles and Radford, Eisenhower decided not to intervene in Indochina unless three conditions set by the congressmen the day before were met. A coalition would have to be formed; France would have to confirm the independence of the Indochinese states; and the French expeditionary force would have to remain in Indochina.[11] In a letter sent to Churchill on the same day, Eisenhower specified what he meant by a coalition and unified action.[12] In fact, the American decision of April 4 put an end to Operation Vulture as initially conceived and made the formation of a coalition the new aim of American diplomacy.

It is clear that, in proposing this coalition, Dulles wished to secure the authority of Congress for a more direct form of intervention by the United States in Indochina. But his immediate goal was to establish a political and strategic framework where, as in NATO, France and England would no longer be able to take any diplomatic initiatives (such as negotiating peace in Indochina) without Washington's formal agreement. The "solidarity of the free world" would transcend all national interests. When he addressed the House Foreign Affairs Committee about the foreign-aid program on April 5, Dulles dwelt at length on the problem of Indochina. Stressing the "supreme effort" being made by the Communists to break the fighting spirit of the French and their allies before the Geneva conference began, he added, "That scheme must be frustrated. The Free World must assert its solidarity and its vital interest in maintaining freedom in that part of the world. France and the Associated States must not be allowed to feel that they were alone at that decisive moment. Communist encroachment must be met with a common determination and, if necessary, united action."

11 Eisenhower, *Mandate for Change*, p. 347; Beal, *op. cit.*, p. 207; Sherman Adams, *First Hand Report: The Story of the Eisenhower Administration* (New York, 1961), pp. 121–22.

12 The text of the letter is in Eisenhower, *op. cit.*, pp. 346–47.

Dulles declared that Chinese participation in the fighting at Dien Bien Phu looked very much like direct intervention in the conflict. He listed some information recently received: the presence at Giap's headquarters near Dien Bien Phu of a Chinese General, Li Chen Hou, accompanied by some twenty technical advisers; the installation and operation of the Vietminh telephone network by Chinese personnel; the fact that the Vietminh's radar-equipped 37-mm. antiaircraft guns were served by Chinese crews; the manning of 1,000 Vietminh trucks in the area by Chinese drivers, etc.[13]

In conclusion, Dulles recalled his statement at St. Louis on September 2, 1953: American reactions to Chinese intervention in Indochina "might not be confined to Indochina."[14]

And so the pace was accelerating in Washington. Dulles had clearly opted for "peace through strength." The Alsop brothers noted on the following day that his speech meant war if the Chinese went on helping the Vietminh, and a negotiated peace in Indochina if they did not.

The menacing tone of Dulles's statement and its warning to China suggested that the United States, having found the pretext it was looking for, was about to intervene in strength. But this idea aroused very lively fears and misgivings in France and Great Britain, not only in the press but also in the councils of government.

Dulles's proposal for a coalition of states to defend Southeast Asia was studied at a closed session of the Council of Ministers in Paris on April 6. The French Government decided to reject it.

In its reply, the French Government invoked French public opinion, which would find it difficult to understand anything less than a total commitment to a peaceful settlement of the Indochinese affair and would be angered by anything that looked as though it might block such a settlement. Would the formation

[13] Saigon denied that it had supplied this information. The French General Staff made it clear that no Chinese dead, wounded, or prisoners were identified at Dien Bien Phu. See *L'Information* (Paris), April 8, 1954. For the official text of Dulles's statement, see *Department of State Bulletin* XXX, no. 773, April 19, 1954, pp. 579–83.

[14] *Mutual Security Act of 1954, Hearings, Committee on Foreign Affairs*, pp. 1–25.

of a powerful alliance on the eve of the Geneva meeting contribute to creating a suitable climate there? It seemed unlikely. A threat to internationalize the war might perhaps induce the opposite side to make peace, but it would have to be formulated so as to give China no grounds or excuses for direct intervention in Tonkin, or for hardening its attitude at the conference. French opinion tended to regard the American plan as liable to reduce the chances of an acceptable compromise in Geneva.

The French Government therefore felt that the proposed declaration and the resulting coalition should await the next stage, if it turned out, in the light of the transactions at Geneva, that no agreement with Communist China was possible. In the meantime, the French Government suggested the study of a number of questions, such as the type and strength of the forces the United States might be willing to commit to the defense of Southeast Asia, the nature of the obligations required from the members of the coalition, the conditions under which the guarantee would come into play, etc.

This reply was given Dulles on April 8, and it caused him obvious disappointment and worry. If the United States lacked the full support of its partners in dealing with the dangers threatening Southeast Asia, he said, it would have to decide for itself what methods and policies were best calculated to provide for American security and the defense of American interests.

The British reply, formulated at a long meeting of the cabinet on April 7, was equally clear. It was cool and reticent and basically similar to the French reply. However, Churchill said that he would like to discuss the matter personally with Dulles in London on April 12.[15]

Thus the governments in both Paris and London, knowing the full measure of Chinese pride, thought it unwise on the eve of the conference to threaten China with allied reprisals if it intervened in Indochina. They wished to safeguard Bidault's chances of negotiating with Chou En-lai in Geneva. As Laniel told the National Assembly on April 9, the government intended to ar-

[15] Eisenhower, *Mandate for Change*, p. 347.

rive at the Geneva talks with complete freedom of action, and it was determined not to overlook any opportunity to achieve peace.

Such a wide divergence of views among allies clearly called for a joint study of the situation. London and Paris therefore agreed that Dulles should come to Europe and expound his plan for concerted action, although the British and French governments had already decided to avoid all premature commitments.

Dulles arrived in London on April 11.[16] His talks with the British Government lasted until the morning of the 13th. He explained that he thought it would not be feasible to bring United Nations forces into action, should the need arise. He had therefore suggested the creation of an *ad hoc* coalition, making it possible to launch concerted action without delay, should this be required. A coalition of this kind could be assembled immediately on a very simple basis—for example, by a joint declaration. The conclusion of a formal treaty, on the other hand, would require negotiations followed by the lengthy procedures of signature and ratification. Months might pass, while the situation deteriorated politically and militarily, before anything could be done to check the Communist advance.

Churchill and Eden made it plain that the British Government could not consider joining such a coalition—which the French Government had not asked for in any case—in the immediate future. The chances of success at the Geneva conference were certainly slight, but they must be patiently and fully explored. British public opinion and the Asian members of the Commonwealth would neither understand nor allow any other course of action.

Britain considered that it was dangerous to address a warning to China, because the latter could not abandon the Vietminh without losing face. If China did not give in, and if there were

[16] At almost the same moment, on April 10, Bao Dai left Vietnam for France. On April 12, a decree of the Vietnamese chief of state ordered general mobilization in Vietnam and established a "war cabinet." It was later revealed that two American aircraft carriers armed with atomic weapons were entering the Gulf of Tonkin at that same time.

no other effective means of coercion, it would become a matter of either going to war or giving in. The British thought it safer to seek a compromise.

Nevertheless, the British Government fully agreed that France could not be left to carry on the struggle alone. It was therefore willing to examine, together with France and the United States, the possibility of devising a more general pact for the defense of Southeast Asia. This necessitated a detailed study, which would be directly affected by the results achieved at Geneva.

The joint communiqué published on April 13 at the end of the talks, which was drafted by Dulles together with Churchill and Eden, reflected this point of view.[17] Dulles left London convinced that he had secured British agreement to the immediate beginning of discussions about an *ad hoc* association. American officials even asserted that Churchill had promised Dulles his support for a possible American intervention in Indochina.[18] There was, however, no more talk of issuing a warning to China.

The Franco-American talks, which lasted throughout April 14, merely went over the ground already covered in the Dulles-Bonnet meetings during the preceding weeks.

Although the Secretary of State had expressed the conviction, on several occasions in the recent past (in Washington to Bonnet and in London on April 12 and 13), that the Geneva conference would lead nowhere, he was careful to stress in Paris that his goal was to improve the chances for a solution of the Indochinese question. As he saw it, such a solution could not be achieved until the futility of attempting conquest was brought home to the Communists, together with some inkling of the risks they took in pursuing this aim.

[17] "We are ready to take part, with the other countries principally concerned, in an examination of the possibility of establishing a collective defense, within the framework of the Charter of the United Nations, to assure the peace, security, and freedom of Southeast Asia and the western Pacific.

"It is our hope that the Geneva conference will lead to the restoration of peace in Indochina. We believe that the prospect of establishing a unity of defensive purpose throughout Southeast Asia and the western Pacific will contribute to an honorable peace in Indochina." *The Times* (London), April 16, 1954.

[18] *The New York Times*, April 14, 1954.

Dulles himself was persuaded that the Russians would press Peking for a settlement only out of fear of a general war, which might break out at a time that did not suit them. Thus it was necessary to prove, before the Geneva conference, that the nations of the Free World had made a firm decision to resist the Communist offensive together and in this way create the conditions for a satisfactory solution.

It emerged from his conversations with congressional leaders, Dulles explained, that the United States would be able to increase its share in the struggle only if the other countries concerned recognized that events in Indochina threatened them all. If they failed to do so, it would be extremely difficult to secure the assent of Congress and the American people to United States action in Indochina or to a more active participation in the war.

Bidault accepted Dulles's analysis of the situation but had some reservations about the timing of the proposed moves. He explained that domestic considerations, above all, had forced the French Government to seek negotiations about Indochina. The need to secure an honorable peace, a peace that would not also be victory for Communism, had been forced upon France. Therefore, nothing could be allowed to give the impression that the French Government was not sincere in its search for a peaceful settlement, that it was resigned to failure at Geneva, or that it was on the verge of decisions that would enable it to continue the war in a different form.

Therefore, nothing should be done to suggest that the government anticipated such a failure. On the contrary, France was determined to explore every possibility of a peaceful settlement. Certain indications, however tenuous, gave grounds for hope that the conference could, in fact, achieve tangible results. In any case, the French Government did not wish to lay itself open to the accusation that it had allowed its hands to be tied in advance. France could consider the internationalization of the war only if the conference had clearly failed.

The meeting of April 14 apparently reached no conclusion.

On his return to the United States, Dulles invited the British, the French, and the other Western countries concerned to "preparatory" talks to start in Washington on April 20. He thought he had sensed that, despite their refusal to sign a joint declaration, France and Britain would be prepared to discuss the situation. But on Easter Sunday, April 18, the British ambassador, Sir Roger Makins, warned Dulles that his government had instructed him not to attend. The British Government did not wish such talks to take place until the Geneva conference had completed a detailed study of the chances for peace in Indochina. Dulles was furious and accused the British of sabotaging a meeting they had earlier agreed to hold. This ten-nation conference was transformed at the last moment into a sixteen-nation conference about Korea, in order to save face for the American government.

The American coalition plan, designed to provide political cover for Operation Vulture, appeared to have misfired just five days before the opening of the Geneva conference. On April 20, Dulles was able to tell congressional leaders that American intervention in Indochina was neither imminent nor even under consideration.[19]

[19] No doubt this was the state of affairs Eisenhower referred to on January 13, 1960, when he said that there had never been any specific plan for Indochina. During the debate in the Senate on July 9, 1954, Republican Senators Homer Ferguson and Alexander Smith solemnly denied that the problem of intervention had ever been raised during their various meetings with Dulles. The editorial in *U.S. News and World Report* of August 9, 1954, quoting a highly authoritative source, stated that "the official records show that the United States never was on the verge of a shooting war with Communist China over Indochina."

6

ON THE BRINK

At Dien Bien Phu, the situation worsened every day. Since the beginning of April, General Giap had apparently abandoned his costly massed assaults. Instead, he sought to isolate and strangle the outer French positions by digging a dense network of trenches and approach lines, from which his troops then struck when the opportunity arose. In a succession of local attacks, his infantry infiltrated ever closer to the center of the fortress.

On April 21, the Vietminh again attacked toward the central redoubt and made more progress. By now, General de Castries's positions had been reduced to a circular area less than a mile in diameter. On April 23, the Vietminh reached the middle of the airfield, thereby making further parachute drops impossible. Rain and low visibility were slowing down air activity in any case, and the enemy's very accurate, radar-guided antiaircraft fire had rendered low-altitude parachute drops hazardous for some time past.

On April 21, High Commissioner Dejean and General Navarre decided that the situation was virtually hopeless. "Only outside action could now turn the battle in our favor," Dejean wrote.

He concluded that without such intervention the defense would sooner or later be swamped or, more probably, asphyxiated. General Navarre wrote on the following day that "Dien Bien Phu will not be able to hold out indefinitely without a major operation to relieve it, and air strikes to cut back the Vietminh's logistic support significantly."

In fact, both the Commander in Chief and the High Commissioner put their hopes in Operation Vulture, which, as we have seen, had been shelved but not abandoned. The American Chiefs of Staff had carried their technical planning to an advanced stage. Since early April, two carriers of the Seventh Fleet, the "Boxer" and the "Philippine Sea," had been on station in the Gulf of Tonkin, carrying fighters to cover the heavy bombers from Manila.[1] Meanwhile, the French were hurriedly providing air cover over upper Tonkin and the Thai plateau.

Dulles's veto on April 5 put a damper on these preparations, but the military men on both sides went on trying to work out some way of making the raids without revealing America's participation. Navarre suggested a number of small-scale sorties by aircraft with French markings, or no markings at all, manned by unidentified crews. Admiral Radford rejected this strange suggestion around April 11.

The next proposal was that the necessary B-29 bombers should be turned over to the French General Staff. The French Secretary of State for Air, Louis Christiaens, visited the United States in connection with this scheme, but no French Air Force crews were familiar with the B-29.[2]

For this reason, Navarre proposed on April 14 that the American strikes should not be directed at Dien Bien Phu and should be confined to night raids by a group of 15–20 B-29's against specified targets along the Vietminh lines of communication. This operation could be safely carried out, he believed, by aircraft with

[1] The chief purpose of sending out these carriers was to intimidate China, according to James Shepley, "How Dulles Averted War," *Life*, January 12, 1956. The carriers were "Boxer" and "Essex" according to Fletcher Knebel, "We Nearly Went to War Three Times," *Look*, January 24, 1955.

[2] See Christiaens' press conference in New York, April 13, 1954.

American markings. It might succeed in smothering the Vietminh fighting force, and in any case it would leave the French Air Force free to concentrate on the close support of Dien Bien Phu itself.

These suggestions were by no means unwelcome to the Americans. The contact between Admiral Radford and General Ely had not been broken. General Earle E. Partridge, Commander of the U.S. Far Eastern Air Force (FEAF), visited Saigon on April 14 in one of a series of secret contacts between French and American military staffs. He told Dejean that he had come to study the operational possibilities and chances of success of Operation Vulture from a purely technical point of view, and he discussed the operation at length with General Navarre. When he returned to Saigon from Tonkin on April 17, he told the High Commissioner that if his superiors in Tokyo and Washington accepted the conclusions of his report he would send out one of his assistants to study the operation in greater detail.[3] Thus Operation Vulture remained an immediate possibility from the military point of view.

The operation also seemed to have found a new lease of life in the political sphere. Admiral Radford was not alone in advocating strong action in Indochina and had found a powerful ally in Vice President Nixon. The latter personally and confidentially informed the French ambassador that he entirely shared Admiral Radford's views, and was in favor of massive American air intervention to save Dien Bien Phu.

Nixon, still hoping to reverse the "top level" decision of April 5, confidently took up this new position. Speaking to newsmen on April 16, he said that if a Communist conquest of Indochina

[3] Dejean was also visited on April 22 by General Caldara, Operations Officer of General Partridge's staff, who was going to Tonkin and the upper region to investigate conditions for high-level precision bombing. He stated on his return that the operation was technically feasible. In his opinion, the requisite result could be achieved in the course of three or four nights by 75–80 B-29's each carrying about eight tons of explosives. The operation required only 72 hours' notice; the aircraft would be back at their base in Manila before dawn. French pilots would serve as pathfinders in the B-29 squadrons. At the same time, a senior French officer would be sent to Manila to work out the technical details (radio nets, codes, etc.).

could be prevented by actions that involved the risk of American troops being sent there, the United States Government would have to "face up to the situation and dispatch forces."[4] This statement provoked a lively reaction in congressional circles, and it was necessary to issue an official statement pointing out that Nixon was merely expressing a personal opinion.

On April 21 and 22, Paris learned that the defenders of Dien Bien Phu were now fighting under virtually hopeless conditions. Dulles happened to be in the French capital at the time for discussions with Bidault and Eden about the tactics to adopt at the opening of the Geneva conference. On April 23, Bidault took Dulles aside and showed him a message from Navarre saying that without immediate and massive air support, Dien Bien Phu could not hold out much longer. The fall of the fortified camp would enable Giap to move his forces back to the Red River delta for an offensive against Hanoi before the rainy season. The resulting deterioration in the situation would require France to seek a cease-fire by the quickest possible means. Bidault asked the Secretary of State whether, in these circumstances, the United States could not reconsider its decision of April 5 and authorize Operation Vulture.[5]

The following morning, Dulles and his senior officials spent four hours in drafting a reply to his French colleague's request. The Secretary of State rejected the request of the Laniel government,

[4] Speech to the American Society of Newspaper Editors, reported in *The New York Times,* April 18, 1954. Nixon softened his stand somewhat on April 20; he said that the aim of the United States was to avoid involvement if at all possible and seek an "honorable and peaceful settlement" of the crisis in Geneva. *The New York Times,* April 21, 1954. On Nixon's position, see also Joseph Buttinger, *Vietnam: A Dragon Embattled,* (New York, 1967), pp. 1084, 1086.

[5] According to C. L. Sulzberger's article, "The Day it all Began," *The New York Times,* January 11, 1967, "on (April) 22nd (1954) an activist American policy began to shape up for Southeast Asia." Sulzberger writes that he dined that evening in Paris with Walter S. Robertson, "the courtly, bellicose Virginia gentleman who then, as Assistant Secretary of State for Far Eastern Affairs, virtually ran American policy in Asia. . . . He felt the United States must intervene in Vietnam."

saying that the operation would imply active belligerency on the part of the United States. Such an act of war required the prior approval of Congress, and this could not be obtained in a matter of hours. Moreover, it would first be necessary to reach a political understanding with Great Britain and the other powers that had vital interests in Southeast Asia.

Dulles pointed out that, in the opinion of his military advisers (including Admiral Radford, then in Paris), it was already too late: the proposed raid could not save Dien Bien Phu. Indeed, they suggested that if the camp fell, the strategic situation in Indochina would not be vitally affected.[6] The Vietminh had paid such a heavy price for the attack that the balance of forces would continue to favor the French.

Therefore, Dulles could see no sound military reason why the fall of Dien Bien Phu should force France to ask for a cease-fire, which would seriously endanger the defense of the entire area and lower the morale of the Indochinese people. Provided that a system of collective defense could be organized rapidly, the Secretary of State thought that Indochina could be held by the free nations. Dulles ended with an uncharitable exhortation to the French Government to "react vigorously" and to "surmount this temporary ordeal. If you don't quit, we won't quit."[7]

Even so, the snub was not cruel enough to make the Laniel government give up. The opening of the Geneva conference was only two days away, but the Premier was absolutely determined to try again. On Laniel's instructions, Bidault sent a letter to Dulles during the afternoon of April 24 in which he stressed two points: (1) French military experts estimated that a massive intervention by the U.S. Air Force could still save the garrison of the camp; and (2) the French High Command believed that since the

[6] This is exactly the opinion put forward on the same day by General Navarre; in a 1959 talk with the author, Bidault was to describe Navarre's reports as "sinusoidal."

[7] Sulzberger, *ibid.*, adds that on the same day (April 24) "Dulles saw Bao Dai and obtained his support for the Southeast Asia pact." Lancaster says that "Bao Dai's conduct seems to have been based on the belief that American opposition would prevent the conclusion of an armistice." Donald Lancaster, *The Emancipation of French Indo-China* (London, 1961), p. 317.

Vietminh had concentrated the bulk of its fighting force around the fortified camp, a rare opportunity presented itself to destroy the greater part of it by air action. This was a chance to strike the Vietminh a decisive blow.

Dulles had already left Paris and only received this letter in Geneva on the following day. However, the text had also been cabled to Bonnet in Washington, who passed it that night to Walter Bedell Smith, Under Secretary of State. The latter immediately brought it to the attention of President Eisenhower. Faced with this real SOS from France, the American Government did not refuse again, as many thought it would. Bedell Smith informed Bonnet that there could be quick action if the declaration of intent which Dulles had tried to negotiate in London and Paris were published over the signature of the states involved; he took the agreement of the other powers for granted and everything now depended on London, so Bidault should try to persuade Eden as he passed through Paris on his way to Geneva. Meanwhile, a personal message would be sent to Churchill from America.

The State Department and the various embassies concerned could arrange everything in Washington by Monday, April 26. A congressional resolution—which was already in draft—could be approved by Wednesday, April 28. It would authorize the President to commit naval and air forces in Southeast Asia. Bedell Smith hoped that the negotiations would proceed quickly enough so that the American carrier aircraft could strike before Dien Bien Phu was overwhelmed.

And so, on Saturday, April 24, 1954, the United States declared that it was ready to intervene militarily in Indochina from the middle of the following week—provided only that the British would agree. But London had not yet agreed.

The conference was due to start at Geneva on Monday, April 26, and Anthony Eden was on his way there from Paris on the evening of April 24 when he received the French Government's request for intervention. The British Government was being asked to associate itself, at least symbolically, with the joint action being prepared by the military staffs in Washington and Paris. Eden broke off his journey and hurried back to London.[8] A special cabinet meeting was held at 10 Downing Street the next morning (Sunday, April 25) with the Chiefs of Staff in attendance.

Simultaneously, the French ambassador in London, René Massigli, received from Paris an account of the previous night's conversation between Bonnet and Bedell Smith. He hurried to the Foreign Office and was received by Eden, just back from Downing Street. Massigli informed Eden of the conversation in Washington, stressing the consequences of a British refusal to join in the proposed declaration, especially in the current circumstances. Eden said he was genuinely sorry not to be in a position to help France as much as he would have wished, but his government would not be able to take the course suggested. The proposed operation would have no immediate practical purpose, since Dien Bien Phu could no longer be saved; Admiral Radford had told him so only yesterday, in the presence of Dulles. British military experts did not believe that an air strike could be effective, since the battlefield was so small and the weather was so poor, nor did they believe that attacks on the rear of the Vietminh forces would have a significant effect on the battle. Anyway, such an operation would make negotiations for a truce in Indochina impossible and would certainly cause the war to flare up. Yet neither France nor the United States seemed ready to make the effort needed for victory. In these cir-

[8] Anthony Eden (now Lord Avon) refers in his memoirs to the events of April 24, but his version is rather different. He says that Dulles had prepared a letter informing Bidault that, in view of the very serious threat hanging over the Expeditionary Corps, the United States was prepared to send armed forces to Indochina and internationalize the conflict in Southeast Asia, if France and its allies asked for this. Dulles asked Bidault whether he agreed that the letter should be sent officially; Bidault, after hesitating for several minutes, acquiesced. Eden writes that René Massigli, French ambassador in London, told him on April 25 that the letter had been sent. Anthony Eden, *Full Circle* (London and Boston, 1960), pp. 103–4.

However, the only letter of which there is any trace in the French archives is the one we have analyzed above (part of the original text appears in J.-R. Tournoux's book *Secrets d'Etat*). Could it be that the Bidault-Dulles conversation about this hypothetical letter (a conversation that followed Bidault's dramatic account of events in Indochina) was basically intended to shake Eden and to force British agreement, since the United States could not then go beyond the limits that Dulles actually did spell out in his letter?

cumstances, the only realistic policy was to seek a cease-fire immediately in Geneva. Britain would unreservedly support the search there for peace.

On the afternoon of the same day (Sunday, April 25), Admiral Radford arrived in London carrying a "personal message" from President Eisenhower to Churchill. After conferring with the three chiefs of staff at the Ministry of Defence, he went to Chequers, where the Prime Minister had him to dinner, and then left for Washington during the night.[9]

Eden finally set off by air for Geneva in the evening of the 25th. Bidault came to greet him during his short stopover at Orly, and Eden left him in no doubt about British intentions, being even more outspoken than he had been with Massigli. He made it clear that the British Government was not prepared to make the slightest commitment to military action in Indochina until after Geneva. On the other hand, it would give France every possible diplomatic support to enable the French to secure an honorable settlement of the conflict.

Yet even now, Operation Vulture was not quite dead and buried. Laniel felt he had not yet exhausted the efforts to save Dien Bien Phu. He instructed Massigli, whom he saw during the afternoon of Monday, April 26, to make one final approach to Churchill. After all, American intervention awaited only the assent of the British.

Churchill received Massigli late in the morning of Tuesday, April 27. The ambassador began to tell him that at Laniel's request he was bringing him additional information, but Sir Winston interrupted him—he wanted to hear nothing about the military aspects of the problem. Very moved, at times unable to master his emotion, the old statesman expressed his admiration for the heroism of the defenders of Dien Bien Phu and his sorrow that he could do nothing to save them. The crisis was a tragic one, but he urged that temporary reverses should not deflect the allied governments from their goals or shake their resolution. The British

[9] On Admiral Radford's visit to London, see Bernard B. Fall, *The Two Viet-Nams* (New York, 1966), pp. 229–30; and Victor Bator, *Vietnam, a Diplomatic Tragedy* (New York, 1965), pp. 71–73.

Government had given much thought to the situation, and its mind was made up. The success of the proposed operation was at best extremely doubtful. Moreover, an airstrike would destroy the chances of an agreement at Geneva, on which the hope of lowering tension in the Far East depended. These chances must under no circumstances be jeopardized. The British Government had no alternative but to hold to its decision.

In order to eliminate any possible misunderstanding, Sir Winston went directly to the House of Commons to announce the final decision of the British cabinet. To the applause of the members, who had been alerted by the diplomatic comings and goings of the past two days, he stated that "Her Majesty's Government are not prepared to give any undertakings about United Kingdom military action in Indochina in advance of the results of Geneva."[10]

News of the British refusal had been brought to Washington by Admiral Radford on the morning of April 26, but Bedell Smith also tried one final move. He suggested that it might be possible to secure authority for an immediate military intervention through ANZUS,[11] thus bypassing the question of British consent. Congressmen sounded out during the evening of April 26 were not unfavorable to this suggestion, and so, on the following day, Bedell Smith asked Dulles in Geneva whether he thought it might be appropriate to summon an ANZUS council meeting. Dulles's reply is not on record, but the French Ministry of Foreign Affairs heard nothing more about the matter. Such was the end of Operation Vulture, which had caused more noise and upheaval than many actual operations.

Now that all its efforts had failed, the American Government could do no more than look on as the French military command faced a major defeat in Indochina. The American public's enthusiasm and admiration for the defense of Dien Bien Phu failed to convince Congress to authorize operations that, as the Secretary of State put it, would have brought the United States to "the brink." No doubt it was the British veto that put an end to the

[10] *Hansard* (London), April 27, 1954, col. 1456.

[11] The treaty organization of the alliance concluded in 1951 between Australia, New Zealand, and the United States.

affair; but the American Government itself had been unwilling to run the risk of war. All the evidence showed that American public opinion, which governs the actions of Congress, agreed with the decision not to intervene.

Even the U.S. Government seemed to come around to the British point of view. While several "hawks" were taking their seats at the conference table in Geneva, the "doves" were raising their voices in Washington. On April 29, just as the National Security Council was preparing to hear Admiral Radford's report on his visit to Europe, Eisenhower wrote the epilogue to this dangerous moment of history. He said, in effect, that the American Government would wait for the results of the Geneva meeting before undertaking any further steps to help France in Indochina, because it did not wish to prejudice the chances of reaching an acceptable *modus vivendi* at the conference. The United States saw two possible solutions: one, which would be entirely satisfactory—the abandonment of the struggle by the Vietminh—was "unattainable"; the other was "unacceptable," because it would mean the collapse of the whole system of barriers erected against Communism in Southeast Asia. Was there no middle way between these extremes, whereby coexistence with the Communists would become possible, as it was in Europe? Real peace was certainly out of the question, but surely there was some way to reach an agreement that would stop the bloodshed and yet safeguard the Free World's access to Southeast Asia's economic resources.[12]

12 For Eisenhower's April 29 Declaration, see *Public Papers of the Presidents of the United States: 1954* (Washington) p. 428. Between the unacceptable (Communist conquest of the entire region) and the unattainable (a stable relationship with the Communists) there was probably a middle path: "The most you can work out is a practical way of getting along. Now, whether or not even that is possible, I don't know; but when you come down to it, that is what we have been doing in Europe—the whole situation from Berlin all the way through Germany is really on a practical basis of getting along one with the other, no more." In *Mandate for Change*, Eisenhower writes: "Under the conditions then existing, we would probably get not what we would like by way of settlement in Geneva but rather a *modus vivendi*, a pragmatic and workable rather than a desirable arrangement. There was no plausible reason for the United States to intervene; we could not even be sure that the Vietnamese population wanted us to do so." Dwight D. Eisenhower, *Mandate for Change* (New York, 1963), p. 353.

7

BETWEEN THE UNATTAINABLE AND THE UNACCEPTABLE

When the curtain fell on Operation Vulture on April 29, the Asian conference had already started in Geneva.[1] Though it was still busy with the Korean prelude, talks about Indochina would soon begin.

The principal Western participants were not well prepared, and they were still very far from achieving a concerted point of view. Laniel, in his speech to the National Assembly on March 5, had defined the conditions under which France would be willing to discuss a cease-fire.[2] But these conditions seemed to apply only to immediate and direct negotiations with the enemy. Did they still hold, now that the participation of other powers offered new opportunities to safeguard a settlement? In any case, a cease-fire was merely a beginning, and there was no escaping the sequel. Yet the French seemed to have no clear ideas about the ultimate goal of any negotiations or the nature of any future settlement

[1] See below, chap. 8.
[2] See above, chap. 4, p. 67.

in Indochina. Everyone talked of a great peace settlement for Asia, but nobody knew exactly what this was intended to mean; evidently, it was no more than a desperate Grand Design of last-ditch diplomacy. What were France's political aims? What parts of Indochina did it hope to save from domination by the Communists? What schedules and safeguards would be vital to any settlement that might be negotiated? No one had worked out answers to these central questions. Indeed, the veil of secrecy that very properly covered the French Government's "plan" seemed to conceal no more than a collection of pious hopes, illusions, and conflicting daydreams.

Although Laniel had not rejected the possibility of direct negotiations with Ho Chi Minh, the government had given the impression for some time that any such suggestion was shelved. It was felt that direct talks could serve no useful purpose so near to the beginning of the Asian conference[3] and might even severely damage France's interests by arousing suspicion or resentment among its American and Vietnamese allies.

From the evidence available, it seems that the French Government expected direct negotiations to bring about nothing more than a cease-fire at first.[4] Its terms would be considered independently and not as part of a general political settlement, the timetable and conditions for which could be discussed once the cease-fire was in effect. This two-stage procedure was realistic and reliable.[5] The end of military operations would almost certainly lead to a reduction of international tensions by ending foreign intervention or at least slowing it down. And, within Indochina, it might well inspire a process of political evolution in which the imperatives of "national resistance" could yield to

[3] Direct talks might possibly have been very useful at precisely this time, if only to establish the mood and intentions of the Vietminh leadership. Yet in March, Bidault told Savary, in order to prevent him from making just such a contact, "Ho Chi Minh is on the point of capitulating. We are going to beat him. Don't support him by a contact of this kind."

[4] Letter from Bidault to Bao Dai (for the text, see below, chap. 9, p. 135), and author's conversation with Bidault, July 24, 1959.

[5] This solution was advocated by the authors of this book in an article in *Combat* (Paris) dated November 22, 1950.

political considerations better adapted to the real future needs of the country.

However, a majority in the French Government was unwilling to consider a cease-fire unless it included a set of safeguards they felt were essential.[6] An official document spelled out the reasons:

> [Such safeguards are] made necessary by the peculiar nature of the military situation in Indochina. No continuous front separates the contending sides; enemy units are often imbedded in the midst of our military zones; the high density of population, particularly in the Red River delta, renders the problem of security especially difficult; the irregular troops that constitute the bulk of Giap's forces carry on guerrilla warfare over most of the territory.
>
> As things now stand, the acceptance of a cease-fire under conditions other than those put forward by the government would involve grave dangers: the irregular Vietminh troops would remain free to infiltrate all over the peninsula, and the French forces and those of the Associated States could not resist because they would be paralyzed by the cease-fire. As a result, the situation would rapidly become most unfavorable in military terms and very dangerous for French citizens scattered throughout the three states. Rebel infiltrators could also completely paralyze the political and economic life of the three states; the results achieved by the Associated States would rapidly be undone, while misery and disorder spread throughout the area. If the Vietminh became master of the situation and could look forward to gaining complete control, it would lose all incentive to negotiate. A preliminary cease-fire without adequate safeguards would put the peaceful settlement which France seeks virtually out of reach, not bring it any nearer. It is no coincidence that Ho Chi Minh himself asked for this in the interview given to *Expressen* last November.

However, it seemed doubtful that the Vietminh, with the military and political tides running in its favor, would negotiate a cease-fire on Laniel's terms.

After the Berlin conference, the French evidently decided that the Vietminh was able to fight on solely because of aid it was receiving from China. Ho Chi Minh would probably prove ac-

[6] See below, chap. 9, pp. 137–38.

commodating if Peking cut off its support or forced him to negotiate. Peking must therefore be offered the appropriate price for abandoning Ho Chi Minh or putting pressure on him, bearing in mind that Sino-Soviet relations were believed to be undergoing a crisis. For the French, then, the main objective of the Geneva conference was to end Chinese aid to the Vietminh.[7] This was regarded as a good and sufficient reason to negotiate with Peking —a step that Vice-Premier Paul Reynaud had been advocating within the cabinet for some time. Was it, however, still possible to reduce the war to national proportions, to the level of a local rebellion, when its international repercussions were now so disturbing to so many powers?

What price would Peking ask for abandoning the Vietminh? Recognition of the People's Republic of China and its admission to the United Nations? The resumption of commercial relations—especially the supply of capital equipment,[8] which, it seemed, Russia was now dealing out rather sparingly? The neutralization of Formosa or the slowing down of Japanese rearmament? Only the United States had the means to pay stakes of this magnitude. Some pundits suggested that the United States might use this situation as a wedge, to detach Peking from Moscow and enable Chinese "Titoism" to assert itself.

All such notions were illusory. The United States firmly refused to consider any concessions to China; China was still the enemy in Korea and had not yet made a single gesture of good will. While the American political atmosphere remained poisoned by McCarthyism and Walter S. Robertson continued as the Assistant Secretary of State for Far Eastern Affairs, there was little hope that America's attitude might become more flexible in the near future. Moreover, Dulles was redoubling his statements opposing the admission of China to the United Nations, in order to silence

[7] This is how the French Commissioner General in Indochina described the object of the conference to the Vietnamese public. (Note by Dejean, April 27, 1954.)

[8] Bidault, with his customary flair for images, referred to these as "sweeteners." This was an allusion to sugar-refining equipment worth 1 billion francs, which the government had barred from export to China.

the criticism of extreme right-wing Republicans, who had been accusing him of moving toward an Asian Munich ever since the Berlin conference.

But Paris did not lose hope. One influential school of thought maintained that the only true road to peace in Asia led through Moscow rather than Peking, and indeed, the Berlin conference had done something to confirm this view.

This theory was based on two arguments. The first was that Moscow was eager to conciliate France, not for the sake of Indochina (which the U.S.S.R. was willing to leave to its own fate), but because of the situation in Europe and the German question in particular. The Kremlin could not hope to lure the French away from the idea of the European Defense Community (EDC) if it remained systematically negative about Indochina or supported unacceptable and humiliating demands made by its Asian allies. Thus, many political circles in Paris began to consider the questions of Indochina and EDC together: would the Soviets help to end the war in Indochina if France abandoned EDC in return?

These currents of opinion caused lively concern among France's allies. The alarm was such that Chancellor Adenauer made an unexpected visit to Paris at the beginning of March, and C. Douglas Dillon, the American ambassador to Paris, returned to his post even though he was still recovering from an operation.

The Americans and Germans were clearly eager to have France ratify the EDC Treaty of Paris before the start of the Indochina conference. They were well aware that once the talks began in Geneva, the French parliament would refuse to decide about the treaty on the grounds (according to the Gaullist argument) that either ratification or rejection would jeopardize the prospects of an agreement with the U.S.S.R. And this rejection of EDC would disrupt the united front presented by the West. In Europe, it was believed, it would mean the end of the Atlantic alliance. It would also severely shake whatever confidence the American administration still had in France, and it would, finally, establish West Germany as America's bridgehead in Europe. In the Asian sphere, it would deprive France of any hope of American support in its search for a settlement in Indochina. No wonder, then, that Laniel,

Bidault, and Pleven, who were determined to preserve Atlantic solidarity at all costs, took a very firm position at that time. Bidault had already made it clear that "world-wide bargaining" was out of the question. Now, he stressed this again in a speech at St. Etienne on March 26: "We must not trade EDC for Indochina at any price." But, faced with a half-hesitant, half-hostile National Assembly, the government was afraid to put the matter to the test or even to set a date for the debate on the treaty's ratification.

In order to smooth the way, the British and American governments went so far as to offer new guarantees. The United States promised that if the treaty were ratified, it would keep its troops in Europe (including West Germany) "for as long as the area might be threatened" and would agree to prolong the Atlantic pact indefinitely. Britain, for its part, in an agreement signed on April 13, 1954, agreed to keep its forces on the continent.

The National Assembly's "anti-Europeans" and their political allies refused to be swayed by such concessions. Some were eager to end the Indochinese conflict; others opposed EDC out of narrow-minded nationalism or devotion to Moscow. Together, they made ratification so unlikely that it seemed pointless for Russia to trade the rejection of EDC against peace in Indochina and thus risk Chinese and Vietminh displeasure. Russia knew that EDC would be killed anyway, when the French "nationalists" and Communists, from Michel Debré to Jacques Duclos, coalesced in opposition to the treaty.

There was a second argument sustaining the belief that the key to an Indochinese settlement lay in Moscow: the Malenkov regime's need for peace. For in the past year, Moscow had given many hints that it wished a quick end to the Asian conflicts in which China tended to involve the Soviet Union. Peking was, in effect, obliged to react to any serious American intervention in Vietnam. Any Chinese reaction could easily lead to a new confrontation in which Washington might well resort to the use of atomic weapons. This, in turn, would compel the Chinese to ask for Soviet assistance; and so the struggle in Vietnam might yet ignite a worldwide conflict.

Malenkov was calling for *détente,* for international trade, and increased emphasis on consumer goods in the Soviet economy. He was opposed by Nikita Khrushchev, the First Secretary of the party, who evidently had the support of Molotov, Bulganin, and the army. Khrushchev advocated a continued emphasis on heavy industry and gave top priority to the rapid development of nuclear arms. But it would be a long time before the Soviet nuclear threat would be impressive enough to exert a controlling influence on international crises. For the present, this fact compelled the two Soviet factions to follow a common line of prudence and caution. The Soviet press still vigorously condemned the war in Indochina and foretold the approaching downfall of the colonialists, but in private conversations and personal contacts, Soviet officials hinted clearly that a *modus vivendi* must be found. On March 26, 1954, the new counsellor at the Soviet embassy in Paris made significant comments about the subject, and Soviet Ambassador Vinogradov made similar off-the-record remarks about a cease-fire and the creation of a buffer state to certain opposition leaders.[9]

But could the Russians impose their point of view on the Chinese and the Vietminh? Bidault believed that he and France held the trump card that would force Peking and its Vietminh allies to reconsider: the threat to extend the war through more intense American intervention if the Asian conference failed. But to be effective, the threat had to be convincing. The possibility of American intervention had faded with the rejection of Operation Vulture. But, on the strength of existing trends, Bidault was convinced that the United States could not stand aside for ever and that sooner or later it must help the French to contain the Communist drive to the South.

The cabinet was divided over the way in which this trump card should be played. A majority believed that the very prospect of

[9] *New York Herald Tribune,* April 27, 1954. On April 26, Malenkov gave a speech predicting the collapse of the capitalist system in the event of nuclear war, which indicated that he had lost ground to the Khrushchev faction; the latter had gained some allies in Peking, thanks to the Kao Kang affair. On the internal Soviet debate, see Melvin Gurtov, *The First Vietnam Crisis* (New York, 1967), pp. 88–90.

confronting the United States would drive the enemy to look for a compromise, but the threat would be hollow if there were any suggestion that it would never be implemented.[10] Therefore, the Chinese and the Vietminh would have to be persuaded that the war would certainly expand unless they exercised greater restraint.

The majority of Laniel's cabinet thought that the risk of spreading the conflict—and it was a serious risk—must be taken. There was no point in being half-hearted about it. But the ministers tried to comfort themselves with the thought that even intervention by the "Anglo-Saxon powers" would not necessarily lead to the generalization of the conflict. They believed that China would remain passive and would not openly retaliate against American action. These optimistic views appear to have been shared by the ministers who criticized Bidault's policy as well as those who approved of it.

All in all, it was a most difficult political maneuver to carry out: the fear of intervention must be instilled in the enemy without panicking the French people, who were already nervous enough about the probable consequences of tough action. Above all, any suggestion of doubt about the possibility of intervention must be avoided at all costs. It was vital that no one could tell at any given moment whether determination, or a wish to limit the risks, was uppermost in the minds of the French negotiators. Bidault, whose style combined an aura of mystery, a look of assurance, and a gift of ambiguous language, was well suited to the task of bringing off this delicate maneuver. He even made good use of the indignation of his opponents to advance his plan.[11]

[10] Raymond Aron reflected this point of view in *Le Figaro* on April 26: "How can the American threat fulfill its purpose if we let it be known that we do not propose to bring it into action under any circumstances? The extension of the conflict must be avoided as far as possible, but the risk must be taken in order to secure an honorable peace."

[11] J.-J. Servan-Schreiber reported Bidault's remark on April 25, in the presence of a number of bystanders, that he would resign himself to the possibility of a general war in Asia if the Geneva conference failed. A leading member of the French delegation has also told us that during the conference, Bidault talked freely about the "crusade" that the West would sooner or later have to lead against Communist China, and the possibility that fate might decide to give the signal at Geneva. Were these so many acts of psychological warfare?

Nevertheless, the fact had to be faced that France had virtually no cards to play in dealing with China and Russia, except for EDC.[12] Basically, a settlement was dependent on American, Chinese, and Russian good will. Daladier and Mendès-France aired their skepticism in Parliament—why should Moscow and Peking make France's task any easier? Was it not in their interest that France should continue to drain away its strength some 7,500 miles from home? Evidently these skeptics did not view the facts of the world situation in the same light as Moscow and Peking; they did not see that *all* the competing factions in the socialist camp were at least temporarily united in their determination to isolate the United States, while working toward *détente* and peaceful coexistence with France, England, and India.

The intentions of the United States were equally in doubt. Though the MRP ministers behaved as though they agreed with Bidault that a cease-fire might result from the Geneva conference, other members of the government (particularly the Radicals and Gaullists) were less sanguine. These dissidents thought their colleagues were deluding themselves about the genuineness of any American threat to intervene and, above all, about the extent to which the United States really wished to promote a settlement in Indochina. What *was* the attitude of France's allies toward the French dilemma in Indochina? That was indeed a fundamental question.

In London, the search for a negotiated settlement met with neither obstacles nor objections. The British Government had lost all illusions about a "happy end" in Indochina. The deterioration of the military situation there, the growing involvement of the Americans, and the support given to the Vietminh by the Chinese gave London every reason to fear serious complications that, in the long run, threatened to involve the Commonwealth. No one in London still believed that the Vietminh could be defeated. From now on, it was a matter of confining the blaze,

[12] It was also suggested that in return for Chinese "good will," France might concede to China a free port at Haiphong, which would give Yunnan Province an outlet to the sea.

of amputating the infected limb. Northern Vietnam, where the hub of Ho Chi Minh's power was located, was not worth a world war, but Laos and Cambodia, the bastions of Thailand and Malaya, and possibly even southern Vietnam might be salvaged. And so London favored a settlement that would limit the damage, even if it involved at least a temporary partition, as in Palestine, Germany, and Korea.

Such a truce, based on the actual situation on the ground and drawing a line that the Communists could cross only at their peril,[13] would enable Laos and Cambodia to establish themselves as political entities.[14] Without an armistice obliging the contending forces to withdraw to definite lines guaranteed by the Western and Asian powers,[15] Vietnam would not be able to emerge from chaos and find stability. The anti-Communist Vietnamese could assert themselves and secure general support only if the country were truly independent. Without full independence, they would be unable either to re-establish order or to isolate the Communist guerrillas.[16]

Her Majesty's Government, therefore, considered that any settlement would require military and political concessions to the Vietminh; it was almost certain that the Communists would accept a solution of this kind. Moscow and Peking might even agree to the creation of a buffer state in northern Indochina. The Kremlin seemed less than eager for a further extension of Chinese influence in Southeast Asia, even though it had recognized the area as a "Chinese sphere of interest." A buffer state, separating Chinese territory from the Western positions, would help to minimize incidents and clashes and would also give China a greater sense of security. And, indeed, there were indications that no objections would come from the Soviet side. Toward the end of March, an official from the Soviet embassy in London approached

13 *Daily Mail* (London), April 26, 1954.

14 *Manchester Guardian*, April 26, 1954.

15 It was recognized that it would be difficult to draw a demarcation line, but the Laniel suggestion of a regrouping of forces was regarded as a valid proposal.

16 *The Observer* (London), April 11, 1954.

the Foreign Office's under-secretary in charge of Southeast Asian affairs about the possibilities of "partition" in Indochina.[17]

By now, the idea had caught on in influential British circles; even *The Times* took it up. References to the "English partition plan" appeared in the world press, although officials in London naturally denied responsibility for it. In the beginning of April 1954, the British ambassador to Washington, Sir Roger Makins, warned Dulles and Bedell Smith that the United Kingdom had to contemplate the possibility of accepting a compromise with the Communists and said that partition appeared to be the least objectionable solution in Indochina.[18]

The British Government felt that a settlement would need the support of as many neutral Asian powers as possible, so that it would not look like a product of Western imperialism. A forthcoming meeting of the Colombo Pact might provide the appropriate occasion for a diplomatic initiative by its members. Since March 29, India had grown actively alarmed over Dulles's increasingly anti-Chinese stand and his plans for "united action"; now it was urging London to work for a quick and peaceful settlement in Indochina. On April 29, India and China signed an agreement about Tibet; the preamble of this accord set forth the "five principles of peaceful coexistence" which China soon put to good use at Geneva. Thus the possibility of extending neutralism to new areas of Southeast Asia might possibly convince India and like-minded countries to associate themselves with a settlement in Indochina.

In other words, the British had no use for negotiations laden with menace; they preferred to promote a universally acceptable solution, a genuine compromise. However, they may well have impaired the Western position by publicly resigning themselves to this attitude before negotiations started.

[17] This is probably the approach to which Bao Dai referred in his message of April 26 (*Viet-Nam* [Paris], No. 75, May 15, 1954). However, Tran Chan Thanh, then an adviser to Ngô Dinh Diem, mentioned a "partition plan" in a talk with the author in Paris on April 9, 1954.

[18] This did not become public knowledge until Anthony Eden's memoirs appeared in 1960. Anthony Eden, *Full Circle* (London and Boston, 1960), pp. 91–92.

The American position was both more rigid and more vague. The Eisenhower Administration had stated at the highest policy level—in the National Security Council—that no further advance of Communism could be tolerated in Southeast Asia. Indochina in particular was of crucial strategic importance and must be saved, since its loss might trigger a chain reaction leading to the fall of the entire Southeast Asian area. Unfortunately, nobody had taken the next logical step and explained how this disaster could be prevented.

By now, it was widely believed in the United States that most Frenchmen wanted a negotiated end to the war. This possibility confronted the Americans with a cruel dilemma.[19] News from Paris about the mood in the National Assembly suggested that France might give up the struggle in Indochina if the government changed. The immediate reaction in some right-wing American circles was to claim that very important decisions could no longer be avoided and that either the United Nations or some other international coalition would have to take over the fight.[20] Even the use of American troops could not be ruled out in such a case.

This suggestion was repellent to American public opinion. Even the extreme right-wing element of the government led by Walter Robertson, Assistant Secretary of State for Far Eastern Affairs, and supported by the "China lobby" (including such influential congressmen as Senator Knowland) was surprised and dismayed by this suggestion. It was opposed to any negotiations—above all with China—but refused even to consider the dispatch of American troops. But if the French gave up the fight, who could be found to take their place—the South Koreans and Chiang Kai-shek's men? In fact, this right-wing group had already resigned itself to the loss of Indochina, because it refused to contemplate either intervention or negotiation.

The United States had agreed to the Geneva conference because

[19] Senator Alexander Wiley, then Chairman of the Senate Foreign Relations Committee, candidly admitted in New York on March 27 that the West would be in a "terrible fix" if the French did not carry on with the war. *The New York Times,* March 28, 1954.

[20] Report from Washington in *The New York Times,* March 29, 1954.

the French Government needed it for domestic political reasons. But the overwhelming majority of American officials considered it futile and were certain that it would fail. The American leaders were determined to make no concessions to China; therefore, they convinced themselves that the other side would make unacceptable demands and that there would be no further progress. They believed that any political settlement in Indochina, given the prevailing military situation, would amount to handing over control of the entire country to Ho Chi Minh. The members of the National Security Council were well aware of French war-weariness and of the persistent demands for immediate peace in certain political circles in Paris;[21] they simply hoped that the Russians and Chinese would make negotiations impossible by pitching their demands too high.

In sum, the immediate aim of the United States in the spring of 1954 was to encourage the French to carry on with the war and to discourage them from negotiating an armistice with the enemy which could only lead to an "Indochinese Munich."[22] Washington agreed to strengthen its hand and even to run some "calculated risks" (such as strategic bombardments), on condition that henceforth France would act within a new framework, where the "good" whites would help the "good" Asians to battle the Reds. Naturally, Washington—the capital of the free world—would set the tone and regulate the rhythm of the new combat. Dulles's offer of concerted action probably aimed to achieve no more than this.

Some people in Washington were publicly hoping that France would struggle on for another year or two,[23] until a strong Vietnamese national army had been raised, trained, and equipped with American help, after which the great offensive against the Vietminh could finally be launched. Others, who thought that

[21] "Off-the-record" speech by Nixon at the annual meeting of the American Society of Newspaper Editors, April 16, 1954. Quoted in *The New York Times*, April 18, 1954.

[22] Report of a congressional mission, consisting of four members of the Foreign Affairs Committee of the House of Representatives. See *The New York Times*, March 28, 1954.

[23] Statement by Senator Mike Mansfield, March 22, 1954.

complete victory in Indochina was unlikely, believed that only then would the time have come to undertake negotiations.[24]

Yet it was difficult for the United States, which was doing everything it could to avoid entering the war, to discourage France from looking for the settlement it wished. Dulles learned from his talks in London and Paris between April 11 and 14 that the British and French were reasonably hopeful about the outcome of negotiations but did not underestimate their difficulties. When he returned to Washington after sounding out the French, the Secretary of State believed that he had dealt with the serious threats that France would abandon the struggle or negotiate directly with Ho Chi Minh.

Some influential Americans, who understood the military imperatives that were driving France toward negotiation, had already given some thought to the basis for an eventual settlement. They concluded that Laos and Cambodia could serve as buffer zones protecting Thailand only if Vietnam itself could escape Communist domination, at least in the south.[25] They believed that to forestall a "chain-reaction collapse," it was essential to keep certain vital areas of Vietnam free of Communist control. This would require the establishment of strongly held fortified zones covering areas of special strategic importance.

Dulles himself thus came to accept the idea of a cease-fire "on honorable terms consistent with the independence of Vietnam, Laos, and Cambodia."[26] But an armistice seemed to him essentially a way of gaining time—the respite needed to equip and train a powerful Vietnamese army, and to establish a defense system for Southeast Asia which would henceforth be based on Saigon rather than on Hanoi.

24 *Agence économique et financière,* dispatch of March 29, 1954.

25 Hanson Baldwin discussed some similar proposals in *The New York Times,* March 29, 1954.

26 Statement of April 20, 1954, on his departure from Washington for Paris. At the same moment in Cincinnati, Ohio, Vice President Nixon also declared himself in favor of "an honorable and peaceful settlement" in Indochina but said that he would oppose outright surrender to the Communists. *The New York Times,* April 21, 1954.

Thus it was a truce, rather than peace, that the United States was preparing to promote at Geneva.

It was not only the American attitude that caused concern in Paris: the Vietnamese reaction also aroused some misgivings. The talks that had started on March 8 had not yet reached a satisfactory conclusion. Vietnamese independence was still the stumbling block. This time the Saigon government was determined to secure the unqualified recognition of Vietnamese independence and sovereignty which it had been demanding for five years. Only when its freedom was confirmed would Vietnam be able to join the French Union of its own free will.

The Vietnamese representatives had finally succeeded in persuading France that two treaties should be signed virtually at the same time: the first would once again recognize the independence of Vietnam; the second would spell out Vietnam's association with France. However, disagreements continued about the limitations of sovereignty resulting from membership in the French Union, because articles 62 and 65 of the French Constitution vested the conduct of defense and foreign relations in the Union's directing agencies—in other words, in the French Government. The Vietnamese, who were demanding total independence, maintained that they could not be bound by the provisions of the domestic constitution of one of the member states of the Union.

The discussions were deadlocked when Bao Dai arrived in Paris on April 11, at which time Dulles also happened to be there. At this point, the French Government decided to take a broader view of the question and conceded that a solution must be found in the interests of unity in the Free World.[27] It was agreed that the status of Vietnam "within the framework of the French Union" would be defined solely by the terms of the treaty and of conventions negotiated on the basis of complete equality, and not by the provisions of the French Constitution. The cabinet thereby took a severe political risk in relation to its right-wing opponents.

[27] Pleven and Reynaud had already advocated a more flexible and liberal attitude in this connection, while Bidault insisted on preserving all the constitutional prerogatives for the benefit of France.

The French Government, and especially Bidault, had repeatedly stated—at the February 23 meeting of the High Council of the French Union, for instance—that France would make no final decisions concerning Indochina without the formal consent of the Associated States. But it was only on April 23, when the three Western powers were meeting at the Quai d'Orsay to discuss the tactics to be used in Geneva, that it thought of informing Vietnam officially of its intentions. Only a few hours earlier, Bao Dai had asked René Coty, in his capacity as President of the French Union, to call a meeting of the High Council in order to discuss the problem of peace in Indochina, and the response of the government had been negative. The following day, however, Bidault received representatives of the Associated States and told them about the French delegation's plans. Nguyen Quoc Dinh, the Vietnamese Minister of Foreign Affairs, expressed strong reservations. He saw in these plans the beginnings of a scheme for partition[28] and the international recognition of the Vietminh. Bidault gave him a verbal assurance that the possibility of a political settlement based on partition had not been mentioned in the discussions with the British and Americans. He also reaffirmed the intention of the French Government to act in constant consultation with the Vietnamese Government at the Geneva conference. Then he proposed that he and the representatives of the three Associated States should announce that the four states were in full accord and that further consultations would take place *in Geneva.* Dinh refused to sign this document and said that "to do so would imply that we were going to Geneva, which is not yet certain, because Vietnam can go to this conference only if it is genuinely independent. But the treaties are not yet signed." Thus Dinh secured the insertion of the words "*in Geneva or elsewhere.*"

[28] Conversations with Nguyen Quoc Dinh (June 9, 1959) and Tran Chan Thanh (April 9, 1954). The latter, who became Minister of Information in the Diem Government and is now (December, 1968) Minister of Foreign Affairs in the Saigon regime, was convinced at the beginning of April, 1954 that the great powers were moving toward this solution. From this moment, the Vietnamese Right-wing nationalists were to turn decisively toward U.S. support to outflank the French-supported Baodaist regime. Total independence from France was needed to make this turn effective and lasting.

That same evening, a communiqué from Bao Dai's cabinet announced that the Vietnamese Government had decided not to sign the two treaties of independence and association for the time being, even though there was full agreement on the texts.[29] The communiqué declared that it had not been given the firm assurances it required concerning Vietnam's unity and independence, and it denounced the "various plans that would involve a partition of Vietnam," as well as the possibility of negotiations in which France, contrary to the principles of the French Union which it claimed as its own, would negotiate with rebels against the Vietnamese nation or with powers hostile to it. The communiqué concluded with a reference to Geneva, affirming that "neither the head of state nor the government of Vietnam would be bound by any decisions that ran counter to the independence or the unity of their country."

Thus, on the eve of the Geneva conference, Bao Dai's Vietnam, which had much to lose there, reasserted its freedom of action and announced that it might refuse to take part. This threat, if carried out, would put France in an exceedingly embarrassing position. Moreover, Bao Dai (and the United States as well) reserved the right to act outside the limitations of any settlement which might be reached.[30] Clearly, this development foreshadowed further difficulties.

On the morning of Saturday, April 24, 1954, just before the great confrontation at Geneva, the French Council of Ministers met for a final discussion of the French delegation's position. Bidault asked for, and received, a blank check from the government—the same freedom to negotiate that he had been given by every successive government so far (except possibly that of General

[29] This move was welcomed by some influential French experts because it maintained France's legal right to negotiate in Geneva on behalf of the French Union (and thus on behalf of Vietnam also). On this subject see Ngo Ton Dat, *The Geneva Partition of Vietnam and the Question of Reunification During the First Two Years*. Unpublished Ph.D. dissertation, Cornell University, 1963.

[30] This left Bao Dai free to support the Southeast Asia pact; see footnote 7, chapter 6.

de Gaulle).[31] His argument was unchanged: how could the French delegation be tied to a position when it knew nothing about the attitudes the Chinese or Russians would adopt? Nobody could forecast the circumstances in which the talks would proceed, and no tactical opportunity must therefore be excluded *a priori*. This statement met with no objections, and the Council of Ministers formulated no instructions.

The Foreign Minister's freedom of action was limited by only two requirements: he had to report every day to the Premier, who took charge of the Ministry of Foreign Affairs in his absence; and he had to pursue the government's primary goal of an armistice governed by strict safeguards.

[31] Conversation with Georges Bidault, July 24, 1959.

II

THE GENEVA CONFERENCE

8

A LAKESIDE RENDEZVOUS

Did Eden, Molotov, Dulles, and Bidault slip the first volume of *The Possessed* into their luggage as they were leaving for Berlin? One can safely bet that they did not. The remarks of Praskovia Nikolaevna, the embarrassing friend of the General's wife, might well have put them off Geneva as a site for the Asian conference: "This city irks me. . . . Of course, they say that the lakeside climate is relaxing. . . . But this quietness makes for boredom . . . and boredom is irksome. . . . Oh, how Geneva irks me!" But for once, Dostoyevsky would have read badly: our diplomats were inspired indeed when they chose Geneva for their rendezvous, without becoming unduly depressed by the memory of failures suffered there by Briand, Stresemann, and Titulescu.

Everything in the place seemed to encourage a patient search for contact and compromise—the sparkling air from the surrounding mountains, the gentle lapping of the lake, the shady walks along the banks, the restaurants, the *fondue*, the trout, and the phlegmatic, well-informed, and knowledgeable newspapers, delivering each morning a ready-made yardstick of public opinion. Everything seemed to favor negotiation—the imperturbable local inhabitants, the comfortable hotels, the calm of the villas overlooking the Lake of Geneva: a quality of moderation, deliberation, and also freedom in this city where the fire that consumed Michael Servetus had long since died out. Everything seemed suited to a peace conference—the careless flight of the gulls, the light mist over the lake, even the ghosts of Jean-Jacques Rousseau and Madame de Warens. Who could remain unaffected by this pervasive climate of tolerance, by the calm that seemed to soften the very air?

The first delegates arrived on Saturday morning, April 24. The North Koreans landing at the airfield at Cointrin seemed somewhat surprised to find it deserted and to discover that they aroused so little curiosity after coming such a long way. General Nam Il, the tough negotiator of Panmunjom, looked around him for the photographers; seeing none, he quickly made for the long black Zis that was waiting to take him to his hotel. He looked thoroughly disgruntled.

Six hours later, what a crowd there was to meet the Chinese delegation! The American journalists, even more than the others, were trembling with excitement to see this Chou En-lai, Prime Minister and Foreign Minister of China, Mao Tse-tung's right-hand man and already a legendary figure. When the aircraft landed, about four in the afternoon, several men emerged from the cabin and clattered down the stairway. But where was Chou? Suddenly, another man was outlined in the door against the darkness inside the aircraft. He hurried down the steps, followed by two or three others dressed in blue. Which one was Chou? The tall thin one or the squat one? An American photographer shouted: "Chou En-lai! Closer! Look at me!" Taken by surprise, the first man turned around, singled out and cut off from the herd by the cold eye of the camera. His were the instinctive reactions of the great actor and public figure. On the smooth ivory face, deeply lined, with its high forehead, huge mouth, and enormous pointed black eyebrows setting off the large and beautiful dark eyes, there flashed a smile. It was a great, meaningful, ironic smile, showing dazzling teeth. It was a smile that would animate the pages of American magazines and be worth months of negotiations for the

United States' recognition of the Chinese People's Republic. His effect achieved, Chou En-lai sheathed the smile and disappeared into his car, looking stern.

Neither Molotov that evening, nor Eden on the following day, nor even Bidault a day later created anything like this stir. And there was no jockeying for position as a grumpy John Foster Dulles read to the assembled journalists a statement he had just scribbled in the plane concerning the honorable amends that the Communist states should be prepared to make.[1]

Dulles, the mainspring of American diplomacy, was the only delegate to choose a hotel for his residence. Perhaps the Hotel du Rhône, that composition in chrome and concrete, brought to mind some New York colossus like the Waldorf-Astoria. Or perhaps this choice was meant to show that Dulles was merely passing by and that the American delegation would be in constant readiness to leave. The leaders of all the other delegations preferred to live and work in the villas built along the lake shore by patricians of Geneva or by Anglo-Saxons and Slavs who had been voluntary exiles among the meadows and gentle romantic groves. Stories were told of savage in-fighting between the quartermasters of the Chinese and the Soviets, the British and the South Vietnamese, for possession of the most notable residences near Geneva—the *Grand Mont-Fleuri*, the *Villa Blanche*, the *Reposoir*, *Bella-Vista*, the *Bocage*. Molotov had expressed the wish to stay at the *Reposoir*, which once had sheltered Leopold III and the Princesse de Rethy; but the Geneva banker Pieter had discreetly refused to receive him and instead, only a few days later, invited Anthony Eden, who made himself at ease among furnishings upholstered in embossed velvet, admired the collection of Chinese art, and relaxed in the park and under the pergolas.

Molotov, short-sighted though he was, could not fail to see how

[1] He came, he said, on a peace mission that had been made necessary by Communist aggression in Asia: "We hope to find that the aggressors come here in a mood to purge themselves of their aggression." He hoped it would be possible to "achieve a durable peace" that would enable the people of Vietnam, Laos, and Cambodia to "enjoy and perfect the political freedom which is now theirs." *The New York Times*, April 25, 1954.

the Soviet delegation's prestige was diminished in the setting of *Les Chatillons* (whose eighteenth-century charm failed to win him) or the vast, pretentious armchairs and garish decoration of the *Villa Blanche*. Bidault, who evidently did not believe that national prestige was moving in with him, was even more modestly housed. The one intriguing feature at *Joli-Port*, a relatively bourgeois villa leased for him at Versoix by Jean Chauvel, the French ambassador in Bern, was the lone fence that separated it from the house in which Pham Van Dong, leader of the Vietminh delegation, was to take up residence on May 12. As we shall see, Bidault derived less benefit from this arrangement than anybody else.

Of all those taking part in the Geneva talks, Chou En-lai probably took the greatest trouble to live in state. He was, after all, making what amounted to a European debut. At the vast estate of *Grand Mont-Fleuri*, beautiful furniture and carpets from China were now arranged; it had the air of a national museum, the better to present the delegation which represented an ancient and powerful nation heir to thousands of years of civilization. At *Grand Mont-Fleuri*, Chou could also receive the smaller Asian delegations as a host, elder brother, and counselor. The house became a sort of embassy; evidently, he planned to stay for several months, viewing the Geneva conference as the first act in his European performance.

Thus the actors in the coming debate settled down along the banks of the Rhône and the lake before crossing swords. What thoughts preoccupied them? In the august halls of the Palais des Nations—on its ceiling, painted by José Maria Sert, five giants, supposedly representing the five continents, shake hands warily—the first meetings were devoted to the Korean problem. Interest in these was slight, which made it easier to sound out the delegations about their thoughts on Indochina and to estimate which ones opposed a compromise solution and which supported it. In a former five-and-ten-cent-store, now turned into a press center and repainted for the occasion in U.N. blue and white, Asian specialists and veterans of earlier international conferences harbored few illusions about the value of the tips they swapped, or the seriousness of the answers they gave to questions from their younger colleagues.

How would Chou En-lai and Molotov work as a team, now that these two foreign ministers faced their Western opposite numbers together for the first time? As it turned out, they divided the labor. Chou, seconded by the Vietnamese, dealt with purely Asian questions about suspending hostilities, defining demarcation lines, and timing withdrawals; Molotov kept largely to broader matters, such as long-term peace guarantees and the organization of control commissions. It was all done with a punctilious regard for national sensitivities and without missing a single opportunity to point out that China had now joined the great powers and intended to be treated, and to behave, as a member of the club.

The part played by Chou En-lai, fairly inconspicuous though it was during the early weeks of the conference, grew after the beginning of June. There was a sense of constraint about him at first, a stiff quality, a touch of harshness and violence—but his manner gradually eased and his range widened remarkably. His mandarin inheritance, that incomparable tradition of great Chinese civil service and diplomacy, came to the surface, and during the closing days he was clearly one of the dominant figures at the meeting. Molotov, on the other hand, although less inscrutable, abrupt, and monolithic than he had been at previous international meetings, showed signs of aging and weariness. He was not always able to master his moods, good or bad.

The Vietminh delegation was not due to arrive until May 4. What would they be like, these men who had emerged in Geneva, with only a few hurried stopovers on Chinese and Soviet airfields, straight from the Vietminh headquarters in the limestone caves near Thai Nguyen? Their leader, Pham Van Dong, the son of a mandarin, a former history teacher, and a favorite colleague of Ho Chi Minh, was no stranger to most of the French journalists. They had known him eight years earlier in Hanoi or at the Fontainebleau negotiations, where he led the first Vietminh delegation under Ho Chi Minh's direction. But to those who had known him years before, he was now almost unrecognizable, for the years of struggle had scarred him cruelly. It was as though a fearful storm had ravaged his features; like the face of a test pilot exposed to a supersonic blast, his face seemed stretched taut and scored to the limit of endurance; the cheekbones jutted out harshly; the burning eyes were sunk deep in their sockets. In this ravaged face—scarred by sickness perhaps, and by passion and privation as well—only the protuberant mouth seemed to be made of flesh. And the harsh, staccato, often ragged voice matched the face. His disfigurement might well have served as a living witness for those who maintained that the Vietminh, however successful it might be, was in a hurry to come to terms—its troops weary, its food supplies scarce. Who could predict how much suffering an eastern people will endure when freedom is in sight?

The conference saw Pham Van Dong's personality undergo progressive relaxation. Geneva had its calming effect. So did the establishment of his delegation's claims, the contacts with other diplomats, and the consideration shown him by the members of the French delegation during the second part of the conference. Most of those who talked with him appreciated his brilliant intelligence, his stubbornness, and his liveliness in argument. In this academy of world diplomacy, the spokesman of the Vietminh militants proved to be no parvenu. Once his illness was gone and he had learned to put aside his conspirator's reserve, Pham Van Dong's very real talents blossomed. Eventually, he was able to take pleasure in displaying a cultural background that extended beyond Michelet and Jaurès to Montaigne and Voltaire. Toward the end, he even started to smile, and it was Pham Van Dong's joke over the final toasts to peace that journalists remembered as they left Geneva.

He had able assistants as well. Phan Anh, a jovial character, and Hoang Van Hoan, the Vietminh ambassador to Peking, convinced the journalists that great discretion and a history as a guerrilla did not necessarily disqualify one as a lively sparring partner in interviews; Ta Quang Buu and Ha Van Lau, Vietminh representatives on the military commission, made life difficult for their French counterparts, General Delteil and Colonel de Brébisson. Only Tran Cong Tuong, the vice minister of justice, retained his reserve to the end.

It was not so easy to assess the representatives of Cambodia, Laos, and nationalist Vietnam. The Cambodians were alternately petulant and evasive. The Laotians stayed in the shadow of the French delegation, but this indicated tactical discretion rather than disinterest. The delegation from Vietnam (which changed substantially in the middle of June, after Diem replaced Buu Loc as prime minister) were in a patently false position, because their government was obviously convinced that it would be the loser in any political settlement that the conference might reach. The leader of the first delegation, Nguyen Quoc Dinh, clearly held this view; his successor, Tran Van Do, obviously felt that, however bad any agreement might be—particularly one leading to temporary partition—the prolongation of the war would lead to even worse disasters. Bao Dai kept a nonchalant and world-weary eye on the proceedings from Evian, where he received numerous American emissaries and far fewer French visitors.

Bao Dai hardly needed to convert the Americans to a skeptical view of the situation. Dulles had so little faith in the possibility of an agreement that he flew home to Washington only a week after reaching Geneva. Two of the more important American delegates harbored still stronger prejudices against negotiation; these were Assistant Secretary Robertson and U. Alexis Johnson, American ambassador in Prague. Johnson succeeded in astonishing even Bidault by the density of his unthinking anti-Communism.

It was the continuing presence of Walter Bedell Smith as leader of the American delegation that made it possible to preserve cohesion in the Western camp: without him, the West's fragile unity might easily have been shattered by such a surfeit of anti-Communist frenzy. General Bedell Smith had been Chief of Staff to Eisenhower during World War II; after the war, he served as ambassador to Moscow and director of the Central Intelligence Agency before being named Dulles's chief assistant at the State Department. With his clergyman's face, his abrupt language, and his field-soldier's bearing, he was hardly the image of a supple and accommodating diplomat. His sudden and violent blasts of temper were all the more surprising from an officer normally almost puritanical in his restraint. Moreover, he had been a "hawk" during the April argument over Operation Vulture. But his natural common sense, his first-hand knowledge of the capabilities and thought processes of the Communists, and his long association with Eisenhower combined to make him more careful, if not more conciliatory, than his colleagues.[2] He knew that in the circumstances, it was the strong who could afford to wait, and he practiced his patience by marching off to the lake, a fine marine cap on his head and an old army jacket on his back, to dangle bait over the pike.

Geneva was a familiar battlefield—or theater—for Anthony Eden. He knew every corner of the Palais des Nations; such stars as Lord Curzon, Austen Chamberlain, and Maxim Litvinov had taught him the secrets of this speechmaker's seraglio long ago. He had learned here at first hand the price to be paid for surrenders and for sanctions unequally applied. He was unsurpassed in his ability to distinguish between a crippling compromise and the concession that clinches a deal, between an opening to peace and the respite before a war.

In fact, he was the pivot, or rather the broker, of the negotiations throughout the ten weeks of the talks. This was partly due to his personal talents, his long experience, and his determination to succeed. But it also stemmed from Great Britain's position as the only Western power maintaining diplomatic relations with Peking and from its links (through the Commonwealth and the Colombo Plan) with the aspirations of the Asian continent. These influences impelled Britain to press for an end to the war in Indochina, even while it worked to build a barrier along the eastern frontiers of Laos and Cambodia against the Communist drive toward Malaya. But all this may be an over-elaborate analysis of an entirely empirical attitude.[3]

Eden also played a leading part in the conference in his capacity as co-chairman, a duty he shared with Molotov. It was an odd

[2] In the very first days of the conference, he confided to some members of the French delegation that partition at about the 18th Parallel would probably be inevitable.

[3] Eden's memoirs show that the Foreign Secretary regarded his work in Geneva mainly as a trial of strength with Dulles, whom he wanted to convince that by risking a war against China in 1954, America was picking the wrong enemy, on the wrong ground, at the wrong time.

formula—yoking together in one team the man in the hat and the man in the pince-nez—but the results were not bad. The Russian and the Englishman took turns at deciding when to begin or adjourn debates, whether to call on delegations to speak or overlook them. Between them, they somehow kept the whole enterprise on the move.[4]

Eden had reliable assistance. At his side was his permanent under-secretary, Denis Allen, embodying the Foreign Office's flawless technique and capacity for getting and dispensing information. To his right was Lord Reading, Minister of State for Foreign Affairs, big china-blue eyes shining with Victorian fervor, a bald head crowned with a few wisps of snowy hair, plump cheeks like those of a well-fed baby. Reading was like an imperial breakwater in this troubled Asian sea, the living symbol of an unsinkable, untroubled, and somehow touching Britain. Sir Humphrey Trevelyan, on Eden's left, ashen-faced and skeletal, was a striking contrast. Sir Humphrey was Her Majesty's chargé d'affaires in Peking, and he had previously advised the Government of India on foreign relations. Of all those present on the Western side, he knew Chou En-lai best, and he made good use of this acquaintance. The disturbing light of well-informed intelligence flickered in his dark eyes.

Georges Bidault, leader of the French delegation, arrived in Geneva last of all. The little man had leapt to the platform of the Cornavin railroad station on Monday, April 26, only a few hours before the Korean meetings were due to start. His hair was unkempt, his eyes were puffy from lack of sleep, but his voice was as cutting as ever. Before leaving Paris for Switzerland, he had seen both Dulles, on Saturday, and Eden, on Sunday, in dramatic confrontations. There was tension both in NATO and in the National Assembly, where every direct hit on the airfield at Dien

[4] In fact, the question of the chairmanship was an extremely delicate problem. Eden and Molotov agreed as early as April 28 on a simple formula for the *Korean* conference: the first session was to be chaired by the Thai Prince Wan Waithayakon, the second by Eden, and the third by Molotov. Since Thailand was not taking part in the Indochina conference, the formula was easily simplified. Eden's and Molotov's co-chairmanship supplied a happy solution to the problem created by the presence of China among the great powers.

Bien Phu was a telling blow against the Laniel government. A few hours earlier, London had vetoed Operation Vulture out of hand, while Eisenhower and some close associates were accusing Bidault of trying to drag America into a venture that could only end in atomic war.

This was, in fact, the theme of many editorials concerning the start of Bidault's mission in Geneva. But Bidault himself took no notice. He was completely self-assured—or completely absorbed in trying to impress his adversary with his self-assurance. Nor did he seem to worry about his disagreement with the man who should have been his closest colleague, Marc Jacquet, Minister for the Associated States and long an advocate of direct negotiations with the Vietminh. The two had often clashed in the past, and they failed to come to terms either politically or personally in Geneva. Jacquet's robustness, his cheerfulness, and his salesman's common sense exasperated Bidault, who finally secured his recall.

Apart from Frédéric-Dupont, who acted as a go-between in June, Bidault's team was composed of professional diplomats: Jean Chauvel, de Margerie, Raymond Offroy, Jacques Baeyens, Jean Laloy, Jacques Roux, Folin, and Claude Cheysson. The first two in particular had long been regarded by their department as "international class" diplomats, fit for the most important negotiations. From start to finish, Chauvel proved to be one of the finest players at the meeting. He had the long face of a Renaissance prelate; leaning over his papers and maps, he injected into the discussions a constant flow of ideas, suggestions, and bold proposals. He was a diplomat in the great classical tradition; when he found himself in the kind of international conference that once was thought to have vanished with the nineteenth century, he displayed a sovereign talent.

Talented military men were closely associated with every stage of the talks. Colonel Jacques Guillermaz, a heavy man with a high complexion and a thick thatch of hair, had been military attaché in Nanking and Bangkok, spoke Chinese, and was personally acquainted with Wang Ping-nan, one of Chou's assistants. Colonel de Brébisson, thin and reserved, left his mark throughout the negotiations and became one of the chief architects of the agreement. General Delteil stood for the strictest soldierly tradition; he headed the military commission. Professor Gros, legal counsel of the Quai d'Orsay, managed, even during the most arid discussions, to maintain the detached but watchful look of a great bridge player; he took a leading part in the drafting of the conference documents.

The French delegation made its headquarters at the villa of *Le Bocage*, but its meetings took place at *Joli-Port*. Bidault held long sessions with his delegation in the great salon, where inappropriate columns supported the ceiling and impersonal English paintings adorned the walls. Occasionally, they met in the park, under the tall, romantic trees. Here, too, Bidault received visitors for private discussions, and these soon became a mainstay of the entire, peculiar conference.

During the first few weeks, the sixteen representatives at the Korean talks and the nine participants in the Indochina debate met more or less regularly. Then, little by little, the conference began to come apart at the seams. Its Secretary General, Jean Paul-Boncour, who had represented France in China and Thailand before he became an international civil servant, did everything he could to stop the drift, but the conference crumbled into a succession of casual meetings over cups of tea, meals in Geneva's best restaurants, and official dinners. Despite his position, his knowledge of Asia, and the legacy of his father's long diplomatic career at Geneva, Paul-Boncour found himself confined to a purely technical role. Molotov, one of the co-chairmen, refused to recognize his official position, though no one was quite sure why; and Bidault did not even seem to notice his existence.

Isolated villas, "impromptu" visits, meetings that gradually turned into more or less secret confabulations—all combined eventually to set the style of the Geneva conference. It was a matter of subtle nuances, navigation by dead reckoning, whispered secrets; of good meals, oblique moves, and walks in the sun. The mixture had something Swiss in it, something Asian, and something British. Yet these nine characters in search of peace might easily have chosen more sterile methods and less productive paths.

9

THE TWO OF CLUBS AND THE THREE OF DIAMONDS

The Korean prologue to the conference hardly raised a flicker of interest. Everyone was completely skeptical. The Western diplomats had at last agreed to sit down at the same conference table with the Chinese and North Koreans, but there was no risk whatsoever that they might actually negotiate. The armistice had been signed; the fighting was not likely to start again. The two worlds seemed content to accept the stabilization of their positions along the 38th Parallel.

But the approaching debate on Indochina had everyone aroused. It was time to get it under way, and that required agreement about who would participate. The Western side had decided some days earlier, in a sudden but unpublicized burst of realism, that a Vietminh delegation could be admitted. The Democratic Republic of Vietnam did not rank as an "interested nation" from the Western viewpoint; it was merely a "rebel group." But it was the adversary in the war, and, if an armistice were to be discussed rather than just the ending of Chinese aid, representatives of the enemy would have to be present. Also, the Soviet Union would probably refuse to talk with the Associated States, whose political legitimacy it had always denied, if the Vietminh, which had been recognized as the Vietnamese government by all the People's Democracies, were not represented as well.

Bidault wanted to sound out the intentions of his adversaries on this question, and he received Molotov at *Joli-Port* on April 27. The Russian foreign minister was in an excellent mood, and a relatively cordial conversation lasted for forty minutes. "This is the beginning of the beginning," said Bidault. At a second meeting on the following day, the agreement was practically settled. Without raising any objections, Molotov agreed to recommend to his allies that the Big Four, Communist China, and the three Associated States all take part in the conference; not unexpectedly, he asked that Ho Chi Minh's government also be represented. Bidault replied that he wished to think it over before giving an answer.

The fact of the matter was that Bidault had not yet secured Bao Dai's agreement to the admission of the Vietminh, and he needed time. Bao Dai had not even revealed whether he would take part in the conference, in spite of a personal appeal by Jacquet in Evian.

Telephone calls followed, impatience, and irritation. On April 30, Bidault sent his *directeur de cabinet*, Pierre Falaize, to Evian on an "information mission." Bao Dai was pressed to nominate a delegation with the least possible delay and to give his answer concerning the admission of the Vietminh. This French request was personally supported by the American Ambassador to the Associated States, Donald R. Heath.

As we have seen, the Vietnamese head of state and his ministers felt that Vietnam could not appear in Geneva as a French satellite.[1] In order to confront Vietnamese public opinion, and Ho Chi Minh as well, Bao Dai knew he would have to make it clear that he was fully independent. He stated his terms: Vietnam would

[1] Conversations with Prince Buu Loc (June 6, 1959) and Nguyen Quoc Dinh (June 9, 1959).

agree to go to Geneva to discuss the possible participation of the Vietminh only if it were invited to do so by the three Western powers, with which it would first have to hold a preliminary conference.

Bidault persisted—time was short—but Bao Dai turned a deaf ear. As a gesture of "good will" and to make contact easier, he did allow his Foreign Minister, Nguyen Quoc Dinh, to move to Saint-Julien (a French town near Geneva), but he made it clear that the minister would not cross the frontier until the letter of invitation reached him.

In the end, the Vietnamese conditions were accepted. Dinh was officially invited to confer with the Big Three, and he reached Geneva on May 1. On the evening of Sunday, May 2, Chauvel visited Gromyko to inform him that Vietnam agreed to Vietminh participation in the conference, provided it was not taken to imply legal recognition in any sense. Official invitations went out the next day to Vietnam, Cambodia, Laos, and the Democratic Republic of Vietnam. Nguyen Quoc Dinh's discussion with Bidault, Eden, and Bedell Smith also took place on May 3, and it seemed that the conference could begin before the end of the week. But there was more trouble to come.

Bao Dai suspected that France was moving toward support of partition in Indochina, and he now requested "clarifications" and "guarantees" concerning the unity of Vietnam. In fact, the French had not even considered the possibility of partition as a lasting solution. It was morally out of the question, and, in any case, Vietnamese of every political persuasion were uniformly opposed to it. All that was openly under consideration was a "re-grouping" of the contending forces—an exchange of territories held when a cease-fire came into force, so that the areas occupied by each side could be consolidated and the front stabilized. An attempt would then be made to reach a political settlement, though there was little hope of success; Korea, Palestine, and Germany were not encouraging examples.

Bidault finally decided to give Bao Dai the requisite assurances in writing, despite the marked reservations of his staff, who wished to preserve the delegation's freedom of action.[2] On May 6, he wrote to the Vietnamese head of state reaffirming "the intention of the French Government to act in Geneva in constant consultation with the Vietnamese Government" and went on:

> The French Government does not presently propose to seek a final political settlement here. Our task, as indicated by the Berlin communiqué, is to establish peace in Indochina.
>
> Our object, therefore, is to secure a cease-fire as part of an armistice incorporating the guarantees required by the three Indochinese states, France, and those allied powers having general interests in common with ours in Southeast Asia. This armistice must not prejudice the nature of the final settlement, the study of which can be undertaken at a later date, when the conditions of peace and freedom necessary for holding general elections have been achieved.
>
> Indeed, I am now in a position to confirm to Your Majesty that nothing could be more contrary to the intentions of the French Government than to prepare for the establishment of two states, each with an international role, at the expense of the integrity of Vietnam.

Meanwhile, a mood of relative confidence was emerging at the conference, making the pessimism of the first few days seem somewhat excessive. The first contacts revealed that the Russians were willing to forego debates on procedure, as they had in Berlin, which suggested that they wanted an early start to the meetings. The Russians also gave some observers the impression—as though they were afraid of the effect of Chinese intransigence on the mood of the Western powers—that they wished to arrange direct contacts as soon as possible between the French and the Vietminh, over whom Moscow had a certain measure of control. For this purpose, Molotov and his colleagues used the question of the French wounded at Dien Bien Phu.

[2] On May 3, Dejean—acting on the instructions of the French Government—told the press in Saigon: "The French Government does not intend to seek the settlement of the problem of Indochina on the basis of a partition of Vietnamese territory. Formal assurances . . . were given by the French Minister of Foreign Affairs to the Minister of Foreign Affairs of Vietnam on April 25 and confirmed to him on May 1."

At his first meeting with Molotov, Bidault had urged that the question of evacuating these casualties should take precedence over the question of which states were to take part in the conference. He said that the French commander had granted a truce to the Vietminh at the beginning of the siege for a similar purpose, and he now asked for reciprocal treatment. Molotov seemed to be sympathetic and suggested that the problem should be settled as quickly as possible *in Geneva* by the representatives of the two sides. Were Vietminh representatives already in Switzerland? Bidault, who still refused to "deal with Ho Chi Minh," jumped to the conclusion that the Russians were trying to blackmail him.[3] Days were thus lost, tragically, for reasons of self-esteem.

What attitude should the French delegation adopt when the conference opened? What proposals should it put forward? In those first days of May, everything had yet to be defined. Some experts thought that the Vietminh—or the Soviet Union—would propose an immediate and unconditional cease-fire,[4] thereby gaining the advantage of being the first to make a peace offer and creating a world-wide movement of opinion in his favor. He would then be able to exploit this advantage, and the cessation of hostilities, to secure a favorable political settlement.

Individual points of view within the French Government and military command were all related to this possibility. Those who regarded the over-all military situation as critical and those who were preoccupied with the fate of Dien Bien Phu and its garrison favored rapid agreement on a cease-fire, with a minimum of safeguards or no safeguards at all. Those who took a longer view considered that any armistice should be carefully protected by

[3] A Soviet spokesman had stated as early as April 21 that the U.S.S.R. would ask for the opening of talks between Bao Dai and the D.R.V., because the Soviet Union considered that negotiations between "the two sides directly concerned" constituted the best means of reaching an agreement. This source had added that such an arrangement must be accompanied by the withdrawal of all foreign troops. United Press dispatch, April 21, 1954.

[4] In an editorial on April 7, 1954, *Izvestia* had advocated an immediate cease-fire "to enable France and the Democratic Republic of Vietnam to begin talks."

guarantees and control measures. Bidault belonged to the second school of thought—he was completely opposed to an unconditional cease-fire—and most of his colleagues supported him in this stand. When the French Council of Ministers met on April 24, only one minister—Vice-Premier Reynaud—asked whether the French delegation should not secure a cease-fire at the outset. France itself could not solicit this, he agreed, but it might be possible to rely on proposals advanced by other powers—Reynaud mentioned recent speeches on this subject by Nehru. When asked who would take such an initiative when India was not taking part in the conference, Reynaud replied, "England."

At the meeting of the Council on April 30, Reynaud, supported by Louis Jacquinot, the Minister for Overseas France, returned to the attack and suggested that a cease-fire be requested at the opening session of the conference through the mediation of a third power. In his opinion, direct and immediate contact with the Vietminh would have been preferable. Maurice Schumann, Under-Secretary for Foreign Affairs, argued against Reynaud and supported Bidault; so did the Premier, who took an active part in the discussion. But the government was unable to reach an agreement, and so it was left to the French delegation to devise a plan in Geneva.

Bidault was very tired. He was torn between Geneva and Paris and had little time to spare for this particular question, so the whole work of preparing the French position fell on Jean Chauvel. Chauvel, with the help of Claude Cheysson, one of the two members of the delegation who knew Indochina (the other was Raymond Offroy) and was able to assess accurately the impact of the words about to be used, worked out a plan of action.

After protracted exchanges of views between Paris and Geneva, it finally was decided that the aim should be an armistice backed up with guarantees and controls. However, it was felt that "cease-fire" was a safer term to use than "armistice," since the latter had political overtones and tended to commit governments as well as armies. The agreement between the commanders in chief should include territorial safeguards (regrouping in zones) and political ones (international control and collective guarantees). In Laos and

Cambodia, the objective was to re-establish peace by obtaining the straightforward withdrawal of Vietminh troops.

But, in the meantime, the French military command had already formed more precise views on the subject. General Navarre has complained that he was never consulted about the circumstances in which he would consider an armistice; however, he does admit that he received a questionnaire from Chauvel around the middle of April.[5] We now know that he answered it on April 21[6] and that it was his opinion which ultimately determined the French delegation's position on a number of essential points. Navarre thought that the Vietminh would indeed be inclined to accept (he did not say "propose") a cease-fire "in the hope of taking the direction of the country in hand by legal means." In any case, as a result of the propaganda about the conference, the Vietminh would regard the cease-fire as a success in itself. In particular, General Navarre supplied answers to the two following questions:

> 1. *If the talks were to move toward the allocation—however temporary—of a sphere of influence to the Vietminh, what would be the maximum acceptable limits of such a zone?*
>
> *Answer:*
>
> A. As far as Laos is concerned, it would seem difficult to compromise, except to agree to certain rectifications in the northern frontier.
>
> B. In Vietnam, we could only accept a line of partition along the 18th Parallel, which, while leaving us Hue, the political capital [of Annam], and the city of Tourane [Da Nang], would allow us to anchor our position to a geographic obstacle of military value [the limestone area of Mu Gia and Troc].
>
> C. It would also be necessary to continue the occupation of Hanoi and Haiphong, at least temporarily, and to retain freedom of movement along the Hanoi-Haiphong axis.
>
> *But General Navarre added:*
>
> We must consider the possibility that the enemy will not accept a demarcation line north of the 16th Parallel. This would mean

[5] Henri Navarre, *Agonie de l'Indochine* (Paris, 1956), pp. 296, 303.
[6] Note No. 1809, from the Commander in Chief, April 21, 1954.

giving the Vietminh the whole of the zone we control in central Annam, while retaining under our authority an area as thoroughly "infected" as Quang Ngai.

2. *If such a zone were established, what measures would have to be taken (a) by us; (b) by the Vietminh?*

Answer:

A. Evacuation of the regular forces of each side from the control zones allocated to the other.

B. Disarming or evacuation of regional forces (irregulars and regional battalions).

C. Evacuation of French and Vietnamese civilians wishing to leave the zone controlled by the Vietminh. Guarantee of safety for property and persons remaining on the spot.

Nothing could be more coldly incisive. The conditions for a cease-fire outlined by General Navarre were far from being those of a conqueror, and he stated them more than two weeks before the fall of Dien Bien Phu. After a searching reassessment of the situation, he was ready to evacuate the whole of Tonkin, with the exception—"at least temporarily"—of Hanoi and Haiphong and the highway connecting these cities. He did not even say categorically that the 16th Parallel was unacceptable as a demarcation line; he did think it necessary to comment unfavorably on any settlement that might be based on it.

General Navarre also dealt with the subject of control. He foresaw "the establishment and operation of mixed control commissions, consisting either of neutrals or representatives of the belligerents (the Associated State concerned, the Vietminh, and France)." And he stressed the difficulties that would arise from the tangle of positions held by the opposing sides if there were a cease-fire before a general agreement had been concluded. Finally, he stated that there would be no immediate danger in proposing the complete military evacuation of Laos and Cambodia by both sides.

This statement was far more realistic than the position held by Bidault. General Navarre was, in fact, pointing the way not merely to negotiations with the Vietminh, but to the "military partition" solution that was ultimately adopted. By stating the advantages of the 18th Parallel as the demarcation line, while mentioning the possibility of a temporary partition along the 16th Parallel, he marked out the area of dispute that was eventually to become a key part of the talks.

What trumps did the French still hold, with which they could secure their "honorable compromise"—an armistice including safeguards and controls? Bidault's letter of May 6 to Bao Dai had already put a moral bar in the path of any solution involving the partition of Vietnam under separate governments. What now remained of the Quai d'Orsay's supreme argument, the possibility of American support?

Dulles and his advisers had reached Geneva with the idea that failure was not merely inevitable but actually desirable, since the West was unable to dictate peace for the time being. At the Paris meeting on April 22, they were already talking about "expediting the work" at Geneva.

All the more enlightened elements in American public opinion, as well as the British and French, were greatly perturbed by this negative approach. Walter Lippmann pointed out in the *New York Herald Tribune* on April 29 that "European, uncommitted Asian, and almost certainly American public opinion as well, will insist that an earnest, sincere, and searching attempt be made to negotiate . . . an armistice." He felt obliged to add:

> Unfortunately it is almost impossible, owing to the political situation in Washington, for Secretary Dulles to participate in this effort. Congress has deprived him of the means to negotiate. He can make no concessions to the Vietminh or to Red China. . . . The American position at Geneva is an impossible one . . . so long as the leading Republican senators have no terms of peace except unconditional surrender of the enemy and no terms for entering the war except as a collective action in which nobody is now willing to engage.

Unfortunately, the failure of the Korean conference helped to justify Dulles's pessimism. The North Korean delegate, General Nam Il, was as intransigent as Molotov had been in Berlin two months earlier. The same obstacles cropped up. The dialog proved empty, and Dulles, growing more and more convinced that it was impossible to negotiate with Communists and that he had been wrong in agreeing to meet with them in Geneva, soon began to talk of leaving.

The effect of American domestic politics on Dulles's attitude was even greater. Dispatches from American correspondents in Geneva revealed to the American public that the French and British were determined to talk to the Communists, even Chinese Communists, in order to achieve a settlement. And now Dulles, the puritan representative of a puritan America, was also embroiled in transactions with the Antichrist! A storm broke out across the Atlantic; outrage and even humiliation swept the country: America was losing its leadership. Not only was it unable to stop its allies from taking the downward path to another Munich; it was itself about to go the same way. On May 5, *The Washington Post,* a paper of moderate views, went so far as to suggest that there had been "a humiliating setback." American opinion found it hard to believe that Dulles could not have prevented the move toward a cease-fire, especially after he had been warned against appeasement by leading Republican commentators.[7] The administration and the State Department scarcely reacted at all; thus they let it be understood that it was no longer possible to prevent what they had long sought to avoid. It was France, after all, that was fighting the war. But both the press and Congress were less resigned. Unhesitatingly, they blamed the British Government for this failure of diplomacy, for turning down the suggested collective intervention, leaving Bidault no alternative except a search for the cease-fire they dreaded so much.

But Dulles and his concept of collective action also came under fire. Rumors began to circulate that the Secretary of State would be forced to resign, although the White House naturally denied this. As though to clear Dulles, it was hinted in Washington that he had been concerned about certain trends in French foreign

[7] See, for example, the article by David Lawrence in the *New York Herald Tribune,* April 29, 1954, praising Dulles's speech at the Geneva conference in which the Secretary of State opposed any idea of surrender.

policy which he regarded as excessively conciliatory. Was it true, then, that the Americans had vetoed some of the solutions proposed by the French? Certainly the Americans had not suggested anything more constructive. They had merely said that a partition of Indochina would not constitute an acceptable solution. In fact, the American Government realized more clearly every day that it could do nothing to inhibit the European desire to end the war through a settlement with the Communist East. President Eisenhower's statement of April 29, with its reference to a *modus vivendi*, had already pointed to this realization, and that it helped to unleash a political storm against Dulles merely demonstrated the extent to which the American public and the Congress were living in a dream world.

In this tense atmosphere of impotent bitterness, Dulles left Geneva to return to Washington—on May 3, the very day on which the Vietminh delegation's arrival in Geneva was announced—abandoning the Korean conference and refusing to take part in the Indochina one. As he boarded his aircraft, he told Chauvel that, *above all, the Red River and Mekong deltas must be held, in order to prepare for the coming counterattack in two years' time.* Yet Dulles had told his deputy, Walter Bedell Smith, merely to watch and wait—to allow the French to maneuver as best they could, and to intervene only if a settlement between East and West began to take shape.

In fact, Dulles was outwardly resigned only because he was certain that the French would fail and would be driven back to a firm policy by the Communists' unacceptable demands. He was not throwing in his hand but simply letting the French have their fling. If they achieved the honorable *modus vivendi* they were looking for, so much the better.[8] America would support them in

[8] David Lawrence wrote from Geneva in the *New York Herald Tribune* of April 30: "If somebody can draw a line inside Indochina that is militarily defensible and does not mean the entering wedge for an infiltration of the whole area by Communists, a cease-fire can be worked out at this conference. That is what General Eisenhower described as a *modus vivendi*." Lawrence was very skeptical as to whether such a settlement would work. Marguerite Higgins, also in Geneva, wrote an article in a similar vein in the *Tribune* of May 1: "The United States has indicated that it will join in making military

this if necessary, but it would not associate itself with any settlement.

The advocates of a "hard line" did not like Dulles's skeptical temporizing, and the Secretary of State came under fire from extreme right-wing leaders in the Senate and the House of Representatives as soon as he returned to Washington. Nonetheless, Dulles developed the President's thesis clearly and courageously in a speech televised on the evening of May 7:

> The French have stated their desire for an armistice on honorable terms and with proper safeguards. If they can conclude a settlement on terms which do not endanger the freedom of the people of Vietnam, that would be a real contribution to the cause of peace in Southeast Asia. But we would be gravely concerned if an armistice or cease-fire were reached at Geneva which would provide a road to a Communist take-over and further Communist aggression.
>
> If this occurs, or if hostilities continue, then the need will be more urgent to create the condition for a united action in defense of the area.[9]

On the previous day, the National Security Council had examined the circumstances in which the United States could accept a *modus vivendi* and concluded that the French must yield some ground. Part of Vietnam would inevitably have to be sacrificed, although the two deltas would have to be retained at all costs. A demarcation line would have to be drawn, and Vietminh elements on the French side of it would have to withdraw or disarm. The territorial integrity of Laos and Cambodia would have to be assured and guaranteed. These conditions differed somewhat from those put forward by the French command.

These American attitudes allowed the French diplomats to retrieve some of their freedom of action, but it was not precisely the kind of freedom they had hoped for. The statements of Eisenhower and Dulles in favor of peace cast doubt on the likelihood

---

guarantees for a new frontier in Indochina if some kind of partition plan allotting part of the country to the Communists but containing 'satisfactory safeguards' can be worked out, it is reliably learned."

[9] *The New York Times,* May 8, 1954.

of any American intervention in Indochina, at least for the time being. The threat that should have been Bidault's trump card was now scarcely credible, and the French Foreign Minister might well feel that America's recent withdrawal from the brink had done nothing to help him. But perhaps this situation could be exploited in other ways. The British and Russians could certainly use the occasion to demonstrate in practical terms that the forebodings of the American right wing were unjustified.

The British already felt that it was time to carry out their favorite idea: to associate the Asian powers with a settlement in Indochina. The Foreign Office was well aware that Nehru wanted to contribute to the re-establishment of peace in Indochina. Now it was a matter of persuading India to undertake initiatives openly. On April 29, Eden sent telegrams to the prime ministers of India, Pakistan, and Ceylon at the Colombo conference, asking for their help in formulating proposals for the re-establishment of peace in Asia. The Asians were quick to respond. On April 30, the ministers at the Colombo conference launched an appeal for a cease-fire in Indochina. Was this the lifeline that Reynaud had been looking for?

The problem naturally looked rather different from Moscow. American diplomacy had withdrawn—only temporarily, to be sure—and might well be unable to prevent the British and French from negotiating with the East for the first time since World War II. The Kremlin wanted to exploit this situation quickly. Washington was openly relying on the Communists to make unacceptable proposals and thereby compel the Western powers to reunite. The Russians would have been wrong to overlook this unique opportunity to score a few points. In any case, they certainly realized that inflexibility on their part would force a rapprochement between Paris and Washington, where the Nixon-Radford-Robertson-Knowland clan would regain the upper hand.

From this viewpoint, the American withdrawal clearly did give Bidault a few real trump cards, even if they were not the ones he had been expecting to play. However, the Foreign Minister had not yet come to the end of his setbacks.

In Paris, the National Assembly came back into session on May 4. Indochina was at the top of the agenda. Four questions had been asked; in one, a Deputy named Vallon accused Bidault of nothing less than abusing his authority. The government would naturally try to have the questions adjourned, but the climate in the Assembly was less favorable to it than before the recess. The publicity surrounding Operation Vulture and the danger of an internationalization of the conflict were causing the voters a great deal of worry.

In truth, Indochina was mainly a pretext. The formerly Gaullist Social Republicans (or at least the more extreme among them),[10] their allies among the Radicals and moderates, and the Communists—all were attacking Bidault's foreign policy, as well as his party, the MRP. Premier Laniel was also under attack for supporting his Foreign Minister in Asian as well as in European matters. The opposition had already subjected Bidault's attitude in Geneva to lively criticism; now, the whole range of his intentions was on trial. He was accused of lacking faith in the possibility of peace, or of being unwilling to achieve it, of wishing to prove that negotiation was impossible, in order to secure American intervention that would change the course of the war, and so on.

On the eve of the new session of parliament, Daniel Mayer, Chairman of the Foreign Affairs Committee of the Chamber of Deputies, had gone to Geneva and, on May 3, conferred with Bidault, who apparently did not regard the visit as a sign of distrust. On his return, Mayer emphasized that Bidault was determined to reach a settlement but that his good intentions were thwarted by a shortage of trump cards.

At the parliamentary session on May 4, speakers on the right and left demanded an immediate cease-fire. The Socialists even asked the government to reveal its instructions to Bidault. Vallon accused the Foreign Minister of systematically refusing all opportunities for contacts with the enemy, of conducting a disastrous personal policy, and of "pursuing war rather than peace."

[10] The party of the Social Republicans, formally known as the Union des Républicains et d'Action Sociale (URAS), was formed in early 1953, after de Gaulle had withdrawn the RPF from all parliamentary and electoral activity.

Laniel replied that his government proposed to negotiate, not surrender, that the virtually unilateral cease-fire demanded by the opposition would amount to capitulation pure and simple. An immediate debate on Indochina would delay the opening of the conference and weaken France's position. He therefore proposed that the discussion be adjourned to a later date.

The government had one major argument in its favor: if it fell, the Geneva conference would almost certainly have to be postponed. And under what circumstances could it be reconvened? It was not even certain that all the powers could be induced to attend again, given the attitude of America and Vietnam.

This fear worked wonders. On May 6, the Laniel government was sustained by a vote of 311 to 262.[11] But it could nurse no further illusions: the National Assembly may have thought it had no right to deprive the country of its government at the height of the war and the crux of the negotiations, but that government's fate now hung on the Indochina conference. Bidault had been flatly told to succeed, and he remained a minister only by grace of a suspended sentence.

Yet events in Geneva were about to feed the campaign against him and—what was even worse—end the very fragile and unnatural lull in Franco-Soviet relations. The discussions about the evacuation of wounded from Dien Bien Phu had perceptibly soured. Molotov had advocated direct contacts between France and the D.R.V., but he had not made it clear how these contacts could be established. The Vietminh delegation had arrived on May 4, but when the French tried to contact them through the Chinese on the following day, they got no response. This affected the general mood. Bidault and some other members of the French delegation did not improve matters when they publicly cast doubts on the elementary humanity of the Russians and Chinese.

Bidault became even more suspect in Paris as a result, and the chances of survival of the Laniel government were correspondingly

[11] Supporting the government: 53 Radicals (out of 76), 87 MRP, 37 URAS (out of 75), 94 Independents and Peasants, 40 other. Against the government: 18 Radicals, 28 URAS, 103 Socialists, 95 Communists, 18 other.

diminished. The reprieve it had secured in the Assembly was extremely tenuous. One more military or diplomatic disaster would turn the legislators avidly against the government. And just such an event was at hand.

At 10:00 P.M. on May 7, 1954, the struggle ended at Dien Bien Phu. Overwhelmed by the Vietminh assault, the fortified camp no longer answered radio messages.

The last days had been terrible. The coming of the monsoon had completely altered the conditions in which the battle was fought. Fine rain began to fall on April 29, drenching the ground, turning the foxholes into sloughs and the clay soil into sticky paste. On the evening of May 1, General Giap launched a powerful two-pronged attack against the central position and the southern stronghold "Isabelle." He made more progress. In spite of courageous counterattacks, the garrison was forced to abandon several supporting positions under the relentless fire of the enemy batteries. Its resources and its maneuvering room continued to shrink. By the next day, General de Castries, the commander of Dien Bien Phu, had lost virtually all of his artillery and had only mortars left.

Then, on May 2, the rain turned into a downpour and transformed the battlefield into a lake of mud. The men in the trenches and foxholes were now up to their knees in water. The Nam Yum stream, which flowed through the main stronghold from north to south, began to rise. What would happen when it overflowed its banks? Of course, the rain would also ruin the vast earthworks laboriously constructed by the Vietminh; their network of bunkers and trenches would be flooded, and this might cause a lull. The rain went on falling without a break.

For the defenders, the most serious effect of the bad weather was the lessening of air support. Rain and bad visibility virtually halted air operations. For several days, the transports and bombers were unable to penetrate the thick layer of clouds blanketing the highlands. When the weather improved and they managed to break through, they were forced to fly as low as 500 feet in order to parachute food, ammunition, and medical supplies in a narrow drop zone at the southern end of the airstrip, while avoiding both the lethal Vietminh antiaircraft fire and the surrounding hills that were shrouded in rain and mist. The air force had already taken heavy risks. Now it took still more, knowing how vital it was for the smothered garrison that the drops be accurate, and wanting to show the survivors that the outside world had not forgotten them and was doing everything possible to keep them alive.

The approaching start of the conference and the monsoon's effect on the battle probably impelled Giap to make an end of it. From May 5 on, his artillery, which appeared to have been further reinforced, subjected the garrison to almost uninterrupted fire. At about 10:00 P.M. May 6, after two hours of intense artillery preparation in which "Stalin organs" (ten-tube rocket launchers) were used for the first time, the Vietminh launched the final assault against the central position. After a night of desperate fighting, they captured position "Eliane," which overlooked the remainder of the camp. "Isabelle" was also relentlessly pounded and lost most of its guns. At dawn, the fortified camp was in desperate peril, and it would get no reprieve from the Vietminh.

On May 7, from 1 P.M. on, a flood of men came pouring down from the heights to reinforce the Vietminh assault troops. An inextricable melée spread over the cratered, lunar landscape where clay and mud mired everyone. Waves of attackers flooded the camp, submerging every position that still showed a flicker of resistance. Disregarding the antiaircraft fire, the French Air Force plunged through a break in the weather to carry out a violent bombardment. In spite of it, the Vietminh surged on to attack the center of resistance—the command post and "Claudine." At 4:00 P.M., General de Castries radioed Hanoi that the Vietminh were infiltrating in strength through the support points along the western side of "Claudine." Between 5:10 and 5:30 he communicated for the last time with General Cogny: "The end is coming. We will fight to the last. We shall destroy the cannon and all the communications equipment. Goodbye, General. Vive la France!"

In the evening, the garrison of "Isabelle" tried a last sortie;

it failed.[12] Radio messages continued to be heard until 1:00 A.M. Then there was silence.

Dien Bien Phu had fallen. For fifty-seven days, these men of every race—French, Vietnamese, German, Senegalese, North African—had been subjected to a fearful bombardment, to nerve-racking strain, to cold nights and scorching days and torrential rain. They had held out against an eager and powerfully equipped enemy who was prepared to pay any price to overcome them. And now they had become a crowd of more than ten thousand survivors, forming up for a death march to the prison camps.

This cruel setback had been foreseen since the day the Vietminh vise had closed on the garrison in early January. Yet it was not a strategic disaster, and Dien Bien Phu was not the whole of Indochina. It was not even the whole of Tonkin. It was only a fortress in the heart of the Thai country, where the French had lost 5 per cent of their fighting strength (though, to be sure, Dien Bien Phu had held the best of the Expeditionary Corps).[13]

But it was not possible to consider Dien Bien Phu solely in military and strategic terms. The question now was how France would react, how the fall of the fort would affect the complex of forces militating for and against the war. Would it cause morale to sag or to stiffen? The repercussions of the event could not yet be assessed, but they were certainly going to be heavy in France, in Vietnam, and in the world at large. Clearly, they were unlikely to inspire moderation in the enemy ranks.

A stiffening of Communist attitudes was immediately noticeable

[12] Some elements managed to escape through the jungle in the direction of Laos. They were picked up a few days later in a state of exhaustion by Colonel de Crèvecoeur's column.

[13] Total French losses amounted to about 16,000 men (including 1,500 killed, 3,000–4,000 wounded, and 10,000 prisoners or missing); in other words, six battalions of infantry, seven of parachutists, two artillery groups, one armored squadron, and other units. The losses of the Vietnamese People's Army have been estimated at from 25,000 to 28,000 men, including 8,000 to 10,000 killed. Bernard B. Fall, *Hell in a Very Small Place* (New York, 1967). For the development of the battle, see also Vo Nguyen Giap, *Dien Bien Phu* (Hanoi, 1959); Jules Roy, *La bataille de Dien Bien Phu* (Paris, 1963); Bernard B. Fall, *Street Without Joy* (Harrisburg, 1963); *Contribution à l'histoire de Dien Bien Phu* (Hanoi, 1965); and Pierre Rocolle, *Pourquoi Dien Bien Phu?* (Paris, 1968).

in Geneva.[14] The difficult search for a solution was obviously not going to become any easier. However, as the London *Economist* sagely remarked, there was certainly a middle way between defeat and victory, and it was the task of the conference to find it.

Would Bidault—half-dropped by Washington, under suspended sentence in Paris, and without support in Hanoi—really be reduced, as he put it in those somber days, to playing his hand with the two of spades and the three of diamonds? Had France really lost all its cards, as the best-informed commentators were saying?[15]

Faced with opponents who visibly dreaded complications, Bidault did indeed have a few cards left—the very ones he had always planned to use, even though he had played them rather badly until then. If a solution could not be negotiated in Geneva, the war would most probably be internationalized, because France *must* not carry on alone. That was the key fact. If it could not obtain the peace it needed, France would confront the United States with its responsibilities, as Britain had done in Greece in 1947. Would the Americans then be able to evade the problem without losing their international raison d'être? This was indeed something for Moscow and Peking to think about.

[14] Would the D.R.V., now giddy with success, agree to stop hostilities or even to withdraw from certain areas, in order to facilitate a compromise? The Vietminh's militants and moderates were doubtless still at odds, as they had been in 1946. Which faction was likely to prevail now? It seemed that, for the moment at least, the moderates were closer to the general Communist line than the militants.

[15] See the article by André Fontaine in *Le Monde* (Paris), May 5, 1954.

10

BIDAULT AND DONG LAY DOWN THEIR CARDS

Just after 4:00 P.M. on Saturday, May 8, 1954, the delegates of the nine powers took their seats at the horseshoe-shaped table. The conference on Indochina had begun.

The mood was heavy: twenty-four hours earlier, news of the fall of Dien Bien Phu had spread gloom in Geneva. But, cruel as this setback was for France and its friends, it did not affect the French position quite so adversely as the delegates and journalists asserted. In a sense, it simplified the task of the French delegates by restoring some freedom of action to them. If the agony of the stronghold had continued into the early days of the conference and if there had seemed to be the slightest chance of saving the garrison, the French Government could hardly have refused the offer of a cease-fire despite is earlier decision, even if the proffered guarantees were ludicrous. French diplomacy had lost some trump cards, but it had also shed this intolerable burden.

Eden, who was presiding, called on Bidault to open the debate. It was a daunting responsibility, but it had the advantage of permitting Bidault to take the initiative.[1] In a voice charged with emotion, the French minister first paid tribute to the defenders of Dien Bien Phu and, somewhat naïvely, deplored the predictable fact that the announcement of the conference had intensified the fighting. But then Bidault ventured onto dangerous ground, recalling the civilizing role of France in Indochina and retracing the progress of the war in an attempt to justify it. His picture of the origins of the war—"this conflict that was imposed on us"—bore only an incidental resemblance to historical truth and his vigorous insistence that *the war, for France, was a matter of defense and not a crusade* was convincing only to the converted.

Bidault's audience awoke when, after repeating that the French Government wished *to reach a reasonable settlement that would make it possible to end hostilities,* he outlined what seemed to him the "most appropriate" method by which to achieve an accord. The whole room listened attentively when he began to formulate French proposals for the establishment of a "just and lasting peace" in Indochina: "We propose that the conference start by adopting the principle of a general cessation of hostilities in Indochina supported by essential guarantees of security. . . . These guarantees are intended to preserve the security of the troops of both sides and to protect the civil population against any abusive exploitation of the truce."

France had scored a psychological advantage. It was the first to offer a cease-fire, and its gesture caused an immediate stir among the Vietminh delegates across the table. Bidault went on. Circumstances differed in the three Associated States, he said, and it would be sensible to take these differences into account:

> In Laos and Cambodia, the problem is clear: no civil war, but an unjustified invasion without a declaration of war. . . . Therefore, the solution is to arrange for the withdrawal of the invaders and to re-establish the integrity of the territory. The implementation of the agreement would be carried out under international supervision.
>
> In Vietnam, the situation is very different and far more complex.

[1] The full text of the speech may be found in *Le Monde* (Paris), May 11, 1954.

> It is, in fact, a civil war that we face there. As far as France is concerned, a Vietnamese State exists, and its unity, territorial integrity, and independence must be respected. [Therefore, provision must be made for] a transitional phase, during which a solution for the political problems can be worked out gradually after hostilities have stopped. . . . The immediate problem is to secure a cessation of hostilities and to provide guarantees for it. We feel these guarantees should work in two stages: first the regular units of both sides should be concentrated in clearly defined regrouping zones, while the other [irregular] forces are disarmed. Then the implementation of the agreement should be put under the supervision of international commissions. . . . The agreement . . . should be guaranteed in appropriate terms by the states taking part in the conference.

Bidault went on to propose that the member nations of the Geneva conference guarantee the agreement in all three Associated States and concluded by saying that any violations should be regarded as cause for immediate consultations among these nations, with a view to taking appropriate measures either collectively or individually.

The French plan was, then, essentially military, and Bidault emphasized that the formulation of conditions for a political solution was a matter for the Vietnamese Government. France, at any rate, did not intend to discuss political problems with the Vietminh: "If the party that has organized armed forces to battle the state of Vietnam has been admitted to this conference in order to reach agreement on the cessation of hostilities, this should not be interpreted as implying any form of recognition on our part."

It was now the enemy's turn, but the enemy was not yet ready to lay down his cards. Pham Van Dong rose only to demand in violent tones that the "democratic Khmer Issarak and Pathet Lao governments" be admitted to the conference. According to Dong, these "governments" had "liberated" vast tracts of the national territories of Cambodia and Laos; they had created a "democratic authority" and raised the standard of living of the masses, who supported them and viewed them as the embodiment of national aspirations. The future of Cambodia and Laos could not be decided in their absence. Molotov and Chou En-lai immediately concurred.

Bedell Smith demanded the immediate rejection of Dong's proposal on the grounds that the question of participation in the conference had been settled some days earlier in accordance with the Berlin communiqué and there could be no question of going back on this agreement.

A confused debate followed. "Should we be discussing the admission of governments that are nothing more than phantoms?" asked Bidault. "Monsieur Bidault has already described the D.R.V. Government in the same terms in the past," replied Pham Van Dong harshly. In a short and neat intervention, Sam Sary, the Cambodian representative, assured the conference that "the Democratic Government of Cambodia exists only in the imagination of the ministers of the Eastern bloc," and asked Molotov whether he would accept the presence of the Polish government in London at a conference.

Bedell Smith and Eden suggested a closed meeting of the four Berlin powers to resolve this procedural point. This only made things worse: as might have been expected, Molotov retorted that if the point were to be discussed in restricted session, then five, not four, powers should attend. China was one of the powers mentioned in the Berlin communiqué, it had invited the Vietminh to attend the conference, and its presence was therefore essential. (Molotov's statement revealed that the invitation to the Vietminh, which Russia alone had been asked to transmit on May 2, had been sent under joint Chinese and Soviet signature. Bedell Smith protested.)

Thus, at their very first meeting, the nine were confronted with proposals that were difficult if not impossible to reconcile. Eden thought it best to adjourn the session until the afternoon of Monday, May 10.

Meanwhile, the West's united front had already begun to crack. As soon as the first meeting was over, the Vietnamese delegation voiced marked reservations about the proceedings. They claimed they had been consulted about the French proposals only two hours before the meeting. They denounced them as a step back from Laniel's speech of March 5, and a particularly dangerous one, since they would inevitably lead to partition—a possibility the nationalists refused to consider, as did the Communists at that time.

Monday, May 10, was the Vietminh's day. For two days, the conference had been expecting the Vietminh representatives to make a humanitarian, or at any rate a political, gesture in favor of the wounded at Dien Bien Phu. As soon as the meeting opened (with Molotov as chairman), Bao Dai's Minister of Foreign Affairs, Nguyen Quoc Dinh, asked that the question of evacuating the wounded be given priority "for humanitarian reasons." Pham Van Dong gave the expected reply: "The Government of the D.R.V. is ready to permit the evacuation of all the seriously wounded at Dien Bien Phu. Representatives of the two commands will take practical measures on the spot to effect their repatriation."[2] A direct contact between the French and the Vietminh would thus be established in Vietnam, rather than under the eyes of the conference.

Bidault immediately accepted the proposal, though not without pointing out that he had made the same suggestion as soon as he had reached Geneva. Then Dong began his speech—a two-hour monologue beginning with a lengthy history of Vietnam's problems, dating from the beginning of the colonial period. In truth, his picture of the immediate origins of the war was nearer to historical reality than Bidault's. It was easy for the speaker to remind his audience that the Vietminh had tried to negotiate even after the struggle started but that France had set conditions that amounted to the Vietminh's complete surrender. Why? Because, Dong claimed, France and the United States wished to liquidate the D.R.V. and replace it with a puppet government. Dong disposed of the Vietnamese Government in a sentence: "It represents only itself, and those who have created it and will liquidate it."

Dong next rejected the Bidault plan, saying it stemmed from an "outdated colonialist outlook" that totally neglected the political aspect of the problem and dealt only with its military side, albeit without taking account of the real military situation. After a violent denunciation of "American intervention" in Indochina,

[2] These assurances were unfortunately not followed by all the results that might have been expected.

Dong put forward the D.R.V.'s proposals under eight headings.

1. Recognition of the sovereignty, independence, and territorial integrity of Vietnam, Laos, and Cambodia.

2. Conclusion of an agreement concerning the withdrawal of all foreign troops from the territory of the three countries, in accordance with schedules arranged by the belligerent parties. Before troops were withdrawn, the stationing of French forces in certain limited sectors of Vietnam would be arranged. These troops were not to interfere in the local administration of the areas in which they were stationed.

3. Organization of free general elections in all three countries, with a view to setting up a single government in each. These elections would be prepared by "consultative commissions" comprising representatives of "all the democratic organizations." No foreign intervention would be permitted. Pending the setting up of single governments in each country, and after agreement had been reached concerning the ending of hostilities, each side would administer the areas under its control.

4. A declaration by the D.R.V. of its intention to study the problem of its free association with the French Union, as well as the conditions governing such an association. Similar declarations would be made by the Cambodian and Laotian governments.

5. Recognition by the D.R.V., Cambodia, and Laos of the economic and cultural interests of France in the three states. Once single governments were established, these economic and cultural relations would be formalized on the basis of the principles of equality and mutual interest. The nationals of each side would enjoy a reciprocal privileged status, which remained to be formulated.

6. Immunity from repression to all persons who collaborated with the opposite side during the war.

7. Exchange of war prisoners.

8. Implementation of these seven provisions would be preceded by a cessation of hostilities and the conclusion of corresponding agreements between France and each of the three countries in Indochina. This would be done on the basis of a general and simultaneous cease-fire, followed by readjustment of the areas and

territories occupied by both sides; a ban on the introduction into Indochina of fresh troops, arms, and munitions; and the establishment of a control system, consisting of commissions comprising representatives of the contending sides in each of the three countries.[3]

The cards were now on the table. Eden and Bedell Smith felt they should reply to Dong immediately. It was useless, they said, to argue about the origins of the war and the distortions of recent history, as the Vietminh leader had done. What mattered was to reach an agreement. From this point of view, it seemed to them that Bidault's proposals represented a constructive effort, because they were inspired by a concern for the preservation of the freedom and independence of the people of Indochina. A simple cease-fire was clearly impracticable and could not lead to a peaceful solution. Therefore, the conference should work toward agreement on an armistice that would specify the conditions of control and implementation. Eden and Bedell Smith hoped that the conference would study Bidault's proposals immediately and adopt them as a basis for discussion.

Attention now focused on the French delegation's reactions to Pham Van Dong. Jacques Baeyens, Bidault's spokesman, in an impromptu press conference held after the session, said: "The Vietminh proposals are very clever—even attractive. They are also very specious. . . . The Vietminh is less interested in ending the war than in swallowing Indochina *in toto*. It is clear that, if the Dong plan were accepted, the three states would eventually have Communist governments, with results that anyone can forsee." He pointed out that the Vietminh plan denounced America's intervention but did not breathe a word about China's. True, it offered to respect French economic and cultural interests, but what value could be attached to such an offer? As for the suggestion that a united Vietnam could associate itself with the French Union, it could only be compared to the idea of the U.S.S.R.'s offering to join NATO.

[3] The full text of the Vietminh proposal, as well as excerpts from the speeches of Pham Van Dong, Bedell Smith, and Eden, appeared in *The New York Times*, May 11, 1954.

Unanimously, if hastily, the journalists present concluded from Baeyens's statement that the French delegation had rejected the Vietminh proposals.[4] The news was cabled to Paris, where the papers brought out special editions. Late that night, it was learned in Geneva that Baeyens's remarks had caused a sensation in the government and the National Assembly.[5] Obviously, Paris had not been consulted before the French delegation took its position, which appeared to be chiefly that of Bidault himself. The statement seemed to confirm American forebodings; it also seriously increased the government's difficulties on the even of a hazardous vote, and it intensified public misgivings about the Quai d'Orsay's policy.[6]

The conference members were all the more surprised at the French delegation's reaction because Eden, in closing the day's session, had described the Vietminh proposals as "constructive." Bidault's team hastened to qualify its attitude. That same evening, they let it be known that the Baeyens statement was far from being a simple rejection of the Vietminh proposals. By the next morning—May 11—word had spread that the French representatives had not "rejected" the Vietminh plan at all—on the contrary, they were studying it closely. They did not deny its competence, but they complained that it was a blatant attempt to secure an immediate advantage for Ho Chi Minh; they also expressed doubts about trying to bring three people's democracies into the French Union. The French delegation stressed once again that it would be wrong to make a cease-fire depend upon a political settlement, as the Vietminh seemed inclined to do.

[4] No one could find out whether the general line of what Baeyens said had been worked out on the previous evening or whether it was unrehearsed. Some correspondents claimed that it had been decided in advance to give the Dong proposals a generally negative reception, whatever their nature. Be that as it may, the French delegation was very nervous and gave the impression of having been caught unprepared.

[5] Reynaud was particularly forceful in demanding that the government's displeasure be made clear and that the delegation in Geneva be made to reverse its negative attitude.

[6] *The New York Times* said in an editorial on May 11 that the Vietminh proposals were completely unacceptable, but *La Suisse*, in Geneva, wrote that "it would be very difficult to reject them wholesale."

The Vietminh plan had aroused real interest among the various delegations, for its relative moderation generally belied the gloomy forecasts of certain observers. The Communists had not disqualified themselves by their extremism, as the Americans had hoped. In fact, the American delegation regarded the Dong plan as too subtle and complex to be rejected out of hand, even though its ultimate effect was to demand a French surrender.[7]

Starting on the evening of the 10th, the British delegation did some positive thinking. Eden and his assistants figured that the Dong plan would be backed by the Communists, just as the French plan had been supported by the Westerners. Therefore, they figured that it would also serve as a basis for discussion. Thus it was not a question of rejecting it, but rather of examining the two texts together and discovering the points of agreement, the possibilities of *rapprochement*, the elements of compromise. The British experts took up the challenge immediately.

A compromise began to take shape in the course of various conversations during the day. The Thai foreign minister, Prince Wan, while expressing some reservations about the Bidault plan, suggested to an interviewer that the questions of Laos and Cambodia should be dealt with separately, as they were much less complex than the Vietnamese problem. The Prince thought the French should stay in Indochina until a date that could be decided upon as part of the general settlement; the D.R.V. delegation, in any case, denied that it had asked for their immediate withdrawal. And Hoang Van Hoan, the D.R.V.'s spokesman, told a French reporter: "Point Two of the plan we have presented provides for the withdrawal of French troops within time limits to be mutually agreed upon. Clearly, we were not considering an immediate withdrawal, since the same paragraph provides that French troops will not interfere in local administrative affairs in the areas in which they are stationed."[8]

[7] When a Washington journalist asked Dulles on May 11 whether the Vietminh proposals were unacceptable, he replied that he would not wish to be as categorical as that, because the proposals did not seem wholly unacceptable to him.

[8] *Paris-Normandie* (Paris), May 12, 1954.

Elements of a possible basis for compromise were beginning to appear: separate consideration of the questions of Laos and Cambodia, as requested by the French; an armistice covered by an international guarantee; the continuing presence of French troops until a stable regime was established; adequate protection of French economic and cultural interests; and general elections under international control.

The meeting on May 12 was marked by the "hawkish" statement of Bao Dai's minister of foreign affairs, Nguyen Quoc Dinh, and by Eden's very constructive intervention in the debate.

Bidault had confined himself to military problems; now, Dinh set out the nationalist Vietnamese conditions for a *political* solution. He began by castigating the errors committed by the Vietminh in the struggle for independence and highlighting the achievements of successive Bao Dai governments: national unity (the return of Cochin China), the formation of a national army, the creation of an administrative service, and diplomatic recognition by thirty-five foreign states. "History will tell whether it was necessary to introduce Communism, which is the most advanced form of imperialism, in order to put an end to colonial domination; and whether, in order no longer to be a French colony, it was necessary to become a satellite of China."

To show that the Vietminh's struggle for independence was now pointless, Dinh revealed the two Franco-Vietnamese treaties, which the two countries had agreed to but had not yet signed. (The first was an independence treaty containing four articles whereby France recognized Vietnam as a fully independent state; the second was a treaty of association between Vietnam and France.)

After expressing the categorical opposition of his government to any partition, "direct or indirect, final or provisional, *de facto* or *de jure*," and once again stressing the need for international supervision of any cease-fire, Dinh put forward a seven-point proposal for a political settlement:

1. The only state qualified to represent Vietnam is the state represented by His Majesty Bao Dai.
2. This state has only one army, the National Army, into which

the soldiers of the Vietminh may be integrated in accordance with conditions to be defined, and under international control.

3. Free elections, under United Nations auspices, will be carried out "within the framework of the state of Vietnam and under its jurisdiction" when the Security Council agrees that the authority of the state is acknowledged throughout its territory and the requisite degree of security prevails.

4. A representative government will be formed, after these elections and in accordance with their results, under the authority of His Majesty Bao Dai.

5. The state of Vietnam will guarantee that no reprisals will be taken against those individuals who collaborated with the Vietminh.

6. Vietnam will receive international guarantees of its political and territorial integrity.

7. Vietnam will receive U.N. assistance to develop national resources and raise its population's standard of living.

These proposals lacked any trace of realism. In effect they demanded the unconditional surrender of the enemy on the day after his greatest military success. They met with a polite but icy reception. Only the American delegation, in the person of Bedell Smith, felt obliged to give it open support.

The time had now come for China to reveal its point of view. Chou En-lai naturally supported Dong's proposals, describing Bidault's as having a "colonialist outlook" that ignored the true strength of the D.R.V. Successive French governments had committed grave faults in Indochina in the course of the years, and now they had a bill to pay. China could not remain indifferent to events along its frontiers, to the danger that the war might spread, and to the unceasing efforts of the United States to raise tension and create aggressive blocs in Southeast Asia. It was high time that France and the United States, which had given the Declaration of the Rights of Man and the Declaration of Independence to the world, granted the independence which the nations of Indochina were claiming.

It took Eden five minutes to put things back on the track. With a weary smile, he deplored the time wasted by these successive enumerations of historical facts with which no one else agreed. He suggested that it might be useful to extract from all the lengthy speeches the few practical points on which quick agreement seemed possible: everyone recognized the need to secure an orderly cease-fire and he also assumed that everything necessary would be done on behalf of the wounded of Dien Bien Phu.[9] Eden therefore felt justified in asking both sides the following questions:

1. Was there agreement that the opposing forces should be regrouped in certain defined areas? It had seemed to him that there was no great divergence between the views of France and the D.R.V. on this point, while the Vietnamese delegation had rejected this solution as being likely to lead to partition.

2. Should not the question of Laos and Cambodia be dealt with separately? Points of view differed on this question, but it seemed practical to approach it independently. The Laotian and Cambodian governments maintained that the "revolutionary governments" exercised no authority on their territory. Moreover, they rightfully considered the Vietminh forces as invaders, who might have the support of isolated individuals but not that of the population as a whole. These governments considered the situation in their countries very different from that prevailing in Vietnam.

3. Who was to define the regrouping zones in Vietnam? Would it not be appropriate to entrust this task to the commanders in chief in the field, while requiring them to report to the conference?

4. Once the regular forces had been regrouped, was the conference agreed that irregular troops should be disarmed? This proposal had not met with any objections.

5. Were all agreed on the principle of international control? If so,

6. What form should it take? The British delegation favored U.N. control, Eden added. And the five Colombo conference powers also believed that the United Nations should supervise the implementation of decisions taken in Geneva. Eden made it clear that, when he referred to U.N. members, he did not necessarily

[9] Saigon announced on May 11 that General Navarre had received instructions from Paris to enter into contact with General Giap in order to arrange for the evacuation of the wounded at Dien Bien Phu. Measures were taken for the transfer of 1,300 men.

mean the combatants or the powers sitting at the conference table. The U.N. supervisors might be a different group of countries altogether. The U.N. membership was large enough so that those present at Geneva could find some countries acceptable to all for service in control commissions.

The nine powers then adjourned for two days to give themselves time for reflection. What were, in fact, the chances of reaching a compromise, after these three days of negotiations? Despite the evident differences, the British delegation believed that agreement was possible. The Vietminh had not been as unyielding as expected, and, although Chou En-lai had supported Dong's proposals, he had stressed that they "could" serve as a basis for negotiations. The use of "could" rather than "must" seemed significant to the more hopeful observers. And it was also clear that Bidault was now definitely "condemned to negotiate," for Laniel's government had obtained a further reprieve in the National Assembly on May 13 only by pointing to Eden's efforts to reconcile the different positions.[10]

The representatives of the Big Three agreed that Eden should make contact with the chief Communist delegates during the course of May 13. It was time to discover whether the Russians and Chinese were willing to discuss military questions—particularly a cease-fire—as a matter of priority. At this stage, it seemed, the best way of starting real negotiations, of discarding polemics and monologues, was the tried and true method of secret negotiations. This was what Eden was going to suggest.

The next morning, Eden, affable as ever, met with Chou En-lai and then Molotov. While he was thus engaged, the British Government let it be known through every unofficial channel at its disposal that, if China and the U.S.S.R. did not prove conciliatory, Britain would go ahead with the United States and France and sign the Southeast Asian mutual-security pact, with all the con-

[10] Laniel had been forced to ask for a vote of confidence once again. He won by a hair's breadth, with a 2-vote majority (289–287). This time, 42 instead of 28 members of the URAS voted against him. He could now count only on the MRP, the Independents, and the Peasants; the Radicals were more and more split.

sequences that would involve. The "exploratory" talks, thereby, also became something of a test.

The session of Friday, May 14, did indeed see the quiet beginnings of a transition from harangue to practical negotiation. Bidault was the only listed speaker. He had prepared a speech that included three concessions to the Vietminh point of view, but Molotov, who was presiding, "forgot" Bidault and gave himself the floor instead. For twenty-five minutes, he denounced France's "colonial war," railed against American intervention, and cast doubts on the genuineness of the independence granted by France to the three Associated States. He then came to the French plan, whose chief defect, he argued, was its failure to deal with political problems. Ending the war could not be separated from the solving "of at least some of these problems." Molotov could not accept the French proposal that an agreement at Geneva must be guaranteed by all the powers taking part in the conference, while any breach of the agreement would lead to consultation and a resort to individual or collective measures. In keeping with traditional Soviet tactics, Molotov was prepared to consider only collective measures.

While expressing his "solidarity with the plan submitted by the D.R.V.," Molotov nevertheless recognized that it made no provision for the supervision of an armistice by international organizations. Therefore, he proposed that, "to help the parties to apply the clauses of the agreement covering the cessation of hostilities, the organization of a control commission composed of neutral powers should be provided for in the agreement." There should be no differences of opinion, he added, about the composition of these commissions. In conclusion, he said, his delegation was certain that "the conference would also examine any other proposals calculated to facilitate the re-establishment of peace in Indochina." The Vietminh plan was therefore not the only admissible one as far as they were concerned.

"Neutral commissions"? "Taking other proposals into consideration"? The East had clearly taken a step forward. It had long been obvious that the West would not accept the mixed control commissions advocated by the Vietminh and would only agree to international control. Now it looked as though Molotov were entering the game. It seemed that Russia was coming to share the Anglo-Saxon conviction that France and the Vietminh should no longer be left to work things out alone. The negotiators hoped that France would reply to this Soviet gesture in a conciliatory and constructive way, and Bidault did not disappoint them.

To be sure, he began his speech in his usual cutting manner, with an attack on Molotov's "diatribe." But he went on to say that the French delegation had made a careful study of Dong's proposals. Calmly, he re-emphasized the difference between the situation in Vietnam and that in the other two states, where it was a simple matter of the presence of foreign troops. In Vietnam, the movements of the Expeditionary Corps depended on the course of the fighting and would continue to do so until peace was re-established. Once this had been done, however, the French Government would not consider keeping its troops in the country against the will of the legal government. Bidault made it clear that, subject to agreement with the governments concerned, the French Government was prepared to consider the withdrawal of its troops from Laos and Cambodia if the invaders also withdrew.[11] Since a cease-fire would be easier to arrange in Laos and Cambodia than in Vietnam, it would be logical to start with those countries. And, he emphasized, the military problem should receive the highest priority: "The French delegation does not think that agreement on a political settlement should precede, and thereby delay, the implementation of a military settlement. It does not deny that the two are linked but considers that the former should be a result rather than a preliminary condition of the latter."[12]

In response to the Eden questionnaire, Bidault made it clear that:

1. The problem of Laos and Cambodia should be treated sepa-

[11] This proposal conformed with the position adopted by General Navarre in his note of April 21. See above, chap. 9, pp. 138–40.

[12] As to Dong's proposals about Vietnam, Bidault repeated that they failed to take account of the facts: the government of the state of Vietnam was the only legal government.

rately, and Vietminh forces must be withdrawn from both countries.

2. In Vietnam, the troops on both sides must be regrouped in designated zones. The definition of these zones was a matter for the conference after it had consulted the commanders in chief.

3. France had proposed international controls. It was prepared to consider any suggestions concerning the composition of the control commissions. If international control was accepted in principle, then perhaps mixed groups representing the combatants could operate under the authority of international commissions and carry out actions required by them.

Bidault thus indicated that he would not insist on international control being carried out by the United Nations, and that he might accept the idea of an armistice guaranteed either individually or collectively by the powers taking part in the conference.

Both sides had thus dropped a little ballast, but these early concessions required some adjustments by each. Would the D.R.V. agree to the combination of mixed commissions and international control? Molotov had accepted the principle of international control by neutrals but had implicitly rejected the international supervision of elections, a point which France considered important. He had referred to a collective guarantee of the armistice by the powers taking part in the conference, whereas Bidault had indicated his preference for individual guarantees, although he had not excluded outright the possibility of a collective one.

Molotov closed the meeting with an important announcement: the next meeting, which would take place on Monday, May 17, would be in closed session; each minister would be accompanied by only three advisers. Real negotiations could therefore begin.

The British initiative had achieved its object. At any rate, it had shown that the Soviet delegation was open to certain arguments and might already be prepared to facilitate a settlement in Indochina.

In order to counteract Franco-American scheming[13] and prevent it from jeopardizing the compromise they had already roughed out,

[13] This subject is dealt with in Chapter 12.

the British now launched the three-pronged diplomatic action they had had in the offing for some time. First, they very gingerly advanced the idea of partition, knowing the Russians were basically in favor of it but the Americans needed to be converted. Simultaneously, there was a perceptible *rapprochement* between Eden and Molotov; both were eager to reach a compromise quickly, because both were uneasy about their allies.[14] Perhaps, too, they saw more clearly than the rest the dangers inherent in any extension of the conflict in Southeast Asia. Finally, the British Government played all its trump cards and brought the Southeast Asian neutrals, above all, India, into the game.

On Saturday, May 15, Bidault and Bedell Smith met with Eden at his residence. Tactics were reviewed in the light of the previous day's events. Molotov had made considerable concessions on May 14, but this did not necessarily mean that the Communists had abandoned their designs on the whole of Indochina. Could they now be persuaded to settle for control of only a part of it? If they were willing to do so, negotiations might start in earnest.

Two issues would make it possible to sound out the intentions of the opposite bloc: the priority to be attached to a cease-fire and the separation of the Vietnamese problem from that of Laos and Cambodia. If the Communists were still unwilling to accept a quick cease-fire and the *de facto* partition of Vietnam, then Geneva was merely a psychological-warfare operation as far as they were concerned and they were determined to fight on and attack the Red River delta in strength while the military situation was favorable to them. Similarly, if they refused to separate the Laos-Cambodia issue from that of Vietnam, and pressed for the admission of the Khmer Issarak and the Pathet Lao to the conference, this would indicate that they intended to push on beyond their current positions and impose Communist governments on both countries. If this proved to be the case, it would lead to certain inescapable conclusions.

By now, the French and the Americans privately agreed with

[14] It was during this period that a member of the British delegation remarked to a Soviet diplomat, "We both have difficult allies."

the British. The Americans also wished to achieve a miltary settlement first, even if it meant avoiding any political settlement later on—in other words, they had accepted the idea of temporary partition in their hearts,[15] but the three powers had not yet reached agreement on a demarcation line.

Meanwhile, the British diplomatic maneuvers reached their next stage, and India appeared on the scene. Nehru had yielded to pressing requests from London. On May 15, he announced that India wished to contribute to the re-establishment of peace in Indochina and was prepared to play its part in finding a solution. New Delhi made it clear—and the Indian ambassador in Washington, Gaganrihari Mehta, confirmed this to the American Government on May 16—that, if all the parties concerned (France, nationalist Vietnam, the D.R.V., and China) requested the Indian Government to dispatch a mission to supervise a cease-fire or truce, and if the Big Four accepted such intervention, India would not withhold its cooperation. Moreover, Nehru's personal negotiator, Krishna Menon, was preparing to leave for Geneva.[16]

At an improvised press conference on the evening of Saturday, May 15, a spokesman for the Soviet delegation disclosed part of an exchange of correspondence between Molotov and Bidault concerning the evacuation of the wounded. The French delegation counterattacked, publishing the full text of the letters and stressing that the Vietminh, despite its promises, was not evacuating the Vietnamese wounded at Dien Bien Phu. Moreover, the Vietminh had also demanded that Route 41 be neutralized as a condition for this evacuation, to which the French had agreed, but now the Vietminh was using the road for large-scale troop move-

[15] We have already noted Bedell Smith's remark to a member of the French delegation, during the early days of the conference, that some form of partition was more or less inevitable.

[16] There was talk on Sunday, May 16, of a British "Asian Locarno" plan, to be supported by political guarantees and mutual undertakings signed not only by the Big Five but also by the member countries of ANZUS, by the countries of the Indochinese peninsula, and even, the British hoped, by India, Pakistan, and Indonesia. Apparently, the British believed that such a pact would allay the fears aroused in Asia by the Dulles plan for a Southeast Asian treaty.

ments in the direction of the Red River delta, while failing to evacuate the wounded. Bidault had asked Molotov to bring these facts to the attention of Pham Van Dong so that the latter could intercede with General Giap as a matter of urgency. The Russian minister replied by once again advising Bidault to approach the head of the D.R.V. delegation directly.

Yet on May 15, eleven days after the arrival of Ho Chi Minh's representatives in Geneva, Bidault had not yet exchanged a single word with Dong, although he had known him eight years earlier when Dong had led the D.R.V. delegation at the Fontainebleau conference. The French minister gave everyone the impression that he not merely was failing to seek direct negotiations but was actively avoiding all contact.[17]

In order to make it plain that France would not give in to "blackmail about the wounded," the French staff at Hanoi announced on the afternoon of May 17 that the evacuation of the wounded from Dien Bien Phu was suspended and that bombing of Route 41 between Dien Bien Phu and Son La would be resumed from midnight on May 18.

As a result, the first closed session of the nine began in an atmosphere of renewed tension on the afternoon of May 17. Once again, the question of the wounded took priority. At the start Bidault eloquently recalled that under the terms of the agreement reached on May 10, there was to be no discrimination by race or nationality during the evacuation. Dong replied that the agreement of May 10 did indeed cover *all* the troops under General de Castries's command. Bidault took note of these assurances.

Next it was Molotov's turn, and he went to the heart of the problem. In a very relaxed manner, he suggested that instead of studying the French and Vietminh plans separately, which would raise a delicate question about which of them should be considered

[17] Five years later, in July, 1959, Bidault told the author that such contacts are completely pointless—particularly "working" lunches and dinners: "One just wastes one's time at them," he asserted; "however, it was at such a dinner that I taught Molotov that there are seals in Lake Baikal." He added, in a more serious vein: "Why would I have seen Pham Van Dong? I had nothing to learn from him. I knew he had only one idea—to throw us out!"

first, the conference should take them together as a basis for discussion. This may have been a minor concession, even a purely formal one, but it confirmed the existence of a certain flexibility in the Soviet delegation, which probably reflected a wish to take immediate advantage of America's quiescence.

Dong again refused to separate military issues from political problems; nonetheless, it was agreed that the French and Vietnamese plans would be discussed simultaneously and that military questions would be given priority, since they were the only ones raised in both sets of proposals.

And so, it seemed, the preliminaries were at an end. The links, however tenuous, had now been made. The shadowy and broken outlines of a settlement started to emerge through the unending monologues, the relentless pleadings, the propaganda speeches, and the Stalinist diatribes.

But what exactly did the Vietminh want? Dong had made it clear that his government would agree to a cease-fire only if the D.R.V.'s political conditions were accepted. Would General Giap try to force France's acquiescence by striking decisive blows in Laos or Tonkin?

11

MILITARY MOVES IN INDOCHINA

Painful and costly as it was, the fall of Dien Bien Phu was amplified out of all proportion by the French press and government, in political circles, and in the emotions of the French people. The government, which had turned the fort into a symbol, a sort of Verdun, now seemed to be doing everything it could to emphasize the pathos of its fall, as though trying to drown its own errors in a sea of grief.

The defeat struck harshly in military circles. Everyone feared that Dien Bien Phu was only the prelude to other, even more bloody, reverses and that it might even lead to the collapse of the entire French position in northern Indochina. What would happen if the Vietminh, in order to maintain or increase its pressure on the Geneva conference, launched a general assault against the entire perimeter of the Red River delta before the rainy season?

Three of the men who were then chiefly responsible for French policy in Indochina have since tried to prove that these fears were groundless and that there was no urgency about concluding an armistice. General Navarre writes that "as soon as the fortress fell, there was a considerable slackening of enemy pressure on all fronts.

This slackening demonstrated the Vietminh's state of exhaustion and its inability to exploit immediately on the strategic level the victory it had just won." Navarre does admit that the enemy was concentrating on the area of Phu Ly, in the Red River delta, and on certain posts in the southern zone, but he claims that the Hanoi-Haiphong communications complex had become relatively quiet again. He concludes:

> The situation was in hand in the Indochinese theater of operations as a whole. We had serious local difficulties, but there was no immediate danger. . . . An attack against the delta was theoretically possible after June 20, but there were no serious indications that it was impending. On the contrary, a fair amount of information was reaching us about both the state of attrition of Vietminh units and the intentions of the enemy command, all of which made us think that the enemy was incapable of endangering our position.[1]

General Cogny told an Agence France Presse correspondent on May 9 that he did not believe there was "an immediate danger in the delta." He added that, in view of the considerable losses they had sustained at Dien Bien Phu, the enemy forces would doubtless be unable to move 200 miles from the Thai country to the Red River delta before the rainy season, which was imminent. He was confident that the Vietminh forces would rest in their bases for some weeks, once they reached the delta. "As a result," concluded the commander of the French forces in Tonkin, "a major Vietminh operation in the delta cannot logically be anticipated until September."[2]

Lastly, Premier Laniel, who carried the main responsibility for the conduct of the war, was the most categorical of all:

> If our losses were heavy, those of the attacker were higher still. . . . His two best divisions were out of action. His cadres had been seriously reduced. . . . Our Expeditionary Corps's superiority in equipment was as crushing as it had been before the battle. The balance

[1] Henri Navarre, *Agonie de l'Indochine* (Paris, 1956), pp. 262–63.

[2] *L'Information* (Paris), May 11, 1954. Agence France Presse dispatch from Hanoi, May 10.

> of forces had not been disrupted in any sense. . . . We had been given a certain respite; whatever happened, the enemy was unable to take the offensive again before autumn.[3]

The actual situation seems to have been rather different. Although some scattered sectors of the front did indeed experience a lull of sorts after the fall of Dien Bien Phu, a comprehensive analysis of all information that has since become available (and has been thoroughly cross-checked) shows that, contrary to these assertions, the enemy did not relax his efforts. He put increasing pressure on a string of small French and Laotian posts in northern Laos, between Dien Bien Phu and Luang Prabang. He was active in southern Laos, around Pakse, and clashed sharply with the French in several engagements near Phan Rang in southern Annam. But the Red River delta, where tens of thousands of peasants were at that moment harvesting their rice, remained his basic objective. The Vietminh sought to pin down as many French troops as possible by daily harassment, so that it could then seize food stocks in a very large number of villages.

In the north, on the Hanoi-Haiphong road, the Vietminh was not content with ambushes, which it set on every road in the country. For the past two months it had taken to mine-laying, and although this had not yet seriously interrupted the flow of supplies to the capital, the situation could fairly quickly become dangerous. Roads were closed every evening at 6:00, and they could not be re-opened until noon the next day, or even later. Every morning, it took five or six hours to clear the mines and fill in the trenches dug across the road during the night. Every night, the Vietminh started over again, laying their mines and digging their trenches; every morning, the French dug up the mines and repaired the cuts. And nearly every day, some trucks were blown up by mines that had been overlooked.

During the two weeks after the fall of Dien Bien Phu, official communiqués of the general staff in Tonkin mentioned "increased acts of sabotage and harassing operations on the road and railroad

[3] Joseph Laniel, *Le drame indochinois* (Paris, 1957), p. 104.

connecting Hanoi and Haiphong."[4] And Hanoi, which had never before even considered the possibility, began to dread encirclement. Once again, the sound of guns could be heard in the city; the Vietnamese People's Army was probing the outer defenses of the perimeter, near Son Tay.

But it was the situation in the southern part of the Red River delta that aroused increasing anxiety. The enemy launched violent attacks around Phu Ly,[5] proving that he could bring highly trained and very aggressive regular elements into action in the delta before his divisions at Dien Bien Phu had even had time to move. Vietminh regional units were also very active in the area bounded by Phu Ly, Nam Dinh, Thai Binh, and Hung Yen; even the Ninh Giang sector was not spared.

The chief threat lay elsewhere, but it was on its way. The Vietminh main force had regrouped at Dien Bien Phu and started to descend on the delta. It began to move on May 13, and by May 19 the leading elements were already in Moc Chau, 50 miles west of Hoa Binh.

Although its aircrews were exhausted, the French air force tried to block this movement. It attacked the Vietminh convoys and the lines of communication, particularly Route 41, without interruption, but these raids merely slowed Giap's troops by forcing them to move at night or in bad weather.[6] All evidence indicated that the enemy divisions would be back in position around the delta by June 15 or 20.[7] The crucial question was whether they would be in condition to launch a general assault.

One can understand why the situation was viewed with anxiety

[4] *Le Monde* (Paris), May 11, 1954.

[5] The May 14 communiqué of the French High Command referred to "heavy losses on both sides." On May 12, four Vietminh battalions attacked a French battalion between the posts at Yen Phu and An Xa. An Xa was besieged for three weeks and fell on May 21. Yen Phu was isolated by floods and surrounded; a large-scale operation was necessary to relieve it.

[6] Navarre, *op. cit.*, p. 263.

[7] General Navarre confirmed the arrival of the 308th and 312th Vietminh Divisions, as well as the Heavy Division, in the area of Yen Bay, Phu Tho, and Thai Nguyen, and of the 316th and 304th Divisions in the area of Thanh Hoa, between June 10 and 20. He added, "These were the normal rest and regrouping areas of these divisions." (*Ibid.*)

in Paris. There were even signs of panic—the word is used advisedly—in certain influential political circles. The parliamentary debates of May 10 and 12 showed the National Assembly's grave concern for the safety of the Expeditionary Corps.

In this anguished and uneasy atmosphere, the National Defense Committee met on May 14 and 15. It first heard an account by General Ely of the causes and future implications of the defeat at Dien Bien Phu. This was followed by a wide-ranging and forthright debate about the military situation and the action it demanded.

It was generally agreed that the French military position had seriously deteriorated. Giap could be expected to exploit his advantage to the full and attack the delta quickly. From this point of view, the threat to Tonkin might easily be more serious than it had been before Dien Bien Phu, because the Expeditionary Corps had lost its spearhead, the best parachute and Foreign Legion units, in the battle. Its mobile reserves had virtually disappeared, while the dispersion of the French forces in the delta left them exposed to fresh attempts at encirclement. The need to keep the forces in the field at full strength taxed the resources of the French command and prevented it from rebuilding the mobile forces the situation demanded. Moreover, Vietminh agents had been working on the population with their usual fierce energy and forceful arguments for some weeks, and this raised the fearful possibility of a popular uprising. The Vietnamese Army was the target of unbridled propaganda as well as armed attacks. This, combined with the demoralizing effect that Dien Bien Phu and the opening of the Geneva conference must have had on it, gave reason to fear a total collapse in the sectors where it operated alone, such as the southern part of the Red River delta.

In these circumstances, a contraction of the defense perimeter seemed inevitable, for it was doubtful whether the French were in any condition to hold the whole of the delta. But how much should they shorten their lines? Should they evacuate single posts or entire sectors? Should they abandon the southern region of the delta, including the triangle of Phu Ly, Phat Diem, and Thai Binh? Should they consider withdrawing to the Hanoi-Haiphong axis or even to a bridgehead at Haiphong, if Vietminh pressure increased?

Everyone now realized that the safety of the Expeditionary Corps was at stake and that it would, therefore, have to be freed of all responsibility for local defense. But was this possible under the circumstances? If vital areas were abandoned in mid-conference, the last chance for the French to achieve an honorable compromise might well be ruined. The enemy might be encouraged to exploit his advantages even more, to become more enterprising in military operations and more unyielding in negotiation.[8]

Pleven and de Chevigné insisted that a decision had to be made; the Minister of National Defense felt strongly that the enemy must be discouraged from delivering further blows while the Geneva talks were in progress. Extraordinary precautions must be taken to strengthen Bidault's position at the conference and to safeguard the Expeditionary Corps against further Vietminh assaults, even if these precautions seemed disproportionate at the time. All the members of the government agreed that the Expeditionary Corps had to be reinforced. Immediately after the fall of Dien Bien Phu, two parachute battalions and a *Corsair* fighter-bomber wing had been ordered to Indochina, and these units were already on their way. On May 12, a further order was signed by Laniel, Pleven, and Jacquet: one Algerian *groupe mobile,* three AMX armored-car squadrons, one additional B-26 bomber group, and supporting units were to leave immediately.[9] But this was not all.

On May 6, when the fall of Dien Bien Phu was imminent, General Navarre had listed the reinforcements he would need to continue operations if the conference collapsed and the Vietminh intensified the war. These included twenty-five mobile battalions,

[8] Some ministers wondered to what extent France could depend on American support if the military situation got worse. A communication the French Government had just received from Washington was not encouraging in this respect. See below, chap. 12, pp. 194–95.

[9] Between May 1 and May 31, 4,008 men left for Indochina, of whom 3,600 were replacements and 408 were reinforcements. Another 5,275 left between June 1 and June 20, of whom 2,072 were replacements and 3,203 were reinforcements.

five artillery groups, three battalions each of engineers, armor, and antiaircraft artillery, as well as three medium bomber groups and three helicopter groups. In terms of manpower, this represented 1,000 officers, 3,000 noncommissioned officers, and 30,000 enlisted men. Unfortunately, there was another problem which General Navarre had already mentioned. The Expeditionary Corps was operating among a population in which even the loyal elements, let alone the passive and neutral ones, might suddenly change their attitude if they became convinced that a Vietminh victory (or a French withdrawal) was imminent. The Ministry of Defense asked that the equivalent of three divisions should stand by on full alert to support the French forces in Indochina if such a change of heart occurred. These troops would not be used for offensive operations but would permit the French forces to redeploy in an atmosphere of consolidation rather than defeat.

The dispatch of these three divisions was bound to have a powerful psychological impact in France and Indochina. On the other hand, it would seriously weaken France's military capability at home and in North Africa. It stirred fears that if France sent so many troops to Asia without quickly replacing them, America would decide to hasten the rearmament of West Germany, with or without EDC, to make up for the shrinking number of French troops in Europe. Pleven therefore asked the government to advance the call-up of the second levy of draftees in the 1954 contingent, in order to "re-establish the level of strength required for the defense of Europe and the protection of sovereignty in North Africa."

Such a decision was likely to cause serious political repercussions, and the ministers had misgivings about its timing. Laniel asked for time to think it over and to determine whether the local military situation really justified such precautions. On the one hand, it was essential—and Reynaud was particularly insistent on this point—that another Dien Bien Phu (at Hanoi, for example) be avoided at all costs.[10] Neither public opinion nor parliament would tolerate another such defeat, and, if one occurred, the government would

[10] Conversation of the authors with Paul Reynaud, June 15, 1959.

be brought down immediately. On the other hand, a rapid contraction of the positions in the field, combined with assurances about American support if the Geneva conference ended in stalemate, might make it unnecessary to call the draftees prematurely or send them to Indochina.

Therefore, the National Defense Committee agreed on a directive to General Navarre, drafted by the Chiefs of Staff Committee, which directed him to draw in his defensive perimeter around the Red River delta. The Committee also decided to send to Indochina a special mission consisting of Generals Ely, Salan, and Pélissié.[11] They were to study the situation created by the fall of Dien Bien Phu, consider immediate requirements, and assess what the long-term needs would be if the Geneva conference failed to produce an agreement. In case of emergency, they were empowered to take whatever decisions the situation on the spot required. The Committee's operational directive was entrusted to General Ely, who was to pass it on to General Navarre. This document, which had wide implications, became, in fact, the political testament of the Laniel government.

Three days later, on May 18, the three generals landed in Saigon. General Ely explained to Navarre, who had come to meet him at Tan Son Nhut airfield, that "the only purpose of his journey" was to hand him the government directive he had brought.[12] This directive is given in full in the Premier's own book. It harshly contradicts all the optimistic statements we have already quoted. It reads:

> 1. Your plan of action in the present period must have as its chief aim, *taking precedence over all other considerations, the safeguarding of the Expeditionary Corps.* Therefore, you must take account of the real capabilities of the enemy, which may increase

[11] General Salan, a former commander in chief in Indochina, was then inspector general of overseas French forces. General Pélissié was attached to the general staff of the French Air Force.

[12] Navarre, *op. cit.*, p. 268, and Paul Ely, *L'Indochine dans la tourmente* (Paris, 1964), p. 131.

further through Chinese aid despite the attrition he has suffered at Dien Bien Phu.

2. Your plan, in broad terms, should be designed:

a) to clean up the situation in central and southern Indochina south of the 18th Parallel (in order to prepare for the withdrawal of the defense south of this line, should the situation require this in the future). *To the north of this line, no political consideration must be allowed to take precedence over military considerations.*

b) to make whatever contractions of your field positions are necessary to restore the balance between your forces and those of the Vietminh in the Tonkin delta. The strength of the armed forces in this area must be limited to the minimum necessary to safeguard the Expeditionary Corps, so as to provide sufficient reserves in case of a threat in central Annam.

The first stage of this contraction will concentrate our forces in the developed part of the delta. If a second stage is necessary, our forces will fall back on the stronghold of Haiphong, which backs on the sea, and therefore can rely on the navy for firepower and supplies. You will devote particular attention to considerations governing the operations of the air forces in order to ensure ground and antiaircraft protection for the bases in Tonkin and the strengthening of the air force infrastructure in the stronghold of Haiphong. The number of airfields available in Haiphong should be raised to four in the shortest possible time.

3. In general, you must avoid all dispersal of our forces and ensure that the necessary regrouping is carried out, so that there will be no danger that the battle of Tonkin will cause such attrition of the Expeditionary Corps as to compromise the general situation in Indochina.

In putting this plan into action, it is your responsibility to make effective arrangements for ensuring the safety of French citizens and of those elements of the Vietnamese population that may be imperiled, particularly the families of Vietnamese fighting in the ranks of the Franco-Vietnamese forces.[13]

Ely explained to Navarre that the French Government expected the first stage of withdrawal (abandonment of the southern and

[13] Laniel, *op. cit.*, pp. 106–7, and Ely, *ibid.*, pp. 129–30.

western parts of the Red River delta) to be carried out in a very short time, that is, ten to fifteen days. However, the second stage (evacuation of Hanoi and retreat to Haiphong) should only be undertaken on direct orders from the government or, in case of very heavy enemy pressure, on the initiative of the commander in chief.

Navarre had some objections. Although he accepted Points 1 and 2 (*a*) he was not entirely in agreement with Point 2 (*b*). He himself had long stressed the advantages of establishing the line of defense at the 18th Parallel. He had even conceded the usefulness of some contraction of the positions in Tonkin so that some forces could be spared for redeployment south of the 18th Parallel.[14] But he felt that premature evacuation of the southern and western areas of the delta could have dramatic results. He pointed out that these withdrawals would change the war map to the disadvantage of France at a time when the talks at Geneva had hardly started. They would deprive the Vietnamese Army of vital sources of recruitment. Finally, and above all, evacuation would have such an effect on morale that it would no longer be possible to rely on Vietnamese support, and, at the same time, the French negotiators in Geneva would be deprived of all freedom of action.

Navarre maintained that, from the military point of view, these withdrawals were not immediately necessary. They were likely to be far more dangerous than an attempt to hold existing positions, because, as soon as the enemy—unavoidably—got wind of their preparation, he would make things difficult for the French. It would be much harder for the French to defend themselves during a withdrawal than while standing firm in their present lines.[15] At worst, Navarre thought, the immediate threat would consist of attempts by Vietminh units arriving from Dien Bien Phu to infiltrate the Red River delta, and the expected reinforcements would be sufficient to put a stop to these.

[14] General Navarre admits that he had suggested such measures in a letter to the government (*op. cit.*, p. 269). This confirms certain press reports. See J. R. Tournoux, in *L'Information* (Paris), May 15, 1954.

[15] It seems that this was also General Cogny's opinion.

As General Navarre saw it, the contraction of French positions on the ground should only be considered in the autumn, if the talks in Geneva reached deadlock and if the latest reinforcements did not seem sufficient to hold the territories for which the French were responsible. He felt that, in the meantime, the French should hold their positions and not draw back anywhere, so as not to tempt the enemy to attack; this would not rule out shortening defense lines locally and abandoning numerous isolated posts.

However, as the government directive was not subject to argument, Navarre suggested that he should regroup the Expeditionary Corps around Hanoi and the Hanoi-Haiphong road but make the Vietnamese army responsible for defending the south and west of the delta. General Nguyen Van Vy, the head of the Vietnamese imperial military secretariat, had given his agreement to a solution on these lines.[16]

After thinking the matter over for a few days, Ely gave his personal sanction to this interpretation of the directive, which he regarded as not being out of line with the spirit of the French Government's decisions. As he saw it, the withdrawals ordered by the government were mandatory only for the Expeditionary Corps. The commander in chief retained full freedom of action in his employment of the armies of the Associated States.

The three generals carried out their tour of inspection very rapidly—spending four days visiting key points in Tonkin—and set off on May 23 for Paris (where they arrived only on May 25 because their aircraft needed repairs). The views they brought back about the seriousness of the situation seem not to have tallied completely.[17]

The Committee of National Defense met again on the evening of May 26 to hear their report. By the very next day, enough information about this meeting had leaked out to make a reconstruc-

16 This decision was implemented six weeks later under the code name Operation Auvergne. Mendès-France's government did not know of its existence and was informed only when it was already well under way.

17 According to Frédéric-Dupont, Ely foresaw the evacuation of Hanoi within two or three weeks; Salan was even gloomier. Frédéric-Dupont, *Mission de la France en Asie* (Paris, 1956), p. 148.

tion of its outlines possible.[18] In the main, the generals confirmed the picture of the situation put before the Committee on May 14 and 15. They had found that the French war map had deteriorated very much more than they had expected. Casualties had been heavy during the previous two months. The Expeditionary Corps had lost its "mailed fist," its best assault elements, at Dien Bien Phu. The strategic reserve had practically vanished. Many isolated posts were at the mercy of enemy attacks, several had already fallen, and others were gradually being smothered.

Events had also affected the morale and cohesion of the Expeditionary Corps, and, though the results varied from unit to unit, there was now a crisis of leadership. The Vietnamese Army was still putting up an honorable fight, but it was being undermined by Vietminh propaganda. Dien Bien Phu had had a profound effect on the civilian population, and the enemy was capitalizing on its triumph. There was good reason to fear that the population, in anticipation of an imminent Vietminh victory, might suddenly transfer its allegiance. In strategic terms it appeared that Giap, encouraged by his success at Dien Bien Phu, was determined to exploit it thoroughly and was driving his forces toward the delta and Hanoi. Information received during the previous few days

[18] See *Le Monde* (Paris), May 27, 28, and 29, 1954. The weekly *L'Express* published in its issue No. 54 of May 29, 1954, a summary of the "impressions and recommendations" of the three generals under the title "The Ely-Salan report." *L'Express* explained that this report was obtained from "an excellent source and in his own words." This issue of *L'Express* was immediately confiscated, at the request of the Minister of National Defense, and legal proceedings were begun against a person unknown for divulging secret military information. However, Agence France Presse had by then distributed to its subscribers in the provinces a substantial summary of the document, which appeared in numerous dailies (*Paris-Normandie, L'Est Républicain,* etc.). Those considered responsible for distributing the document were soon afterward dismissed by the director of AFP.

A search carried out in the offices of *L'Express* during the night of May 27 unearthed some documents. Two days later, Marc Jacquet, the under-secretary responsible for relations with the Associated States, handed his resignation to Laniel, while making it very clear that the documents found that originated in his department were in no way secret. It was learned later that the *Express* report was actually an account of a conversation between an *Express* writer and General Salan. The case was shelved under the next government, on the instructions of General Koenig, Minister of National Defense.

suggested that he was positioning his units to encircle the delta. Part of the Vietminh force coming from Dien Bien Phu along Route 41 had branched off toward the northeast, to the Nha Phu sector. Thus, the possibility of a general Vietminh offensive against the delta could not be ruled out in spite of the rains and the effects of attrition and fatigue on Giap's fighting force.

It was now a matter of using the forces available in a defensive but highly mobile capacity in those areas that were considered vital. The generals believed that the developed part of the delta could and should be held—for the time being, at any rate—even at the cost of pulling back the lines in the southern part. A withdrawal to the Hanoi-Haiphong axis should be contemplated only as a second stage, if the situation deteriorated further. The mission had already taken certain measures on the spot. All the *groupes mobiles* that were scattered or operating in nonessential areas were being regrouped in the north: this had enabled General Cogny to rebuild reserves amounting altogether to about one division.[19] Limited withdrawals had started all around the delta. Every available force was being repositioned on the outskirts of Hanoi and along the Hanoi-Haiphong road. In addition, reinforcements were on their way to strengthen the defenses of the delta. Nevertheless, the generals had no confidence that these measures would be sufficient. The General Staff would be able to save what could be saved only if it were given the means to do the job.

Yet the limit of available resources had now been reached. The units in West Germany, France, and North Africa could no longer provide the required manpower. It seemed clear that the call-up requested by Pleven on May 14 could no longer be avoided. The rapid dispatch of large conscript units to southern Vietnam could release regular troops that were stationed there for the northern theater of operations. The generals claimed this would prove an effective means of restoring the military situation in the field and would thereby contribute to the success of Bidault's negotiations

[19] Laniel indicated that Ely drafted and handed to Navarre two military directives, dated May 20 and 22, that were approved by the National Defense Committee on May 26. According to him, these gave precise executive orders (*op. cit.*, p. 107).

in Geneva. If, on the contrary, the government were to delay sending these troops for more than four weeks, it would risk further serious defeats for the Expeditionary Corps and a resulting breakdown of the Geneva talks. The military situation could not be divorced from the diplomatic one.

Equally, it would be essential to strengthen the Expeditionary Corps if the Geneva meeting failed. Whether the intention would then be to evacuate certain areas in safety or to hold on and resist or even to recapture the initiative, conscript troops would have to be called upon.

And so, two weeks after its first deliberations, the French Government was again faced with the hard facts it had attempted to escape. Laniel and Bidault, among others, did not share the general pessimism about the situation in the Red River delta; they believed that the French command there still had considerable resources at its disposal and retained appreciable capabilities for action and movement, provided it were not tied down by considerations of politics or prestige. Laniel made this clear: "The commander in chief must take care to avoid another Dien Bien Phu at Hanoi. He must make his decisions on the spot in the light of military developments. It is his responsibility to choose the time and method of withdrawing from Hanoi if the situation demands it."[20]

Two days later, on May 28, the Council of Ministers approved the measures taken to reinforce the Expeditionary Corps. It considered the proposals made by the Committee of National Defense with a view to forming several operational divisions as part of a general reserve. And, most important, it resigned itself to decreeing a phased but rapid call-up of the second batch of conscripts in the 1954 contingent. This decision did not mean that conscripts would immediately be sent to the Far East; they were, instead, to be called on to replace career soldiers transferred from units in Europe and North Africa to the operational divisions of the newly created general reserve.

Three days later, the government made a decision the Premier

[20] *Ibid.*, pp. 107–8.

had wanted to make immediately after the fall of Dien Bien Phu. It decreed that, in such a period of crisis in Indochina, civil and military powers should—as in 1950, after Cao Bang—be concentrated in the hands of a single individual. It therefore ended the assignments of Navarre and Dejean. Because Marshal Juin refused the post, General Ely agreed—in a spirit of commendable self-sacrifice—to take on supreme responsibility in Indochina at this most daunting moment of all. He was appointed Commissioner General *and* commander in chief by a decree dated June 2, and he left France for Saigon on June 6.

The army leaders had confronted the Laniel cabinet with its responsibilities. In order to avoid the worst, and not deprive Bidault of any of his trump cards during the next few weeks, the cabinet had taken a series of measures that would doubtless shield the Expeditionary Corps against disaster for the duration of the summer, or at any rate for the duration of the conference. But what then? The government knew the alternatives well: either the conference would achieve a negotiated settlement, or the war would have to be internationalized, which would imply further military efforts by France. It was convinced that the threat of the latter development was one of Bidault's strongest cards in Geneva. Therefore, it had been trying for more than two weeks to obtain the necessary assurances from the United States.

12

BIDAULT'S TRUMP CARD

Two weeks previously, Bidault had thought nothing of refusing to associate himself with the American plan for a guarantee in Southeast Asia; now, he bitterly complained to his colleagues that Washington had deprived him of the vital trump card: the threat of American power.[1] Indeed, the French believed that President Eisenhower's statement of April 29 had seriously weakened the entire Western position—convincing the Russians that the United States was resigned to the prospect of at least part of Indochina coming under Communist control.

The President and Secretary of State were troubled by these comments, for they had immediately understood Bidault's need to re-establish his "position of strength." In a message to Dulles on April 30, Eisenhower had made a point of repudiating the pessimistic interpretations put upon his speech and had stressed once again that American policy had not changed. Dulles informed Bidault of these assurances and added that the President

[1] Daniel Mayer, who had been sent to Geneva by a parliamentary committee, reported, just before the conference began, that Bidault was willing to negotiate but was hampered by this lack of trump cards.

was willing to help the French and Vietnamese to improve their position.

Dulles believed that only a policy of firmness could effectively support Bidault. On the evening of May 2, just before returning to the United States, Dulles assured Bidault that he would do everything in his power to help France during the conference, and after it if it led nowhere. He confirmed this in writing the next day, adding that it would be difficult to reach a peace settlement without a valid alternative in case the Communists failed to put forward honorable proposals. He hoped and believed the United States could make a contribution to this alternative, he said.

The alternative in Dulles's mind was clearly the Southeast Asian security pact. But would it aim at intervention in Indochina or withdrawal to a new line of defense? In its search for a negotiated settlement, could France count on America or not?

For the time being, at least, the Americans had apparently decided to divide the Indochinese responsibilities.[2] The search for an acceptable settlement was left to France and the Associated States; the creation of a framework for collective action guaranteeing this settlement, or even achieving it, was up to the United States. For both foreign and domestic reasons, the Eisenhower administration had to give first priority to such a pact: it would highlight America's determination to resist Communist expansion in Southeast Asia; it would provide an international guarantee for any negotiated solution of the Indochinese conflict; and it would offer the best pretext for American intervention if Geneva ended in failure. For the present, the State Department and White House felt that America's main role was to reinforce the Western position and provide additional leverage in Geneva. Even preliminary contacts about the security pact would instill caution in the Communists, convince the Vietminh that they could not hope to win the war, and remind the French that the game was not yet lost.

For this reason, Dulles met with the ambassadors of all the countries involved—Great Britain, Australia, New Zealand, the Philip-

[2] See above, chap. 9, p. 143.

pines, Thailand, and France—when he returned to Washington. Later, the net was cast even wider. The State Department did not want its plan to look like a "white man's enterprise"; in response to British objections (or British advice), it sought to associate Asian countries with it—especially the five Colombo powers. Robert Murphy, a deputy under-secretary of state, called on their ambassadors to explain the reasons for the American initiative, stressing the purely defensive nature of the proposed pact, and asking them to sound out their governments. A psychological operation was in progress: the U.S. Government expected nothing from India and Indonesia, the two pillars of Asian neutralism, but it hoped for moral support from the other three. Yet even this was denied it. The Colombo powers turned a deaf ear to the American advances.

While this string of consultations was in progress, Dulles managed, for better or worse, to define a foreign policy during a television interview. Then, on May 8, he had a long conversation with Ambassador Henri Bonnet. Dien Bien Phu had fallen the day before, and this event had already affected American policy to some extent. Dulles repeated his hope that France would manage to conclude the armistice, but he clearly did not believe this would be possible. In his opinion, a victorious Vietminh would turn down any compromise that did not put it in a position to dominate the whole of Indochina sooner or later. Dulles was determined to press on with his plan for a pact—if necessary without Great Britain, which was still reluctant.

Bonnet gathered that Dulles hoped for immediate talks about how to halt the Communist drive to the south. In reporting the conversation, he suggested that it might be possible to take advantage of this American frame of mind. Perhaps, France could now discover what the U.S. attitude would be, if—"contrary to our wishes"—the Geneva conference did not end the hostilities or if the military situation in Tonkin suddenly deteriorated so badly that France had to ask for American help.

Bonnet had not yet been able to assess the effect that the fall of Dien Bien Phu had had on the Congress or the American public. In the United States, as in France, the publicity of the previous weeks had artificially inflated the strategic importance of the fort, and now a wave of gloom swept through large sectors of American opinion: Indochina was lost; the French would let everything go; it was only a matter of weeks. The interventionists lamented—Indochina was the hinge of Southeast Asia; a chain reaction was about to take place; the house of cards was going to collapse. The Alsop brothers wrote that the loss of Indochina now seemed probable and this event would have a tremendous psychological effect on the expectant masses of Asia. And so the prospect of another major Communist victory in Southeast Asia unfolded before a public virtually transfixed by it. Would Southeast Asia, with its tremendous resources, follow China into the Kremlin's orbit? Chiang Kai-shek's defeat had sealed the fate of the Democratic Party in 1952; the fall of Bao Dai might well do the same for the Republican Party in 1954.

Dulles tried to dispel this dangerous mood of public alarm and prevent the effects of humiliation and frustration from gathering momentum by suggesting on May 11, during his first press conference since his return from Geneva, that Southeast Asia might possibly be secured even without Indochina.[3]

Given the diplomatic atmosphere at the time, this was a resounding, even sensational, statement. Dulles sensed almost immediately that his words would be misunderstood: it would be assumed that the United States had resigned itself to the partial loss of Indochina or had abandoned it completely to its fate. Right away, he tried to restore the balance, but it was already too late. The news, flashed across the Atlantic by French and British press agencies, panicked French diplomatic circles. It reached Geneva early on May 12 and was brought to Bidault while the conference was in session. Bidault saw at a glance that the backbone of his case had collapsed and his position had become untenable. He was heard to mutter something about a "stab in the back."

[3] *The New York Times,* May 12, 1954, and *Department of State Bulletin,* XXX, no. 778, May, 1954, p. 782. On the significance and context of this statement, see Melvin Gurtov, *The First Vietnam Crisis* (New York, 1967), p. 121.

After a glance through the text, Bidault passed a note to Bedell Smith from his seat at the conference table, demanding an immediate clarification by Washington. At about eleven that evening, Bedell Smith sent his French colleague the full text of Dulles's statements; it gave the French delegation a moment of reassurance. Dulles's clarification at least proved that the American position remained *more or less* as it had been on May 7. In effect, the Secretary of State had said that the system of collective security that the United States was trying to organize in Southeast Asia was intended to safeguard *all* the area if possible, and its essential parts in any case. The United States had not abandoned the Associated States; on the contrary, the U.S. Government wished them to participate; indeed, without them, the defense of the area would become more difficult. He added, "But I do not want to give the impression either that, if events that we could not control and which we do not anticipate should lead to their being lost . . . we would consider the whole situation hopeless, and we would give up in despair."[4]

Dulles's prime object had been to reassure public opinion and Congress by refuting (without direct reference to it) the interventionist slogan that Indochina (above all, Tonkin) was the key to Southeast Asia. If Indochina were lost, wholly or in part, American public opinion should not be allowed to believe that all of Asia had been lost with it. But it did not seem to occur to the U.S. Government that it could still prevent this loss by a bolder and more clear-cut policy.

Amid all these clarifications and reclarifications, one point stood out: Indochina remained important to the United States but no longer vital. This change of emphasis colored every calculation from then on. The fate of Indochina was being decided on the battlefield, in Geneva, and in Paris—places outside American control—and the United States neither could nor would enter into any firm agreements concerning it. The American position could

[4] *The New York Times*, May 12, 1954. Secretary of Defense Charles Wilson, who was particularly hostile to any suggestion of intervention, said, as he left on an inspection tour of the Far East, that, like Dulles, he thought the loss of Indochina would not inevitably bring about the loss of all of Southeast Asia.

be plainly stated: as long as France does not throw in its hand in Indochina, it will support France as far as it can; if France yields and Indochina falls into Communist hands, it will depend on the collective-security system to limit the damage. America does not want to abandon the Associated States, but its attitude depends on the participants' will to resist; it will only help those who do not give in.

In France, where the intricacy of Dulles's moves was seldom well understood, political leaders and the press considered that his remarks, even when "clarified," had deprived Bidault of one of the last cards left to him. The well-known French columnist Pierre-René Wolf asked in *Paris-Normandie* on May 12, "Are we to go on tearing up one by one the few trumps we still hold? It might be time to put this question to Mr. Dulles." The French Government had already decided to do precisely this. The diverse groups within it were united in agreeing that the American Government should be asked at once whether it was giving up the defense of Indochina—yes or no. The French representatives in Geneva could not adopt a realistic attitude until they knew the answer. On the evening of May 12, after a meeting of the Council of Ministers, Laniel summoned Ambassador Dillon, requesting an immediate statement from the U.S. Government on the attitude it intended to adopt if an honorable armistice proved impossible to secure in Geneva or if the military situation deteriorated further before the end of the conference. Schumann instructed Bonnet to put the same question to the State Department.

This was not a demand for American intervention as some commentators have called it. After so many confused and conflicting statements by high political and military officials in the United States, Laniel's cabinet simply wished to know where it stood vis-à-vis the leader of the Atlantic alliance. In brief, it was a matter of obtaining the "threat of intervention" without which, Bidault believed, he would be unable to induce a conciliatory spirit in his opponents. He needed to be able to sound the thunder without allowing the lightning to strike.[5] And, when all was said and

[5] Conversation between Bidault and Bedell Smith on May 23, 1954.

done, he needed to convince the Americans that, if the war flared up again, France could no longer fight on alone.

It is not clear that the French Government had carefully weighed the dangers involved in the step it took. Failure to obtain this threat of intervention would once again weaken the Western position by revealing the divisions among the allies and the rancor aroused by equivocations and refusals. And if, contrary to all expectations, the interventionists in Washington won the day and gave the French the assurances they wanted, this might create an even more serious crisis, in which control over events would pass from Geneva to Washington. In order for it to be useful rather than harmful, the sounding-out operation would have to be conducted in complete secrecy. Did anyone seriously believe that this was possible?

Bonnet raised the question with Dulles on May 13. Dulles again told him that he thought it necessary to have an alternative that would be helpful in the negotiations and available to fall back on if the need arose. He said the American Government was well aware that France could no longer fight on alone and that the burden had become too heavy. If the Geneva conference did not achieve a cease-fire, it would doubtless be necessary to discuss and define the *conditions* of an *eventual* American intervention in the war, both from the political point of view (relations with the Associated States, war aims, etc.) and in military terms (planning and carrying out operations, command structure, training the Vietnamese Army, etc.).

In any case, Congress would have to give advance approval to any military action, and it would not agree to the commitment of American troops unless certain conditions were fulfilled. These conditions did not yet exist, Dulles added, and once again he repeated them: "real" independence for the Associated States, the creation of a framework for collective action, and a prior warning by the United Nations.

Despite Dulles's admonitions, the French request caused acute embarrassment in Washington, for the American reply would have a decisive influence on French actions at Geneva. Either a refusal to come to a decision or another postponement would force

Bidault to accept the least unfavorable armistice terms that the Vietminh was willing to offer.

But which was the right decision? It was no secret that the American leadership was very much divided over the Indochina question. The interventionists, including Admiral Radford and Vice President Nixon, believed that the "Free World" would have to fight unless it were willing to surrender Indochina, Thailand, Burma, and Malaya to the Communists. Indochina, with ten French divisions in action and a Vietnamese army undergoing training, offered more favorable conditions for intervention than the countries farther south. If China persisted in its "indirect aggression," there would have to be a strike "at the head": China would have to be attacked and bombed without any of the "vain scruples" that had paralyzed American action in Korea. It was a clear-cut and direct approach (stemming, apparently, from Admiral Radford and a few senior officers of the Strategic Air Command, rather than from the Pentagon as a whole). The interventionists were opposed by a group of prudent and semiprudent officials led by Charles Wilson, Secretary of Defense, and including such senior officers as General Matthew Ridgway and General Nathan Twining. They had given Indochina up for lost, and they believed in letting the French negotiate independently while they tried to set up a strong line of defense capable of stopping any further Communist advance.

There was very little elbow room for Dulles between these two groups. He was, undoubtedly, sincere in wanting to help France quickly by obtaining some sort of joint allied declaration, as the first step toward a collective commitment that would enable the President to ask for congressional approval to act in Indochina. Most commentators predicted that Congress would grant such approval, subject to the fulfillment of certain conditions. These conditions, of course, were the ones Dulles had described to Bonnet. But had Dulles suggested these conditions to the congressmen, or had they imposed them on him? Whatever the answer, the prospect of elections in November did not exactly encourage Congress to take bold decisions that might involve shedding the blood of "our boys." The American public's opposition to a new Asian entanglement forced Dulles to consider not only the exigencies of the world situation but also the Republican Party's electoral strategy.

In these circumstances, everything suggested that the U.S. Government would again try to stall. The rainy season, which interrupted all military operations, would in any case give American diplomats time to assemble the proposed alliance.

Moreover, any plan for intervention would surely include numerous conditions designed to intensify the French effort, while giving America the military responsibilities that the French had heretofore obstinately refused to relinquish, including the actual direction of the war as well as the training of the Vietnamese forces. This was made clear when Dillon handed Schumann the American reply to the French request on May 15. It listed the conditions that would have to be met before American intervention in the war could be *contemplated,*[6] should the Geneva conference break down:

1. France and the three Associated States should address a request for assistance to the United States.

2. The same request should be addressed to Thailand, the Philippines, Australia, New Zealand, and Great Britain. The United States was prepared to act if the first two gave a positive answer, the next two showed active interest, and the last did no more than consent.

3. The United Nations should approve the enterprise in response to a request by Thailand, Laos, or Cambodia for the dispatch of observers to discover or forestall any attempt at aggression.

4. The French Government would reaffirm the complete independence of the three Associated States. It would be made clear that this independence could go as far as secession from the French Union.

5. As long as common action was in progress, the French Government would undertake not to withdraw its troops, it being

[6] According to Laniel, Dillon informed the French that Eisenhower was ready to ask Congress for the necessary authority if certain conditions were fulfilled. Joseph Laniel, *Le drame indochinois* (Paris, 1957), p. 110.

understood that the American contribution would consist mainly of naval and air forces but might also include land forces.

6. Agreements would be made between the United States and France for the organization of the command structure, the distribution of assignments, and the training of the Vietnamese army.

7. The request for assistance would have to be approved by the French Parliament.

These, it must be stressed, were the conditions set by the U.S. Government for the mere *study* of the possibility of intervention. Laniel has written that they did not strike him as "unacceptable,"[7] but they were in fact both cautious and greedy, and could be relied on even more than the rainy season to provide time for the preparation of a possible intervention, or to conceal second thoughts.

In any case, the mission of Ely and Salan gave the Americans an excuse to defer all decisions until their return from Indochina. The measures decided on in Paris had made an excellent impression in Washington. The French war efforts would give the American administration a new argument for convincing Congress either to provide additional aid for France or to decide on joint action. On the other hand, it did not seem possible to ask that GI's be sent to Indochina so long as French conscripts were not already in action there.

In the meantime, the hostility of American public opinion to any commitment induced even the interventionists to behave more cautiously. On May 16, for instance, Senator Knowland said during a television interview that he would favor American intervention in Indochina only if the Chinese Communists appeared there in force. He added, thereby completely contradicting what he had said on May 4, that in his opinion it would be a serious mistake to send troops to Asia. On the same program, Senator Mike Mansfield, a Democrat, opposed to the dispatch of American troops to Indochina because, he said, the Vietminh could obtain from China and the Soviet Union more troops than the United States could commit. In conclusion, both senators urged the Asian countries to conclude

[7] *Ibid.*, p. 120. The substance of these negotiations became known to the public fairly quickly: see the report from Paris entitled "French Contacts with U.S." in *The Times* (London), May 21, 1954.

a defense pact among themselves. The defense of the continent was their responsibility; the United States and its allies could not go beyond a supporting role.

In other words, caution, reticence, and embarrassment became the keynotes in Washington. How could the policy-makers in Paris still retain so many illusions?

Throughout these transactions, the British Government had been most reticent of all. On May 10, the day after the conversation between Dulles and Sir Roger Makins, Selwyn Lloyd had confirmed that he was not to be moved: there would be no British commitment of any kind until the results of the Geneva conference were known. It was obvious that he did not wish to take part in talks about collective action in Southeast Asia at that time. Moreover, the secrecy surrounding the latest Franco-American contact did nothing to placate the British cabinet,[8] which, naturally, had been aware of the proceedings and was hurt at being excluded.

The British press reacted quickly and, in general, rather sourly. (Certain papers such as the *Daily Herald* were outspokenly critical.) Although the members of the government succeeded in moderating their ill humor, it was pointed out that these backstage contacts put Eden in a false position in Geneva and threatened to handicap his attempts at conciliation. Since Bidault and his allies appeared to be seeking no more than a simple armistice, the Vietminh might well suspect that the only aim of the Western maneuvering was to give the United States time to prepare for intervention. British opinion very nearly considered these "Franco-American initiatives" as attempts to torpedo the chances of peace.

Moreover, the British leaders had an uncomfortable feeling that they were being subjected to a kind of blackmail by the Americans. Snippets of information leaking from Washington suggested that the deteriorating military situation in Indochina might impel the Americans to speed up the negotiations. An agreement might be concluded "even without Great Britain" and, if it seemed neces-

[8] These feelings were exacerbated when Reuters cabled from Washington on May 13 that France had asked the United States for immediate assistance in Indochina. See *L'Information* (Paris), May 15, 1954.

sary, action might be taken. According to the Alsop brothers, Nixon and Radford thought the Commonwealth countries should not be invited to join discussions, because they would tend to delay action. Other dispatches suggested that the U.S. Government might disregard Great Britain and try to extend ANZUS westward by drawing Australia and New Zealand into the South East Asia pact.[9]

Sir Winston Churchill did not allow himself to be intimidated. On May 17, he briefly indicated to the House of Commons, which was showing active concern, that his government had learned about the Franco-American talks only from the press. He repeated, cooly but forcefully, that Great Britain remained opposed to any promise of intervention in Indochina as long as the outcome of the Geneva conference remained in doubt.

In Geneva, Bedell Smith had already had a talk with Eden and had assured him that failure to inform Britain of the talks had been an "error." He had categorically promised Eden—as Bidault was to do some hours later—that the Franco-American contacts would not be allowed to hamper his efforts thereafter. Being a good sport, Eden went to Paris with Bidault some days later, to celebrate the fiftieth anniversay of the *Entente Cordiale*.

When more extensive information reached the British from Makins, in Washington, they realized that the contacts were largely semi-official and exploratory, their main purpose from the American point of view to stiffen the French Government's resolve. And, indeed, it *was* this that prompted the White House to make an official show of its determination to set up a barrier in Southeast Asia—unilaterally, if necessary. President Eisenhower spoke on this subject at his press conference on May 19. Only a system of collective security could lay the political foundations needed to resist Communist aggression, he said. Australia[10] and New Zealand were Commonwealth nations directly interested in such an alliance. A collective-defense agreement could be set up with the Asian nations

[9] It was already being said in Washington that, pending signature and ratification of the pact, a simple joint declaration would be sufficient to justify a request for Congressional approval of a possible air-sea operation.

[10] We have already seen that Australia favored a collective system.

concerned. Without British participation, it would not be as satisfactory as one might wish, but it could still be realized, Eisenhower said. In other words, Britain, like Indochina, remained important but was no longer essential.

What element of bluff was there in the Americans' intricate game? Could it be that, to help Bidault, they thought it necessary to persuade the enemy (who was aware of British reluctance) that America could do without Britain's agreement? Yet, Dulles had included British agreement among the conditions governing a possible future American intervention. Once again, therefore, the fate of the entire operation was made to depend on the British Government. This may have been arranged in order to forestall the American advocates of intervention; it certainly provided an excellent alibi. If nothing came of the project or if the threat failed in its effect, Britain would again bear the responsibility before Congress, American opinion, and history. The United States would have made a show of supporting Bidault's firm line and could rest with an easy conscience.

By his single-minded determination to regain a position of strength, Bidault had succeeded in arousing British misgivings and stimulating Anglo-American dissensions. In return, he had obtained nothing but words, and very insubstantial words at that. How could he have hoped, in any case, that the U.S. Government would adopt a clear-cut attitude when, with six months to go before the elections, American public opinion on the subject had not even begun to crystallize?

It must be stressed, however, that under the circumstances, France could not tolerate further uncertainty. Sooner or later, the British and Americans would have to be warned that they could postpone a strategic decision no longer. If the French were no longer willing—or able—to carry on the fight in Indochina, someone would have to take their place, or all the fragile regimes in Southeast Asia would fall as a result of either invasion or infiltration. No Asian country, not even India, Pakistan, or Indonesia, had either the resources or the will to assume this role.

The vacillating inflexibility of the American Government—unable to accept the reality of Communist China or contemplate a lasting concession to the D.R.V. or to guarantee effective military assistance to France and the Associated States if negotiations led nowhere—could only encourage the opposite camp to push its advantage as far as possible. This militated against both possibilities of peace: the peace that might result from negotiations, and that which some still hoped to impose by force.

Yet, however shadowy the threat of intervention may have been, the very fact that talks had been initiated in Washington had an immediate effect on the course of the conference in Geneva.

13

TOWARD PARTITION

One step forward, one step back. After three weeks of talks, public confrontations, and not-so-private contacts, the nine powers in Geneva began to wonder whether they had not strayed onto the "road to Panmunjom," as one representative put it. To be sure, there had been certain overtures on both sides; Molotov had made some concessions on May 14 and 17. But psychologically, if not politically, the conference was wallowing in the trough of a wave, despite the experts' claims that it had made significant progress. Public interest was flagging, and, as diplomatic notes went to and fro, the proceedings gradually sank into a morass of diplomatic procedure.

What, in fact, was it all about? About peace in Asia. . . . About battles being fought—from the wooded slopes on the edge of the Laotian and Tonkinese forests to the sticky ricefields of the Red River delta. . . . About wounded men rotting to death in Dien Bien Phu[1]. . . .

The issues of the prisoners and wounded cut across the con-

[1] The agreement signed between the two commands on May 13 had virtually been abrogated. See above, chap. 10, p. 169.

ference's somewhat detached ceremony and generated something near to self-reproach; they became a kind of scandal. By introducing imbalance, urgency, and emotion into the work of a conference that otherwise would have been capable of ticking on forever, like a good Swiss clock, these issues were to trigger the real debate and force France and the Vietminh, the two real protagonists, into communication with each other.

As we have seen, Bidault had twice prompted Molotov to intercede with the leaders of the Vietnam People's Army for a speedier evacuation of the wounded from the captured fort. Molotov smugly replied that the issue was outside the Soviet delegation's competence and that Bidault would be well advised to address himself to the Vietminh delegation. At the closed session of the conference on May 17, it was agreed that the evacuation of the wounded from Dien Bien Phu should be discussed privately between the French and Vietminh representatives. Consequently, Colonel Brébisson, Jacquet's chief of staff, was authorized on May 19 to meet a Vietminh representative in Geneva. Their discussion, which took place that very afternoon, was to cover the fate of the wounded of Dien Bien Phu and a possible exchange of prisoners. Less than two weeks after the fall of the fortress, a French officer was talking to Colonel Ha Van Lau.

It would have been hard to find two individuals more representative of their kind. Colonel Michel de Brébisson was a colonial soldier with a cavalryman's style—thin, gangling, with a lean, ruddy face and an earnest look that combined candor with conscientiousness. Here was a real Indochina veteran: from the day in November, 1945, when he had disembarked at Saigon at the head of the Metropolitan Regiment of Colonial Infantry—"the premier regiment of France"—he had been constantly involved in the war, first in the field, then in the military secretariat. He was a true soldier, incapable of intrigue and therefore likely to win the confidence of his opponents. Ha Van Lau, a former clerk in the French colonial administration, had once been declared an "excellent element" by his French superiors. He had become political commissar of the formidable 320th Division after commanding the South Annam Vietminh zone, where he had been the direct opponent of de Brébisson. (Might this in itself have created a kind of soldierly understanding between them?)

Seldom, in fact, had war separated two inflexible opponents less. Their meeting on May 19, 1954, inaugurated the most fruitful stage of the Geneva negotiations. Very little is known about the substance of the first conversation, apart from unofficial statements that its tone was "courteous and almost cordial." But, from the next meeting on, the Vietminh officer gave more and more hints and glimpses of possible ways to make progress. Thus began a long dialogue within the military committee (which met only in closed session after the middle of June, at first semi-officially and later officially)—an underground current of negotiation between soldiers that ran parallel to the protracted debates of the nine powers and proved relatively more fruitful, at any rate until July 10. Several of the clauses of the final July 21 agreements originated there.

Ha Van Lau's and de Brébisson's first meeting came in a week that seemed otherwise barren. The Communists, as we have seen, had given the impression of being in a conciliatory mood at the session of May 17, despite the harsh tone adopted by the head of the Vietminh delegation; they had avoided all debate on procedural matters and, in fact, had adopted the Western agenda.[2] But the very next day, at the second closed session, Pham Van Dong, supported by Molotov, launched a vigorous plea that the Khmer Issarak and the Pathet Lao be given recognition in principle before any other subject was debated. The Vietminh leader refused, with the same asperity, to contemplate any withdrawal of the Vietminh forces in Cambodia and Laos. Eden spent an hour with Chou En-lai during the morning of Thursday, May 20, but was unable to move him on this issue. The Khmer and Lao resistance movements might be weak but—so Chou gave him to understand—there could be no question of settling the fate of their countries without them. It began to seem that Peking and

[2] See above, chap. 10, pp. 169–70.

its allies were aiming at a form of partition in Cambodia and Laos.

If this were so, what should be done? The representatives of the three Western powers met to discuss the problem. Once again, the British were entrusted with the task of trying to make the opposite side understand which paths led toward agreement and which did not.

That evening, Eden dined with Molotov and warned him in his inimitable way—poise blended with a carefully cultivated shyness—that the Russians and Chinese would be well advised not to push their luck too far. The military situation might be very favorable to the Vietminh at the moment, but time was not necessarily working for the Communists. The United States had ducked when faced with the French Government's demands for intervention and military support, but they would not do so again if the French and Vietnamese suffered more severe setbacks. Eden managed to convey to his dinner companion that Bedell Smith's latest telegrams to Washington displayed a marked shift of emphasis in favor of increasing the Western military potential in Indochina, rather than continuing the talks in Geneva.

As a negotiator, Molotov was not given to admitting that threats, however oblique, moved him; Eden was therefore careful to take no credit for the relaxation that set in at the next day's session.

France's proposals for regrouping military forces in Vietnam had at last been formulated. As Bidault saw it, the zones within which the troops on either side would be regrouped needed to be fairly large, so that their perimeters could be effectively inspected and a rash of incidents avoided. However, their nature and geographic position must not foreshadow a partition of Vietnam in any sense whatsoever, even militarily. The contending sides would remain face to face in Tonkin, Annam, and Cochin China, one or more zones being allocated to the Expeditionary Corps and the Vietminh in each area. The long shape of Vietnam on the map would thereby come to look like a leopard skin, and this is the tag that came to be attached to the French plan.

The argument for this plan was that each side would remain

in those vital areas in which it intended to retain a foothold. The plan would maintain opposite poles of attraction from which political activity could radiate. The military forces would be secure in these zones, and refugees would find asylum there. There would be time for tension to simmer down; it might even prove possible to keep the balance in future elections.

The drawbacks were much more numerous. It was easy to predict bitter bargaining over the selection of zones, with each side demanding sectors controlled by the other on the strength of doctored maps. The borders would be disproportionately long, giving rise to endless incidents of friction and requiring an army of inspectors (no less than 80,000, according to one estimate). There would also be the risk of losing everything, because the nationalist zones would be surrounded by the Vietminh, who would certainly infiltrate them and subject them to heavy pressure. In spite of all these weaknesses, the "leopard-skin" plan remained the official doctrine of the French delegation until the fall of the Laniel government.

Molotov was careful not to condemn it outright, and his realistic and thoughtful speech was favorably received. In his mildest manner, he put forward a five-point program calling for a cease-fire, regroupment in zones, measures to prevent further reinforcement of the belligerents, methods of supervising these arrangements, and an international guarantee of the agreements. These proposals seemed very close to the French plank—so close, in fact, that Bidault praised the objectivity of his Soviet colleague and agreed that the Russian plan should serve as a basis for future discussions.

Molotov next extended his peace offensive on another front. On the following evening, he invited Walter Bedell Smith to the *Villa Blanche*. (Eden and Bidault left Geneva for the weekend to report home on the progress made during the first weeks of the conference.) The only immediate echo of the meeting between the leader of Soviet diplomacy and the former ambassador to Moscow was the reported comment of the latter to one of his colleagues: "I have just dined with the angel of peace." But flickers of irony were difficult to catch on the lined, clean-shaven face of the Under-Secretary of State. It was later learned that in the course of this conversation, Molotov had indeed adopted a bland and most benevolent tone and had gone so far to please his American guest as to complain that Chou En-lai was "a difficult partner" who made excessive demands.

That night, another visitor flew in to Geneva. Krishna Menon was little known outside New Delhi, the United Nations, and Labour Party circles in London, and when photographers' flash bulbs lit his strange fakir's silhouette, young journalists whispered to their elders, "Who is that?" Nehru had sent his close confidant to consult with Eden, it was said, to build bridges between the Western delegations there and his Asian friends. The gesture may also have been intended to show the world that British diplomacy in the Far East had the support of the 500 million Asians involved in the Colombo plan.

Krishna Menon brought no proposals with him, and there was no plan in his pocket. It has been suggested that his talks with Chou En-lai persuaded the Chinese to accept the thesis that the Cambodian-Laotian situation was radically different from that in Vietnam and that each therefore required a specific solution. It has also been suggested that his talks with Bedell Smith made acceptance of the idea of partition less difficult for the Americans. But Krishna Menon was so wordy and so full of his own importance that it would not be safe to measure the effect of his activity by either the length or number of his conversations. Darting from one contact to another, chatting and interfering, he played the part of a "germ carrier," as one Geneva delegate put it. Peace germs were what he carried, according to some; germs of discord, according to others.

It was certainly no more than a coincidence that several encouraging signs were noted on May 24, the day after Krishna Menon's arrival. This was the day on which Bidault, responding further to Molotov's five-point proposal, put forward only one amendment and two additions. He suggested that international guarantees of any agreement should be individual, rather than collective as Molotov proposed, so as to avoid a right of veto, and that the disarming of irregulars and the exchange of prisoners be specifically mentioned.

It was not the near similarity of Soviet and French working proposals, or even the first—purely formal—contact between Bidault and Chou En-lai that interested observers most, however, but a statement made to the correspondent of *Le Monde*, Jean Schwoebel, by Hoang Van Hoan, the Vietminh delegation's spokesman and ambassador in Peking. Schwoebel asked him whether the People's Army command would accept a cease-fire only on the assumption that a political agreement already existed, and the Vietminh diplomat replied, "The cease-fire must be achieved first. We set no preliminary political conditions. If, in Mr. Dong's plan, the political proposals come before those dealing with the cease-fire, that is only a matter of presentation." The French journalist wondered whether he had heard the answer correctly. It was so important and so new that he asked Hoang to repeat it, and he received the same reply with equal clarity.

Thus, one of the French objectives had been achieved; the Vietminh representatives had fallen into line with the concession made by Molotov ten days earlier. There was now agreement that military questions took priority. The negotiations were definitely making progress, and the methods of the conference were taking shape, though as yet only dimly.

On May 25, a new issue appeared on the horizon. It was known in advance that Pham Van Dong's speech in closed session would be important, but what he had to say was so striking that two experts in the French delegation hastily took notes for the benefit of Bidault and Chauvel, so that they could discuss the speech without waiting for the full text. In the fifteen-minute address, delivered in Dong's typically staccato and emotional manner, they noted a few key sentences about the demarcation of the zones on which a cease-fire could be based:

> The adjustment would be made on the basis of an exchange of territories, taking into account considerations of area, population, politics, and economics, so that each side would acquire zones representing a single holding that would be relatively large and would facilitate economic activity and administrative control in each re-

spective area. As far as possible, the demarcation line should follow geographical features or other reference points which are easily recognizable on the ground, and it should be drawn so as not to interfere with communication and transport within the respective zones.

Of course, this was not, cards down, an open offer of partition. But how else could one understand an expression such as "zones representing a single holding," the use of "demarcation line" in the singular, and the stress on "economic activity and administrative control," both of which would necessarily be much more difficult in the "leopard skin" solution proposed by the French? Coming out of the meeting, Cheysson clutched de Brébisson's arm and spluttered, "This time, Colonel, it is partition—and *they* are offering it!"[3]

The best-informed commentators interpreted Pham Van Dong correctly. In an editorial for May 27 entitled "Toward Partition?" *Le Monde* said, "In fact, Mr. Dong has now come round to partition, which, as we have often said, represents the only possible compromise formula." And *The Times*'s correspondent wrote, "The proposals look toward a form of partition for Vietnam. . . . There is now a general feeling here that, in spite of all the caveats that such a conference requires, the Communists probably do wish to reach agreement."[4] Pierre-René Wolf put things plainly in *Paris-Normandie* the next day: "If one refused this suggestion of partition, one might—consciously or otherwise—be refusing a cease-fire. By insisting on an armistice with badly defined zones, one might well be preparing a quick triumph for Ho Chi Minh. Faced with gangrene or amputation, one should choose amputation."

It soon became plain that the Vietminh was resigned to the thought of partition, and only Bidault's prejudices prevented ac-

[3] Most of the French experts regarded partition as inevitable and preferable to all other outcomes. But it was virtually impossible for any French negotiator to propose partition, because of the ties between the governments in Paris and Saigon. Hence the impact of the Dong offer—the Vietminh would take responsibility for it.

[4] *The Times* (London), May 27, 1954.

tive exploration of these offers for two weeks or more after Pham Van Dong had spoken. Was the thought of partition too disconcerting for the Western leaders? Would it irritate the Vietminh's great allies? The subject was often touched on in unofficial conversations, bandied from one continent to another by political observers (notably Walter Lippmann and Robert Guillain [5]), and, as we have seen, given near recognition in diplomatic correspondence.

The British Government already favored it. Eden must have been pleased about the favorable reception given the proposal by his leading Commonwealth colleagues in Geneva—Richard Casey for Australia, Lester Pearson for Canada, and Krishna Menon for India.

The Chinese were careful not to reveal their intentions or preferences. But the government that had already sponsored the Panmunjom agreement must have given some thought since 1953 to the creation of a buffer state on its southern border. Such a state should be neither so small as to become a burden nor so large as to assert its individual outlook or provoke the Americans into retaliation.

This left France, the United States, and the nationalist Vietnamese. Among the last, the merest hint of partition provoked indignation, regardless of the fact that, by mid-1954, the country could have been united only by the Vietminh. In Washington, the aim was no longer to withdraw to the two deltas in preparation for a 1956 counteroffensive but, rather, to establish a strategic demarcation line, which should, of course, be drawn as far north as possible. For Bidault, it was a question of honoring the promises given to the Vietnamese leaders before the conference began. He believed that the emergence in Vietnam of two states with international standing was intolerable, but, if it was only a question of a *de facto*, purely temporary, strictly military partition, ... He allowed an epigram to form on his lips—as he so often did—even before he had given the matter careful thought: "Let's divide the pear, but we'll keep the half with the stem."

[5] *Le Monde* (Paris), May 7, 1954.

On May 27, two days after Dong's speech, Bidault accidentally met Pham Van Dong and resigned himself to exchanging a few words with him for the first time since the beginning of the conference—not without muttering *sotto voce* to a neighbor, "It's not the first time I've had to shake a murderer by the hand."

That evening, Bidault had Molotov to dinner and enjoyed a pleasant and soothing conversation. According to a later account,[6] the two statesmen eventually found themselves discussing the Lake of Geneva and its fish. Bidault remarked that a fishing party would give him the opportunity to row the short distance to the French shore. His Soviet colleague expressed surprise that France was so near; seizing his chance, he asked, "But what about the fish? Are they French or Swiss?" Bidault, always the good teacher of history and geography, explained (without appearing to notice the allusion to Vietnam) that since the lake was divided into two zones, the fish belonged to the Swiss or the French depending on the bank from which they were caught. Molotov pointed the moral: "In other words, no problem for the fish—the solution is ready-made."

[6] Michel Clerc, in *Paris-Match,* June 10, 1954.

14

WASHINGTON BACKS OUT

The conference had reached an impasse; which way would it go now? Had it been the threat of American intervention that had induced the Vietminh to suggest a compromise based on a temporary military partition? Or was it some other, unknown consideration? The secrecy that had surrounded the Franco-American discussions since May 12 certainly benefited diplomatic activities: the Russians, the Chinese, and the Vietminh might well have feared that the French and American governments would suddenly reach an agreement confirming the alliance between the United States and Vietnam and, thereby, relieve the pressure for peace that Paris was exerting on Bidault.

In fact, the Laniel government had achieved very little since May 12. The preliminary conditions the United States wanted met before it would consider the possibilities of intervention were now the subject of negotiations, mainly conducted in Paris between Schumann and Dillon. These negotiations were far from finished.

Some of the seven conditions put forward by the Americans on May 15 raised no difficulties. Points 1 and 2 (requests for assistance from France and the Associated States) caused no problems, but their implementation depended on how the other conditions were met. Point 3 (a warning by the United Nations) was well on the way to fulfillment. Thailand, acting on American advice, had raised the matter in the Security Council on May 27. It protested that the Vietminh advance in Laos posed a threat to its frontiers and asked for the dispatch of U.N. observers. On June 3, the Security Council put the Thai request on its agenda. France had withdrawn its original opposition to this move, and the Soviet Union was alone in voting against it (but without using its veto). However, a Soviet veto seemed unavoidable when the Security Council came to examine the substance of the request. In the meantime, General William J. Donovan, the wartime director of the Office of Strategic Services (OSS) and now American ambassador in Bangkok, had arrived in Saigon. It seemed reasonable to assume that this almost legendary figure was not traveling as a tourist.

A few days before, another American had appeared there: U.S. Air Force Colonel Edward G. Lansdale, a top CIA agent in the Far East. Lansdale, who had belonged to General Donovan's OSS, had been sent to the Philippines in 1951, in order to help President Quirino's government overcome the Huk rebellion. He had become an efficient and trusted advisor to Ramon Magsaysay, the Secretary of Defense, who became President of the Philippines in 1953. Lansdale had first visited Indochina in the summer of 1953 and had been nominally attached to the American military mission there; he had taken a special interest in counter-guerrilla programs and intelligence work. He had also established relations with some Vietnamese politicians, including Phan Huy Quat, of the Dai Viet party.[1] Then, too, it was shortly after his visit that Ngo Dinh Nhu founded his "Movement of National Union for Independence and Peace." In May, 1954, just after the fall of Dien Bien Phu, Lansdale (who had returned to the Philippines) was called to Washington to address a special group of officials from the State Department and the CIA. According to Wise and

[1] Robert Shaplen, *The Lost Revolution* (New York, 1965), pp. 101–2.

Ross, Dulles was present at that meeting.[2] Lansdale then left Washington for Saigon with instructions from Dulles to find out quickly what could still be done to save Vietnam from Communism.

In Paris, meanwhile, the French Government had serious reservations about Washington's other conditions. It had been fairly easy to reconcile the differences of opinion about Point 4 (the Associated States' independence and right of secession). The State Department deferred to the very firm attitude taken by the French Government, and new instructions sent to Dillon and communicated to Parodi on May 27 opened the way to an agreement on the following procedure:

1. France would sign the treaties of independence and association with Vietnam as soon as possible. At the moment of signature, the French President would affirm that the French Union consisted of free and sovereign states. The President of the United States would then have the opportunity to declare that the independence of the Associated States was a fact. The United States, and other countries as well, could thereafter guarantee this independence.

2. A genuinely national Vietnamese government would be formed. France would find ways to make the Vietnamese Defense Minister feel that he was playing a larger part in the defense of the territory.

3. The Associated States would have a larger share in the American military-aid program.

4. France would make plain its intention of withdrawing the Expeditionary Corps when hostilities ended, subject to any commitments within the French Union that might make it necessary to retain some forces on a reduced scale.

But, during the last few days, the Vietnamese Government had added pressures of its own to those exerted by the United States. The course of the Geneva negotiations had convinced the Vietnamese Government that partition was in the offing, and Nguyen

[2] David Wise and Thomas B. Ross, *The Invisible Government* (New York, 1964), p. 167.

Quoc Dinh thought it was already inevitable. But the Vietnamese nationalists had made it plain that under no circumstances could they associate themselves with such a decision or even accept it. What were they to do if the great powers agreed to this solution? The nationalists were determined not to be handed over to Communist domination as a result of any partition. Only the United States seemed capable at that moment of giving such a guarantee. In order to obtain it, it was necessary to achieve independence once and for all; but for nationalist Vietnam, independence could be granted only by France.

Prince Buu Loc urged this point in his talks with Bedell Smith, Bidault, and Jacquet between May 25 and May 27, but he sensed certain reservations on the French side. He was soon to discover that some of the French ministers had come to fear—in the light of Pham Van Dong's proposals about the French Union—that, if the treaties were signed, they might apply one day to a Vietnam dominated by Ho Chi Minh, that a "people's democracy" might be a member of the French Union.

Buu Loc was on the point of returning to Saigon empty-handed when Reynaud suddenly suggested that the treaties be signed before the Prince left. "We shall only initial them," Buu Loc replied. "Their signature is a matter for our heads of state."

The treaties were initialed on June 4. Vietnam's independence had now been recognized by France for the fifth time, but this time, at least, Vietnam had been recognized as a sovereign state.[3] On the same day, Dulles, in a Washington press conference, said, "France has granted as much independence as possible to the Associated States. If it left Indochina today, this independence would last only a few weeks." Buu Loc left Paris for Saigon on the following day.

Point 6 (Franco-American arrangements concerning the Vietnamese Army) was, of course, closely linked with Point 4. Here

[3] The first article of the treaty read, "France recognizes Vietnam as a fully independent and sovereign state endowed with all the powers recognized by international law." Thereafter, the word "Vietnam" could mean the State of Vietnam as well as the Democratic Republic of Vietnam, since the question of legitimacy of power remained unresolved.

again, the Americans and the Vietnamese nationalists were moving in similar directions. Buu Loc urged that the army should be put under autonomous command immediately, to demonstrate Vietnam's sovereign status, and indeed, by May 27, the Franco-Vietnamese Military High Committee had already decided to broaden Vietnamese responsibilities in operational matters. The French Government also seemed to have agreed that American advisers should undertake the training of Vietnamese combat divisions as soon as a special agreement had been signed between the Vietnamese authorities and American representatives—a development expected at any moment.

Point 7 (ratification by the French parliament of the request for assistance) seemed politically dangerous in the extreme. "Presenting such a program to the National Assembly would literally be asking for the government to fall," one of his staff said to Bidault on June 1. Laniel spoke to Dillon, and then Bidault met with Bedell Smith, in a coordinated attempt to induce the United States to abandon this requirement. But Bedell Smith only re-emphasized Washington's determination to have the French parliament ratify any agreements, so that, as he put it, their permanent character might be protected against the vicissitudes in the life of governments. The French negotiators prudently marked time on this delicate issue.

But it was Point 5 (retention of French forces in Indochina and character of the American contribution), far more than the issue of ratification, that was to prove the stumbling block of the negotiations. When Dillon first listed the seven points on May 15, Schumann pointed out the obvious French objections to the American demands. As Washington proved inflexible during the next few days, Bidault approached Bedell Smith in Geneva; the latter was rather encouraging, although he said he was personally opposed to the commitment of American land forces to the Asian theater.

The substance of his advice[4] was that France should not worry if any future intervention by the United States were limited to air and naval action, because the Marine Corps (up to six divisions,

[4] This conversation took place on May 24.

each of 20,000 men) could be brought into action without committing an act of war within the meaning of the Constitution. Congressional authority would not be necessary in such a case. For several weeks, the Laniel government held to the hope of at least obtaining assurances about commitment of the Marines (assurances such as those the Lebanese Government was to obtain in three days in 1958).

As to the future of the French effort in Indochina, on May 28 Dillon showed Schumann the new instructions he had received from Washington. Compared with the earlier proposals, these went a long way toward meeting French requirements. Point 5 had been redrafted as follows:

> France will enter into an undertaking which clearly states that:
>
> 1. The forces of the United States and other countries contributing to joint action will supplement the French forces rather than replace them.
> 2. While collective action is in progress, both the French forces now in Indochina and those reinforcements that have already been committed will be retained there throughout, with the following provisos: (*a*) the normal rotation of troops will continue and (*b*) the forces of France and the other countries taking part will gradually be withdrawn as the national armies develop and the military situation improves.
>
> Lastly, no country taking part may withdraw any troops without first consulting the other countries involved.

The French cabinet did not consider even this draft acceptable. On June 5, Bidault put another, "improved" text to Bedell Smith; the American reaction was evasive.

While these discussions and negotiations kept illusions alive at the Quai d'Orsay, the French ambassador in Washington, Henri Bonnet, assembled various facts and rumors into a picture that was to temper the optimism prevailing in Paris.

The debate in Washington between militants and moderates was reaching a climax. The interventionists had undertaken a major drive, and two themes emerged from their statements. The first was that, if there was to be fighting, it should be now and not later.[5] The implications of the second were even more dangerous: if intervention was to be decided on, there should be nothing half-hearted about it. It must lead to victory and must not be hamstrung by the notions of "sanctuary" or limitations on the use of the most effective weapons. Admiral Radford, a champion of intervention, was reported to have argued, in an executive session of the House Foreign Affairs Committee on May 26, that, if the United States joined an allied action in Indochina, the campaign would involve use of atomic weapons to win final victory. (The admiral did acknowledge that the decision on whether to intervene was a political one and outside his competence as a military commander.)[6] General Mark Clark stated, on another occasion, that, if the United States did intervene, it would have to do so without restrictions, and to win.[7] A few days later, Arthur J. Connell, National Commander of the American Legion, went even further and said that, if the United States intervened, the Legion would support an all-out effort, including the bombing of the Chinese bases from which the Communists in Indochina were supplied.[8] And MacArthur's former chief of intelligence, General Willoughby, also declared that he—and many others—favored using atomic weapons.[9]

Clearly, the interventionists were not thinking of a repetition of the Korean war. Intervention in Indochina, as they saw it, could well be the beginning of total atomic war, which would overflow the limits of that theater in order to eliminate Peking as the nerve center and power plant of Asian Communism.

To the great annoyance of this group, President Eisenhower had so far not taken a position on this issue. It was not that he was afraid of a refusal by the Congress. Dulles had told Bonnet he was convinced that the President could obtain Congressional

[5] See the speech on May 27, 1954, by Admiral Carney, Chief of Naval Operations, to the National Security Industrial Association. The text was published in *The New York Times*, May 28, 1954.

[6] *The Times* (London), June 2, 1954, from information leaked by a Democratic Representative.

[7] *L'Information* (Paris), June 29, 1954.

[8] *Le Monde* (Paris), June 9, 1954.

[9] *The Times* (London), June 2, 1954.

approval within twenty-four hours for any measure clearly in the national interest. But Eisenhower did not think an appeal to the Congress was either urgent or necessary.

The President continued to act with circumspection, in marked contrast to Truman's response to similar threats in Greece, Turkey, and Iran in 1946–47. The reason was that Eisenhower and his advisers believed they could sense the mood of the country more clearly than Dulles, the State Department, or the Pentagon. They daily became more convinced that neither the public nor the Congress (which was receiving heavy mail from the voters) would accept another entanglement like the Korean War, or a new commitment of American soldiers to the paddies of Asia, for the sake of a police action of doubtful moral standing. The idea of intervention in Indochina had been unpopular from the first, and it was even less popular now.

Reasons other than the "pulse of the country" contributed to the President's cautious attitude, one of the strongest being the opposition of a majority of the military leaders. In their opinion, the envisaged intervention could not long be confined to an air-sea operation. The action would expand quickly and unpredictably, and, at the time, the United States lacked the resources to conduct even a limited land war in Asia. In this sense, America's devotion to the strategy of massive retaliation had robbed it of much of its military flexibility.

Generals Ridgway and Twining were the most forceful opponents of intervention.[10] Ridgway estimated that eight American divisions would be required for a decisive victory over the Vietminh; these troops were simply not available.[11] He also feared that any intervention by American forces in Indochina would induce China to send in even stronger forces and that this would ultimately force an unlimited effort on the West. General Twining

[10] *The Times* (London), June 15, 1954. On General Ridgway's opposition, see also "What Ridgway Told Ike: War in Indochina Would Be Tougher than Korea," *U.S. News & World Report*, June 25, 1954, and General Matthew B. Ridgway and H. H. Martin, *Soldier: Memoirs of Matthew B. Ridgway* (New York, 1956), pp. 274–78.

[11] At that time, the United States had only twenty divisions spread from Korea to West Germany. *L'Information* (Paris), June 11, 1954.

did not wish to commit the U.S. Air Force to operations in which it might be prevented from striking at the centers of enemy power, as it had been in Korea. As to the Navy, it appeared to have no wish for intervention, despite Admiral Carney's fiery speeches.

Finally, the influence of the Secretary of Defense, Charles E. Wilson, turned out to be extremely important. It was well known that he and George Humphrey, Secretary of the Treasury, had been thoroughly opposed to any suggestion of intervention from the start. Wilson returned from a tour of inspection in the Far East[12] on June 2, and the National Security Council met on the very next day to hear his report. Wilson's main thought—which he had expressed in the past and would express again—was that military means were not in themselves an adequate counter to Communism in the world at large. "We cannot destroy false ideas with bullets," he said in an address at Columbia University on June 8.[13] In his opinion, colonialism and its consequences were still at the root of the Indochina crisis.[14] The French were in their present predicament, many Asians thought, because they had not granted real independence to Vietnam and had failed to attach due importance to nationalism. The advance of Communism was largely due to this lack of understanding. In Indochina, he assured his listeners, most of the problems were far more political than military.[15]

Wilson concluded that the United States could not intervene under present circumstances without, in Asian eyes, appearing to make common cause with colonialism in its death throes. The independence of the Associated States must, therefore, be put beyond all doubt. Then and only then would it perhaps become possible, given time, to wean from Communism people who had probably joined it for lack of any better alternative. The main thing was to prevent China from intervening; that would be the end of Indochina. In any case, America must regain the confidence of those Asians who had been shaken, or turned against it, by its

[12] Wilson had not been able to visit Indochina.
[13] See *L'Information* (Paris), June 12, 1954.
[14] Report from Washington in *The Times* (London), June 4, 1954.
[15] *L'Information* (Paris), June 4, 1954.

minatory and anti-Chinese stance. It must make its will for peace shine forth.

Wilson's report gave the White House fresh grounds for persevering in its caution. Wilson's influence began to grow quickly in Washington, suddenly creating a climate unfavorable to intervention. It was not long before the effects were felt in Paris.

Although Churchill had once more assured the House of Commons that British policy would not alter until the end of the Geneva talks, the British—who did not wish to go on being scapegoats forever—finally agreed to the holding of military talks at the chiefs-of-staff level about Southeast Asia. As far as they were concerned, however, it was understood that these talks would be confined to a technical study of the problems posed by the defense of Southeast Asia and that they would not, under any circumstances, be binding on the governments concerned. In other words, they would clear the ground for political decisions whose time was yet to come. To emphasize that these were routine consultations and not preparations for a security pact, the British asked that no Asian general staff (Philippine or Thai) be associated with the talks, and this was agreed on. Therefore, the participants included representatives of only five powers: the United States, Great Britain, France, Australia, and New Zealand.

The talks, held in great secrecy in a small conference room in the Pentagon, opened on June 3. The delegations were very small. Admiral Carney led the U.S. delegation; Field-Marshal Harding, the British; and General Valluy, the French.

The discussions soon showed the hollowness of the hopes to which the French Government was still clinging. Fundamentally, as Valluy stressed, the work of the conference largely depended on the answer to the basic question of whether the French army could hold Tonkin. The discussions soon revealed that, in order to hold the Red River delta, the Expeditionary Corps would need more air support and the assistance of land forces. The senior officers present quickly reached agreement on the scale of forces and resources required, but, when Valluy asked where these reinforcements might be found, the embarrassed silence of his colleagues made it clear that, in the short term at least, France must continue to depend on its own resources. Soon, it was apparent that the United States, the only power capable of providing the necessary air support, would make it available only as part of a joint effort. As to land forces, none of the English-speaking nations felt able to provide them. The British, though they did not say so, regarded the conflict as primarily a French and Vietnamese one and believed that these two powers had not yet committed all their resources. The Americans stated unequivocally that the defense of Asia was a matter for Asians. In spite of the assertions of Bedell Smith in Geneva and Dillon in Paris, the American Chiefs of Staff had not the slightest intention of sending Marines to Southeast Asia.[16] The Australians and New Zealanders pleaded the numerical weakness of their armed forces. In short, none of these states would do anything immediately; they all would need time to prepare a worth-while intervention. But France needed immediate help.

General Valluy insisted several times that the white powers had to show solidarity in this critical moment. An allied guarantee of the Red River delta would have a decisive effect in Geneva and would certainly contribute to securing an armistice on honorable terms. His plea fell flat. France was left to its own devices. Everything indicated that the Anglo-Saxon general staffs were resigned to the imminent loss of Indochina and, therefore, unwilling even to consider the possibility of risking the few divisions available to them.[17]

[16] In the course of this conference, Radford suggested to Valluy that South Korean troops be used instead of U.S. Marines. Dulles, who was told of this by Bonnet, found it unthinkable that the French should reject such an offer. America, he said, would refuse no offer of help that might enable it to secure victory. President Syngman Rhee had already offered a South Korean division to France, as reported in *The New York Times,* February 14, 1954; France did not accept the offer.

[17] The talks ended on June 9. No final communiqué was published; apparently, the conference resulted in a report to the five governments involved. After reviewing the resources available to the non-Communist powers in Southeast Asia, the experts analyzed the various possibilities (overt intervention by China, complete collapse of French defenses in Indochina, institution of an effective armistice with a clearly defined demarcation line, etc.) and listed the steps necessary to deal with each development. In other words, they defined the strategy to be adopted if the Geneva conference failed.

Nevertheless, the rapid decline of the military situation made it likely that President Eisenhower would ask Congress, before its current session ended, for authority to intervene in Indochina if necessary. The battle for Hanoi was drawing near, and this gave the interventionists fresh hope, because they thought that the defense of the northern capital would arouse U.S. public opinion. It would then be easier to demand energetic action to break the Communist offensive. Thus, new pressures were already being brought to bear on the President to induce him—at long last—to come to a decision. But the White House remained immobilized; it wanted to help France achieve an honorable armistice, but its eagerness was balanced by its reluctance to battle a powerful popular aversion to any commitment of American troops in Asia.

In view of all these factors, Bonnet held out little hope for a decision in favor of intervention, at least in the near future.

In the meantime, the assurances that Schumann was hearing in Paris made him rather impatient with Bonnet's doubts and fears. Dillon told him on June 7 and 8 (with the approval of "the highest level,"[18] as he put it) that, if the United States decided not to commit land forces in Southeast Asia, it might, nonetheless, "consider the participation of Marines in a military action prepared in advance within the framework of a general plan of operations."

These words were reported to Bonnet, and they convinced him that he had to clear up the matter once and for all. What was the reason for the contradictions that had been cropping up for weeks now between what was said in Washington, on the one hand, and in Paris and Geneva, on the other?

At a press conference on June 8, Dulles added one more to the long chain of ambiguities he had been putting together for three months when he virtually adopted Wilson's point of view in saying that the United States did not contemplate unilateral action in Indochina "unless the whole nature of Communist aggression" in Asia changed and that, in consequence, the government would not ask Congress to authorize action in Indochina.[19] This was a

[18] Who could this have been, apart from Vice President Nixon?
[19] *The New York Times,* June 9, 1954.

sensational and fateful statement (its importance in the context of Geneva will become clearer in the course of the next chapter), and its immediate effect in Washington was considerable.

It was in these circumstances that Bonnet finally succeeded in obtaining a clear explanation from Dulles. Bonnet was a good diplomat, and he reported to his government that this conversation had been "as lively as it was friendly." In fact, on this occasion, Dulles was brutally frank. He said, in effect, that France wished to acquire an option on unleashing an American operation—that it wanted to be able to call the forces of its ally to the rescue at its convenience and in its own good time, if things went badly at Geneva or in Indochina. But, the Secretary of State said harshly, "The United States cannot lend itself to this game."

Bonnet then asked whether or not the United States was prepared to commit Marines in Indochina. The Secretary of State replied that discussions on this subject were futile at that stage. If the United States entered the war in Indochina, it would do so with the firm resolve to win, and it would not stop short of victory. Troops, including Marines, might be used, but there was no way of predicting more precisely what forces would be employed. The U.S. Government could not make any commitment.

The conclusion the Laniel government would finally be forced to draw from this forthright statement was obvious: the American Government was not prepared to enter publicly into any commitments about military intervention in the Far East. It was, therefore, impossible to base any policy in Geneva on an inflexible position. It would be necessary to compromise.

In addition, the French Government was informed on the following day that the U.S. Government wished to retain its freedom of action until the end of the current negotiations. American spokesmen also indicated that the Pentagon intended to remain free to decide, at the time when intervention might be requested (in other words, when all the conditions put forward on May 15 had been fulfilled), whether the military situation in Indochina still offered enough favorable possibilities to make action worth taking.

To remove any lingering doubts, President Eisenhower confirmed, during a press conference on June 10. that he did not contemplate asking Congress for authority to take any special action in Indochina. American intervention in Indochina, as Reuters immediately informed the four corners of the earth, now seemed to be definitely excluded. No doubt this evasive action was founded on wisdom, but it was not calculated to ease either the endeavors of Bidault in Geneva or the position of the Laniel government in Paris.

Dulles felt obliged to explain the "retreat." On June 10, in Seattle, he told the annual convention of Rotary International that Great Britain was responsible for the failure of the proposed actions. He also threatened another "agonizing reappraisal" of American foreign policy (aimed at France, this time) if the EDC treaty were not ratified.[20] On June 11, he made a similar speech in Los Angeles,[21] which he repeated on television on June 12: all of America's efforts to save Indochina through concerted action had been doomed, he said, by the reticence of its allies, just as Stimson's efforts had been thwarted in 1931 during the Manchurian affair.[22]

These were only pretexts. In fact, Dulles, when he left Washington for the west coast on June 9, had known for at least two days that French supremacy in Vietnam had ended and that power in Saigon would "change color." Moreover, Moscow had obtained the same information at almost the same moment.

Immediately after initialing the Franco-Vietnamese treaty on June 4, Prince Buu Loc left for Saigon. He was faced at once with a new political organization, the "Front for National Safety," which had been created on May 27 by Ngo Dinh Nhu (who had founded the "Movement of National Union for Independence and Peace" the summer before). This front, composed of the

20 *The New York Times,* June 11, 1954.
21 *The New York Times,* June 12, 1954.
22 Dulles's attempts to create a British scapegoat were made easier by Chalmers M. Roberts's editorial in *The Washington Post,* June 7, 1954; however, they were severely criticized by James Reston in *The New York Times,* June 13, 1954. Reston said "This picture, omitting any reference to Congressional or White House opposition to using force in Asia . . . is one of the most misleading oversimplifications ever uttered by an American Secretary of State, but it allocates blame and furnishes an alibi."

Catholics of the center, some of the Caodaists and the Hoa Hao, the northerners of Phan Huy Quat's Dai Viet party, and a few other nationalists, was demanding the immediate establishment of a new regime to fight the Communists and insisting that only Ngo Dinh Diem was qualified to lead it. The successive arrivals in Saigon of Colonel Lansdale on June 1 and General Donovan on June 3 were directly connected with this move by Nhu.[23]

Since May, Bao Dai had been negotiating in France with Ngo Dinh Diem.[24] The result of American insistence, the cooperation of some French Catholics, and Bao Dai's calculations was that at the beginning of June, the ex-emperor finally agreed to place the former mandarin at the head of the government.[25] From that day on, Dulles felt reassured and "resigned himself" to partition. He no longer saw any need for the United States to intervene on behalf of a moribund colonialism or to fight for the "unity" of that distant country. The opening move had been made, the principal pawn had been advanced; and given patience and wise maneuvering, it should lead to the establishment in Southeast Asia of a political and strategic system that was wholly under American direction.

[23] See above, p. 211. After a week in Saigon, Lansdale had decided that only Diem had sufficient suppoft to salvage the situation. Wise and Ross, *op. cit.*, p. 167.

[24] On the Ngo family and Diem's career, see Bernard B. Fall, *The Two Viet-Nams* (New York, 1966), pp. 234–45; Shaplen, *op. cit.*, pp. 105–13; and Georges Chaffard, *Indochine. Dix ans d'indépendence* (Paris, 1964), pp. 21–26.

[25] According to direct and well-informed sources, Bao Dai, who had never liked or trusted Diem, believed that the moment had come to "raise the mortgage" personified at that precise moment by his former minister. Bao Dai entrusted Diem with power in such dramatic and difficult circumstances that one would have had to be a bit oblivious to accept it. (Diem himself once admitted that he had no "competition" then. Denis Warner, *The Last Confucian*, New York, 1963, p. 66.) Bao Dai reportedly said at the time that Diem would be "finished in three to six months" and totally discredited. But in giving power to Diem, Bao Dai knew that he was also bringing the Americans over to his side (at least temporarily) and that he was considerably improving the position of the Vietnamese nationalists vis-à-vis the French. According to the same sources, it became clear in the course of Bao Dai's talks with the American's that Diem was the candidate of the Department of State (and even of the Dulles brothers), but that influential elements within the CIA were not hiding their preference for Phan Quang Dan.

15

BIDAULT LEAVES THE GAME

In Geneva, on the afternoon of Tuesday, June 8, Molotov rose to speak. He had returned five days earlier from a short visit to Moscow,[1] and it was rumored backstairs in the Palais des Nations that Moscow had authorized him to work out a sensible solution to the Indochinese problem with his colleagues; talk of a *détente* filled the air. Bidault had spoken before Molotov, and his summary of the results already achieved had left his listeners surprised by the balance, moderation, and unaccustomed optimism of his views. But Molotov's first sentences told Bidault that he was being confronted with his own failures; his belated overtures were being rejected with calculated brutality:

> The task incumbent upon the participants in the Geneva conference is heavy with responsibility. They must endeavor to stop military operations as soon as possible and contribute to the re-establishment of a solid and lasting peace in Indochina. . . . It is impossible to overlook the fact that the participants obviously do not all

[1] He was supposedly rushing home to see his newborn twin grandchildren. However, the aircraft of the Soviet delegation carried twenty-six passengers on this occasion.

> regard their task in the same light. This can be established by looking at what goes on at the Geneva conference and around the conference while it is in progress. . . . The participants are not unanimous in wishing that peace should be re-established as quickly as possible in Indochina. In fact, while taking part in the Geneva conference one may set oneself the task, not of re-establishing peace in Indochina, but of proving that it is impossible to reach agreement. . . . But those who are striving to prove the impossibility of an agreement have not merely chosen the road that leads to prolongation of the war: they are in fact preparing to extend the war even further, with all the dangerous consequences that involves.

Molotov, much given to plain speaking, went on to denounce the Southeast Asian pact, the military talks in Washington, the Thai attempt to shift the Indochina question from Geneva to the United Nations, and "the fears . . . felt by aggressive people in certain countries that the Geneva conference may succeed." He continued with a lengthy and ponderous indictment of the Bao Dai regime, even blaming it because the defense of Dien Bien Phu had been furnished by "all kinds of foreigners." Then, he fired a tirade point blank at Bidault: "Today we have heard a statement by the head of the French delegation, who said that the Geneva conference had already achieved some results on the road to peace. The significance that can be attributed to this will depend upon what the French delegation does in future to conform with it."

Why was Molotov slamming the door in Bidault's face after treating his old colleague so respectfully during the past month in Geneva? It seems unlikely that East-West relations were reassessed during his visit to Moscow, or that the Russians had attached much importance to the Franco-American talks that had begun on May 12. Molotov must have known of the progress of the French request over the past weeks, if only from the press. No, Bidault drew such a fulminating attack not because the French request had been made but because it had not, thus far, achieved anything.[2] Nothing is more pitiful than a threat that fails to mate-

[2] Dulles's statement of June 8 was not yet known in Geneva, and Eisenhower's was not made until June 10. But the failure of the five-power chiefs-of-staff meeting and the popularity of Charles Wilson's ideas had been well publicized.

rialize. If Bidault had obtained an unconditional promise of American intervention in the event the talks failed, he would have been a respected opponent in Geneva—especially because the beginning of talks in Washington about a Southeast Asia pact, and Laniel's and Buu Loc's initialing of the agreements granting Vietnam unconditional independence, should have strengthened his diplomatic standing. (Of course, there were plenty of critics waiting to tell him that the French "war aims" were shrinking to the vanishing point.) But, now that Bidault had been rebuffed once again by the Americans, the Soviets and Chinese saw him as no more than an opponent who had tried to scare them and had failed to do so. They found him far too heavily burdened with reservations and doubts and much too slow in grasping the importance of the partition offer the Vietminh delegation had made on May 25 (and would confirm on June 10, at the evident instigation of its two powerful partners).

The purpose of Molotov's pitiless admonishment, at a moment when the French National Assembly was starting another debate about Indochina, seemed clear enough. Bidault immediately whispered to one of his colleagues, "He's after my skin." The next day, the *Journal de Genève* editorialized, "Molotov wanted to make it plain to the French parliament that Bidault . . . is not the man with whom Moscow and its partners are inclined to negotiate." A few days earlier, on May 30, François Mitterand had already noted ironically, in the *Courrier de la Nièvre,* that the fate of the cabinet depended on "Mr. Molotov's smiles." Bidault had few illusions when he arrived back in Paris some hours later, puffy with fatigue, pale, a strand of disheveled hair stuck on his damp forehead, a bitter smile on his lips. As long as there was a good chance of compromise in Geneva, the parliament's desire to maintain a French presence at the conference had saved the Laniel government, even though it was weak and torn by dissension. But, as soon as the enemy ceased to regard Bidault as a worth-while opponent, many French leaders decided that the time had come to change crews, even in mid-course. In addition, the enemies of the European Defense Community seized the opportunity to shoot down a team that included Pleven, the inventor of the European army.

On June 9, Bidault stood at the rostrum of the Palais Bourbon and displayed the cavalier courage he had made his own. He tried, naturally enough, to establish the impression that he was about to become the victim of the Muscovite barbarian: "Yesterday we heard an unscheduled speaker attack us—I refer to the Minister of Foreign Affairs of the Soviet Union." Bidault thought it best to broach some subjects before his enemies did so. He went on:

> Some have spoken of a double game at Geneva and of negotiations supposedly started solely in the hope of seeing them fail. . . . If anybody can show that I have committed one action running counter to peace or favoring war, I am waiting for him to rise to his feet and speak. . . . I have been warned that the government would be brought down if I did not bring back the certainty of an agreement. If you believe that another negotiator has a better chance of success, I am ready to hand over the task and its responsibilities to him.

Bidault had challenged one and all to question his eagerness for peace; now, Pierre Mendès-France took up the challenge. The Radical Deputy roundly denounced Bidault for having made so little effort to contact those best suited to help solve the problem —the Chinese,[3] the Indians,[4] and the Vietminh. He went further, accusing Bidault of having played a "diabolical game of poker" with the Americans by asking for the intervention of their air force, since the temptation to merge the Indochinese disasters into a general war was very great. Mendès-France added, "We shall be all the stronger if we cannot be suspected of hidden motives or intrigues. We must be sure of having done everything to secure peace—an honorable peace, which must not be a capitulation."

General Koenig and Jacques Soustelle supported Mendès-France's offensive. Meanwhile, outside the National Assembly, Raymond Aron, in *Le Figaro*, denounced the "diplomatic sleep-walking" that seemed to him to characterize the French delegation's activities. In

[3] Curiously enough, Bidault refrained from revealing that he had held a conversation with Chou En-lai on June 1. He had taken extraordinary precautions to keep this meeting secret.

[4] Bidault pointed out that he had met with Krishna Menon.

L'Information, Geneviève Tabouis, a careful observer of events in Geneva, claimed that only a "change of climate"—a move away from the immobility displayed by the French representatives, who had refused to make the necessary contacts—would produce practical results. Then came another blow for Bidault: in the *New York Herald Tribune* of June 8, 1954, the most articulate spokesmen for the "big stick policy," the Alsop brothers, forecast a "massive attack" by the Vietminh against Hanoi and the rest of the Red River delta around June 20.

During the night of June 9, Laniel's government found itself in a minority by 322 votes to 263, but the question of confidence had not yet been raised. Obstinacy was Laniel's ruling virtue, and he set off in search of some loophole. According to the rules, he was not forced to resign unless his opponents mustered 314 votes against him in a vote of confidence, and, if they did, he could dissolve parliament. Laniel relates that Bidault, who had already returned to Geneva, sent him a telegram that said, "If there are 313, tell them I stay put. If there are 314, tell them it's dissolution."[5] But the Radicals in the cabinet, Edgar Faure and Martinaud-Deplat among others, refused to stay on in these circumstances. The government was collapsing as much from internal division as from the blows of its opponents.

At this point, an ebullient person burst upon the Paris scene, direct from Geneva: Frédéric-Dupont, appointed minister for the Associated States only a few days earlier, in place of Jacquet, who had been forced to resign at Bidault's insistence. Late in the morning of June 11, Frédéric-Dupont dragged Laniel off to the Elysée Palace to inform the President of the Republic of a "tremendous offer" the Vietminh had made in Geneva.[6] The Premier and the Minister asked that an extraordinary meeting of the Council of Ministers be called to arrange to adjourn the debate in the National Assembly, in view of the impending success of the negotiations and the imminence of peace in Indochina. Unfortunately

[5] Joseph Laniel, *Le drame indochinois* (Paris, 1957), p. 114.
[6] See below, chap. 16, pp. 233–35.

for Laniel and Frédéric-Dupont, Bidault did not agree with them.

Bidault, in Geneva, had been given only a sketchy account of the offer by Frédéric-Dupont. He was, in any case, too exhausted to appreciate immediately the implications of the step Frédéric-Dupont had taken. The next morning, as soon as he had been filled in by Chauvel, he called the Elysée, as well as several of his more sober-minded colleagues, to stop Frédéric-Dupont's venture and assure all concerned that the success the latter claimed, although not without interest, was no more than one episode in a protracted dialogue. Bidault's categorical condemnation applied to both the intentions and the methods of his colleague.

Frédéric-Dupont knew little about the ways of international negotiations—the hints, the quiet pressures, the disappointments, the tactical moves, and the influence of pure chance. He was also enormously eager to secure a quick and spectacular result. And so he had mistaken a bold peace feeler—valuable only so long as it remained secret and allowed a French negotiator to reply in similar terms—for genuine peace conditions. Once Frédéric-Dupont's meddling was ended, the discussions in the military commission (following the meeting between de Brébisson and Ha Van Lau on May 19) continued to bear fruit.

Nevertheless, Frédéric-Dupont's activities nearly succeeded in saving the government. Even an observer of the caliber of *The Times*'s correspondent in Paris wrote, on June 11, "Twenty-four hours ago, most people had written off the Laniel Government. . . . Tonight Paris is full of new and exciting rumours, caused by the unexpected arrival this morning from Geneva of M. Frédéric-Dupont. . . . It is generally supposed that M. Frédéric-Dupont is the bearer of a new proposition made to him by the Vietminh delegation at Geneva. . . . If these rumours are well founded, there may be a surprise in store . . . about the fate of the government."[7] As it turned out, the Vietminh delegation's very abrupt denial of a United Press dispatch carrying parts of the Frédéric-Dupont "proposal," as well as some final bungling by Laniel in the debate on the question of confidence, wiped out the effect of Frédéric-Dupont's

[7] *The Times* (London), June 12, 1954.

move and delivered the death blow to the government, which was again defeated on June 12, by 306 votes to 296.[8]

As if to reconfirm Bidault's elimination and contribute an American push to his fall, Eisenhower had said two days earlier that he did not contemplate asking Congress for the right to take any initiative whatsoever in Indochina. Meawhile, at two consecutive press conferences held at San Francisco and Los Angeles on June 10 and 11, Dulles—who was described by *Le Monde*'s Washington correspondent as being in the process of resigning himself to partition—revealed the conditions under which the United States would commit itself to military action in Indochina on the French side. And in *The New York Times* of June 9, 1954, James Reston, well informed as always, asserted that the possibility of U. S. intervention in Indochina was "fading."

And so Bidault was dismissed not once but three times—first by the leader of Soviet foreign policy, then by the French National Assembly, and finally by those on whose intervention he had founded his last hope.

[8] On this occasion, 33 Radicals and 44 URAS (includng Soustelle) voted against the government.

16

VIETMINH AND CHINESE INITIATIVES

The most productive stage of the Geneva conference began very quietly, on June 9, 1954—just one day after Molotov's indictment had shaken Bidault and spread dismay among the participants. We have stressed the importance of the conversations between Colonel de Brébisson and Colonel Ha Van Lau, who had already reached an agreement about the fate of the prisoners and the wounded on June 2. The next day, the military committees went to work. Three committees were established—one for each of the states in Indochina—under the chairmanship of General Delteil and Ta Quang Buu, the Vietminh vice-minister of national defense; they included, in addition to de Brébisson and Lau, Colonel Fleurant and, as the representative of the Vietnamese nationalist army, Colonel Le Van Kim. The basic tasks of the military committees were to determine the terms for a cease-fire and to map the regrouping areas for the two armies.

Although the nationalist Vietnamese blocked any immediate progress, the military committees operated in a relatively relaxed atmosphere and, above all, under conditions of secrecy much more favorable to confidential exchanges than the plenary sessions of the nine powers. This gave Chauvel (who headed the French delegation after Bidault had left for Paris on June 8) the idea of sounding out Vietminh intentions, particularly on the issue of partition, through the military committees—a matter of which Bidault hesitated a great deal before finally authorizing Chauvel to act, since he had been much less impressed than Chauvel and most of the French delegates by Pham Van Dong's May 25 speech.[1]

And so, at about 1:00 P.M. on Wednesday, June 9, Colonel de Brébisson took Colonel Ha Van Lau aside after a session of the military committee and said that Chauvel had suggested that they discuss the full significance of what Dong had said on May 25. He asked, in particular, about the expression "exchanges of territory" and whether such exchanges would be based on other than strategic and tactical considerations.

The reaction of the Vietminh military delegate the next day showed that Chauvel and de Brébisson had hit the nail on the head. Dong had shown the most lively interest in de Brébisson's questions and the ideas he had expressed during earlier meetings, Lau said, because these appeared constructive and conducive to "peace with honor." Lau added that since these questions led to the heart of the matter—in other words, to the allocation of zones—it was important to arrange secret conversations attended by himself and Ta Quang Buu, a member of the Vietminh government, on one side, and Delteil and de Brébisson, on the other. Lau, who was clearly impatient, said that the sooner the meeting was fixed the better, but he left the choice of time and place to the French.

That very evening, between 10:00 P.M. and midnight, the extraordinary meeting was held on the outskirts of Geneva, in an isolated villa that had hastily been rented for the purpose. It is customary to talk about the tortuous ways of Asian diplomats, but Buu—a former scoutmaster and history teacher, well informed in military subjects, a firm-looking man with a prizefighter's neck and shoulders and a square head topped by a thick mop of black hair—went straight to the point. Brusquely, he unfolded a map of Indochina and put his hand on the Red River delta with the gesture of a

[1] See above, chap. 13, pp. 206–7, for Dong's speech.

Roman emperor. "We need this," he said. "We need a state; we need a capital for our state; we need a port for our capital."[2] Could not Mr. Buu go into more detail? This gesture . . . the north . . . a capital . . . a port . . . and what else? Buu, refusing to be drawn out, simply dwelt on the importance his government attached to central Vietnam and the area of Hue. He refused to elaborate.

The French representatives asked him whether his proposal was not tantamount to splitting the country, and Buu replied that it was only a question of a temporary, purely military partition, since provision was being made for elections throughout Vietnam. These elections would make it possible to unite the country by legal means, and the Vietminh was determined that they should be held.

The French then asked what territorial compensation the Vietminh envisaged in return for the evacuation of French Union forces from Tonkin, but to this question Buu would not give an immediate answer. Delteil and de Brébisson made it clear that partition could not even be contemplated in Paris or Saigon unless the French and the Vietnamese nationalists secured control over the whole of the country south of the 18th Parallel. Buu cut short this discussion and proceeded to talk at length about the advantages of the discreet bilateral procedure they were following, as opposed to the drawbacks of the conference and supervision by the nine powers. He was insistent about the desirability of keeping their conversations secret. Colonel de Brébisson made a point of impressing upon the Vietminh representatives that achieving a peace mattered more to them than it did to the French Union forces: if the Geneva talks failed, the battle in the Red River delta would burst out again with renewed violence and wreck whatever the fighting had spared so far, particularly if the conflict was internationalized, as seemed likely. Buu's and Lau's eagerness to hold these talks in the military committees clearly suggested that Vietminh officials had discussed the same possibility among themselves.

Buu's proposals were the most novel and daring put forward

[2] Accounts of this conversation vary. Was the word "Tonkin," for instance, actually mentioned? It is certain that Buu pointed to the area of northern Indochina on the map.

since the beginning of the Geneva conference. Since Bidault was in Paris for the National Assembly debate, Delteil and de Brébisson awoke Frédéric-Dupont and Chauvel immediately (it was now 4:00 A.M., June 11) to report Buu's proposals. We have seen how Frédéric-Dupont subsequently telephoned and then rushed off to Paris, hoping to cut short the debate in the National Assembly, save the Laniel government, and appear as the author of peace. We also know how Bidault did his best to stop his colleague's activities (although he did telegraph General Ely in Saigon on June 11 to ask him whether partition could be considered; the favorable reply he received on June 13 contributed to the more flexible attitude he adopted around June 15).

Either the Vietminh military delegates did not care about Frédéric-Dupont's sensational revelation of their secret proposal or they thought that the denial published by the delegation's spokesman provided sufficient cover. At any rate, they resumed contact with the two French officers at the same villa on June 12.

As Buu and Lau appeared pleased that their disconcerting proposals of June 10 had not been rejected outright, the two French officers urged them to declare clearly and publicly that the Vietminh had abandoned all interest in Laos and Cambodia and would, therefore, withdraw its troops from those two countries. Delteil and de Brébisson made this a French condition for any settlement. They added that the withdrawal of Franco-Vietnamese forces from the Red River delta could be considered only if the Vietminh withdrew its troops to positions north of the Porte d'Annam—in other words, north of the 18th Parallel.

The French officers also insisted on learning the other side's intentions concerning the French base at Haiphong, French commercial interests in Tonkin, and the fate of the Catholic population in the areas of Phat Diem and Bui Chu. They added that religious freedom must be respected in these areas. Buu said that his government would not think of advancing an agreement that failed to "conform with the honor of the belligerents," and that the best possible solution would be achieved by a direct understanding between France and the D.R.V. Government. Regarding French interests in Tonkin, he made a point of promising that not only financial investments but also cultural institutions and activities would be respected; evidently, he intended to give his French colleagues something of a lesson.

At the third secret meeting, which was held on the evening of June 13 and was cloaked with the same precautions as the two earlier encounters, the Vietminh delegates took a step backward. Buu felt it necessary to point out that the French stipulations about Laos and Cambodia might put an end to the conversations. How could the Vietminh declare that it was abandoning its interest in countries where it had never openly admitted having intervened? And how could the Pathet Lao and Khmer Issarak movements establish a working agreement with the royal governments of these countries, if France and the Vietminh did not contribute their good offices? This, incidentally, was the first time Buu had resorted to the propaganda double-talk that Dong used regularly at the meetings of the nine powers.

Buu then confirmed that Haiphong was, indeed, the seaport his government regarded as vital. Unambiguously, he accepted the principle of a phased withdrawal of troops by both sides. He also insisted that the partition could not be a final political settlement, saying that he and his friends relied on the proposed elections to reunite Vietnam in their favor.

Two further meetings, on June 17 and 22, did not produce as many fresh ideas as the earlier conversations. Undisguised urgency remained the outstanding feature of the Vietminh spokesmen's efforts to obtain a clear-cut decision from the French on the military partition of Vietnam. They stressed that there was not the slightest chance of an armistice or substantial negotiations until the French made a categorical declaration on this issue. The two French officers could do no more than repeat to Chauvel that there should be no delay in formulating a French policy to take account of the enemy's relatively favorable attitude.

The crucial decision to base the search for an armistice and peace on the temporary partition of Vietnam was to be made in Paris on June 24, at a meeting presided over by the new Premier, Pierre Mendès-France. After that meeting, the military talks were official, although they still remained secret. With the resolute backing of the new French delegation, they gradually became part of the main body of negotiations, and they no longer provided the striking contrast they had shown earlier with the general course of the Geneva conference. But it was the first five secret and unofficial meetings that had dragged the conference out of the mire and kept the prospects of peace open despite the futile or negative official confabulations. On June 10, Molotov seemed to have blocked all progress, but, on that same day, the crucial contact was made and the Vietminh's basic conditions were elucidated: a preference for face-to-face negotiations with French representatives; a demand for military partition of Vietnam; emphasis on Vietnam proper, as distinct from Laos and Cambodia, which, it now appeared, might be treated as separate issues. (What was even clearer than the Vietminh's program was its determination—indeed, its haste—to start negotiating. Buu and Lau had demonstrated their eagerness to reach a satisfactory solution when they did not break off contact after the Frédéric-Dupont episode.) During the remainder of the conference, this clarification of Vietminh intentions proved invaluable to the new French negotiators.

Nonetheless, neither the Vietminh initiatives nor all of Chauvel's diplomatic experience and instincts seemed sufficient to save the Geneva conference. By mid-June, it appeard destined for a long slumber. "Bidault's refusal to discuss the political issues has condemned the conference to frustration, at least for the time being," wrote a *Le Monde* correspondent on June 12.[3] As Frédéric-Dupont's revelations had produced no official reaction from the Communists except an abrupt denial from the Vietminh, commentators were driven to gloomy analyses of the latest speeches by Molotov and Dong. And they seemed less inclined than ever to make the one concession without which even the British could not seriously commit themselves to negotiations: a recognition that the cases of Laos and Cambodia were radically different from that of Vietnam and must be dealt with separately, since the Vietminh forces there were foreign invaders and must simply be withdrawn.

[3] See also Philippe Devillers's interview with Phan Anh in *L'Express* (Paris), July 10, 1954.

Eden no longer talked of anything but leaving, and he let it be known that all he was looking for was a graceful formula for breaking off the talks. His speech on June 11 was largely a warning, and his conversation with Molotov on June 12 produced nothing. Bedell Smith took the likelihood of failure more seriously than Eden, who merely intended to let deputies temporarily carry on the conference. As *The Times* pointed out on June 11, "The disturbing fact is that no agreed plan is yet ready to counteract the effects of a breakdown of the conference. . . . For these reasons a sudden decision to break up the Geneva discussions would be no gain to the Western Powers."

On June 15, Eden associated himself with the initiative taken by Bedell Smith that effectively shut one side of the double doors at Geneva: the sixteen powers taking part in the Korean talks, stalemated because of the persistent refusal of the three Communist states to agree to the principle of general elections under U.N. control, officially declared the Korean negotiations ended by default. It would be an understatement to say that Chou En-lai was thunderstruck by this attitude on the part of Eden and his colleagues. His face, usually resembling a mask carved in old ivory, showed signs of agitation bordering on frenzy. Could it be that the Eastern bloc did not set the tone of the conference, call its tune, and control the opportunities it offered? Was he going to be robbed of months of negotiations, with their innumerable opportunities for international contacts? Would the Chinese People's Republic fail in its first appearance on the stage of modern diplomacy?

On Wednesday, June 16, *The Times* said that "it seems to be taken for granted that the Geneva conference will be adjourned before the weekend." The U.S. delegation let it be known that it would leave on June 24, and the White House announced that important talks between Eisenhower, Dulles, Churchill, and Eden would begin on the same day. The President of the French Republic had asked Mendès-France to form a government, but most commentators thought it unlikely that the National Assembly would accept him. Meanwhile, Bidault had announced that he was returning to Geneva. Was he planning to pull the conference down with him?

It is quite possible that it was not these developments that prompted Chou to act as he did, but everything indicated they had been the decisive factor. On the morning of June 16, Chou asked to see Eden, and a British spokesman described their conversation as "important." That afternoon, at a closed conference session on Indochina, Chou made a speech that *The Times*'s correspondent immediately described as "remarkably conciliatory." He said he was in favor of a withdrawal of all foreign troops from Laos and Cambodia, not just the withdrawal of French troops, in which case there would have been nothing new in his statement. He made it clear to members of the Western delegations—particularly to Bidault, when he returned next day—that he also regarded the Vietminh forces as "foreign."

This was the most constructive remark yet made by any delegate during the official talks in Geneva, for it lifted the heaviest burden inhibiting the progress of negotiations. Its value was enhanced a few minutes later when Molotov made a concession about the next most important point at issue—the question of armistice control—in suggesting that the representatives of Communist states could form a minority in the proposed control commission and that Indonesia could join India and Pakistan opposite Poland and Czechoslovakia.

It was clear that Chou En-lai's statement was a deliberate attempt to rescue the conference, and Chou's opposite numbers got the point immediately. Chauvel described his speech as "very interesting," and Bedell Smith said that it was "reasonable."

Chou's initiative was particularly interesting to those who were aware of the progress being made at the military talks. It was clear to all concerned that the Communist powers, having been denied all the advantages they had hoped to gain from the Korean talks, were determined not to leave Geneva without securing a settlement in Indochina. "The situation now offers real possibilities for an understanding . . . particularly, as Mr. Eden said last night, if both sides were to consider a real solution in terms of the territorial partition of Indochina."[4]

[4] Geneviève Tabouis, in *L'Information* (Paris), June 18, 1954.

The Swiss press, however, perhaps with more ingenuity than good sense, tried to find other purposes behind Chou's gesture. The *Neue Zürcher Zeitung* editorialized on June 17, "The main purpose of the concession made by the opposite camp is to enable the new [French Foreign Minister] to decide what direction he should give to French policy in Asia, a policy that will have a determining influence on the decisions Sir Winston Churchill and President Eisenhower may be called upon to take." It should be borne in mind that Mendès-France had not yet won the National Assembly's approval or announced his decision to take over the post of foreign minister.

Bidault, who had returned to Geneva for less than two days on June 16, might have shown some resentment that his opponents had opened to his successor a number of avenues that had remained closed to him. But one would have to attribute to him a meanness alien to his nature in order to imagine him capable of ruining the chances of future negotiations for those who followed him. His cutting intransigence and his passionate unrealism were those of a patriot far too aware of historical precedents to forget the importance of national continuity. France would still have to play its cards after he had gone. He spent his last few hours in Geneva as though no changes were expected at the Quai d'Orsay.

Observers were somewhat puzzled that Bidault should behave more like his own successor than like the Bidault of past weeks. He launched into more intense and, above all, more constructive diplomatic activity at that time than during the whole of the preceding period. He not only rushed off to Geneva on June 16, when Chauvel had informed him that the conference was threatening to collapse, but he also spent a long time talking to Molotov and, on June 17, had a second conversation with Chou, which ranged more widely and was more fruitful than the first. In the course of this talk, Chou clarified his concessions concerning Laos and Cambodia. And, although Bidault still refused to talk to Dong, he formally authorized the continuation of the secret military talks, provided they remained strictly *ad referendum* (in other words, only to inform the head of the delegation), even though these conversations were clearly pointing to the partition of Vietnam.

All the observers at the conference noted that it was another man who left Geneva early in the afternoon of June 17 to attend the debate on the investiture of Mendès-France—"a different man, alert and sure of himself,"[5] who said, according to *The Times*, "I have not wasted my time in coming to Geneva. We have done good work." His face was smooth; he had a mischievous glint in his eye; his gestures were firm—he was, indeed, a different person during his last twenty hours in Geneva, and no one there would have questioned his determination to achieve a sensible peace in Indochina.

It is, therefore, only fair to say that during those two days, Bidault helped Chou retrieve the conference from the impasse that his own inflexibility and reservations had done much to create. As a caretaker minister, he worked to save what, as an office-holder, he had jeopardized. Why did he do it?

It will be recalled that during the June 9 debate in the National Assembly, when Bidault had challenged his opponents to prove that he had not done everything possible to achieve peace, Mendès-France had retorted that Bidault's refusal to talk to some of his fellow representatives in Geneva must be held against him and had somewhat cruelly cast doubts on Bidault's will to succeed. It is hardly surprising that, as he relinquished his post, Bidault did his best to ensure that his moves for peace would carry a little more weight and be a little more numerous. When the accountants are coming, it is most important for the books to balance.

But the behavior of an experienced diplomat should not depend on whims and points of vanity. Bidault's evolution from haughty reserve early in May to feverish activity in those final hours in June may well have stemmed from a political analysis of changing circumstances. He evidently had gone to Geneva at first with a strong feeling of skepticism. Perhaps he had wanted to demonstrate that no agreement with the Communists was possible. Perhaps he had wanted to allow the Americans time to prepare for military inter-

[5] Pierre Artigue, in *Paris-Normandie* (Paris), June 18, 1954.

vention or set up a Southeast Asian pact. Or perhaps he had wanted time to obtain a cease-fire before Dien Bien Phu fell or—when it had fallen—before Giap's divisions laid siege to Hanoi or cut the road to Haiphong. But the repeated disappointments he had suffered in June, at the hands of his American partners—Dulles as much as Eisenhower, and even Nixon, in June—had forced him to realize the inadequacies of a diplomacy founded on intimidation.

These mortifications had caught up with Bidault at a time when the atmosphere of the conference was affecting him and when—despite the diatribes of Molotov and Dong—opportunities had appeared that no experienced diplomat could leave unexplored. His exchange of telegrams with General Ely between June 11 and June 13 may also have modified his outlook.

In fact, everything suggests that Bidault, who had gone to Geneva convinced that the undertaking was pointless—even noxious—had come to ask himself, after six weeks, where France's real interest lay. "He developed doubts," as one of his colleagues put it very simply. It was while he was in this state of indecision, and at the same time enjoying the freedom his caretaker's status gave him, that he had been confronted with Chou's major offer of June 16. He had done little to encourage the Chinese concessions, but, when they appeared, they could not be overlooked. And so it happened that Bidault, the erstwhile diehard, became a diligent negotiator for a few hours and provided a smooth transition from his own activity during the early weeks of the conference to that of Mendès-France, whom he had so often denounced as a "defeatist."

17

MENDÈS-FRANCE: ONE MONTH TO MAKE PEACE

At about three in the afternoon, June 17, 1954, Pierre Mendès-France, Radical-Socialist deputy for the Département de l'Eure, former under-secretary of the treasury in the first Blum government (1938), former minister of the economy under General de Gaulle (1944–45), ascended the rostrum of the Palais Bourbon. Four days earlier, in the evening, President René Coty had summoned him to the Elysée Palace and asked him to form the sixth cabinet in the life of that parliament. If he succeeded, Mendès-France, who had consistently denounced the evils of the war for the past seven years, would be in a position to end it. He has since described how he resisted the President's offer for several hours, struggling, as he said, like "M. Seguin's goat."[1] Nevertheless, he left the Elysée after another session the next morning as Premier-designate.

One year earlier, he had failed by thirteen votes. Since then, the

[1] Conversation with Pierre Mendès-France, December 20, 1958.

French political situation had changed markedly, the Indochina problem had become critical, and military developments there had cruelly confirmed his forebodings. In spite of these changes and in spite of the fact that in June, 1954, he was clearly the man of the moment, his chances of gaining acceptance from the National Assembly seemed little improved. According to the experts, he could expect 290 votes or, at most, 295. But one sentence in his solemnly presented declaration of policy electrified the deputies who had hesitated until then between curiosity and distrust: "I promise to resign if, one month from now, on July 20, I have failed to obtain a cease-fire in Indochina."

When Mendès-France left the rostrum, the estimates of his probable support had risen to 310 votes. But the Communists immediately undercut any advantages he might have gained by announcing that he was the first Premier since the spring of 1947 whom they would support—a poisoned gift indeed. During the late night session, the Premier-designate found the antidote: "When the barbarians invaded Athens," he said, "they burned all the houses, sparing only that of Pericles, thereby condemning to the vindictiveness of his fellow citizens the man whom they most hated and who had been of service to his country." This profession of faith by an anti-Communist and a lover of classical culture could not fail to win the votes of the middle-of-the-road deputies, caught between their fear of appointing a strongman and their longing to hear the notes of a cease-fire ring out in Indochina. At 2 A.M. on June 18, Pierre Mendès-France became Premier by 419 votes to 47, with 143 abstentions.

Since June 14, Mendès-France, with his voracious zest for work and the concentrated zeal he was known to bring to bear on his lawyer's briefs, had immersed himself in a thorough study of the situation in Indochina. He had first met with the military leaders: General Ely's return was scheduled for June 20 and could not be advanced so that they could meet before the investiture debate, but he talked for a long time on June 14 and 15 with General Guillaume, Chief of the General Staff; Generals Blanc and Fay,

Chiefs of Staff of the army and air force, Admiral Nomy; and Jean Mons, Secretary-General of the National Defense Committee. He also carefully reviewed the dispatches from Ambassador Chauvel, who sent de Margerie from Geneva to confer with him, and he called on Bidault and Frédéric-Dupont on their return from the conference. Bidault gave him a fairly friendly welcome but told him, "It's harder than you think. . . . You have illusions about those people."

This first study, carried out between his nomination and his investiture, showed that the military situation was extremely dangerous—indeed, desperate—and that it might deteriorate dramatically during the coming weeks. In addition, there was the problem of long-term damage to the national defense organization. The news from Geneva, on the other hand, continued to improve; both the official debates (Chou En-lai, as we have seen, reversed his position on the Laotian and Cambodian question on June 16) and the secret military talks sounded encouraging.

This analysis led Mendès-France to formulate what immediately became known as the Geneva "wager"; it was criticized by his political opponents, but to the man in the street it sounded like a pleasant intrusion of the spirit and methods of sport into the mysterious world of diplomacy. The world press welcomed it as a bold new departure. What induced Mendès-France to put forward this "ultimatum addressed to himself"?[2]

The new prime minister was deeply disturbed by his conversations with the senior officers. He has since admitted that, though he had long been worried about the course of the war in Indochina, he had never suspected the true state of things as described by Generals Guillaume and Blanc: the Expeditionary Corps was threatened with real catastrophe during the few weeks left before the rainy season; Hanoi was practically indefensible; the Haiphong road was in danger; a furiously contested and murderous withdrawal was in the offing. Above all, the French Army was so badly disorganized that it would take years to rebuild it as a major force.

[2] The phrase is André Siegfried's.

"We must act quickly," said the military leaders, "we must make them put their cards on the table as soon as possible."[3]

Meanwhile, experts in Asian affairs claimed that, although the Geneva conference had started moderately well, it could easily turn into another Panmunjom, which had lasted two years. It was unlikely that the Chinese could be made to hurry. They knew how to drag things out to help the Vietminh improve its war map, while stopping short of anything that might provoke atomic retaliation by the Americans.

What could be done in the circumstances? The advantages of setting a time limit for the negotiations seemed vastly to outweigh the disadvantages. By proclaiming this limited period for negotiations, Mendès-France hoped to create a psychological situation very nearly equivalent to a truce. Any enemy offensive operations during these four weeks devoted to the search for a settlement would alienate world opinion. As things stood, only the Vietminh was capable of attacking, but there would be nothing to stop the French from adjusting their positions and carrying out whatever regrouping and withdrawal seemed necessary. A scaling down of military activity would do nothing to hamper the French, but it would help to immobilize the enemy.

[3] In the National Assembly session of July 22, 1954, Mendès-France said:

"Between the time when I was designated by the President of the Republic and the time when I presented myself before you a few days later, I held long conversations with our military leaders. As a result, I became convinced that, if the war were to go on, our Expeditionary Corps, which was in a difficult position in northern Indochina, would be in danger if large reinforcements were not sent to it without delay; the dispatch of conscripts would become mandatory unless an armistice could be concluded very quickly.

"I hinted at this in my investiture statement. I was to repeat it explicitly before you at this rostrum two weeks later.

"After what I have just said, it will perhaps be easier to understand that what was called a 'wager' . . . in reality meant something quite different. If we had not concluded a cease-fire agreement within those thirty days, our young men would indeed have had to go, and even then, until they landed in Indochina, we could not have been certain that the Expeditionary Corps would not remain exposed to the most serious dangers.

"This is the explanation of the time limit of one month, which has caused some surprise . . . in France and abroad—an explanation I could not give in public at that time without revealing to the enemy the weakness of our military order of battle and the precariousness of our positions."

This strange ultimatum to the winner of the last battle—an attempt to impose a partial truce on an enemy elated by his own success—obviously involved as many political drawbacks as military advantages. Thus, it was not surprising that the diplomats considered "a month to make peace" somewhat too little, although the soldiers thought it rather too long.

Having made the wager, Mendès-France set about selecting his team, informing France's allies of his intentions and discovering theirs, and drawing up a detailed balance sheet of what his predecessors in Paris, Geneva, and Saigon had left him. He entrusted the Ministry for the Associated States to Guy La Chambre, a former minister for air and a member of what might be described as the aristocracy of the Radical Party, who had served on the commission of inquiry on Indochina set up after Dien Bien Phu under the chairmanship of René Mayer, and who was therefore well informed on Far Eastern questions.

Mendès-France retained Jean Chauvel as the head of the French delegation in Geneva because he valued the ambassador's clarity of mind, his boldness in action, and the rigorous principles on which his diplomatic doctrine was founded. He also confirmed the assignments of Delteil and Colonel de Brébisson. As negotiations progressed, Claude Cheysson was given increased responsibility; he was a young diplomat with first-hand knowledge of Indochinese affairs, acquired while serving as an adviser to the Vietnamese Government, and he had thus far been restricted to a purely technical role. The Premier's closest associates—Ambassador Philippe Baudet, Georges Boris, Pelabon, Soutou, and Jean Laloy—all cooperated, in Paris and Geneva, in furthering the negotiations; General Ely, in Saigon, kept in constant contact with them.

On June 20, Eden and Bedell Smith left Geneva for London and Washington. Before they went, Chauvel persuaded them to secure their governments' official acceptance of a condition the French regarded as vital: that any future armistice would be negotiated in three separate committees, thereby stressing the different problems affecting the three Associated States and the special nature of the Vietnamese settlement. Both Eden and Bedell Smith stopped over in Paris and were received by Mendès-France. Eden already knew Mendès-France well enough to look forward to co-operation with him; Bedell Smith, however, shared the general American distrust for the French "new deal" (the cordiality of Eisenhower's letter to Coty a few days later did little to compensate for its note of admonishment), and evidently Mendès-France failed at first to win him over. But the head of the American delegation was as interested as Eden in the Vietminh suggestions about partition and was also reassured by Mendès-France's declared intention not to weaken the Atlantic alliance or to neglect any aspects of the negotiations involving military support.

Eden promised to return to Geneva well before Mendès-France's month was over, but Bedell Smith was reluctant to make a similar promise, maintaining that the presence of Ambassador Johnson lent appropriate weight to American representation in Geneva. This disappointed Mendès-France, who firmly believed that only unqualified Anglo-American support would enable him to extract conditions acceptable to the West and the state of Vietnam from the Communist powers.

The appointment of a new and independent head of the Saigon government did not make the French Government's task any easier. It is an interesting coincidence that Mendès-France and Ngo Dinh Diem came to power within a few hours of each other. Diem, the head of an important Catholic family from the Hue region, had resigned his post as minister of the interior in 1933, in the first national government of Annam under Bao Dai. Although Bao Dai had offered him the premiership three times during the intervening years, Diem had refused every offer until now. An uncompromising nationalist and declared anti-Communist who prided himself on his American connections, Diem enjoyed a reputation for virtue and courage almost unrivaled in Vietnam. If he had accepted the responsibilities of government at last, it meant only that the voice of Vietnamese nationalism would be even louder and more strident than before.

For Mendès-France, the appointment of this difficult partner—

whom he would certainly not have chosen if he had had any say in the matter—had certain advantages that were to become obvious later. Diem's prestige eventually enabled him to agree to peace terms that a less respected Vietnamese leader could not have persuaded Vietnamese public opinion to accept. In addition, the new Vietnamese minister of foreign affairs, Tran Van Do, proceeded to represent his government in Geneva with valuable degrees of moderation, dignity, and realism.

Having formed his team and sized up his partners, Mendès-France turned to a detailed study of the state of negotiations at the moment his month's grace began. A close look at the file revealed no hopeful conclusions.

The official negotiations had yielded tangible results only during the last few days. On June 16, Chou appeared to have agreed that the Laotian and Cambodian problems were essentially different from that of Vietnam and should be dealt with in accordance with different principles under a separate procedure. This was a fundamental concession to the Western powers, as well as to the Laotian and Cambodian governments—a concession that Molotov and Pham Van Dong were to accept.

Molotov had already agreed on May 14 that military problems should take priority over political ones—a point taken up again ten days later by the Vietminh diplomat Hoang Van Hoan in an interview given to *Le Monde*. Then, on June 16, Molotov hinted—and he confirmed it in a conversation with Bidault the next day—that the Communists might alter their position on a third point of disagreement, that of the composition of the international control commission. Molotov abandoned the principle of equal representation of Communist and non-Communist states in this agency and granted the latter a majority by allowing the addition of Indonesian representatives.

On three important issues, therefore, agreement was well on the way: separation of the cases of Laos and Cambodia, priority for a cease-fire, and the composition of the international control organizations. But this was still far from the solution of what were to become the most important issues of all and were already seen as such by the best-informed observers: the military partition of Vietnam and the date of elections intended to bring about the eventual reunification of the country.

The Vietminh military delegation's June 10 suggestion about partition was already regarded as the major event of the conference. But the value of this offer was limited by the fact that the French delegation had still not accepted the principle of partition, even if purely temporary, and continued to support the Laniel-Bidault proposal for "leopard skin" regrouping zones. (This was made very plain by Bidault's reaction on June 11, when Frédéric-Dupont described the Vietminh offer as a success for France. Bidault still refused to accept partition and considered it during his last few days in office only on the condition that General Ely would support it.) Opting for partition was, in any case, only half the answer: there remained the problem of deciding where the demarcation line should be drawn. By June 20, neither Buu nor his colleague had yet said anything specific on this subject to his French contacts. They did so only on June 28, when they made a discouraging demand for all of Tonkin and indicated the liveliest interest in central Vietnam as far south as Hue—in other words, down to the 16th Parallel.

As to the elections, which would enable the advocates of partition to temper their cynicism, the only reference to a date was a delay of six months mentioned by Pham Van Dong in a private conversation. This did not at all suit his French opponents, who had very little confidence in the ability of the nationalist state to stand up under Communist pressure. They estimated that at least a year and a half would be needed to prop up and arm the Saigon regime before it faced its formidable competitor.

It was now a question of bridging the gap between the Communist point of view and those of the Western powers, including the French Union. At least some of the stages on the road to an armistice had been covered during the first six weeks of the talks. Technically speaking, progress had been made and doors remained open, but the greater part of the task still lay ahead. Moreover, it was necessary to generate at least a minimum of confidence, without which one could not induce the Communist negotiators to make the necessary moves.

It may be impossible to describe and contrast the way in which two statesmen approached the same problem, but it is tempting as well. On June 29, 1954, André Fontaine wrote, in *Le Monde*, that "because of Bidault's visible revulsion at having to negotiate with them, Molotov, Chou En-lai, and Pham Van Dong were always convinced that Bidault, while seeking an armistice, was in reality trying to create a truce to cover American preparations for armed intervention." Bidault's plans were probably intended less to rekindle the war than to support the negotiations, but, as luck would have it, his opponents knew about them and distrusted him all the more as a result. When Mendès-France took charge of the negotiations, he clearly proposed to present a different image in Geneva. Bidault's policy was founded on the American alliance, was backed by the constant threat of U.S. Air Force intervention, and operated within the framework of an essentially multilateral conference. Mendès-France patterned his international and Asian policy on Britain's, drawing its military strength not from the United States but from the French nation itself (by means of the threat to dispatch French conscripts to Indochina) and using bilateral meetings rather than collective conference methods. From now on, the French Government looked more to the Rue Saint-Dominique[4] than to the Pentagon, to London and the Commonwealth than to Washington, and preferred personal contacts, even with the enemy, to plenary sessions in the Palais des Nations.

There was another difference: Bidault's policy had been one man's prerogative, somewhat in the style of the "king's secret," and it needed no buttressing other than Bidault's personal talent, sense of history, and nationalist convictions; Mendès-France, on the contrary, openly sought the support of public opinion and relied on the public's yearning for peace. Mendès took pains to keep the French people informed—broadcasting to them every week, in his calm, even voice—and apparently drew real comfort from their

[4] Where the French Defense Ministry is situated.

support. And, of course, this gave him great strength vis-à-vis his opponents: the murmuring of the masses could be heard off stage at Geneva, and the world could know that France wished for peace and that its representative harbored no bellicose intentions.

Less than a week after taking over the government, Mendès-France boldly put these ideas into practice, asking Chauvel whether a quick initial contact with one of the opposing negotiators in Geneva might be useful. Chauvel advised him against meeting the head of the Vietminh delegation—he had himself arranged to meet Dong on June 22—but he told him that a talk with Chou En-lai, who had expressed a wish to meet the new French Premier, would have great advantages.

Relations between Chauvel and Chou had already become cordial, after a rather curious beginning. Chauvel constantly passed the Chinese delegation in the hallways of the Palais des Nations—one day, Chou glanced at him; on the next, he suggested by a gesture that he and Chauvel might share a secret; the day after, he smiled; on the fourth day, he finally stopped and indicated to Chauvel that he wanted to see him. These Peking Opera tricks delighted Chauvel, who knew a good deal about Chinese ways—he had served in China thirty years earlier—and they served as a pleasant introduction to more serious and fruitful meetings.

A difficulty arose: Chou did not want to go to Paris so long as his government was not recognized by France, while Mendès-France did not want to go to Geneva, because he felt it was too early to join the conference "circuit." Dijon was suggested. Then, the heads of the various delegations decided to follow Molotov's example and go to Berne to thank Philipp Etter, the President of the Swiss Confederation, for the wonderful welcome shown to all those taking part in the Geneva talks. It was decided that Mendès-France should also pay his respects to President Etter, and Chou agreed to join him there. The meeting was arranged for the afternoon of June 23 at the French embassy.

That day, Chou left off his dark, high-collared tunic—the garb that Mao Tse-tung has turned into the uniform and symbol of the Chinese revolution. Wearing a gray business suit and a new tie, he looked younger and more relaxed than usual, a diplomat at ease in the French embassy's patrician atmosphere. Whatever he may have thought about Mendès-France's reputation, however, he did not greet him with any great cordiality—starting off by saying that China feared neither threat nor provocation and considered both invalid as means of negotiation.

Mendès-France realized, of course, that this broadside was not personal and was not aimed at him, and Chou went on to make it clear that, in his opinion, and in accordance with French wishes, military questions should have priority over the resolution of political issues in Indochina. With an excellent grasp of the subject and much finesse, he proceeded to outline his government's policy toward the three countries of Indochina. Mendès-France, who was keenly concerned about this issue and eager to throw as much light as possible on any differences among the Peking government's attitudes toward the three states, noted immediately that Chou had definitely agreed to separate the cases of Cambodia and Laos.

Chou stated plainly that his government and the Vietminh proposed to recognize both kingdoms and that he would follow a policy of nonintervention toward both. But he emphasized that the fact that China and the D.R.V. respected these countries' independence did not mean that another power such as the United States could turn them into "bases for aggression." In order to provide for national unification, he said, both royal governments should grant recognition to the "national resistance movements" for the sake of national unity. Here, he distinguished the case of Cambodia, where he admitted that the resistance groups were less significant, from that of Laos, where he thought that regrouping zones should be given to the Pathet Lao forces and even went so far as to add that Vietminh forces which had penetrated Laotian territory might be withdrawn after an armistice.

Chou made clear his preference for direct contacts between French and Vietminh representatives and suggested that the other delegations should generally limit themselves to helping the talks along. Mèndes-France agreed; he had long favored bilateral exchanges. However, there were still many obstacles to overcome concerning the two Vietnamese governments. Mendès-France particularly stressed international control and the elections that should be held in Vietnam after a suitable interval, and he asked Chou whether he was genuinely in favor of very large regrouping zones in Vietnam.

To this Chou's answer was somewhat oblique: the Chinese delegation was sparing no efforts to encourage direct contacts between the D.R.V. delegation and the Vietnamese nationalist representatives. Much could be expected from such contacts, particularly since Vietminh terms were, according to him, extremely reasonable. Mendès-France once more stressed the political and psychological barriers to cooperation between the nationalist Vietnamese and the Vietminh. Moreover, he argued, the talks between the military delegations in Geneva were not progressing quickly enough, because both sides suffered from a lack of instructions. He assured Chou that his next round of consultations—notably with General Ely that very evening—would put him in a position to lay down a line that the French representatives in Geneva could follow. Indeed, Mendès-France added, the preliminary agreements reached by the military representatives could serve as a basis for a general settlement.

Chou then returned, rather warily, to the question of regroupment zones which he had refused to be lured into answering earlier. His preference, he said, was for the formula involving large zones; did Mendès-France have "concrete ideas on this subject"? Mendès-was cautious: a "horizontal cut . . . had been contemplated," but the Vietminh officers saw it "a great deal farther south than the actual situation warranted." Mendès-France added that, as far as he was concerned, everything else depended on the settlement of this problem. Chou was quick to agree and remarked, "this [is] also Mr. Eden's opinion." The military delegations, he thought, should reach agreement "within three weeks," after which the foreign ministers could return to Geneva. Was Chou trying to embarrass Mendès-France by setting a time limit so near to the one fixed by Mendès for the settlement of *all* outstanding problems? With a touch of asperity, Mendès-France remarked that three weeks "should be regarded as a maximum."

Before taking his leave, Chou expressed the hope that Mendès-France would soon find it possible to talk to Pham Van Dong.

Mendès-France reminded him that Chauvel had met with Dong only the day before and gave him to understand that he himself might soon make contact. Thereupon, the two men parted, apparently pleased with each other. Observers gathered that they had "understood each other very well."[5] All things considered, this was not an overstatement.

Arriving at Villacoublay that evening, Mendès-France told reporters, "One can regard the course of the Geneva conference in the near future with optimism." Simultaneously, the Chinese delegation issued a communiqué stating, among other things, that, on the strength of their conversation, Chou and Mendès-France "were in a position to foresee that there would be progress at the Geneva conference."

The conversation between Mendès-France and Chou, and the first contact between Chauvel and Dong, had enabled the French to size up their opposition. The time had come for the new head of the government to lay down a line of action for French diplomacy. The peace objective was reasonably within reach, but the price to be paid for it must be fixed and then firmly defended.

On June 24, the day after his return from Berne, Mendès-France gathered together the four men who knew most about the course of the negotiations and their international implications: General Ely, the commissioner-general in Saigon; Ambassador Chauvel, head of the French delegation in Geneva; Guy La Chambre, Minister for the Associated States; and Alexandre Parodi, Secretary-General at the French Foreign Ministry. It took two sessions—altogether, little more than three hours—to work out the diplomatic and military policies to be followed by France during the next few crucial weeks, and to specify the instructions that Chauvel and Ely would follow in Geneva and Saigon.

Chauvel summed up the situation for the benefit of those present. First, he stated, a careful study of the documents and the experience of nearly two months of talks and debates in Geneva had forced him to conclude that at least a temporary partition of

[5] *Le Monde* (Paris), June 25, 1954.

Vietnam was inevitable. None of those present thought it right to object—least of all General Ely, who had recommended this solution to Bidault ten days earlier. From this moment on, the "military" partition offered by the enemy, which all serious observers regarded as the only solution capable of bringing the fighting to an end, became the official doctrine of the French Government.

Chauvel then asked the two questions bound up with the issue of partition: where should the demarcation line be located, and when should the general elections be held? Nobody, in fact, was prepared to accept a lasting partition or to renounce reunification—at least in public. Chauvel reported that the military experts had recommended a provisional frontier at the 18th Parallel, running along the crest of the limestone mountains forming the Porte d'Annam and reaching the sea at Cape Ron—a natural barrier that would provide a reasonable line of defense if the enemy were to take the initiative in renewing hostilities. As to the date of the elections, however, Chauvel was more reticent. It was obvious that the Vietminh wished for an early poll. But it was most important to make a clean break between the military problem of putting an end to hostilities and the political issue of reunifying the country. Chauvel hinted that it might be possible to arrange things so that the documents did not specify a date and confined themselves to affirming the principle that elections should be held in the future.

Mendès-France then asked about the bishoprics in southern Tonkin and the fate of Haiphong.

General Ely suggested that the bishoprics should be neutralized. If, in return, the Vietminh asked for special status in one or more zones south of the proposed demarcation line, the dangers involved in such a concession could be minimized by the application of some kind of neutral military control.

On the matter of Haiphong, Chauvel suggested a three-stage solution: first, the French forces would withdraw to Hanoi; then, they would withdraw from Hanoi to Haiphong; and, finally, they would be evacuated by sea. Mendès-France argued that France would have to hold on in Haiphong for a year or two, if only to provide cover for the Expeditionary Corps, but Ely quietly replied that it would hardly take more than a year to evacuate all of the Red River delta, and, therefore, it would be better not to stress these technical arguments too much in dealing with the enemy.

Since Guy La Chambre was now responsible for relations with the Associated States, he naturally reflected Vietnamese misgivings. Diem had not been informed of the results of the meeting in Berne on the previous day, and officials in nationalist Vietnam remained convinced that no one considered their advice or their concerns and that their future was held cheap. La Chambre was therefore given instructions to inform Ngo Dinh Nhu, Diem's brother and his closest adviser, about the conversation with Chou.

"We must go fast," Mendès-France remarked at this point. "Not only because of the time limit we have set for ourselves, but also because the situation is quite favorable. Everybody is more or less undecided at present and is searching for the way. If France displays determination and indicates clearly what it regards as important, what it will not surrender at any cost, and what concessions it is prepared to make, it will reverse the present situation and regain the political initiative at the negotiations."

Before Mendès-France closed the meeting, Chauvel reminded the diplomats once more of the need to keep Washington informed of French moves—if only to gain the agreement of the Saigon government (whose pro-American tendencies were already apparent) to the proposed arrangements, especially to the principle of temporary partition. All of those present agreed.

Instructions were prepared for Chauvel as a result of this first meeting and approved at the second meeting that evening. Chauvel was authorized to open full-scale negotiations with Pham Van Dong, with three objects in view: (1) the regrouping of the opposing forces on either side of a demarcation line located in the vicinity of the 18th Parallel; (2) the evacuation by both armies of the bishoprics of Phat Diem and Bui Chu, which would be placed under neutral control (compensation of a similar kind could be conceded to the Vietminh in the southern zone); (3) the retention of Haiphong for as long as possible under French control, in accordance with military requirements arising out of the regrouping of French Union forces.

Henceforth, the aim was partition, and it became a matter of forecasting its political and psychological implications and estimating its dangers. General Ely drew attention to this aspect of the problem at the second meeting and suggested that, during the danger period, when this decision to partition Vietnam was likely to damage French prestige, especially in the nationalist south, France should put itself into a state of "supersecurity." This could only be achieved by starting to send conscripts to Indochina. Even if they arrived late in the day, the mere announcement of their dispatch would strengthen both the French position in Indochina and the hand of the French delegate in Geneva. "Is this your opinion?" Mendès-France asked Chauvel.

"Yes. The announcement of this decision would have valuable results. And we have so little time left that not many men would actually be transferred."

"But isn't this just banging our fists on the table?" Mendès-France objected. "The diplomatic effects might be the opposite of those we are aiming for? Should I have mentioned this possibility to Chou En-lai yesterday in Berne?" Then, turning to General Ely, "Couldn't we organize an airlift to Indochina and fly out regular army reinforcements instead?"

General Ely agreed that both measures could be taken simultaneously, but he insisted that the army in Indochina had to feel that France was behind it. Nothing would make this clearer than the dispatch of conscript units, even if only a few.

"In that case, I shall accept my responsibilities," concluded Mendès-France. "There will be great difficulties in the Assembly, but I will put it to the meeting of the Committee of National Defense next Monday."

An objective had been chosen—partition, at least provisionally; a procedure—dialogue with the Vietminh, within the framework of the Geneva conference; and a means of pressure—the possible dispatch of conscripts. And so the French Government's policy was defined. Twenty-six days remained before the deadline.

18

A DISAPPOINTING TÊTE-À-TÊTE WITH THE VIETMINH

Chauvel resumed contact with Pham Van Dong[1] on June 25 to inform him of the French Government's intentions. Would the new policy decisions make substantial negotiations possible from now on? The Vietminh minister—relaxed, almost smiling, and clearly interested—told Chauvel, "We might settle it within ten days or so." It was a pleasant suggestion but one in which there seemed to be little solid ground for hope.

Now that both sides had accepted the idea of partition, the military delegates had to work out its terms in detail. The military committee's meetings became official, although still secret, and were made part of the main talks; this meant that the participants were bound by any agreements reached. The urgency with which Ta Quang Buu and Colonel Lau had pressed for recognition of the principle of partition should have meant that, after the decision made in Paris on June 24 and communicated to Dong the next day, the Vietminh representatives would push on boldly with the

[1] At Chou En-lai's residence.

dialogue. But, instead, the French military delegates now met with a series of slowdown strikes, as one observer put it. What did this mean? Chauvel had at last mentioned partition, Dong had claimed that no more than ten days were needed to reach agreement, and now the Vietminh representatives suddenly displayed every sign of calculated indifference. Clearly, the spirit that moved Buu and Lau had changed since the second week in June. Then, they were all boldness and drive; now, they were uncommunicative, fussy, and niggling.

Despite this, a meeting was arranged for June 26. The Vietminh delegates startled their French colleagues by leading off with a peculiar remark. The meeting between Chou and Mendès-France was certainly a happy initiative with solid political implications, they said, but why should the Democratic Republic of Vietnam not be treated on the same footing? Why had nobody at the ministerial level been sent to Geneva to contact the Vietminh delegation? That would indeed prove to us, said Buu, that with the formation of a new government French policy had really changed.

Delteil did his best to explain that an ambassador, especially one as high-ranking as Chauvel, was a valid representative of his government, but the Vietminh spokesmen refused to budge. Their attitude was all the more surprising because Dong, the head of their delegation, had manifested none of these misgivings on the previous day and had not expressed to Chauvel any wish that Mendès-France or a cabinet member should hurry to Geneva.

Worse was in store two days later, on June 28, when rumors circulated around the French delegation that the day's meeting would be a crucial one. True to form, Buu went straight to the point. The French had, in effect, accepted the principle of regrouping in two large zones, he said, and had suggested that the demarcation line run along the 18th Parallel. "Now here is our proposal. . . ." Delteil caught de Brébisson's eye: at last, the Vietminh spokesman was about to show his cards. Instead, he slapped them down on the table. Without batting an eye, Buu proposed that the provisional frontier be drawn slightly to the north of the 13th Parallel.

The French officers were startled. They knew that the Vietminh counterproposals would not tally with their original suggestions, but they had never dreamed that five parallels, nearly 350 miles, and a population of nearly 2 million would separate the two proposals. Delteil immediately replied, in the firmest possible tone, that such vast divergences made it virtually pointless to go on with the talks. He stressed that a partition line at the level of Cape Ron was regarded by Paris as the basic condition for an agreement to regroup into two large zones. This was essential in order to satisfy the honor of the army, the interests of the population, the future of the French Union, and the requirements of states allied to France. Buu retorted that the Vietminh command could not surrender areas such as those around Qui Nhon and Faifo (Hoi An), which it had held since the conflict started. There was something to this argument, but it did nothing to keep the dialogue going. Another meeting the following day bogged down in the same way. Nobody budged.

Vietminh demands now proliferated. Buu and Lau stated that their government could not accept a delay of more than three months for the evacuation of the French Union forces. A few days later, this shrank to two months. They even demanded that, when the French had evacuated the north, their own forces be allowed to remain in the south for a while. Their Pathet Lao friends in Laos, they now claimed, must be granted virtually sovereign rights over the eastern half of the country, particularly the Bolovens Plateau, the richest province of all. Delteil and de Brébisson went from disappointment to dismay. Were these the same men they had met with on June 10?

This change in the Vietminh attitude, which has intrigued all those who have since attempted to unravel the threads of the Geneva negotiations, can be traced to a number of causes. The first was psychological: so much had been said and written about Mendès-France, the man of "peace at any price" (the right-wing press in Paris campaigned against him on this slogan), that the Vietminh negotiators had come to believe it was time to stiffen their terms. They had thought there had been a political upheaval in Paris that had brought a "peace party" to power; it is not surprising that they could hardly conceal their astonishment at finding the same French team facing them across the conference table.

Their misapprehensions lasted less than three weeks, until Mendès-France had secured the support of his allies and was able to come to Geneva ready for peace but armed for battle.

Until the last days of June, the Vietminh remained convinced that it faced a helpless opponent at the conference and could afford to speak more firmly. The Communist command then discovered, without being able to do anything about it, that the French General Staff in Hanoi was evacuating the entire southern part of the Red River delta, including the celebrated bishoprics of Phat Diem and Bui Chu. This was Operation Auvergne, militarily a necessary and successful operation but distressing in human terms (even though all but a few dozen of the Catholics who asked to leave their Vietminh-occupied villages were successfully evacuated) and diplomatically costly, since it made the Vietminh think that, by negotiating for the neutralization of these areas, the French were bargaining with something they no longer owned.

It should be borne in mind that this operation had been decided upon at the important meeting of the National Defense Committee on May 14 and 15, under the previous government, and that Ely and Salan had strongly supported it when they returned from their tour of inspection in Indochina. It is, nevertheless, surprising that the General Staff, which was so firmly convinced of the need for this operation, should have failed to give the new government a clear warning that it was about to take place; this change in the military situation came at the height of negotiations over this very area and caught the Mendès-France government on the wrong foot. It hampered the French not only in their dealings with their opponents but also in their relations with the Saigon government.

In fact, the contacts between the French and the Vietminh at that time were obviously governed by what Buu and Lau used to call, with quiet irony, the fluidity of the military situation. Indeed, it would have been surprising if this factor had not loomed disproportionately large under the circumstances, especially in the eyes of an army as "supercharged" as General Giap's.

There is yet a third element in the picture: the removal from the scene of the powers that, in the minds of the "inventors" of

Geneva, were supposed to surround and moderate the Vietminh on the one side and support and strengthen France on the other. While Molotov was in Moscow, studying documents, Chou made some encouraging statements to the Laotian and Cambodian delegations and set out immediately on a triumphant tour across Asia, which took him from New Delhi to Rangoon and Peking. He stopped for a short time in southern China, where Ho Chi Minh joined him for consultations lasting two days.

If the brakes were off the Vietminh, it was also far from clear how the Anglo-American powers were bringing their weight to bear. Everything awaited the forthcoming results of the Eisenhower-Churchill meeting. Mendès-France was confident about Eden's attitude toward the policy agreed upon in Paris on June 24 and knew he could count on British approval and help. But, in Geneva, British diplomacy had become rather colorless of late, while the American delegation had not let a day pass without a show of bad temper or contempt. One day, Donald Heath, Ambassador to the Associated States and one of the most important American delegates, announced his departure; no one was in a better position to impress the leaders in Saigon with the urgent need for major concessions. The next day, Ambassador Johnson, the interim head of the delegation, informed Chauvel that his government could not agree to the presence of even a single Communist representative on the international control commission then under consideration, even though he had admitted two days earlier that the French compromise solution was justified.

This American move did not prevent Chauvel and his colleagues from achieving the only progress made during this period, by drafting what was to become the definitive plan for the armistice commission. The inclusion of India, Canada, and Poland in the commission made it possible to resolve the knotty problem of international control.

In fact, it became clearer every day that direct talks between the French and the Vietminh could only have paid off handsomely if the military situation had been kept stable, if the French High Command and parliament had cooperated with the Premier and General Ely in their efforts to send conscripts to Indochina, and if the nationalist Vietnamese delegation had remained neutral toward the French negotiators while the talks were in progress. However, when Dejean went on July 4 to inform Bao Dai that negotiations were about to start between Chauvel and Dong, the Vietnamese head of state showed great restraint, accepting the principle of partition and dwelling mainly on the safeguards necessary for southern Vietnam.

During those early days of July, a kind of anguish once more overcame French observers at Geneva. Only three weeks were left, and France's opponents were not passing up a single opportunity to underline a demand or add a requirement, while France's allies left it in growing solitude. None of this seemed to shake Chauvel's composure, however, a composure in which irony was a constant element. Discussions with his colleagues, contacts with his opponents, even the official session of the conference—all stimulated his lively mind, and his reports were brightened with colorful vignettes in the classical style. But, dauntless though he was, Chauvel surely drew comfort from Mendès-France's letter, dated July 2:

> We can appreciate all the obstacles you are meeting, and we are glad that you do not allow yourself to grow weary, despite the uncertainties and complexities of the negotiations. I think, as you do, that for the moment we must "hang on" without showing signs of excessive uneasiness or impatience. It is obvious that our opponents are gambling on the July 20 deadline. They think we are in a hurry. We are, but we are not so rushed that we will grasp whatever is offered (for instance, the 13th Parallel). Therefore, I am not worrying about the difficulties we have met during the last few days or the deadlock they have caused. At worst, we will pick up the threads again around July 12, or possibly even later. The cards will not go down on the table until the evening of July 19.

Both the Premier and the diplomat knew that nothing would be done until the last few hours. But it was essential to be armed for the occasion when it came, to secure the support of some and the neutrality of others, and to weaken the enemy's positions in addance. The game might take only a few hours to play, but the cards must be dealt before it could begin.

While Chauvel redoubled his contacts with the Soviet and Chinese missions, Mendès-France sought to make good use of a favorable change in the Anglo-American mood that had appeared after the Eisenhower-Churchill talks. Above all, he worked to overcome tremendous American prejudices. The disappointing confrontation with the Vietminh had not been fruitless, for it had taught the French representatives the importance of closing ranks with their allies at the critical moment. This did not prove the superiority of the conference technique as opposed to bilateral discussions; rather, it was a reminder that all negotiations have many aspects and that a statesman must always find support in the reality of the moment.

In this instance, the reality was an extremely dangerous military situation, combined with the Vietminh's haste to make its pressure irresistible; it was also the determination of the two great Communist powers to end the fighting in Asia in order to give China a chance to breathe and start on the constructive stage of the revolution that the Chinese people had been promised; and, finally, it was the British and American refusal to let themselves be dragged into a general war over Vietnam, and their anxiety to find a resolute partner in Paris.

19

BRINGING THE ENGLISH AND THE AMERICANS INTO FRANCE'S GAME

When Churchill and Eden landed in Washington on June 24, they found their American hosts full of anger, despite the torpor induced by a terrible heat-wave. Not only had the British opposed all military action in Asia during the previous two months and made polite gestures toward Red China, but Eden had publicly expressed a wish for "an Asian Locarno" just two days before his arrival. Washington was profoundly irritated by what it regarded as an apologia for appeasement. The American press was furious, and the photographers crowded around Dulles at the airport to see whether he would refuse to shake hands with his British colleague. Not since the war had Anglo-American relations passed though such a serious crisis; we are on the verge of a breakdown in relations, said an editorial in a leading Washington daily.

But, only five days later, the two governments sent identical notes to Paris outlining a plan for settling the Indochina question. This document, which has since become known as the "Seven Anglo-American Points," was, in fact, one of the most important contributions to the ending of the Indochina war, as well as one of the most reasonable approaches to the problem. It is hard to know whether to credit this sudden evolution in the American attitude to Churchill's powers of persuasion or to Eden's skill.

The British leaders' journey to Washington aroused interest rather than apprehension in Mendès-France and his colleagues. Mendès-France sensed an affinity between his own views and Eden's, while his meeting with Bedell Smith had revealed no basic conflict of views. For the French, therefore, it was a question of influencing the Washington talks *in absentia*, of deriving every possible advantage from a situation in which the active good will of one of the parties could outweigh the sullen reticence of the other.

Relations between Paris and Washington had changed greatly in the two months since Operation Vulture had been abandoned. When Mendès-France took over the Foreign Ministry, he found a telegram from Ambassador Bonnet in Washington, stressing the "deepening rift" between France and the United States.[1] On June 26, therefore, he instructed Bonnet to deliver a twofold communication to Dulles and Eden. He was to inform them of the fresh turn taken by the talks between Chauvel and Dong; he was also to convey to them the Premier's wish for a public show of harmony among the allies. Mendès-France, in effect, was saying to Washington and London, "I shall be stronger in confronting my Communist opponents in Geneva if I can appear there as the negotiator for the West as a whole."

This diplomatic move, the information about the face-to-face meeting in Geneva, and the arguments presented by Bonnet all made a great impression in Washington. By June 29, Bonnet was able to send Paris the seven-point memorandum in which Britain and the United States listed their conditions for respecting any future agreements. It said, in effect, that in order to secure the approval of the two governments, any Indochina agreements must:

1. Preserve the integrity and independence of Laos and Cam-

[1] Statement by Mendès-France in the Chamber of Deputies, July 25, 1954.

bodia and provide for the withdrawal of Vietminh forces from both countries.

2. Secure at least the southern half of Vietnam and, if possible, an enclave in the Red River delta; the demarcation line should run no farther south than Dong Hoi (just north of the 17th Parallel).

3. Not impose upon Cambodia, Laos, or the secured part of Vietnam restrictions that would lessen their prospects of maintaining stable non-Communist regimes, particularly restrictions upon their right to have sufficient forces for internal-security purposes, to import arms, and to call upon foreign advisers.

4. Contain no political clauses likely to result in the loss of the secured areas to the Communists.

5. Not exclude the possibility of later unification of Vietnam by peaceful means.

6. Provide for the transfer, under humane and peaceful conditions and with international supervision, of all those who expressed the wish to move from one zone of Vietnam to the other.

7. Arrange for an effective system of international control.

It would be an understatement to say that this document caused great satisfaction in Paris. In effect, it approved the instructions Mendès had given Chauvel on June 24 and represented Washington's acceptance of the principle of partition. Better still, the Anglo-American points were somewhat less rigid than the French plan about both the location of the demarcation line and the sectors to be neutralized. It therefore left the French a fair amount of room to maneuver, provided stronger support for them, and, thanks to the Americans' pledge, gave them additional leverage with the nationalist Vietnamese when the time came to induce them to accept terms that were essential but unpalatable.

This astonishing document, foreshadowing the agreements of July 20, was, no less astonishingly, kept secret. This secrecy was itself convincing proof of the existence of a common Western doctrine, for any leaks about the document would have weakened Mendès-France's diplomatic line of defense. In any event, it did contain certain ambiguities. The requirement stated in Point 4 (no clause of any agreement must involve the loss of the secured areas) could hardly be reconciled with the suggestion in Point 5 (possibility of reunification of Vietnam), since it was obvious that any attempt at reunification, especially by means of general elections carried out under international supervision, involved a danger of complete Vietminh success. And what exactly did the Americans and British mean when they stated that they were prepared to "respect" a future agreement? At the request of the Quai d'Orsay, a high American official gave the following interpretation two days later: "This term signifies that we would not oppose a settlement that conformed to the 'seven points.' It does not mean that we would be disposed to guarantee such a settlement." Several days later, however, Bedell Smith told Bonnet in Washington that in this instance "respect" was equivalent to "recognize" and the agreement described would, in the opinion of his government, rank as a settlement.

There was no suggestion that this granted the French Government *carte blanche* or unconditional support. But Mendès-France and his colleagues would have been well content with this reassuring document if Dulles's agreement to it had not been followed by a real onslaught against Mendès-France in Washington and in American circles close to the U.S. embassy in Paris. The China and Bao-Daist lobbies in Washington as well as certain French groups that were irreconcilably hostile to Mendès-France learned of the "seven points" agreement and considered it a bonus improperly awarded to the head of the French Government. They now tried to break it up and to ruin Mendès-France's credit—already under attack by one clique—with the Secretary of State and other high American officials.

During the early days of July, for example, a rumor was launched in American circles in Paris which claimed in all seriousness that Chou and Mendès-France had jointly decided on French evacuation of the Red River delta during their meetings in Berne on June 23. To any well-informed person this was absurd; nevertheless, it gained enough credence to become the object of an official dispatch to Washington. During the next few days, it was whispered that the French had accepted, in principle, a plan of partition leaving Hue in Vietminh hands and had agreed to elections within six months. Another story claimed that half of Laos was to be left to the Communists.

A high-ranking diplomat named Douglas MacArthur, Jr. (a nephew of the general and a supporter of the interventionist doctrines of Senator Knowland and Admiral Radford) was a notable sounding-board for this poison campaign in Washington. Dulles, who was not armed against such propaganda by any natural feeling of sympathy for Mendès-France, apparently gave some credence to the rumors. He told Bonnet he was seriously afraid that the French representatives in Geneva would retreat from concession to concession and allow the demarcation line to be pushed back from the 18th Parallel to the 16th, the 14th, or even the 12th!

Mendès-France knew he would have to fight back, and he also knew that no public statements, even those as firm as the one he made in the Chamber of Deputies on July 7, would suffice. He had to convince the American diplomats that France would not surrender to the Vietminh anything that it could hold without extending the war, and that it was determined to create viable Indochinese political entities capable of counterbalancing Communism. In addition, he had to persuade the United States to send a representative of ministerial rank to Geneva. This was necessary to convince the Communist powers that the Western alliance had a united policy not only for the negotiations but also in the event that negotiations failed.

But in spite of Bonnet's representations in Washington, Mendès-France went empty-handed to Geneva on July 10 to lead the French delegation in the final stage of the talks. Washington would not grant the slightest promise about either the preliminary consultation he wanted or the presence of a senior American representative at the conference. On July 11, Ambassador Dillon gave Mendès-France a message from Dulles. This message claimed that the French would be unable to persuade the Communist powers to accept the "seven points" of June 29, which represented the minimum acceptable to the United States even though it represented the best that the French, and probably the British, could expect. Therefore, it would be more damaging than useful if a high-ranking American were put in the position of having to disassociate himself from an agreement and to voice moral strictures about allies who had been driven to accept an unfavorable settlement.

American obstinacy seemed impervious to any argument. Mendès-France was therefore preparing to tackle the last stage of the negotiations with only Eden's support when he was surprised to receive another visit from Dillon, who said that Dulles would be happy to talk with him.

"Is he coming to Geneva?" asked Mendès-France. Dillon replied that Dulles would prefer to meet in Paris, as he was still hesitating about going to Geneva.

"We mustn't let that stand in the way. When could we meet?"

"He could be in Paris tomorrow," Dillon replied.

And so it was that Mendès-France, who had hardly settled in Geneva, left again by air for Paris on the afternoon of Tuesday, July 13, accompanied by Eden.

Dulles landed in Paris slightly ahead of his impromptu host. The first meeting took place at the American embassy. The Secretary of State, with his fresh complexion, his sharp eyes, his thin smile, and his heavy jaw, looked like a great consultant called in from afar to examine a very sick patient. Mendès-France's features were almost ravaged by fatigue. The two men quickly tackled the heart of the argument.

But it was only after dinner at the Hotel Matignon, with Eden also present, that the tilting between the Secretary of State and the head of the French Government began. "P.M.-F." had recovered. Speaking English with a skill that had been polished at twenty international monetary conferences, he went straight to the point that concerned him most—the dispatch of a high-ranking American to Geneva. But Dulles, rather oddly, diverted the conversation to the need for economic aid to Vietnam and observed that the Vietminh would certainly object to such support being given to the part of Indochina saved from Communism. Mendès-France denied this. "What our enemies oppose," he pointed out, "is the establishment of American military bases in Vietnam, Laos, and Cambodia." Dulles replied that he knew about that kind of propaganda, those cries of "*U.S. go home!*" "What they are after is the eradication of all American influence and presence," he said, looking nettled. "How do you expect them to agree that we should provide economic aid to their neighbors?"

Dulles then returned to the main subject and spoke frankly about the question of a U.S. guarantee for the future agreements. He said that the United States could not announce that it would intervene in this or that circumstance. A degree of uncertainty must be allowed to hover over the subject. Therefore, it would be best for an American delegate of intermediate rank to play the role of the "wicked partner" at Geneva. America was particularly anxious to avoid giving the impression that it was abandoning France or standing against it. Dulles asserted that he had come to Paris mainly to show that there was no misunderstanding between America and France, but also to convince the French that his proposals for American participation in Geneva were the best. Mendès-France was quick to reply:

> Do you realize that the absence of an American minister in Geneva delights the Eastern delegations? And do you know that the mere announcement of your coming to Paris and of our meeting tonight has spread dismay among the Communists at the conference? This morning, Pham Van Dong came to see me and asked me not to leave Geneva. He looked completely lost. He even offered me important concessions and suggested that the demarcation line should be moved up to the 16th Parallel. . . . Your presence in Geneva, or that of the Under-Secretary of State, would strengthen the Western position, while your absence convinces our enemies that a wedge has been driven between the allies for the first time since the Second World War.

Eden warmly approved, but Dulles was not yet convinced. He said that any agreement the French would sign in Geneva was bound to be bad. America could not be present without looking as though it was supporting a new Yalta. Mendès-France responded: "But we need your presence so that the agreement will not be bad, so that it will conform to the Anglo-American 'seven points' of June 29. If we fail—and your absence would contribute to that—the war will start again, and soon, before the conscripts we have decided to send arrive, the Vietminh will score further successes, perhaps decisive ones. The situation will be critical by September." Dulles pointed out that the American Government was not inclined to take military action—which Mendès-France had not suggested in any case—and added moodily that America had no direct interests in the area. "What we are asking you to do," Mendès-France persevered, "does not involve signing a treaty with the Communists or even joining them in any commitment. We are asking you to enable us to obtain better terms by being present in Geneva and by letting it be known that a violation of the agreement would involve a serious risk."

The French Premier doggedly returned to the aims of the negotiations, to the results already achieved, and to his determination not to give away any vital interests. He unfolded a map and asked the Secretary of State to follow the movement of his fountain pen upon it: "This is where they want to draw the demarcation line, there, near Faifo (Hoi An, just south of the 16th Parallel) . . . and this is where we hope to finish up, here, close to the 18th Parallel."

"What? Is the map upside down?" asked Dulles, somewhat baffled. "I don't understand—your line is farther north than mine. Are you asking for more than we are?"

Mendès-France could not suppress a smile. Yes, indeed—on certain points the French plan was more demanding than the Anglo-American one (which does not mean that it was more sensible).

A meeting was arranged for the following day at the Quai d'Orsay, to set the terms of a communiqué. But before they parted, Dulles had given the eagerly awaited promise: If his state of health did not make it impossible, Bedell Smith would represent the American Government during the last stage of the Geneva conference. Mendès-France and Eden glanced at each other; the match was won. Dulles muttered with a wry grin that made his face look even longer: "The guy is terrific!"

Next morning, Mendès-France sent a letter to Dulles formally noting that Dulles recognized "the basic right of France and the Associated States to decide the terms of settlement of a war in which they were the only belligerents on the non-Communist side."

The Franco-American memorandum, drafted after the July 14 Bastille Day Parade (which Mendès-France attended at Coty's request, despite a grossly overloaded timetable), conceded a number of valuable points to the French but also contained a clear warning. The document stated that the United States, recognizing the right of those directly involved to accept terms other than the "seven points," was prepared to respect terms that accorded with those seven points but should not be asked to respect terms that, in its opinion, significantly differed from them. It added that the United States might publicly disassociate itself from anyone who accepted widely differing terms.

However, the important thing was that the United States had assumed its share of the burden: it would treat any "respectable" agreement as though it were a commitment stemming from the United Nations Charter and would seek to establish a collective defense organization, together with the other nations concerned, to safeguard the peace. This gave the "seven points" the force of a Western doctrine and thereby powerfully strengthened Mendès-France's position at Geneva.

Mendès-France could leave for the Geneva conference with the feeling that he was now negotiating for the West as a whole. Nothing was better calculated to confirm him in this opinion than the letter he received from Dulles on arrival in the Swiss capital. In it, Dulles said that he admired and respected the rectitude with which Mendès-France approached the vital problems confronting them. Lack of decisiveness was the worst of evils, and Mendès-France had done much to remove it. He should know, at this moment when he was about to take historic decisions in Geneva, that France's many friends supported him with their hopes and prayers. Dulles added that he was happy that they had found a way of showing support for France in Geneva without, he hoped, infringing on principles or running the risk of a later misunderstanding.

20

SCALING THE PARALLELS

We must now go back a few days to understand the sequence of events during the "ten days that reassured the world."

On July 8, Molotov returned to Geneva for the final stage of the conference. Eden was expected on July 12, and Chou En-lai on July 10, the day chosen by Mendès-France to open the battle. From now on, time was reckoned in hours, not days.

The pace was set from the start. As soon as his old Dakota landed at Cointrin airfield in the twilight of Saturday, July 10, Mendès-France held a brief conversation with Faure, who had come from his nearby property in the Jura on his way to Paris, where he was to take over as acting Premier. Then Mendès-France dove into a black Citroën, stopped at *Joli-Port* for a quick briefing by Chauvel about his contacts with Dong and Buu during the last few hours, and sped on to *Villa Blanche*, where Molotov received him. The last stage of the talks had begun; two hundred and forty hours to go . . . .

The meeting at *Villa Blanche* was reasonably friendly. Molotov gave a token of his good will toward the new representative of France by letting Paris press photographers loose in his residence for the first time. He even essayed a few words in French. Mendès-France, in turn, impressed his host by proposing a toast to Franco-Soviet friendship.

But neither of them was inclined to dwell on externals or to waste time on details. The conversation went straight to the heart of the problem: the demarcation line between the two Vietnams. (Molotov had already hinted that any difficulties concerning Laos and Cambodia could easily be overcome.) Mendès-France naturally maintained that the French proposal for a line at the 18th Parallel conformed with reason, the laws of geography, and the interests of all. But Molotov had briefed himself better than his colleagues suspected and objected that the Democratic Republic of Vietnam had controlled several provinces south of the 18th Parallel since the war began. Mendès-France replied:

> The existing situation matters less than the political balance which must be achieved. We must concentrate on mapping out two large regrouping zones. We must trace the line that will cause the least friction—in other words, the shortest line possible. The most suitable provisional frontier lies near the 18th Parallel. And let us not forget that we shall have to persuade all those taking part in the conference to accept this agreement. It is unlikely that the nine powers will agree to any line other than one passing near Cape Ron.

Molotov was clearly interested but by no means convinced. He refused to commit himself further in an area that he felt his opponent knew better than he did. Instead, he digressed to Europe, hinting that he would be glad to discuss subjects outside the scope of those under consideration in Geneva. Was this an approach to "global bargaining," which Bidault had rejected even before he was offered it—the French Government's abandonment of EDC in return for a "good" peace in Indochina? Mendès-France cut off this line of argument and deferred discussion of extraneous subjects by invoking the need to observe an order of priorities. At that, the two sides parted; the French, at least, felt fairly pleased.

The next morning, Mendès-France arranged for a meeting to review the situation. Like Bidault, he had gone to live at *Joli-Port*,

Chauvel's residence. The "English-nanny" style of this edifice, its lack of comfort, and the genteel oddity of its interior decoration did not bother him—anyway, he could hardly see the house for the papers accumulating within it. But, like his predecessor, he was very sensitive to the beauty of the setting, the charm of the lawn that sloped gently down to the lapping waters of the lake, and the sight of three lime trees leaning miraculously over the bank as gracefully as three bathing girls. It was a stage set for the daydreams of a lonely walker, where ladies in flowing dresses might at any moment emerge from some eighteenth-century mansion to wave ribbons at gentlemen in powdered wigs; for the moment, it was thronged with scurrying diplomats in dark suits.

The meeting under the lime trees began just before nine o'clock. How did things stand for the French? Chauvel began with an account of his meeting with Dong the previous day—the first such meeting requested by the head of the Vietminh delegation (who had probably been prompted by Molotov). Chauvel paid less attention to the technicalities of the conversation than to Dong's warm, almost confiding, manner.[1] He compared Dong to Ho Chi Minh at the 1946 conference: "conciliatory, almost friendly; but immediately afterward, his colleagues talked a different language."

It was time to look at the balance sheet. Four rather meager aims had been achieved so far. In May, the Vietminh had agreed with the French delegation that military problems could be discussed separately and that it would be possible to arrange a ceasefire in advance of a political agreement. A few days later, the opposition agreed that supervision of an armistice could be entrusted not only to "mixed commissions" but to an international commission, as the Western side suggested; later, it accepted a commission that included a majority of non-Communist members. In June, the opposition converted Dong's May 25 hint about partition into a concrete proposal and agreed to separate the issue of Vietnam from that of Laos and Cambodia, which would simply be evacuated by Vietminh forces.

[1] Despite these sentiments, however, the Vietminh representative proposed the 13th Parallel as a demarcation line that same day.

But there had been no progress toward fixing a date for the evacuation of Tonkin by French Union troops, or for elections to reunite Vietnam after the "military" partition. Nor was there agreement about the exact composition of the international control commission or, last but not least, about the position of the demarcation line. There had not been even a mention of general guarantees for an agreement, safeguards for individuals and French property in the north, or how the various delegations would be bound by the individual agreements and obligations.

Mendès-France and his colleagues agreed that their goals remained those agreed on in Paris on June 24: to save the Expeditionary Corps, and to ensure the existence of political forces capable of stemming the Communist advance in Indochina. Therefore, their efforts should be directed at three basic points: locating the demarcation line as far north as possible; delaying the date of the general elections as much as possible, in order to give the nationalist state a chance to establish itself; and securing the most distant possible deadline for the evacuation of French troops to the south. To emphasize France's commitment, they decided that the preparations for the dispatch of conscripts to Asia should be publicized. (The week before, recruits in Marseilles had been inoculated against Asian diseases with this very purpose in mind.)

The fate of Cambodia and Laos was not forgotten at *Joli-Port*. But in their case, the basic questions—how to separate their problem from that of Vietnam, and how to persuade the Vietminh forces to evacuate their territory—had already been answered by Chou's statements to Bidault on June 17 and to Mendès-France on June 23. The Cambodian theater of operations had never been important, and Laos was beginning to be evacuated, according to information received from Vientiane. Moreover, it was difficult to discuss the Laotian problem sensibly. While Chou and Molotov displayed praiseworthy moderation, the Vietminh made absurd demands. For instance, on July 9, the Vietminh military delegation suddenly demanded that Laos be split in half and tried to secure territorial rights for a few hundred Khmer Issarak guerrillas in Cambodia. To all this must be added the weird behavior of the royal Khmer delegation, whose presence in Geneva became increasingly unclear up to, but not including, the last night of the conference.

And so, when Mendès-France received Dong on July 11, he was able to employ full knowledge of the facts in his long-awaited dialogue with France's adversary. The man who walked toward him over the grass beneath the trees was no longer quite the fierce campaigner with the hunted look whom Bidault had taken such trouble to avoid. Dong had become less tense, more supple—rounder, somehow. His gestures were smoother and his speech less breathless. Was this the result of meeting almost daily with Chauvel, or was it the wholesome air of Versoix? Could the change in his physical appearance be attributed to a decent tailor in Geneva or to Swiss cooking? The son of the Tonkinese mandarin had lost some of his warrior's stiffness and regained a little of the ease befitting a member of the court at Hue. A slight smile sometimes hovered on the heavy lips that resembled a wound in his anguished face, and a flicker of amusement—or irony—occasionally lit his eyes beneath the bushy eyebrows.

Dong added little to what he had told Chauvel the day before and what his military colleagues had said a day earlier to Delteil. Real contact had been made in personal terms, but Mendès-France found his opponent less than accommodating when it came to the substance of the argument. Dong's only reply to the plea for partition at the 18th Parallel was that his military colleagues had just made a concession by offering to move their line from the 13th to the 14th Parallel. As to time limits for the evacuation of the French forces and methods of regrouping, Dong's proposals were now even further from the French proposals than those he had recently outlined to Chauvel.

Mendès-France began to wonder whether, like the Greeks, Dong should not be feared most when he was bringing the gift of his smile. But he pulled himself together, remembering the rules of the game he himself had started, and reminding himself that his adversary was determined to hold the highest trumps for the last rubber, during the final hours.

On the next day, July 12, when Dulles was due in Paris, attention focused on nationalist Vietnam. It was time to stop playing hide-and-seek with the Saigon regime, a game which could so easily result in a dangerous outburst or a gesture of despair by Diem. Eight days earlier, as we have seen, Dejean had told Bao Dai about the plan for partition and the negotiations with the Vietminh, but this information did not seem to have reached his ministers. When Donald Heath, the American ambassador in Saigon, handed Diem a personal message from Eisenhower and brought him up to date on the situation, Diem was utterly amazed. Had things really gone this far? Had the military situation deteriorated to this extent? Was it not enough that the evacuation of the bishoprics should have dealt a terrible blow to his prestige —as a Catholic and a nationalist—almost as soon as he became President? Now an attempt was being made to impose a partition of the national territory on him: Diem was shattered and told Heath he would have no part in such a policy.

In Geneva, Tran Van Do accepted the same information more calmly. Do, who had once been thought to hold views close to those of the Vietminh, and who concealed remarkable subtlety and political experience beneath his look of incurable melancholy, well knew how weak his resources had become once the American Government subscribed to the "seven points." As far as essentials were concerned, he skillfully confined himself to avoiding mortgages on the future until the very last hours of the conference, and he displayed great outward dignity.

The next day, July 13, was truly crucial. Mendès-France saw Chou and Dong, and Tran Van Do met with Dong as well. Mendès-France, Eden, and Alexis Johnson left for Paris, where Dulles was converted to the ideas and methods of the head of the French Government. It was indeed one of the most important days of the conference.

Mendès-France was meeting Chou for the second time. Since their encounter in Berne, the Chinese minister had visited New Delhi and Rangoon and had met Ho Chi Minh somewhere in China. This naturally led Mendès-France to ask whether he had found his conversation with Ho fruitful. "I found that all those I met had an equal desire for peace," Chou replied with a placid smile.

As had Molotov two days earlier, Chou led the conversation to the problem of the demarcation line. "Why not show good will?" he asked blandly. Mendès-France retorted with an improved version of the case for the 18th Parallel which he had put to Molotov: "No other line has the same advantages. Look at the map. You will object that the Vietminh holds an area between the 13th and 16th parallels. But France holds provinces between the 16th and 18th—so that if we accept a line on the 16th Parallel, you will receive the nationalist areas and the nationalists will receive the Communist areas." Chou listened impassively; then he suggested that each side take a few steps toward the other, although "this does not mean that each must take the same number of steps."

Everything suggests that this conversation, together with the effect of the announcement that Dulles was coming to Paris, had something to do with the sudden change in the Vietminh attitude that soon followed. An hour later, Dong received Mendès-France and Chauvel. He had informed them in advance that he had something important to tell them, and now he suddenly offered to accept a demarcation line at the 16th Parallel—a jump of nearly 200 miles in four days. Mendès-France refused to be impressed; he remarked rather coldly that such a line would deprive nationalist Vietnam of Hue and Tourane (Da Nang), which were of vital importance to it, and leave Colonial Route 9, the only means of access from Laos to the sea, in Vietminh hands. When Dong suggested that special rights of access to this road could be granted to the Laotians, Mendès-France retorted that past experience in Germany concerning access to Berlin hardly encouraged him to think much of this offer.

A little later, as Mendès-France's aircraft was taking off for Paris, Pham Van Dong received his nationalist counterpart, a surprising and rather encouraging occasion. Pham Anh, Vietminh Minister of Industry and Commerce and a member of the northern delegation, had long been a close friend of Tran Van Do's brother, and as soon as he arrived in Geneva, he had passed on a suggestion to Do that the two foreign ministers should meet. "How could brothers of the same race refuse to meet each other?" Do replied. And so it was that Pham Van Dong and Tran Van Do met face to face, equally frail and solemn in appearance, equally consumed by worry over their lacerated homeland. It was a first contact, regarded as promising by both sides, rather than a political discussion.

The two ministers did, however, discuss the question that concerned them most: the general election intended to secure the ultimate reunification of the country. For the first time, Pham Van Dong made the concrete suggestion that elections take place within six months, a period he had hinted at earlier in private conversations. Do was careful not to protest, but it was obvious to him, as well as to his French and American allies, that it would be impossible to compete at the polls while the Vietminh still retained the momentum of its victory.

This argument was used the following day by Tran Van Huu when he called on the head of the Vietminh delegation. For several months, this former nationalist Vietnamese President had been employing his crafty bonhomie, his political experience, and his connections in Paris and Saigon to promote a policy of appeasement and compromise. The Vietminh leaders were glad to welcome the round little man with the high-pitched voice and eyes darting out from under heavy lids, who came to preach moderation to them. "Look," said Huu, "you can't hope to get a frontier on the 13th Parallel, elections within six months, and the embarkation of French troops within three months. Be more modest; you will serve your country better that way." Dong listened attentively. He did not comment and very politely saw his visitor back to the steps of the villa.[2]

While "the boss" was away, the French delegation put Bastille Day to good use by amending the first draft of a general agreement on the cessation of hostilities, which had been put together two days earlier. New differences of opinion had appeared during recent meetings of the Franco-Vietminh military committee. Buu had demanded the complete evacuation of French Union forces within three months, while the French representatives had sug-

[2] Conversation with Tran Van Huu, January 22, 1959.

gested a "technical" delay of 310 days with an additional "psychological" delay of 70 days.

The Vietminh military representatives were also demanding that air and artillery units be the first to leave and that equipment should be embarked last. Moreover, they suddenly refused to continue withdrawing the Vietminh units that were still inside the French perimeters, although this had been the keystone of Dong's plan of May 25. Now, they insisted on keeping these units in position near the Hanoi-Haiphong road while the evacuation was in progress. These Vietminh demands contained too many afterthoughts for the French delegation, which decided to put forward a practical and satisfactory draft of its own to counter these immoderate demands.

21

ONE HUNDRED AND SIXTY HOURS TO GO

It was late afternoon on July 15 when Mendès-France landed in Geneva for the second time, aglow from his "American success" in Paris. But beside the lake, nothing had moved since July 10. The conference had "exploded like a shell"[1] and now resembled a fantastically complicated ballet—a ballet consisting largely of *pas de deux*. Everywhere, beside the waters streaked by the flights of startled gulls, long black cars sped along tree-shaded avenues, carrying preoccupied gentlemen from villas to hotels. There were no less than thirteen meetings, asides, and encounters during that long day of July 15: Eden and Mendès-France, Eden and Molotov, Eden and Krishna Menon, Eden and Sananikone, Eden and Tep Phan, Chou En-lai and Menon, Mendès-France and Menon, Menon and Alexis Johnson, Menon and Molotov, and on and on.

But none of the day's *tête-à-têtes* was more important than the one after dinner at *Joli-Port*. Mendès-France was returning the hospitality Molotov had shown him on July 10. The latter showed little trace of the displeasure aroused among the Communist dele-

[1] Raymond Cartier, *Paris-Match*, July 24, 1954.

gations by the tripartite talks in Paris on July 13 and 14—although his smile was perhaps not quite so wide and friendly as it had been the night of the dinner at the *Villa Blanche*—and Mendès-France got neither the cutting remarks nor the sulky looks that Molotov occasionally indulged in.

After dinner, the two men made their way across the lawn to a table under the lime trees. Between them was a red lamp and a map of Indochina; Andronikov, the interpreter, was at their side. From the drawing room, their assistants watched a conversation that was obviously punctuated by long wordless gaps. "Mr. Molotov has an extraordinary capacity for silence," Mendès-France was to say later. "I think he can stay facing you for hours without a single word. It puts you in a rather difficult position. . . . I spread out my arguments before him and he just sat there, smoking one cigarette after another without answering. It was exhausting." Molotov rose only at half past one, after more than three hours of this strange face-to-face encounter.

Nothing definite came from these silences around the scarlet light, amid the dancing mosquitoes, gradually scattered by the cool night air. The two men leaned over the map of Indochina, using the red lamp as a paperweight to keep it from fluttering in the breeze. But Mendès-France's finger did not move along the same line as Molotov's; the latter maintained that the 16th Parallel would be the best frontier and that special arrangements could be made both for Hue and Colonial Route 9. Molotov was also strongly opposed to the suggestion of enclaves within the two large zones. Was there no crack in this rock? Not content with stubbornly defending the Vietminh representatives' first line of retreat, Molotov also supported their new demands concerning the evacuation of Haiphong and agreed with them that the delays suggested by the French officers were too lengthy. He showed greater moderation about the elections, insisting that a date for them must be officially stated in the documents but indicating a willingness to agree that the issue could be the subject of further discussions.

An hour later, Chauvel cabled the Quai d'Orsay: "This conversation has produced no concrete results." Yet on the following day, when a close colleague of Mendès-France met a member of the Soviet delegation and referred, with a touch of bitterness, to the fruitlessness of the meeting, the Russian diplomat looked astounded and told him that his minister had been delighted by his latest contact with the head of the French Government.

The two statesmen were to meet late that afternoon at Eden's residence. It had been agreed that at this meeting they would draw up a sort of catalogue of points on which there was agreement and problems that still required a solution. It was rumored that, in the Soviet draft memorandum, the blanks indicating no agreement were twice as numerous as in the British and French drafts.

Once again, the task of summation fell to Chauvel. He recapitulated that the settlement should consist of three cease-fire agreements, one for each of the countries involved; that the French delegation had circulated a draft agreement on July 12, which had been answered by Soviet counterproposals on July 15; and that Mendès-France's staff had produced a new draft which took Molotov's comments into account.

Mendès-France then briefly reviewed the continuing differences about the demarcation line: two parallels still separated the opposing sides. He dealt with another point at issue—the date of the elections—and recalled that the latest Soviet proposal suggested the end of 1955. He repeated that he preferred not to fix a date. He felt that a mixed authority should be empowered to select a date in the light of existing circumstances and that only the basic principles governing the authority's choice should be defined in advance. The question of the eventual supervision of the agreements raised problems, concerning both the composition and the powers of the proposed commissions, that were still under study.

Molotov now raised the bid. In rather polemical tones, he pointed out that other points of disagreement existed: the evacuation of French forces from the north, he said, must be carried out in six months, not twelve; Laos and Cambodia must promise not to join any military alliances and must forbid the establishment of military bases on their territories. Eden responded that the regrouping of forces in Laos should under no circumstances involve any form of partition or fragmentation of the kingdom's sovereignty.

Molotov insisted that a date be fixed for the Vietnamese elections. On the problems of the demarcation line, he stressed that the Vietminh had made a great concession by drawing back from the 13th to the 16th Parallel and pointed out, as he often liked to, that the latter had been used in 1945 to separate the British and Chinese spheres of interest after Japan's defeat. When all was said and done, he said, they were discussing a very transitory phase preceding the reunification of Vietnam. He finished on a somewhat milder note by recalling that it was he who had suggested the formula that gave the non-Communists a majority in the control commission.

The net result was cordial disagreement on essentials and grudging agreement on details. The three men met again the next day, July 17, in slightly happier circumstances. Eden took this opportunity to obtain agreement in principle regarding a formula for the control commission, based on an idea in the French draft of July 12: this organization would consist of one representative of the Colombo powers (Asian neutrals), another from the Communist countries, and a third to be appointed by the Western powers. Mendès-France argued that he could subscribe to this formula only if majority rule rather than unanimity—which would have given the right of veto to the Communist representative—was applied, except in clearly defined cases.

But before this fairly positive meeting ended, Molotov gave his two partners some cause for concern: in his capacity as co-chairman of the Geneva conference, he asked that a secret session of the nine powers be called for the following day, Sunday, July 18. The conference had not met for a month; was this reminder that it still existed a danger signal and a condemnation of the method of individual meetings chosen by Mendès-France? Would Molotov launch a diatribe against the American delegation and bring the structure so patiently erected since June 29 tumbling down in ruins? It was a silent and anxious French delegation that filed into the Palais des Nations that Sunday afternoon.

What was Molotov after? Sitting by Eden, he said nothing that

Bedell Smith (who had arrived in Geneva two days earlier but still looked exhausted) might wish to contradict. "Honorable agreements" and "respect for treaties" were mentioned on every side. What purpose did this ceremony fulfill? Suddenly, a touch of drama came from the most unlikely quarter: Tran Van Do rose to protest, with restraint but in a voice cracked with emotion, against the partition of his country and the way in which the fate of the Vietnamese was being decided. But Molotov's congenial speech had caused such great relief that little notice was taken of Do's moving address.

That evening, Mendès-France felt a kind of weariness flooding through him. His colleagues had just told him that Radio Peking had mentioned an impending agreement and a favorable outcome, but there was still so much to settle. He wrote to Faure: "I am trying to put the date of the election as far back as possible. Needless to say, our enemies are particularly tough on this point and they find a good deal of comfort and support even among the neutrals. In general we have been becalmed for three days and—without really believing it—I occasionally wonder whether we are not going to founder within sight of land."

Only forty-eight hours to go . . . .

Mendès-France talked to Colonel Brohon, sent by General Ely to inform him of the latest military developments—which did not encourage any indefinite prolongation of the conference. He sent telegrams to Saigon in an attempt to learn more about the nationalist government's state of mind, and he received Eden and took him to see Chou.

After a luncheon at *Joli-Port* with Albert Sarraut, President of the Assembly of the French Union and a former governor-general of Indochina, Mendès-France set off to spend most of the afternoon with Bedell Smith at the Hôtel du Rhône. Did this mean progress or was there some new hitch between Paris and Washington?

New difficulties had indeed arisen. For one thing, Diem had told the U.S. ambassador in Saigon that, with only the slightest American encouragement, he would take a stand against the proposed agreements and denounce all Vietnamese obligations to France; the ambassador had tried to talk him out of such extremes. A more serious difficulty arose when Dulles, on being informed of the newest version of the draft agreements, declared that they did not comply at all with the "seven points" of June 29 and singled out as unacceptable the proposed neutralization of Laos and Cambodia, as well as the compromise which would allow a Communist nation to be one of the three members of the armistice commission. He kept on repeating: "No Communist can be neutral."

It appeared that the cordial, even enthusiastic, partner of July 13 was now ready to veto the agreement that several of P.M.-F.'s colleagues believed to be imminent. On top of all this, a telegram arrived describing the situation in the Red River delta (where a profound uneasiness was undermining the nationalist Vietnamese units) as grave and the developments in the south (where general guerrilla activity was starting again) as disquieting.

Toward the end of the afternoon, Dong invited a few dozen journalists, most of them French, to his pleasant residence at Versoix. Leaning against a great oak tree, he looked frailer than ever.

"Well, Monsieur le ministre, will there be an agreement by tomorrow night?" they asked him.

"Tomorrow night? Why tomorrow night?"

"Well . . . you know that Mendès-France has undertaken . . . ."

"Oh, we'll manage to agree. . . . Tomorrow? . . . Perhaps another day!"

"But Mendès-France might have a political accident in the meantime."

Dong laughed—a huge laugh out of all proportion with his narrow frame. "One recovers from that sort of accident quite easily!"

Apparently this was only a joke. Three hours later, clearly eager to waste not even a minute, Dong was seen poring over a map of Indochina with Sarraut and Mendès-France. The Parallel, once again . . . . Around Hue, the map was striped like the face of an African witch doctor. Suddenly a member of Mendès-France's staff burst in—Tass was reporting that agreement had been reached. "Deny it," snapped Mendès-France. He had just gained sixty miles on the map and had succeeded in prying Dong loose from the 16th Parallel. But the one day remaining would hardly be enough to balance the scales a little more in France's favor.

On Tuesday, July 20, the flower sellers on the Place du Molard, the old gentlemen and elderly spinsters strolling along the lake shore feeding the gulls, the idlers on the little isle of Jean-Jacques, even the engineer of the Ouchy ferry—all of them asked or whispered: "Is it tonight?" But the game was not yet over.

Mendès-France rose early and left *Joli-Port* to set up shop at *Le Bocage*, the large villa that had been the official seat of the French delegation since April, in order to be near the documents and the center of debate.

How could agreement be reached that night? There were loose ends of disagreement about the demarcation line, about the dates of the elections and the embarkation of the French troops, and about the composition of the control commission. It was still necessary to secure Washington's agreement and Diem's "forbearance." There was also an important formality: General Ely would give the "go-ahead," but he was a conscientious commander and insisted on being informed in advance about the essentials of the documents he was asked to approve. And the Cambodian and Laotian agreements had not even been drafted. The morning of July 20 saw the last of the bargaining sessions. Dong returned, followed by Eden and Molotov. Molotov was tired—one might have said edgy, if it had been anyone else—and clearly eager to be done with it. Mendès-France sensed that he would lend all his weight to peace at the eleventh hour, a peace which he himself had foreseen when he made his wager on June 20 and which he had stalked ever since, with grim determination. His last task was to persuade Chou to go along with him during the final arbitration. And so, Mendès-France's last luncheon engagement in Geneva was with Chou, and it went on until after four in the afternoon.

Ever since the day in June when he saved the conference by stating that the questions of Laos and Cambodia would be treated separately, Chou had played an increasingly effective part in the negotiations. His manner had been rather cramped when he first reached Geneva in late April, but he had grown more authoritative and relaxed. He lacked Dong's fire and Molotov's monumental stability, but he generated a special sense of good fellowship, together with a lively charm and a searching intelligence. He did not put on a show of activity, and he intervened only at crucial moments, but then the centuries-old heritage of Chinese diplomacy came into its own. Still, the Communist militant was never very far beneath the surface. Even the blandest smile could suddenly harden and stir visions of "The Long March," the toiling masses, the re-education camps, the relentless revolution, and the goal that must be reached.

The day before, Chou had cleared the way for negotiations about Laos by persuading the Vietminh delegation to drop its demand for a Pathet Lao regrouping zone, which would have been tantamount to the partition of the kingdom. On the final day, Mendès-France wanted him to pressure Dong once again for further concessions on the demarcation line, the date of the elections, and the time limits for the evacuation of the French troops.

But Chou had something else in mind. What interested him most was not the creation of a Communist state on China's southern frontier or the size of such a state; his chief concern was to ensure that there would be no American military base anywhere near the Chinese frontier. This way why he wanted to head Mendès-France toward some form of neutralization for Indochina. But such a formula would have been incompatible with the third stipulation in the "Anglo-American seven points," which specified that there must be no restriction upon the capacity of the three states to maintain stable non-Communist regimes. Moreover, Mendès-France made it clear to Chou that Laos and Cambodia would have to be completely independent.

Still, during the conversation, the two men worked out a formula to circumvent this obstacle: the only alliances expressly forbidden to the states of Indochina would be those regarded as contrary to the United Nations Charter. This was a sizeable concession on China's part and a great encouragement to Mendès-France. Meanwhile, a telegram arrived from Washington announcing that

Dulles had withdrawn his objections to the clauses concerning the defense of Laos and Cambodia; he was satisfied that they did not involve neutralization. And so, Chou agreed to accompany Mendès-France to *Le Bocage*, where Eden and Molotov were to join them. It was now a matter of persuading Dong to raise the demarcation line a little higher on the map and to put off the date of the elections.

A visitor entering the great drawing room of the villa a little before five o'clock would have discovered a surprising sight: sitting in chairs casually scattered around the large table, amid a *décor* better suited to a village wedding, Eden, Mendès-France, Molotov, and Chou surrounded Pham Van Dong. Perspiring, anguished, looking almost hunted, Dong was bending over a map of Indochina—mile by mile, Communist Vietnam was shrinking northward.

Impassively, Molotov waited for the appropriate moment to launch his compromise solution. It was obvious that he had long expected to arbitrate a compromise demarcation line at the 16th Parallel between the Vietminh, who demanded the 13th or 14th, and the French, who held out for the 18th Parallel. He had pointed out repeatedly, as we have seen, that this line was selected, after the Japanese defeat, to divide the British and Chinese spheres in Southeast Asia. (Everything that brought that epoch back to him —the days when the war ended, his country triumphed, Japan was defeated, the days when the fate of the world was settled with a slide rule, and the fair days of San Francisco—all this was to Molotov's taste.) At the beginning of July, however, during a conversation he and Chauvel had arranged between two senior Soviet officers and de Brébisson, the latter had succeeded in convincing the Russians that, among other disadvantages, a demarcation line at the 16th Parallel would deny Laos the use of its vital link with the sea, Colonial Route 9. Molotov had tried to counter this argument by suggesting that special arrangements could be made for the use of the road, but we have already noted how little enthusiasm the French expressed when Pham Van Dong made this suggestion. On July 13, Chou had persuaded Dong to give up the

14th Parallel and settle for the 16th. Molotov felt obliged to support his allies' demand to begin with, but he still wanted to play the part of arbitrator. Chou had made Dong surrender two parallels; Molotov would only ask him for one. Now, on July 20, Molotov let it drop: "Let us agree on the 17th Parallel."

Eden and Mendès-France exchanged a quick look. The 17th Parallel was within 50 miles of the line proposed in the Anglo-American "seven points," which had been accepted as the Western terms for a settlement at the Paris meeting on July 14. The end was in sight. Mendès-France had virtually run out of arguments to counter Molotov's proposal.[2] Dong, now looking as though nothing further could be wrung from him, except his last breath, nevertheless found the strength to demand that, in return for this concession, a date be fixed for the elections. Mendès-France tried to maintain that it would be better not to be too specific; but here, as on the demarcation line, he failed to secure all he was bidding for. Dong demanded elections within six months, the latest Soviet memorandum provided for elections within sixteen months, while six weeks earlier, Bidault's experts had wanted to hold them after eighteen months. "Two years?" said Molotov. Mendès-France agreed, and Eden no longer even tried to hide his satisfaction.

It was 5:15 in the afternoon of July 20. The news spread fast—agreement had been reached! Everyone began to prepare for the solemn session in the Palais des Nations at which the armistice texts would be signed and the final declaration of the nine powers adopted. In the excitement of the moment, little thought was given to the fact that although compromise had been achieved on the more conspicuous and sensitive points, a number of issues were still in dispute. The agreements dealing with Laos and, above all, Cambodia had barely reached a first draft and had not yet received explicit approval.

Never mind! The Pathet Lao, it was agreed, would have no "reserved zones" in Laos. As to Cambodia, it had been decided weeks ago that the Vietminh should simply evacuate it. The two

[2] General Ely had just agreed in a telegram that partition was feasible on the 17th Parallel.

royal governments, then, had virtually secured recognition by Peking and Moscow. Only formalities remained; let the experts make one last rush before the night was out. The main thing was to get the armistice agreements and the concluding document initialed before midnight. The definitive texts could follow later.

22

THE CLOCKS OF THE PALAIS DES NATIONS

The Geneva conference had already provided a script that any good writer of thrillers would have been proud to sign. From the arrival of Chou En-lai—the sardonic debut of the Chinese revolutionary, dressed in worker's blues, at the exclusive club of modern diplomacy—to that of Pham Van Dong, borne direct from the caves of Thai Nguyen to the Palais des Nations; from the machinations of Bidault, seeking a "Little Guernica" near Dien Bien Phu, to the sudden Vietminh offer of partition; from P.M.-F.'s wager, to John Foster Dulles's lightning dash to Paris and the sudden transformation of Molotov, "Mister Veto," into a virtuoso of compromise—the talks had been brightened with every flashing twist and turn that the regiment of journalists camping in Geneva could have wished for.

A dozen of them were discussing it late in the afternoon of July 20 at the blue and white bar of the press center. Now that the fever had abated, they talked about the prospects of Mendès-France's government, newly reconfirmed in office as a result of its success in Geneva, and about the future of the European treaties.

Everyone was relaxed. Even the American journalists and the correspondents of Paris papers least inclined to "Mendèsism" were visibly satisfied. Tomorrow would be the first day of real peace in the world in fifteen years.

Someone mentioned that yet another meeting was taking place between Eden, Molotov, and Mendès-France at the British Foreign Secretary's residence. Another hitch? No, of course not; at most, some teamwork to get the documents into shape. What could go wrong now, anyway? What problems were left, except to choose between whisky and schnapps? Whether to go home by rail or air. Whether to attend the ceremonies that night in a dark suit or working clothes. Someone drifted into the bar with the news that the session at which the joint declaration was to be announced had been postponed from 9:00 to 11:00 P.M. "That's just a stunt," one of the journalists cracked. "That way the bet will be won on the stroke of midnight. There is a bit of Phileas Fogg in P.M.-F."

There was more to it than that. At eight, Eden called the French delegation to say that Molotov had telephoned him in a fury: Sam Sary, speaking for the Cambodian delegation, was telling the "big powers" that he wouldn't sign. What? Cambodia? What was the matter with them? The draft agreements had reached them two days earlier. Why should they wait until the last moment to publicize a disagreement there had been plenty of time to discuss? Eden went on to say that Molotov was bitter, and that he was convinced it was all an American move to keep Cambodia out of the agreements in order to establish bases there. Molotov was demanding an immediate meeting of the heads of delegations. Eden said that they would meet at his residence immediately.

Half an hour later, Sam Sary confronted the massed big guns of international diplomacy. A short, tawny man with ragged wisps of hair, he clutched the arms of his chair as he hammered back in a harsh and strident voice at Molotov, Eden, and Mendès-France: "No, I will not sign a document that infringes upon the sovereignty of my country. No, it restricts Cambodia's freedom to make alliances or to let anyone it thinks fit have bases on its territory. No, it cannot be done."

"But why didn't you raise these objections earlier?" was the joint reply. "Besides, the documents entitle you to call on the forces of the French Union and forbid only those alliances that are not compatible with the United Nations Charter. Your security is assured, and you know it."

"We want to be free to do what we like! We want to be able to set up American bases in Cambodia. . . . We want to be able to fight Communism in every possible way."

"But don't you see that you are threatening the whole balance of Southeast Asia, peace in Asia, the peace of the world?"

"I am not like the rest; I am not scared of Communism or the great powers." The little man would not budge.

What gave him all that energy? A glance at the ranks of the nationalist Vietnamese delegates showed a few ironical smiles. Was it the Americans? Walter Robertson, the assistant secretary of state, whom one might have suspected of staging the incident, had already left Geneva. A messenger rushed off to Bedell Smith, who was ill in bed. Visibly upset by the whole business, Bedell Smith sent another mediator to tell Sam Sary that his country would be safe, that a multilateral Southeast Asian defense pact was being prepared. Though the documents that affected Cambodia were not every satisfactory, the threat was not so great that Cambodia needed to oppose them. Dulles had given his agreement to the draft treaty . . . and so on.

It made no difference. Time went on. Eleven o'clock came and went. In the brightly lit hall of the Palais des Nations, the growing crowd began to wonder what was happening and to fear the worst. Only forty-five minutes to go . . . only half an hour . . . no delegation had yet shown up. At midnight, a few French and British diplomats came by, looking exasperated. "The Cambodian won't sign. Eden, Mendès-France, and Molotov are in conference with him, looking for a compromise formula. If one can be found, the session could still take place at about 2:00. It may be possible to initial only some of the documents."

But if the armistice were not signed until dawn, what would happen to the Mendès-France cabinet? Someone looked at the clocks—they still showed midnight! Who had stopped the clocks?

In the Palais des Nations, it remained midnight that long night through.

Pham Van Dong rushed in, his face distorted by fatigue and glistening with perspiration. A slight pause for the photographers, and he disappeared into the hall where the ceremony was due to take place. A moment later he came out again. No one knew what to think.

Meanwhile, in the drawing room of *Le Reposoir*, Sam Sary was winning his battle. His outrageous, ingenuous, and cocky stand was having a strange effect on Molotov. The Soviet leader seemed to sense that Sam Sary was *not* a tool of the Americans, that he really *was* fighting his own battle, that Cambodia was acting with the impertinent audacity of a nation too weak to take careful account of any balance of forces. Molotov was no sentimentalist, but, judging from his quizzical look, the Cambodian attitude struck him as half touching and half comical. He softened visibly. If this were really not a move engineered from Washington, if this little man were since and honestly demanding his rights, his request could be considered.

Some formula had to be found to bring the business to an end. What Sam Sary wanted, Molotov was told, was to retain his freedom to call on a foreign power other than France to defend his country, to establish bases. "Bases? Out of the question, quite out of the question," the Soviet minister repeated. "But certain forms of joint defense might be considered. What if Cambodia could call on support from abroad if there were specific threats, a real danger?"

By now, it was past two in the morning. Feverishly leafing through the papers before him, Sam Sary declared—and he was not joking—that he had another seventeen demands to make! But the concession just made by the intractable Molotov was so great that he was forced to yield, and he promised to sign "in the morning." He had scored a major point; who could have foreseen that the Russians and the Chinese would agree to possible American intervention in Cambodia in the event of an ill-defined threat?

"Well now," said Molotov, "I hope that everybody is content at last?"

Mendès-France raised his hand: "I have something to add."

"What—again!"

"Yes. One cannot deny to Laos what one has just granted Cambodia. A matter of simple justice."

Molotov made a wry face. Then suddenly, all patience spent, he said, "All right—Laos too."[1]

All that now remained was to prepare the closing ceremony. It was to be devoid of all pomp: Tran Van Do had asked, on behalf of the Vietnamese delegation, that there be no celebrations in connection with documents that would shatter the unity of his country indefinitely.

Since midnight, Mendès-France had been carrying in his pocket a telegram from General Ely authorizing General Delteil to sign the armistice agreements in his name. Just before 3:00 A.M., he went to look for Delteil, who was waiting for this moment in a small reception room on the first floor. "I know that what I am asking you to do is a painful task for an officer," said Mendès-France, looking grave. "But you know as well as I that there is no other way out and that tonight's agreements are the best we can secure. They are not contrary to the honor of our army, or to the national interest, or to our commitments to our allies."

Delteil's cold exterior concealed deep emotion, but he agreed. He knew that everything the Premier had said was true—he had been too closely involved with both the fighting and the negotiations to doubt it. But to be the officer who was duty-bound to sign this heart-rending document . . . . His face white, his steps deliberate, he walked to the great hall where a horseshoe-shaped table had been set up. The time was 3:20 A.M. Only the military delegates were present; the "political" representatives would meet for the official closing ceremony later that day.

After signing the cease-fire agreement for the Vietminh, Ta Quang Buu rose beaming from the table and turned to Delteil: "And now, General, I hope that you will agree to take a glass of

[1] Conversation with Mendès-France, December 20, 1958.

champagne with us." The head of the French military commission stood up, pale as a corpse: "You will understand that I cannot accept." Walking rather stiffly, he left to join his colleagues.[2]

Meanwhile, the hall and the passageways brimmed with excitement, the sadness of some mingling with the happiness of others. The French delegation held an improvised press conference about the conditions under which the cease-fire would come into force, while the American delegation handed out a short communiqué referring to "the progress made toward peace."

July 21 was dawning; it was time to start the clocks again. Tomorrow there would be no more fighting in the rice fields. The war in Indochina was over.

Nothing was signed during the session on July 21.[3] The documents consisted of "unilateral declarations" and a "final declaration" which was regarded as an "act of the conference" implicitly agreed to by the nine powers. This nonsigning made it possible to spare the American delegation the ordeal of having to countersign a document with Chou En-lai. The negotiators had been skillful and ingenious down to the last minute. The Geneva conference had discovered a new form of peaceful coexistence—that which results from tacit agreement among the parties to a negotiation; and a new form of legal obligation between states—an unsigned treaty.

[2] Only the two armistice agreements for Vietnam and Laos were initialed during the night of July 20 by General Delteil and Ta Quang Buu; the Cambodian armistice was signed later that morning. The military situation was in fact different in Cambodia, since there were hardly any French troops there and the Khmer general staff was not subordinate to Saigon. This enabled the Cambodian General Nhiek Tioulong to sign the agreement relating to his country.

[3] This made it possible to pretend that the organization of elections in Vietnam within a time limit of two years was a mere proposal.

23

THE COMPROMISE

Eight years of war, four hundred thousand dead, three months of negotiations—all this was summed up at dawn on July 21, in a handful of austere documents. What did their words mean, in return for so many dead? The only valid judgment one can make is one that relates to the actual situation. The political map set forth in the documents had to reflect the war map that had been drawn by years of struggle, six months of Vietminh battering-ram techniques, and a sharp increase in Chinese aid. On July 20, 1954, while the final bargaining in Geneva played with the location of the demarcation line and the date of the elections, the military situation in Vietnam deteriorated to the point where a cease-fire was essential, regardless of Mendès-France's wager.

In the north, the Vietminh could put 120 well-armed battalions in the field against 80 French Union battalions, one-third of which were Vietnamese units overwhelmed by an entirely understandable wave of despair. The superior equipment of the French and the fact that their General Staff had the only air force in the theater could not make up for the strategic semi-paralysis induced by their obsessive need to keep the escape route to Haiphong open at any price, which forced them to concentrate all their effort and attention on this line. Despite this, observers thought the Expeditionary Corps could be concentrated at Hanoi only at the price of a very hard, very costly, and very hazardous battle. On July 6, Marshal Juin had suggested the evacuation of Hanoi to the French Government.

In central Vietnam, the Vietminh had just scored a major psychological and strategic success at An Khe (An Tuc, just south of the 14th Parallel) that was less publicized than the fall of Dien Bien Phu, but nearly as rewarding for him. This blow and the failure of Operation Atlante had reduced the French command to impotence in central Vietnam; and in the south, where the balance of forces favored the French more than it did in the north, guerrilla warfare had begun again with purposeful intensity. This added to the state of confusion among the populace, who had not turned against the French because of Dien Bien Phu but might well be swayed to the Communist side by the Vietminh's terrorist activities.

In Laos, the situation was improving, and most reports indicated that the Vietminh troops were on their way back to Tonkin. But it was obvious that this movement would be reversed if hostilities started again; and the French Union forces were too weak, after the costly attempts to rescue the survivors of Dien Bien Phu, to bar such an invasion effectively. In Cambodia, where there had been hardly any war news for more than a year, the Vietminh had just attacked with unprecedented boldness. A single engagement a few days earlier had cost the French Union forces fourteen dead —a small casualty list, perhaps, but a revealing one.

The sum total of these observations led a French officer to remark in Geneva on July 16: "An agreement, however unsatisfactory, is preferable to no agreement at all." Given the situation, was the agreement unsatisfactory?

The documents published at the end of the Geneva conference included three separate military agreements covering Vietnam, Laos, and Cambodia. There was also a "final declaration" by the nine powers, six "unilateral declarations" (two by the Cambodian Government, two by Laos, and two by France), thirteen final speeches (each of the nine spoke, and Tran Van Do, Mendès-France, Tep Phan, and Bedell Smith each spoke twice), and two letters exchanged by Pham Van Dong and Mendès-France.

The "unilateral declarations" covered some very important commitments: they bound the Laotian and Cambodian governments not to enter into military alliances incompatible with the principles of the United Nations Charter and the Geneva settlement and not to invite foreign support except for the "effective defense" of their territories.

The speeches were of relatively little interest. The leaders of the Communist delegations took the opportunity to salute "a victory of peace," and the leaders of the other delegations paid homage to the good will of the partners and observed that the results of their labors would be judged by the ways in which they were put to use. There are noteworthy passages among these texts, however, including Tran Van Do's final solemn protest against the partition imposed upon his country; Bedell Smith's emphasis on the American Government's great interest in having genuinely free elections in Vietnam; Tep Phan's assertion that Cambodia had "legitimate rights and interests in South Vietnam"; and, finally, Mendès-France's insistence on France's strong interest in the maintenance of religious freedom in the bishoprics of Phat Diem and Bui Chu (this last statement led Pham Van Dong to make a commitment of sorts about this subject in his speech).

The "final declaration," which, as we have said, bore no signatures whatsoever, simply took note of the other texts. It decided only one issue, albeit an important one: it set the date of the Vietnamese elections for July, 1956. There were to be consultations on this subject between the "representative authorities" of both zones from July 20, 1955, onward.[1] The most important documents were the three agreements "on the cessation of hostilities," one for each of the three countries of Indochina.

1. *The military partition of Vietnam.* The agreement signed by Delteil and Buu, to be worked out in detail by French and

[1] Was this a decision, a hope, or a promise? We have seen above (chap. 22, p. 300) that a certain lack of definition in this document opened the way to a variety of interpretations.

Vietminh delegates meeting at Trung Gia, stated that the Vietnam cease-fire should come into force on July 27 in northern Vietnam, on August 1 in central Vietnam, and on August 11 in southern Vietnam. Within a period of fifteen days after the above dates, the forces of the opposing sides were to disengage and concentrate in their respective "provisional assembly areas." The evacuation of forces from the provisional assembly areas to the general regrouping zones on either side of the 17th Parallel would be carried out in "successive monthly installments." Each side was given a total of 300 days to complete its evacuation to its own regrouping zone.

Once the two sides had completed their movements, the two armies would be separated by a provisional military demarcation line located near the 17th Parallel, along the Cua Tung River, 6 miles north of Colonial Route 9—the road leading to Savannakhet, in Laos, which had been the subject of so much hard bargaining between Molotov and Mendès-France.

Prisoners of war and civilian internees were to be released by both sides within thirty days of the cease-fire. Both sides bound themselves not to take repressive measures against any individual for activities during the hostilities, and it was explicitly stated that, in both the north and the south, people could opt for the zone of their choice throughout the 300-day period set aside for the redeployment of troops.

From the time the agreement came into force, it was forbidden to bring into Vietnam war matériel intended to reinforce either side, or to set up new military bases. No bases under the control of a foreign state would be allowed in Vietnam, and neither zone was permitted to belong to any military alliance. Finally, in order to supervise the implementation of the agreement, the parties concerned were to set up a Joint Commission, which would be supervised by an International Commission. The latter was to consist of representatives of India, Canada, and Poland.

2. *The disengagement of Laos.* The cease-fire was to come into effect in Laos on August 6. The French and Vietminh forces were given four months to evacuate the country, but the French could retain two bases, with a total of 3,500 men, and the Laotian

National Army could retain 1,500 French instructors. The Pathet Lao units would be concentrated at twelve provisional regrouping areas and then given four months to choose between being re-absorbed into the rest of the population or transferred to one of the two provinces—Samneua and Phong Saly—they had occupied during the hostilities. Control of these provinces was to return to the royal administration under the same conditions as the rest of the country. The Laotian Government declared unilaterally that until the elections—planned for the summer of 1955—the former rebels would have special representatives attached to the royal administration.

3. *The pacification of Cambodia.* The cease-fire was to come into force in Cambodia on August 7. However, the process of integrating the Khmer Issarak into the population was to be quicker; it was given one month to comply. The three-month time limit for the evacuation of French and Vietminh forces was also shorter than in Laos. No regrouping zone was provided for in Cambodia. In effect, the agreement meant the unconditional liquidation of the state of war, which, in the southern kingdom, was largely an artificial creation.

The fact that China and the Soviet Union took part in the preparation of the agreements meant that the royal regimes at Luang Prabang and Phnom Penh secured real recognition from countries which they might well have regarded as their most formidable enemies.

As in Vietnam, Joint Commissions were set up in Laos and Cambodia. They were supervised in each of the three countries by tripartite international commissions, which were chaired by the Indian representatives and normally made decisions by a majority vote; unanimity was required only in cases of violations which "might lead to a resumption of hostilities." If any of the parties refused to comply with the requests of the international commission, there was a right of appeal to the supreme authority, the nine members of the Geneva conference.

We have said that these documents could only be judged in relation to the military situation. They should also be measured against the intentions and hopes of the various parties at the start of the talks.

For Laos and Cambodia, the documents signed on July 20–21 seemed close to the best that their representatives could have hoped to obtain. Of course, the Vietminh demands were exorbitant. It was absurd to claim entire provinces on behalf of the Khmer Issarak, when it hardly existed as a fighting force. Any settlement in Cambodia had to result in the re-integration of Cambodian nationals into the population and the evacuation of Vietminh forces. Both of these goals were achieved within a short time. The French representative was forced to agree to certain limitations on Cambodia's freedom of diplomatic action; the draft agreements imposed a restraint that some regarded as a kind of imposed neutrality. But Sam Sary's daring move during the final night gave his country such complete freedom of action that only aggression appeared to be forbidden to this peaceful little country.

Laos might feel painfully restricted by the provision granting the Pathet Lao rebels the right to assemble, for the time being, in the provinces of Phong Saly and Samneua. But since the administration remained—at least theoretically—in the hands of the government in Vientiane, the demands made by Chou up to July 19 were far from being fulfilled. The two provinces were indeed Communist "regrouping zones," but it was up to the government to ensure that they would not last. It had French bases, French instructors, and the right to call on a foreign power for "effective defense" in case of danger. In other words, the Laotian kingdom emerged from the war without too many painful ties or heavy mortgages on the future. This was very different from partition pure and simple, the fate that the Communist powers had intended for Laos, and the Vietminh had been in a better position to enforce partition in Laos than in Cambodia.

To make a sensible judgment about the agreement relating to Vietnam, one must first decide about the principle of partition. If one is opposed to partition, the agreement negotiated is clearly deplorable. It should be borne in mind, however, that by the end of June, 1954, few opponents of partition remained. On June 29, Dulles himself, until May a determined advocate of withdrawal to the two deltas, had countersigned the seven-point Anglo-American memorandum that explicitly recommended partition. The most senior officers of the French General Staff had supported this solution for several months before agreement was reached. Frédéric-Dupont, the arch-conservative French negotiator, took pride in being responsible for the negotiations that led most directly to it, and Bidault—during his last days as minister of foreign affairs—made his acceptance dependent only on General Ely's, which reached him on June 13.

As far as the Vietnamese themselves were concerned, the attitude of complete rejection adopted first by Prince Buu Loc's government and then by that of Ngo Dinh Diem (Bao Dai appeared to have withdrawn his objections during his interview with Dejean on July 4, 1954) deserved great respect and was often moving. No Vietnamese worthy of the name, whether nationalist or Communist, could cheerfully contemplate the partition of his country, even for a limited time.

But if the principle of Vietnamese unity had been asserted unyieldingly in 1954, the result would certainly have benefited those who won at Dien Bien Phu. The Vietminh's hardened troops, their fifth columns guided by political militants, and their propagandists skilled in manipulating public opinion were dominant throughout the country. What could the Bao-Daist regime put into the struggle against Giap's soldiers, Truong Chinh's militants, and Hoang Quoc Viet's trade unionists? Seldom has there been a clearer case of the stronger and the weaker vessel.

If, on the other hand, one accepts the principle of partition, it is possible to appreciate the results that were obtained by employing it. It did accomplish the two main French aims: it saved the Expeditionary Corps, and it gave the nationalist state a last chance to establish itself and to offer a convincing alternative to Communism behind the relative protection of a solid frontier.

Consider the various attitudes at the end of June, when the French decided in favor of partition (the meeting of Mendès-France, Ely, Chauvel, La Chambre, and Parodi on June 24) and when the Vietminh at last disclosed its intentions concerning the demarcation line (the conversations between Delteil and Brébisson, Buu and Lau on June 28). And then consider the results achieved.

1. *The demarcation line.* From June 10 on, France demanded that Vietnam be partitioned at the 18th Parallel, at the Porte d'Annam and north of the Giang River.[2] But at the end of June, France's Anglo-American allies gave it a "respectable" line of retreat by referring (in their seven-point memorandum) to a frontier near the 17th Parallel, at Dong Hoi.

The Vietminh first demanded partition at the 13th Parallel and took twelve days to shift to the 14th Parallel. On July 13, Pham Van Dong conceded the 16th Parallel under converging pressures from Chou and Dulles, whose arrival in Paris seemed to make a great impression on the Communists. Mendès-France and Sarraut attempted to nibble away even further at the Vietminh claim. During the night of July 19, the French extracted a few more miles, and, during the afternoon of July 20, Molotov very nearly met the Anglo-American terms of June 29 by adjudicating on the 17th Parallel.

The 18th Parallel would undoubtedly have made a better frontier. The limestone hills of the Porte d'Annam, which extend into Laos, and the Giang River, running well south of the Parallel, provided a good natural defense line and separated two fairly clearly differentiated areas. This would have been a perfect outcome for the talks. As it was, the result achieved represented an 80 per cent success for the Western representative.

A high Quai d'Orsay official who took part in the talks but never entirely lost his independent judgment has said:

> The agreements of July 20 represent a sort of transfer to the map of the military situation at that time. . . . This transfer favored us in several ways. The military situation was extremely shaky; we were unable to hold Hanoi. The command had just informed us that even the dispatch of two conscript divisions would not enable us to [do so]. The city could be cut off from Haiphong in a single day. We were told that the withdrawal of the garrison under fire would

[2] This was Navarre's suggestion in reply to Chauvel's questions dated April 21, 1954, although he also considered that the demarcation line could be drawn considerably farther south. See above, chap. 9, pp. 138–39.

have been very costly. Even the base of Haiphong itself, toward which we would have had to withdraw, was riddled by a fifth column swollen by a large number of refugees. The fact of the matter seemed to be that if a regrouping of forces had been carried out in the rather narrow confines of the delta after we had evacuated the southern provinces of Nam Dinh, Phat Diem, and Bui Chu, the Vietminh would have had to evacuate the equivalent of two regular divisions from the areas which we had claimed to control. Moreover, we were vulnerable to any incident in the south because our forces were concentrated in the north. Considering all this information, one is entitled to think that the division of the country at the 13th Parallel would have more accurately reflected the true state of affairs than the partition on the 17th Parallel which we achieved.[3]

2. *The date of the elections.* French policy at the end of June was to put off the elections as long as possible, or even to avoid fixing any date for them (Mendès-France was more demanding in this respect than Bidault), and to leave the responsibility for them to the International Commission. The Vietminh scarcely varied its position and constantly demanded that the delay should not exceed six months. On July 15, the Soviet delegation put forward a compromise formula for elections at the end of 1955. The argument went on until five in the afternoon of July 20, when everybody agreed to Molotov's proposal (in which Eden seems to have played an important part) for a delay of two years. It is worth remembering that the American experts and the author of a note issued by Bidault's team during June wished to secure a delay of at least eighteen months.

[3] On July 23, 1954, Mendès-France made the following statement in the National Assembly: "On May 15, 1954, the Committee of National Defense gave General Navarre precise instructions that once again defined the line of our military policy: 'You should clean up the situation in central and southern Indochina south of the 18th Parallel'—we are within a hundred kilometers of this in Vietnam, and the whole of Laos has been saved—in order to prepare for withdrawal south of this line should the situation require this in the future. North of this line no political consideration must be allowed to take precedence over military considerations.' And so the best-informed recommendations all led to the same conclusion. For a long time, the specialists in the problem have recommended to us precisely that line of separation for which we secured recognition, not without some trouble from our opponents in Geneva."

In this case also, the result was not quite what the French representatives were trying to achieve, but observers agreed at the time that if a two-year delay did not enable the West to create a buffer state in southern Indochina, the whole undertaking was doomed in any case. It should also be added that, as the elections were written into the joint "final declaration," France was no more responsible for their organization than any of the other eight members of the conference. Responsibility did, in fact, lie with the international commission, which made decisions on a political subject such as this by a majority vote, there being only one Communist member out of a total membership of three.

3. *The phasing of the Expeditionary Corps's evacuation.* The French proposed a delay of 310 days for "technical" and 70 days for "psychological" purposes, and the parallel disengagement of the two armies. The Vietminh military delegates suddenly went back on their proposals of early July and demanded evacuation within three months. They were most persistent about this, but their opponents extorted from them a delay of ten months (300 days instead of 380), together with the obligation to disengage. The latter provision ensured that they could not maintain a threat against the Franco-Vietnamese lines of evacuation in the Red River delta, which would have been unbearable.

As to the clauses dealing with the future defense capabilities of Vietnam—which were of the highest interest to Washington—it was specifically stated that neither side could augment its equipment. This allowed the nationalists to increase the numerical strength of their forces, but the Vietminh, which had more troops than it required, was thus barred from building an air force or navy. The ban on the establishment of foreign bases on Vietnamese territory certainly hampered the Americans more than the Chinese or Russians, but the permission to replace equipment as it became obsolete was particularly welcome to the Pentagon, as was the understanding whereby foreign instructors were tolerated.

Given the military situation and the vociferous claims of both sides when the talks began, the result achieved during the night of July 20 were a clear improvement on the forecasts made by the majority of Western observers after Dien Bien Phu. This does not include those American journalists who had neither witnessed the war nor allowed the negotiations and who shamelessly shouted "Munich!" They probably did not know that the Munich agreement of September, 1938, was intended to avoid a threat of war, whereas the nation that signed the Geneva armistice had exhausted its strength after eight years in the rice fields of Vietnam.

"I would not like anyone to have illusions about the substance of the agreements that have just been signed in Geneva. The text is sometimes cruel because it embodies facts that are cruel. It could not have been otherwise."

Thus Mendès-France presented the results of Geneva to France when the National Assembly met on July 22. More rigorously than his political opponents, he itemized everything that made it impossible to regard these agreements as a national success. He was content to point out that they were simply the least undesirable outcome of a totally deplorable situation.

Mendès-France believed that even such a sober report on his mission would not protect him from attack. But in fact, attacks were rare. Former Minister for Indochinese Affairs Jean Letourneau, a right-wing Catholic who had been the embodiment of the opposite policy for the previous four years, might have been expected to make the harshest attacks on the agreements. Instead, he was honest enough to tell his fellow legislators: "Knowing the affairs of Indochina as I do, I feel that I do not have the right to criticize the terms you have obtained."

Approval also came from the moderates in the Assembly, including men who were hardly regarded as defeatists and men who had actively supported the Baodaist experiment. Jacques Fourçade, a right-wing independent, said: "I do not doubt that the effort you have made, which has been crowned by success, is the result, not of some wager that had to be won at all costs, but of the will and good will of a man who is sincere and courageous in what he undertakes." And Henri Bergasse, a conservative, added: "We shall not show ourselves to be bad sportsmen by refusing to honor the skill and resolution with which you have surmounted the numerous and difficult obstacles in the record time you set yourself."

Despite the hard (and partly justified) criticism of ex-Major Raymond Dronne, who was with General Leclerc and Colonels Repiton and Crépin during the first attempt at coexistence with the Vietminh in 1946, and of Bidault, who tried unsuccessfully to prove that the Geneva documents imposed actual neutrality on the three Associated States of Indochina, thereby contravening their interests and violating Article 62 of the Constitution,[4] the Geneva documents were approved with large majorities in three successive votes on July 23.[5]

A full review of the response to the Geneva agreements in the press would be out of place here. Of all the comments inspired by the end of the conference, we shall quote only that of a conservative Parisian paper seldom blinded by political passion and definitely not prejudiced in favor of Mendès-France. On July 21, 1954, *Le Figaro* wrote:

> We are in mourning. Half our positions in the Far East are lost, and the remainder are severely shaken. The free world, which must concede a new territory to Communist expansion in Asia, is also in mourning. But once things had gone this far, a failure by Mendès-France in Geneva would have made the immediate future look dark and stormy indeed.
>
> Let us be grateful to him for succeeding. Soon, French blood will no longer flow in a hopeless battle.
>
> M. Mendès-France has worked hard and well for his country in Geneva. It would be unjust to permit him to bear alone the burden of surrenders that had already been written into the record before he came to power. It would be equally unjust to forget—and we can be sure that he would not think of doing so himself—that his predecessors in Geneva undertook the task, started the talks, and sketched out solutions.
>
> The negotiations of the last days were conducted with authority and clarity, with rigorous precision, and above all with that un-

[4] Bidault sometimes asked himself whether he would have been able to achieve better results (conversation with Philippe Devillers, July 24, 1959).

[5] Vote number 2569 produced 569 votes for the government and 9 against; 2570 produced 455 for and 86 against; and 2571 produced 471 for and 14 against.

tarnished and direct good faith which, in Mendès-France, is a great strength.

If the terms are cruel, at least they leave no stain on our honor and do not jeopardize that western unity whose destruction would represent the only irreparable disaster.

If it is a sign of virility that a painful amputation has been carried out with determination, if it indicates a willingness to overcome the setback and to triumph over the obstacles heaped in the path of France's destiny, then we may hope that our dead in Indochina, to whom we must dedicate this day of national meditation, will not have been sacrificed altogether in vain.

On July 21, when reporters asked him to comment on the agreements, President Eisenhower said he would not criticize what had been done in Geneva because he had no alternative solution to suggest. The most lucid assessment came from the two diplomats who, throughout the conference had been the most patient and inspired craftsmen of agreement. "There is no good end to a bad business," Chauvel concluded. And, during the night of July 20, Anthony Eden tried to put the same thought in a more positive form: "The agreements," he said, "are the best that our hands could devise."

III

AMERICA TAKES OVER

24

THE MANILA PACT

> In these two years [September, 1954, to July, 1956] can be found the roots of the critical political and military situation as it has existed in Vietnam since 1960. In 1954 and 1955, the U.S. could still have charted a different course. But once it chose the direction it did in 1954 and proceeded in that direction through 1956, it became a captive of its policy and committed to its continuation. . . . it is still committed to it.
>
> Victor Bator, *Vietnam, A Diplomatic Tragedy*

The basic object of the Geneva conference had been to put an end to the fighting in Vietnam. This had been Bidault's stated aim; he was in no hurry to achieve a political settlement, least of all by means of elections.[1] While the diplomats completed the attempt to reconcile their points of view as best they could by the shores of Lake Leman, the work of the military committee

[1] See statements by Bidault during the French parliamentary debate on December 20, 1954. *Le Monde* (Paris), December 22, 1954. The essentially military nature of the Geneva agreements is also indicated by the preamble to the final declaration. *Department of State Bulletin* No. 788 (Washington), August 2, 1954, p. 164.

was continued in Vietnam by two military delegations. They met at Trung Gia, northwest of Hanoi, to settle the practical arrangements for the armistice. Their first task was to disentangle the two armies, which had virtually wrapped themselves around each other during eight years of fighting in the rice paddies and jungles.

The operation was completed without major incidents, thanks to the determination of both sides to end the conflict and to the strength of military discipline as well. Fighting stopped as agreed, on July 27 in the north, on August 1 in central Vietnam, on August 6 in Laos, and on August 11 in southern Vietnam. The troops then moved to their allotted regrouping zones, which were to be evacuated within the time limits stated in the Geneva agreements.

An exchange of prisoners was decided upon and organized at Trung Gia on August 14. It started on August 18, and was considered officially closed on September 5. More than 11,800 French Union combatants, most of them captured at Dien Bien Phu and handed over in appalling condition, were exchanged for 65,500 members of the People's Army. No less than 21,000 French Union soldiers were missing, including 13,000 Vietnamese; few of them were ever heard of again.

The International Control Commission was quickly set up and its first team arrived in Hanoi on August 10. It met with President Ho Chi Minh and General Giap in Thai Nguyen on August 12. The ICC's teams helped with the unscrambling and the regrouping and dealt with disputes, but the bulk of the work was carried out by the joint Franco-Vietnamese commissions.

Even at this early stage, however, the political, strategic, and diplomatic aspects of the settlement were becoming more important than its purely military results.

The day after the conclusion of the agreements, the Ho Chi Minh government dispatched short directives to its three territorial administrations (north, central, and south). These clarified the general line adopted by the D.R.V. authorities, stressing three points: (1) The Geneva agreements were signed as a result of a victory by the democratic forces. (2) The Republic had secured peace and taken a decisive step toward the complete liberation of the territory. (3) The government was actively enforcing scrupulous respect for the spirit of the agreements and asked the French to act in a similar way.[2]

The government of the Republic was obviously putting its faith in democracy. It certainly considered that it had won in the field, and it also displayed confidence that it would win the elections due to be held in two years' time in accordance with the agreements. There was little optimism about this election in the West; all observers in Europe and America forecast a Vietminh victory in 1956. The West considered that France had, in effect, secured a breathing space in Geneva, a reprieve to save face while it withdrew its administration and achieved a new *modus vivendi* with the D.R.V.

Dejection was in the air, and the cold blast of defeat blew in the South. Collapse was in the cards.[3] The friends of France felt abandoned. On August 12, when one of Mendès-France's most trusted advisers returned from a special mission to Vietnam, he ended his report as follows:

> The situation in Vietnam has quickly degenerated. . . . The South can be consolidated only by seeking the support of the sects and calling on Vietnamese personalities who have taken part in earlier governments. *The test of success in this sense would be the continued partition of Vietnam beyond 1956* [italics added].
>
> We must therefore abandon any hope of seeing the establishment in the South of a liberal, socially concerned, and progressive regime operated by honest and energetic men, which would provide a focus of attraction for the North Vietnamese and make it possible to seek the re-establishment of unity outside Communism.

[2] Max Clos, *Le Monde* (Paris), December 12, 1954. The key to an understanding of the D.R.V.'s policy on the eve of the Geneva agreements is Ho's report to the Sixth Conference of the Central Committee of the Lao Dong Party on July 15, 1954. Ho Chi Minh, *Selected Works* (Hanoi, 1960–62), Vol. II. See also "Appeal made after the successful conclusion of the Geneva agreements," July 22, 1954, *ibid.*, IV, 17.

[3] The situation in Vietnam (North and South) at the beginning of August was accurately described in articles by *Le Monde*'s correspondent, Max Clos. *Le Monde* (Paris), August 6, 10, and 19, 1954.

Even the chances of setting up a Syngman Rhee type of regime in the South are limited. . . .

We can assist the nationalist government in South Vietnam by keeping armed forces there, by supporting the establishment of the Vietnamese Army, by granting generous technical and economic aid, and by encouraging a policy of total independence.

The documents now available (there are already a good number) indicate that by mid-August, several of Mendès-France's close advisers had reached the same conclusion: if the agreements were implemented, if democratic freedoms were granted to the population of the South and free elections were held in 1956, the southern zone of Vietnam would be "lost." Since past sacrifices made such a responsibility too painful to accept, or even to contemplate, everyone felt free to suggest a solution of his own.

Before he left Geneva, Mendès-France considered sending Sainteny (who had negotiated the agreements of 1946) to re-establish contact with the Ho Chi Minh government as soon as possible. Since the People's National Front (the Lien Viet, formerly the Vietminh, governed by the Lao Dong) seemed certain to win at the polls in 1956 and to reunite Vietnam thereafter, Sainteny's mission suggested that the French Government was shedding its illusions and adopting a realistic attitude. In fact, if it were able to overcome its reactions to defeat, France could re-establish perfectly correct relations with its former enemy and pave the way to cooperation with the Vietnam of the future, whatever the result of the elections in 1956.

Such a policy could well lead to a gradual normalization of the relations of France and its Western allies with Communist China. A movement in this direction, foreshadowed by Mendès-France around July 15, seemed to have been understood and appreciated by his Minister for the Associated States, Guy La Chambre.

Jean Chauvel gave a report full of nuances and prudent advice to a senior member of the French Government on July 30. He stressed that the situation had become somewhat more stable—thanks to the Geneva agreement—that France now had two years at its disposal, and that the most important thing at present was to prevent a tilting of the balance in favor of the North. This could be achieved, he suggested, by methodically consolidating the South, making it a center of attraction and reorganizing it politically and militarily. American help should be used for this purpose, but without allowing the Americans to take charge; in particular, their military aid to Vietnam should be channeled through the French. Chauvel suggested that a reliable external guarantee should be sought for the agreements in the form of an Anglo-Franco-American understanding covering the area, but without making the Associated States parties to such a pact. He also recommended concerted diplomatic and military action to involve the greatest possible number of states in maintaining the status quo and fostering peaceful coexistence. He stressed that none of these activities should infringe upon the recent agreements. In conclusion, he recommended extreme caution: the development of relations with Hanoi must not be allowed to upset Western solidarity, nor should the reaffirmation of the Western alliance close all doors to Hanoi.[4]

The main trend in the French establishment was quite different. Its spokesmen, chiefly diplomats and military men, were each more "Atlantically minded" than the others, and their views differed only by the merest nuances. It was already clear to all of them that the southern zone could be saved only by resisting the "People's Party," by relying on a pro-Western Vietnamese minority and the armed forces at its disposal, and, ultimately, by utilizing American support.

America's intentions were already clear. As we have seen, America had refused to associate itself fully with the final declaration of the conference. This grievously disappointed the French Government, which strove from then on to secure from Washington a guarantee of the agreements outside the Geneva framework. Such a guarantee might be provided by the Southeast Asia pact that had been mentioned throughout the negotiations between the Western powers during the past three months and already

[4] The U.S. Department of Commerce suspended all export licenses to the northern zone of Vietnam, including the French enclaves of Hanoi and Haiphong, on July 26. *Department of State Bulletin No.* 789 (Washington), August 9, 1954, p. 212.

had caused behind-the-scenes talks between the French and the Americans. When General Walter Bedell Smith, the American representative in Geneva, took leave of his French partners on July 21, he said: "We must get that pact."

In his press conference on July 24, Dulles had said that the "important thing from now on is not to mourn the past but to seize future opportunities to prevent the loss in North Vietnam from leading to the extension of Communism throughout Southeast Asia and the Southwest Pacific." He added that a line could be drawn by the members of the proposed pact which would include free nations as well as Cambodia and South Vietnam. "Transgression of this line by the Communists would be treated as active aggression calling for reaction of the parties to the Southeast Asia Pact."

In the days that followed, the State Department approached the French and the British in order to settle the details of a declaration announcing the forthcoming conclusion of a Southeast Asia "security pact." August 7 was suggested as the publication date for this joint statement.[5] These moves, and the intentions they disclosed, struck the French Government as most inopportune and extremely dangerous. The French Government was acutely aware that the cease-fire had not even begun in South Vietnam and that the armistice so laboriously achieved in Geneva might suddenly be jeopardized. On August 3, a word of caution from Chauvel to Mendès-France proved very effective; but that same day, France announced its willingness to join the Southeast Asia Pact.[6] As it

[5] During this period, there was a good deal of talk in high French circles about the "off the record" remarks of Douglas McArthur, Jr., which the French embassy in Washington had reported on July 29 and 30.

[6] Chauvel described America's intentions with great clarity. In his report of July 30, quoted above, he wrote:

> The Americans can only accept the Geneva agreements provisionally. They have reconciled themselves to "respecting" them during the stated two-year period until the elections are held. That is, during these two years they will react to any Communist venture directed against the state of affairs defined in the agreements. But they are in no way prepared to let things take their course when the time comes. As far as they are concerned, the general elections must be prevented by means of any excuse whatsoever. The only purpose of the Geneva agreements, as they see them, is to provide a cover for

turned out, Dulles had to make a rather vague statement on August 7. It seemed clear however, that the Eisenhower administration was firmly committed to a "Containment Policy."

On the other hand, the partisans of the "Roll Back" were again active. A few days later, in an article published in *Look* (announced on August 11 in Paris), former Ambassador William C. Bullitt advocated a preventive war against People's China, with a landing of Chiang Kai-shek's troops supported by U.S. naval and air forces. His stand was praised on August 12 by President Syngman Rhee of South Korea. The British Labour Party Leader, Clement Attlee, was then on his way to Peking, where he arrived on August 14. On August 11, Chou En-lai issued a strong warning about the aggressive character of the South East Asia pact, while stressing the need for "Peaceful Coexistence" in Asia.

Meanwhile, the French Government's plans were rapidly taking shape. Between August 12 and 15, Mendès-France and his group of advisers (Cheysson, Baudet, Chauvel, Ely, and others) concluded that they must secure at all costs an "effective guarantee" for the Geneva agreements from the United States. One of these advisers, while recommending support for the Saigon government, wrote on August 12:

> If, within a year to eighteen months, it should become clear that the government of the South will be crushed when its time comes to confront the North, we should face the consequences and take out of the country whatever has no place in a Communist state.
>
> If such a decision has to be taken, it is essential that the Americans should not be able to denounce it as a unilateral act of defection by France. We must therefore associate them as closely as possible with our policy in South Vietnam. Since the condition laid down by the Americans appears to be the conclusion of an agreement covering Southeast Asia, we must not balk at it. Joint Franco-American action in close association with the British must be pro-

---

the political, economic, and military preparations for the conquest. In May, Dulles thought the preparations would take two years. This reconquest must be achieved, if not through war, then at least by the threat of war; therefore, the pact must create an international force designed either to wage war well or to make the threat of war effective.

moted as quickly as possible in the field of economic and technical assistance to nationalist Vietnam.

Mendès-France's advisers all wanted a strong French influence to continue in South Vietnam, but they wanted it guaranteed, underwritten, and perhaps even financed by the United States (as the war had been). In exchange, they were ready to give pledges to America and join in its global policy for the containment of Communism, the first step being to adhere to Dulles's proposed pact. It seems that Mendès-France made the crucial decisions between August 12 and September 1, since he summarized his September 1 conversation with La Chambre (who was about to leave for Manila) in a note dated September 5 and addressed to a member of the delegation. He added:

> I reject any policy trend in South Vietnam which might in due course lead to an attempt to conciliate North Vietnam. If such a possibility existed, it would rapidly become known and would inevitably influence current action. I would add that in the past all experiments of this kind have invariably proved disastrous.
>
> Much as I have wished that we should be genuinely represented in Hanoi, it is equally essential to preserve the independence of our policy in the South. There must be no misunderstanding on this score. . . .
>
> It is essential that our policy toward South Vietnam must be worked out in conjunction with the United States. We have a number of points at issue with them in other areas. There must be no additional reasons for a clash over Vietnam. Therefore we must take advantage of the Manila conference to examine with them the decisions to be taken and to reach an agreement (which is essential) about a common policy toward Saigon.

Thus, on September 5, 1954, seven weeks after signing the Geneva agreements, Mendès-France was already rejecting all conciliation of North Vietnam in matters that concerned the South. In doing so, was he questioning the provisions of the agreement covering "democratic freedoms" or those concerning "consultations" and "elections"? It is still difficult to be certain. Whatever the answer, it is obvious that France regarded the independence granted to South Vietnam as purely nominal, since the crucial decisions were being made in Paris and Washington. It is equally clear that, contrary to the spirit of the Geneva agreements, the Mendès-France government did not hesitate to encourage the intervention of a third power in Vietnamese affairs. It did so both to release France from its current and future responsibilities and to dispel the displeasure that the European policy of the new French cabinet was causing in the American capital.[7]

Matters now proceeded with relentless logic. Although the French delegates in Manila secured a few formal safeguards, France joined the Southeast Asia security pact prepared by the State Department. As Dulles saw it, this pact would make it possible to meet two related political and military requirements. Its first effect would be to deter the Communists from embarking on another armed operation by creating a line they could not cross without triggering a major conflict; moreover, this would demonstrate the determination of the Free World to pursue its policy of containment toward China and the Soviet Union. The second effect would be to inhibit the neutralist trend that was developing in Southeast Asia with the encouragement of India, Indonesia, and even Britain—a trend that China now appeared to regard in a favorable light.

During the preliminary negotiations, the Americans stressed that Dien Bien Phu and Geneva had, very understandably, sharpened the Communists' appetite. They would inevitably resume their advance as soon as they had consolidated their new positions; therefore, a sound system of deterrence must be set up in time to thwart them.

For obvious reasons, the Americans secured a hearing in Manila, Bangkok, Canberra, and Wellington. Together with Washington, these four capitals were the nucleus of a coalition determined to go it alone, regardless of the reservations and unspoken misgivings prevalent in London. The strains that conflicting assessments of the situation threatened to create within the Commonwealth soon

[7] The French National Assembly rejected the treaty setting up the European Defense Community on August 30.

induced Great Britain to join the pact. As London saw it, it was better to be in—and in a position to keep an eye on the arrangements—than out, and powerless. Besides, the tendency of Australia and New Zealand to turn increasingly to the United States was causing the British some concern. SEATO (South East Asia Treaty Organization) might well become more important than ANZUS (the alliance between Australia, New Zealand, and the United States), and this time England would be one of the organization's most influential members. Pakistan, which the American Government had won over to the SEATO concept, was becoming increasingly pro-Western as India became more neutralist. The recent *rapprochement* between India and China and Russia's support of India in the Kashmir dispute necessarily drove Pakistan into alliances with the West, although it was not in the least interested in Indochina.

In Paris, the Americans predictably made the point that only a pact of this kind could guarantee the Geneva agreements and persuade the Communists in the North not to exploit their psychological advantage and force a decision before 1956. In short, Washington would not agree to underwrite the Geneva agreements, which it regarded as a form of appeasement, unless they were complemented by such arrangements for resistance. Only then would it really be able to commit itself in the South and help the French there.

The more dynamic among the Americans would have liked the new alliance to embrace all the non-Communist states in Indochina, or at least Cambodia and Laos. They pointed out that this would not represent an infringement of the July 20 agreements, which only denied the two kingdoms the right to join coalitions banned under the United Nations Charter—in other words, those that were overtly aggressive.

However, the British and French, and Chauvel in particular,[8] vigorously maintained that, while such a policy might not infringe on the letter of the July documents, it violated their spirit.

[8] France was represented in Manila by La Chambre, Chauvel, Gros, and others.

This, in turn, risked a renewal of tension, from which the new states, deprived of effective safeguards for years to come, would be the first to suffer. Therefore, the French suggested that these states should not be parties to the pact but should instead be passively covered by a special protocol. The suggestion was adopted.

The Manila Pact, which was signed at a ceremony held on September 8, 1954, created the South East Asia Treaty Organization (SEATO).[9] The treaty was basically a declaration of intent. It authorized collective action only in very closely defined circumstances. Indeed, Article IV, the most important of all, stated that:

> 1. Each Party recognizes that aggression by means of armed attack in the Treaty Area against any of the parties or against any State or territory which the Parties, by unanimous agreement, may hereafter designate, would endanger its own peace and safety, and agrees that it will in that event act to meet the common danger in accordance with the constitutional processes. Measures taken under this paragraph shall be immediately reported to the Security Council of the United Nations.
>
> 2. If, in the opinion of any of the Parties, the inviolability or the integrity of the territory or the sovereignty or political independence of any Party in the Treaty Area or of any other State or territory to which the provisions of paragraph 1 of this article from time to time apply is threatened in any way other than by armed attack or is affected or threatened by any fact or situation which might endanger the peace of the area, the Parties shall consult immediately in order to agree on the measures which should be taken for the common defense.
>
> 3. It is understood that no action on the territory of any State designated by unanimous agreement under paragraph 1 of this article or on any territory so designated shall be taken, except at the invitation, or with the consent of the government concerned.

The commitments were embodied in this text, but they were more than a little vague. The contracting parties agreed to *act* constitutionally should they or one of the territories in the area

[9] For the text of the treaty, President Eisenhower's message, and the Secretary of State's report to the Senate, see *Department of State Bulletin No. 805* (Washington), November 29, 1954, pp. 819–23.

(that is, the Associated States) suffer armed attack, but the text did not indicate how this should be done, and the decision would in any case have to be left to the established constitutional bodies. In case of subversion (paragraph 2), the parties were to consult together only in order to establish the policy that should be followed.[10] The Manila Pact powers nevertheless considered that the pact provided a sufficient deterrent and that the *external* protection of the non-Communist states of Indochina was adequately taken care of. The United States had issued its guarantee.

[10] For an analysis of the meaning and interpretation of the Manila treaty's "obligation for consultation," see George McT. Kahin and John W. Lewis, *The United States in Vietnam* (New York, 1967), p. 301.

25

FRANCE'S ASSOCIATE

The Manila Pact dealt in generalities and spoke in relatively innocuous terms, but it brought yet another military coalition into the world. One more organization led by the United States and supported by its allies—in this case the British, the French, and "friendly" Asian powers—took its place beside NATO, ANZUS, and the treaty between the United States and Japan. It covered China's southern flank and looked more like a counter to the settlement negotiated at Geneva than a guarantee of the agreements reached there.

It represented a resumption of the cold war in Asia and was therefore in direct conflict with the very aims that the Geneva conference had tried to achieve: the creation of conditions favorable to a relaxation of tension in Asia; the establishment of peaceful coexistence in accordance with the principles formulated in the agreement between India and China (June 28, 1954); the opening of a way toward the neutralization of Indochina, at least in the military sense; and the normalization of Franco-Chinese relations. China and India were entitled to expect that Britain and France could defend their own legitimate interests in Asia and assert their views on coexistence and the relaxation of tension—if necessary, in opposition to American policy. The signing of the Manila Pact made it plain to Chou En-lai that he had harbored illusions concerning the ability of Britain and France to conduct an independent foreign policy. Disappointment was expressed instantly: Peking and Moscow violently denounced the Manila Pact and characterized it as an aggressive move.

As we have seen, Mendès-France was prepared to accept the Manila Pact in the hope that this would secure American support for his policy in Indochina. He believed that he could "consolidate the Western positions" in Indochina while outwardly conforming with the terms agreed upon at Geneva. But Mendès-France wished to give his policy—in Vietnam as in France—a dynamic character, a sense of reawakening, and an unsullied appearance. In view of this, could his government still afford to support Bao Dai?

Mendès-France was now caught in a web of fatal contradictions. During the Geneva conference, he had promised to respect the complete independence of Vietnam—"a sovereign state"—by claiming to regard the Bao Dai government as legitimate. In theory, this bound him not to intervene any further in that interplay of political forces that made up Bao Dai's Vietnam. But Mendès-France had also concluded a military agreement in Geneva with the only legitimate government of Vietnam—Ho Chi Minh's D.R.V. This agreement entrusted *to France* the administration of the regrouping zone for its military forces, at least until the 1956 elections created a single Vietnamese government for the whole country. At the end of the conference, however, Mendès-France had agreed to evacuate French troops from the South as soon as "the Vietnamese government" requested it. Finally, he had secretly promised the English and Americans that he would do nothing and promise nothing that might lead to Communist domination of the South.[1] All these undertakings were extremely difficult to reconcile: political acrobatics have their limits.

[1] Mendès-France made these pledges when he agreed to the "seven points" in Paris on July 13, 1954.

The first problem was France's promise of genuine independence for Vietnam and noninterference in its internal affairs; it quickly became obvious that Paris could not easily break with its paternalistic habits.

On August 11, 1954, Bao Dai suddenly announced that he intended to return to Vietnam in the very near future. On the same day, Mendès-France received a memorandum from one of his advisers emphasizing that:

> This return must be avoided. Bao Dai is totally discredited in South Vietnam and in France. He has not once asserted his prestige since 1949. His private life, the corruption of his entourage, and his lack of courage are the object of sharp criticism. Everyone knows about his attitude during the Geneva conference. To put South Vietnam under the banner of Bao Dai would mean condemning it to failure and making a gift of the best propaganda points to the Vietminh. It would mean defying the Expeditionary Corps and French public opinion at the very moment when the government has decided to extend its support to the nationalist government.
>
> A new cabinet must be set up in Saigon. It would be unthinkable that this should be done under the aegis of Bao Dai, on his initiative, with his creatures, and by his methods. The benefits of the transfer of administrative responsibilities, above all at the Palais Norodom, must not accrue to Bao Dai.
>
> Contrary to what one might think, the Americans are opposed to the return of Bao Dai. On August 11, Mr. Gibson at the American embassy in Paris asked us to prevent Bao Dai from leaving for Saigon. One of Mr. Stassen's assistants admitted while visiting Saigon a few days ago that it would be difficult to ask Congress to renew aid to Vietnam if Bao Dai reappeared on the political scene.
>
> For all these reasons, General Ely insists that all means should be used to prevent Bao Dai from leaving France. . . .
>
> Unofficial representations should be made to Bao Dai as a matter of urgency, perhaps by M. Dejean, to persuade him not to go home. It might be pointed out to him that the French authorities are determined not to intervene in Vietnamese internal affairs. Therefore, they could not lend their support to the return of the head of state, nor could they maintain order if his return caused demonstrations in Saigon.
>
> We might also let Bao Dai know that if he left for Vietnam

> against our advice he could not hope for any assistance from us should he wish to return to France later on (transfer of capital, means of transport, etc.).
>
> Such an approach might well be supported by the Americans. It would be useful to sound out the American embassies in Saigon and Paris in this regard.
>
> Finally, it would be useful if the press were to comment vigorously about the impossibility of Bao Dai's return.

All this was soon done, and, for the time being, Bao Dai abandoned the idea of returning to Saigon. Nonetheless, the American press unleashed a campaign against the former emperor, claiming that he chose to live in comfort on the Côte d'Azur rather than go home and take part in the political struggle in his own country.

American attitudes were virtually identical with those of the French. In a letter to Mendès-France dated August 18, Dulles expressed his satisfaction with the Franco-American agreement that a solid nationalist government should be formed in South Vietnam. Dulles stressed that such a government must be given firm support in order to avoid a rapid Communist takeover of the South and of Southeast Asia, with all the implications that this would have for Africa.[2] He continued:

> We have asked ourselves here what we could do to help in creating an effective Vietnamese Government. In our opinion, Ngo Dinh Diem has a better chance of rallying and upholding nationalist feeling, at any rate at the start, than the majority of the Vietnamese who seem to be available at present, on the political stage or behind the scenes. We realize that his government needs more realism and experience and a broader geographical basis, but it appears to offer a good starting point for further efforts.

Mendès-France was puzzled. He was also being pressed to support the nationalist government by Cheysson, who had just returned from Vietnam, but he seemed to be wondering where this might lead him. During this same period, he asked La Chambre

[2] Mendès-France was already engaged in an attempt to solve the Tunisian problem; he had visited Tunis with Marshal Juin at the end of July.

some questions that betrayed a certain misunderstanding of the facts about the internal situation in Vietnam.[3]

Meanwhile, in Saigon, Ngo Dinh Diem was floundering. The Vietnamese President had arrived in Vietnam on June 25. He found himself isolated, threatened, and without resources. He could rely only on a close circle of friends—a virtual clan. The French and their agents, the police, the administrators, the soldiers, and the sects all hemmed him in. His only real encouragement came from a number of resident and visiting Americans, including both civilian and military officials. These Americans expressed warm sympathy for the Vietnamese nationalists, stressed that the United States represented their last chance of escaping Communist dictatorship, and hinted that America would support those who resolved to reject the colonial regime still symbolized by Bao Dai, the sects, and the French.[4]

From the beginning, Diem's group was aware of two imperatives. The first was to win over Washington completely. To do this, it was necessary to have a reliable, skilful, and experienced ambassador there. Diem appointed his brother's father-in-law, Tran Van Chuong (who had been Bao Dai's foreign minister in the Tran Trong Kim government), to this crucial post at the beginning of August. He presented his credentials to President Eisenhower on August 16.

Diem's second imperative was to recruit reliable and blindly loyal supporters who would meet with the approval of American officialdom. Diem came from central Vietnam and was rigidly Catholic; he had practically no support in the south. His political constituents were the Catholics in the north who were about to come under the control of the D.R.V. He had to bring the largest possible number of these Catholics south, no matter what the

[3] His message to La Chambre on September 5, 1954, is an instance of this.

[4] One of these Americans was Colonel Edward G. Lansdale of the Central Intelligence Agency. Robert Shaplen, in *The Lost Revolution* (New York, 1965), pp. 103–104, has vividly depicted Diem's entry into Saigon and the first contacts Col. Lansdale made with him. On the lonely position of Diem upon his arrival, his alternatives, and his opponents, see Georges Chaffard, *Indochine. Dix ans d'indépendance* (Paris, 1964), pp. 32–35 and 38–50.

costs, to provide his anti-Communist regime with a mass of faithful supporters. They might be socially rootless, but they would owe him everything. They could be relied upon to be uncompromising because of their fear of the Vietminh, and their anti-Communism would recommend them highly to the Americans.[5] For obvious reasons, Diem and his clan showed little interest in keeping these supporters in the north until the 1956 elections. What they wanted—and quickly—was to provide themselves with a strong "sect" in the south to counter those that had been serving the French and Bao Dai for many years.

With this political object in mind (and with some foreign help), Diem's teams went to work in the north, in the path of the advancing People's Army. As early as June 30, Diem flew to Hanoi and set up a "Committee for the Defense of the North." Hoang Co Binh was its chairman. When the Mayor of Hanoi was dismissed a week after the Geneva agreements, Diem asked the population to rally to the South. However, strong opposition to the exodus had already developed, and the meeting presided over by Diem in Hanoi on August 2 drew only a small audience. It seemed that the number of volunteers to go south would be much smaller than expected. Hoang Co Binh was then dismissed and replaced by a Catholic, Le Quang Luat, who was directed to organize a massive evacuation. He got help from a variety of agents, some of them questionable. Diem's representative in Hanoi (Dr. Tran Kim Tuyen, who was himself a northern Catholic) played a discreet but important role during this period. Diem's teams sought to provoke a mass exodus of Catholic and other economically important elements of the population by playing on their fears and then exploiting a variety of arguments. They found that their task was sometimes made easier by the behavior of the Communists.

Starting in 1950 under de Lattre, the French had succeeded in "compromising" a major part of the Tonkinese Catholic population by 1954. They accomplished this by occupying the bishoprics

[5] America was then experiencing the full blast of Senator Joseph McCarthy's allegations. Ambassador Averell Harriman was one of many public servants subjected to the Senator's accusations.

of Bui Chu and Phat Diem and applying a comprehensive policy aimed at winning these Catholics over to the Bao-Daist regime. It was not difficult to convince these wretched people that their pro-French and anti-Communist attitude would earn them merciless retribution from the new authorities. Desperate, they took flight toward the coast or to the area of Haiphong still in French hands.

The Tonkinese parish priests were brought to a fever pitch of excitement by "integralist" agitators and special agents. They were easily persuaded that the advent of the Communist regime would mean religious persecution, an end to freedom of worship, and the sentencing of priests by special tribunals, as had happened in China. They were told that they and their parishioners should not remain in Communist territory. It was dinned into them that they should seize the chance offered by the Geneva agreements and set out for the southern zone, where they would be well treated, thanks to American aid, by a government headed by a Catholic. As a result, entire villages, led by their parish priests, left their land and their houses to flee toward the coast.

This movement was further intensified by agitators who systematically spread rumors that no holy image, sanctuary, or priest would remain in the north, that the sacraments would therefore no longer be given, and that the Catholics who stayed there would thus be as good as abandoned. (Contrary to reports, the agitators did not claim that the Virgin Mary was leaving the north for the south.)

Agents also spread word that the withdrawal of the "national forces" was only temporary, that sooner or later Saigon, backed by the United States, would again take the offensive to liberate the north, and that the atomic bomb might then be used if China helped the Vietminh. The only way of escaping the atomic destruction intended for the Reds was to flee to the south.

The results were astonishing. First tens, then hundreds, of thousands of refugees trying to reach the south bore down on the Haiphong area, the beaches of Thanh Hoa, and the Red River delta, or attempted to escape to sea in frail craft. The French and American fleets cruising off the coast rescued and transported thousands of these refugees.[6] The "People's authorities" quickly intervened in an attempt to put a brake on this exodus or stop it while they asked the population to think things over. Incidents, some of them violent, resulted. These were interpreted as interference with the freedom of movement and provoked protests that brought the intervention of the International Control Commission.

But these wretched peasant masses, and the members of the wealthy middle class of Hanoi who sought asylum in the south, brought Diem the support of a "politico-religious sect" that was more powerful than the Hoa Hao or the Cao Dai. In addition, the sectarian spirit and narrow-mindedness of many Communist cadres (canbo) contributed greatly to the success of Diem's maneuvers. Some cases of Communist oppression, ruthlessness, heavy taxation, confiscation and requisitioning of property, and impositions of all kinds did much to justify the propaganda of the Diem regime—particularly since news of such behavior spread like wildfire, confirming all fears and forebodings and giving even greater impetus to the flight.

In terms of world opinion, too, the Diem regime benefited greatly from this spectacle of a population on the run from Communism. These hundreds of thousands "voting with their feet" completely destroyed, it was said, the Vietminh claim to represent nationalism or "national liberation" of any sort. The operation profoundly stirred American opinion and aroused the fighting spirit of Catholics all over the world. It also aroused the charitable feelings of Americans and proved to have an immense and lasting effect. The prestige of Diem's regime was tremendously enhanced

[6] On August 6, 1954, the U.S. Government received from the Saigon Government a request for assistance in moving over 100,000 refugees from the north to the southern areas "under control of the anti-Communist Government of Vietnam." The United States replied favorably on August 8. *Department of State Bulletin No.* 790 (Washington), August 16, 1954, p. 241. On the "exodus" from North Vietnam, see Donald Lancaster, *The Emancipation of French Indochina* (Oxford, 1961), pp. 341–46, and Wilfred Burchett, *Au Nord du 17° Parallèle* (Hanoi, 1955), chapter XIV. (This French edition contains pictures of some leaflets distributed to the people in the North to encourage them to go South). See also "The Role of the United States Navy. A Chronology of Events" in R. W. Lindholm (ed.) *Viet-Nam, The First Five Years* (East Lansing, 1959), pp. 63–76.

as a result, but his government was also confronted with a number of practical problems that were far from easy to resolve.

The French Government believed that the Manila Pact represented the American guarantee that it had sought, and therefore it set about elaborating a new policy. By the beginning of September, both Mendès-France's special emissaries and the French High Commission in Saigon had concluded that Bao Dai must be eliminated as soon as possible. They thought this could be done neatly by inducing him to delegate all his responsibilities as head of state to a new and representative successor. They believed that such a delegate-general would be able to form a valid government, harness the sects and the army, and promulgate the sweeping reforms required. The candidate put forward for this post was Professor Buu Hoi. He had just completed a journey in Vietnam in August. He had declared, when he arrived in Saigon on August 17, "a merger of the two regimes in Vietnam is not only desirable, but possible. It will be brought about by the restoration of democratic freedoms, for nobody can prevent them now that the war is ended. Our only guide must be the instinct for survival of the Vietnamese nation." Buu Hoi expressed his regrets that the present government, although it included some eminent personalities, was not "fitting the people's image." He wished the sects to be better represented. Buu Hoi seemed certain of obtaining the support of the sects and the Army, and was well received in many quarters in Saigon.[7]

But Diem and the Americans had been alerted; they began to maneuver in order to impose their own solution. The transfer to Diem of the Norodom Palace (the symbol of French rule) on September 7, the conclusion of the Manila Pact (which was as much of a turning point for the Americans as it had been for the French), and the arrival of Diem's devotees from the north seemed to open the way for action.

On September 11, Diem suddenly dismissed the Chief of the Vietnamese National Army's General Staff, General Nguyen Van Hinh, a key figure of the Bao Dai regime, and replaced him by

[7] *Le Monde* (Paris), August 18, 1954.

General Nguyen Van Vy. The first Franco-American crisis had begun.

The sequel demonstrated Diem's impotence. First, Hinh refused to give up his post. Then Vy declined to take over Hinh's position and was put under arrest. The government asked Hinh to give up all his functions immediately and leave for Paris in a kind of banishment. The Army, however, suddenly displayed solidarity with its leader. Meetings and telegrams of protest followed each other, but even though Hinh had the support of the French and most of the Army, he refused to encourage his supporters, who were demanding quick and decisive action against Diem. Although Diem had hurriedly flown in supporters from Hue, it was obvious that the Army could easily have overturned his regime. But nothing happened, because Hinh made it clear that he did not wish to resort to force.

The threat to the regime now shifted to new ground. On September 16, the three sects—Cao Dai, Binh Xuyen, and Hoa Hao—called for the formation of a new South Vietnamese government and demanded that this time it should be a representative one.[8] The Mendès-France government learned during September 16 that Bao Dai (who was still in Cannes) was thinking of asking the leader of the Binh Xuyen, General Le Van Vien (Bai Vien), to form a government. Cheysson quickly outlined the situation to Mendès-France:

> Unless we take a stand immediately on the solution we wish to see adopted, and do it in full agreement with the Americans, Bao Dai will become sole arbiter of the situation. The head of state will suddenly confront us with a decision we will not be able to alter. It will involve his return to Vietnam and the appointment of a new government, made up as usual of individuals chosen so that their actions will cancel each other out.

Mendès-France was as determined as the Americans to prevent the sects from taking over the Saigon government. He was par-

[8] Lancaster says that Diem took special precautions against a military coup; Lancaster also examines in detail the manifesto issued by the sects. Lancaster, *op. cit.*, pp. 348–49.

ticularly anxious to keep power away from "the leader of the worst of them." Paris therefore asked Bao Dai to defer his decision until it could hear the views of General Ely and the Americans. Bao Dai agreed, thus allowing the French and Americans to make their arrangements and defeat his plan.

Faced with mounting troubles, Diem took evasive action and adopted flexible tactics. He authorized Hinh to retain his post, choose a stand-in, and set his own date of departure for France. At the same time, he confronted General Le Van Vien, who had returned to Saigon on September 17 and was working with Hinh on the composition of a new government acceptable to Bao Dai. With the help of American cash and General Ely's support, Diem bought the good will of the Cao Dai and Hoa Hao. Thus, on September 24, he was able to present a new cabinet that won their acquiescence. The police remained in the hands of the Binh Xuyen—in other words, in the hands of Le Van Vien. But Diem took over the Ministry of Defense, which he had given to General Nguyen Van Xuan four days earlier, and appointed Ho Thong Minh as his secretary of defense.

This complicated compromise provided Diem with a new façade.[9] It bore the hallmark of the new American adviser in the President's office, Colonel Lansdale of the CIA. Acting on his advice, Diem immediately announced a large-scale program of economic and social reforms. Here, at last, was the "good starting point"

[9] In his excellent book *South Vietnam: Nation Under Stress,* (Boston, 1963), p. 21, Robert Scigliano writes: "The Diem Government followed a policy of separating the three groups, which was not too hard to do considering the rivalries which ran between and within them, and of dealing with them one at a time. The government policy owes much to Nguyen Ngoc Tho, a member of Diem's cabinet and later his Vice-President, who had a thorough knowledge of the internal politics of the sects and Binh Xuyen. The general plan was to isolate the Binh Xuyen and eventually to destroy it, while bringing over most of the sects' leaders through persuasion, through promises of political position, and the incorporation of sect troops into the national army, and through outright bribery. In the first move, the united front formed by the three groups in early September, 1954 was broken when Diem brought four Cao Dai and four Hoa Hao leaders into his cabinet later the same month. This maneuver gave Diem time to dispose of his dissident army chief of staff." See also Lancaster, *op. cit.*, pp. 348–52.

that Dulles had wished to find quickly, as he had put it both in his letter of August 18 and in Manila.

The Americans thus scored a great success at the very moment when the French were anxious to define and elaborate a common Vietnam policy with them. In addition, the French wanted to discuss the pressing question of American financial support, which was necessary in order to keep French troops in Vietnam. A French delegation, led by Edgar Faure, Minister of Finance, Guy La Chambre, Minister for the Associated States, and General Ely, the Commissioner General in Indochina, arrived in Washington on September 26, to discuss these questions.

In order to secure continued American financial aid, the French experts pointed out that the end of the Indochina war would enable the United States to achieve a sizeable saving in the $400 million in credits already voted for military aid to France, and that a part of the money thus saved could easily be earmarked for strengthening the defenses of the area. They maintained that the French Expeditionary Corps in Indochina—ten divisions, 185,000 men—was the backbone of Southeast Asia's defense and that it fulfilled an essential requirement of the Western alliance.[10] The French hinted that if they could not obtain this financial assistance, they would have to withdraw considerable forces from Vietnam.

But since the French delegation arrived in Washington only three weeks after the French Assembly had rejected the EDC treaty, its bargaining position was poor: France would obviously find it more difficult to secure a subsidy as "sentry of the West" in Southeast Asia. The Americans were in a highly critical mood, and the Eisenhower Administration had serious doubts about France's real intentions.

It is doubtful that the Mendès-France government harbored any illusions about "American good will," as its predecessors had. Its room for maneuver had been greatly restricted by the decisions

[10] *The New York Times,* September 25, 1954. Ever since 1949, the French Government and General Staff had worked to make French policies an integral part of the American strategic plan. See Philippe Devillers, "Are the Military Credible?" *New University Thought* (Detroit), Vol. 6, No. 3 spring, 1968, pp. 5–7.

of the National Security Council in April and June and by the Anglo-American seven points of June 29, which meant more to Washington than the Geneva agreements. As a result of these American decisions, France could no longer conduct a policy of its own choosing in Vietnam, nor could it yield to genuinely popular, democratic, and national forces there. It could either fall into line with American policies and receive aid or accept a trial of strength.

The bargain had been stated clearly in Dulles's letter of August 18. The Secretary of State said unequivocally that a Diem government would provide a "good starting point" for the policy that the United States proposed to carry out in Vietnam. According to the plan that had been decided upon in Washington, Dulles continued, Eisenhower would send Diem a message assuring him of American support. Thereafter, American economic and military aid to the Associated States would be furnished directly, rather than through the French, as before. This, Dulles emphasized, would be more in keeping with the independent status of the States and would increase their self-confidence. It was in any case an essential requirement of American domestic policy, since Congress wanted aid to be given directly. In this way, Dulles indicated that the United States intended to deal directly with the governments of the Associated States in the future. Dulles also specified that the United States intended to provide military instructors for the armed forces of the Associated States, although this would naturally be done in close consultation with the French authorities. All these measures, however, depended on the achievement of the full independence that France had promised to the Associated States. They would also depend on the stability of the governments receiving aid and their ability to carry out the necessary reforms.

Although it had its own ideas on the subject,[11] the French Gov-

[11] According to a French expert, the main purpose of the French ministerial visit to Washington was the need "to increase the coordination between French and American policies in South Vietnam. We must associate the Americans more and more with the decisions we take there." Thus, all available evidence indicates that, contrary to a view widely held in America, the French government and the French Commissioner General did not oppose

ernment was well aware that the Americans wanted Diem. They wanted him to be entirely independent—at least of the French—so that they could deal with him directly,[12] and they wanted this for very definite policy reasons. Within these limitations they were prepared to help the French help Vietnam.

Thus, when the Franco-American talks began in Washington in late September, the agenda was shaped by Dulles's proposals: direct American economic aid to the Associated States, direct American military assistance without the use of French intermediaries, and the training of local forces by Americans. The military talks were held before the political negotiations. Eisenhower's representatives stated that they were prepared to consider financial assistance to France to help it maintain military forces in Indochina. However, everything depended on the size of the forces that France wished to keep in Vietnam during the next two years and on the degree of real independence it would grant to the states of Indochina.

The French replied that, provided the United States agreed, they planned a gradual withdrawal of their forces from Indochina. The scale and timing of this French withdrawal would be related to the speed with which the Vietnamese forces could be trained and equipped to take their place. The French made it clear that a decisive factor in the transfer of responsibilities to the Vietnamese would be the amount of aid they could expect from Washington.[13] The present French plan was to reduce the Expeditionary Corps

---

Diem, and anybody with a thorough knowledge of the facts and files will agree with Victor Bator's assessment: "Diem could never have survived without French support. He survived because he did receive it. Ely kept the opposition of the three powerful Vietnam sect organizations to Diem within limits and he restrained the anti-Diem activities of the Vietnamese officer corps and the French subaltern commanders by disciplinary measures and similar activities of the French settlers' community by persuasion." Victor Bator, *Vietnam: A Diplomatic Tragedy* (New York, 1965), p. 174.

[12] In the London *Times* some years after, "A Student of Asia" wrote: "In Cannes, Bao Dai appointed Ngo Dinh Diem—as we have since learnt, an American nominee selected by the Central Intelligence Agency. . . ." "Blue Book Reveals Britain's Role. How the Peace in Vietnam Was Lost," by a Student of Asia, *The Times* (London), December 15, 1965.

[13] See Walter H. Waggoner, "France To Seek U.S. Funds for Her Troops in Vietnam," *The New York Times*, September 25, 1954.

to 150,000 men by January 1, 1955, and to 100,000 men by January 1, 1956.

The Americans agreed that the Expeditionary Corps should remain in South Vietnam until the national army was capable of taking over, but they reminded the French that they wished to participate in the national army's training. Ely and La Chambre confirmed once again that the French Government was anxious to evacuate the Expeditionary Corps as soon as possible and accepted, within the limits set down by the Geneva agreement, the principle of U.S. participation in the training of the national armies. This enabled Faure to present his financial requests. The American administration unhesitatingly accepted the principle of American financial aid for the Expeditionary Corps but pointed out that the amount could be fixed only after consultation with congressional leaders—in other words, after the November elections.

The French clearly intended to retain their control over South Vietnamese military affairs for a good while longer on the strength of their contacts within the Vietnamese Army, but Diem was already moving to end their influence. On September 28, during the Washington talks, he informed the United States that he had decided to ask France to withdraw its forces from Vietnam by March, 1956, at the latest. By that date, the French forces would be replaced by a reorganized Vietnamese Army of 250,000 men. The Saigon government therefore requested the United States to make no decisions relating to the Expeditionary Corps without consulting Vietnam.[14] Saigon stressed in its note that the presence of French troops in Vietnam provided useful ammunition for Communist propaganda and that therefore they should leave the country long before the date set for the elections.[15]

[14] American officials in Washington pretended to regard the Vietnamese Ambassador's handling of this matter as clumsy.

[15] Mendès-France had stated on July 20, 1954, that France would withdraw its troops whenever Vietnam so requested. When a reporter asked La Chambre about the Vietnamese request, he replied: "The date is quite within the spirit of what we have in mind." *The New York Times*, September 30, 1954.

As though to demonstrate that the French were no longer wanted, Diem

The French and American negotiators then took up the question of a political agreement, which was far more important than the military agreement. Bedell Smith stated the American political position succinctly.[16] He said that American policy had two basic objectives. The first was to strengthen the anti-Communist elements in Vietnam, and thereby achieve "something constructive," because "our basic policy is to make every possible effort to defeat Communism." The way to accomplish this in South Vietnam was to build a strong and prosperous country as quickly as possible. The second American objective was to prevent any compromise with the Vietminh. Bedell Smith explained that all suggestions of a coalition government, either in South Vietnam or covering both zones, should be rejected, since the formation of such a government would weaken the allied position on the elections, "whether or not elections are ever held."

Regarding relations with North Vietnam, the Americans confirmed that they intended to maintain a consulate there but also stressed the need to organize trade controls quickly. As far as commercial relations across the 17th Parallel were concerned, Bedell Smith bluntly stated that his government was in favor of restricting them as far as possible. He mentioned that at that very moment, other Americans were in Paris, trying to bring the French Government around to this point of view.

Now the delegates approached the main question: Which government should be given joint support in Vietnam? The Americans and the French agreed that the choice was between unsatisfactory alternatives and that, although the Diem solution was not ideal, it was the only one possible at that moment. All agreed that Diem was the most acceptable nominee in moral terms. The

---

told a French journalist: "There is no real Vietminh threat in the south. The rumors about it are without foundation. On the contrary, my information is very encouraging." When the correspondent mentioned the Vietminh's methods of organizing the population, Diem replied: "All that doesn't matter. The mass of the population is profoundly Buddhist. There are a large number of Catholics. No, I am sure that the Vietminh have no chance of success in the south." Max Clos, *Le Monde* (Paris), September 30, 1954.

[16] General Bedell Smith had resigned as under-secretary of state on August 17, effective October 1.

Americans then asked the French whether they would agree to encourage him and back him. Ely and La Chambre replied that they would but pointed out that while Diem had obtained at least the nominal cooperation of the Cao Dai and Hoa Hao sects, he still faced the hostility of the army and the Binh Xuyen, who controlled the Saigon police.

To demonstrate French good will, La Chambre asked Dejean to see whether Bao Dai's influence could persuade the army and the Binh Xuyen to support the reconstituted Diem government. The approach to Bao Dai was made on September 27. To the great irritation of Bedell Smith, it achieved nothing. It was finally decided that Donald Heath, the American ambassador to Saigon, should come to France to support Dejean's further efforts to persuade Bao Dai. General Ely was to accompany Heath on his visit to the ex-emperor. Joint directives to this effect were sent immediately from Washington to Heath and Daridan (the French deputy commissioner general) in Saigon.

The delegates then accepted La Chambre's suggestion that, if the army and the Binh Xuyen could not be persuaded to give their allegiance to Diem,[17] the French and Americans would hold further consultations and decide whether to ask Bao Dai to send Prince Buu Loc to Saigon as his representative. Buu Loc could then preside over the formation of a government of national union, which might include Diem as well as representatives of the other factions.

The Americans made no secret of the fact that they wished to see Bao Dai eliminated, once the legal means were available. This could be done by convening a Vietnamese National Assembly, as soon as one could be guaranteed against domination by Communist elements. The Americans agreed that, for the present, the French were right to insist that there should be no hiatus in the legally constituted authority, particularly in view of the disturbances they might otherwise have to suppress.

Finally, the delegates drafted a skilfully worded joint communi-

[17] The French were determined to resolve this power struggle in order to avoid any public clashes that might make it necessary to bring the Expeditionary Corps into action.

qué. La Chambre secured the omission of a proposed paragraph that included official French support for the Diem government and a violent anti-Communist diatribe as well. Bonnet, the French ambassador in Washington, could not conceal his satisfaction. He believed that the conference—which was also a confrontation—had proved that there was no fundamental disagreement between the French and American governments on major policy aims in Indochina and that the only divergences of view were, as Bedell Smith remarked, of a tactical nature. The main political result of the conference, according to Bonnet, was that both sides had recognized the need to provide the firmest possible foundations for the Diem government.

The joint final communiqué[18] emphasized the usefulness of the Manila Pact and the determination of France and the United States to defend the independence of the Associated States. France and the United States would continue to provide aid for this purpose. France, by agreement with the countries concerned, would maintain its Expeditionary Corps in Indochina, and the United States would consider how it could contribute financially to its upkeep. Aid would be given directly to each of the states by France and the United States, but a study would be undertaken to coordinate action in this field.

But the public communiqué concealed an unpublished four-paragraph protocol that was agreed to and initiated by La Chambre and Bedell Smith on September 29. The following passages from it are specially noteworthy:

> Article 2: We recognize that the Vietminh represents an aggressive Communist force opposed to the ideas and interests of the free peoples of the Associated States, France, and the United States. We will resolutely resist the development of the Vietminh movement's influence or control, while taking into account the positions adopted by the respective governments toward the Geneva agreements.
>
> Article 4: With regard to Vietnam, the representatives of France and the United States agree that their respective governments

[18] The communiqué was published in *The New York Times*, September 30, 1954, and in the *Department of State Bulletin No.* 798 (Washington), October 11, 1954, p. 534.

> should support Mr. Ngo Dinh Diem in establishing a strong anti-Communist and nationalist government. To this end, France and the United States will work to persuade all anti-Communist elements in Vietnam to collaborate fully with the government of Mr. Ngo Dinh Diem, in order to react vigorously against the Vietminh and to build a strong and free Vietnam.

The United States and France were thus united in continuing their intervention in Vietnamese internal affairs, in preparing to deny the will of the Vietnamese people as expressed in elections if this proved necessary, and in pursuing, come what may, a policy determined by the strategic interests of the Atlantic bloc.

Mendès-France's determination to achieve a united Franco-American front in Vietnam was hardly affected by the incidents that punctuated the weeks following the conference. With the help of Generals Nguyen Van Hinh and Le Van Vien, Bao Dai tried to secure key positions in the Diem government in order to at least control it from within. The French attempted to induce Diem's resignation or his subordination to a delegate-general such as Buu Hoi. Both moves were defeated. The American representatives in Saigon were becoming tougher week by week; somewhat surprisingly, they were supported more often than not by General Ely, whom many French officers and officials regarded as "110 per cent Atlantically minded." The Americans were far more apprehensive about the Vietnamese Army, which they regarded as the chief obstacle to absolute power for their protégé Diem. On October 15, Senator Mansfield reported on his visit to Southeast Asia in August and September. This report clearly betrayed the same concern:

> Any replacement of Diem at this time, if it occurs, will probably take the form of a military dictatorship based upon a coalition of the special interests, parties, and groups which now oppose the present government. It is improbable that the substitute will be the kind of government which will be generally supported by the Vietnamese people any more than the pre-Diem governments were. Nor is it likely to be a government capable of sustaining a free and inde-

> pendent Vietnam eventually without foreign support. . . . In the event that the Diem government falls, therefore, I believe that the United States should consider an immediate suspension of all aid to Vietnam and the French Union forces there, except that of a humanitarian nature.[19]

At that same moment, on October 13, 1954, La Chambre was in Saigon for what was apparently a serious attempt to assure Diem of the support of Hinh and the Binh Xuyen. La Chambre was struck by Diem's obstinate refusal to accept such support; he concluded that Diem could not possibly be retained as President and that the "Buu Hoi solution" was therefore necessary. Another Franco-American skirmish was inevitable.

On October 23, yet another conference was held; Dulles, Mendès-France, Eden, and their teams of experts met in the American embassy in Paris. Everyone agreed that the political situation in South Vietnam was deteriorating rapidly, primarily because of the dissensions and rivalries between the leaders of the various factions. Although Diem had failed to show the qualities expected of him, Dulles stressed that he was still "the best man for the job." Dulles indicated that President Eisenhower and the National Security Council had studied the situation in Vietnam and had formulated definite conclusions and precise instructions.

[19] Senator Mike Mansfield, Senate Committee on Foreign Relations, *Report on Indochina, October 15, 1954* (Washington), p. 14. According to David Wise and Thomas B. Ross in *The Invisible Government* (New York, 1964), p. 168, Col. Lansdale "in the fall of 1954 . . . got wind of a plan by several high-ranking Vietnamese Army officers to stage a coup against Diem. He alerted Washington and General J. Lawton Collins, former Army Chief of Staff, was rushed to Saigon as Eisenhower's personal envoy to help Diem put down the uprising." It is not clear how this is consistent with Robert Shaplen's report in *The Lost Revolution* (New York, 1965), p. 115: "In September, Hinh refused to obey Diem's order to leave the country. A few weeks later, when it looked as if Hinh was getting ready to mount a coup, Lansdale took advantage of his old friendship with Magsaysay, who was much admired by Hinh and his staff, to spirit most of Hinh's top officers off to Manila in response to what he told them was 'a special invitation' from Magsaysay. Hinh later pretended to have been duped, but he didn't sound very angry, and this, among other things, indicated that the General wasn't really serious in his coup maneuvers." Some French sources even suggest that Lansdale grossly exaggerated the threat of a coup to induce Washington to act quickly.

Dulles insisted that France and the United States must do more to help Diem and to promote a government of national union under his Presidency. To this end, he said, France must exert stronger presssure "on the military clique" so as to induce it to reach an understanding with Diem. Dulles explained that the United States was ready to support such a government of national union as soon as it was formed. A letter from Eisenhower was about to be transmitted to Diem; it assured him of American support and suggested talks about American aid, as foreshadowed in the communiqué of September 29.[20] In addition, the U.S. Military Group (MAAG) in Saigon was ready to initiate a training program for the Vietnamese forces.

Dulles indicated that if such a government of national union was not formed and Diem was eliminated, the United States would reconsider its attitude to the whole problem. A way out must be found. The deadlock had to be ended, and the military—particularly General Hinh—must be made to abandon their hostility and stop their intrigues. Dulles referred to the Mansfield report and pointed out that Mansfield was very powerful in the Senate, where he was regarded as well informed about Vietnam. If his recommendations were not followed, Congress would not make money available.[21]

[20] This letter, which had already been announced in Dulles's message of August 18, had evidently been drafted and signed on October 1, immediately after the Franco-American conference in Washington; the parallel letter to King Norodom Sihanouk was dated October 2. Shaplen says that this "letter drafted by Young was sent by President Eisenhower to Diem in answer to Diem's request for American aid." Shaplen, *op. cit.*, p. 118. Kenneth Young was then head of the Southeast Asia desk in the State Department.

[21] Shaplen writes (*op. cit.*, p. 118): "What the French were really after was a secret agreement with the State Department to get rid of Diem. In his place, they wanted a more pliable man, like General Hinh or former Premier Tran Van Huu, and their essential objective was to build a bridge to the government in Hanoi that would enable them to protect their economic and cultural interests in the South as well as, hopefully, in the North. This was contrary to the aims of the Americans, as expressed at the highest level by President Eisenhower and Secretary of State Dulles and by a special interdepartmental task force on Vietnam headed by Kenneth Young. With Diem as a nationalist fulcrum, the Americans wanted to build up a single army that would be trained by American officers and could serve as the instrument for pacification in the countryside, where a land redistribution program and

Mendès-France replied that he was willing to support Diem but was not sure that Diem could succeed; plans must therefore be made in case he foundered. Mendès-France added that any action taken must be "within the framework of legitimate authority, which stems from Bao Dai." If Bao Dai was not to return to Vietnam, he could send a delegate-general or viceroy who would embody legality and could act as an arbiter. Mendès-France made it clear that such a delegate-general would act neither for nor against Diem, but would be a head of state, in the same sense as President Coty and Queen Elizabeth. He indicated that he had two or three possible names in mind but did not say what they were.

Dulles replied that he did not believe Diem would be successful if he were not wholeheartedly supported. Therefore, he must be backed 100 per cent. Alternatives should be sought only if he failed; to look for them before the event would immediately precipitate the very action they sought to avoid.

On October 22, Ambassador Heath in Saigon was instructed to hand Eisenhower's letter to Diem as soon as the Paris talks were over. The letter, which was dated October 23, was handed over on October 24.[22] This American initiative was very badly received in France, where it aroused much protest and acid com-

---

other social-economic reforms could be introduced. 'We realized we had to proceed carefully with the French,' Young has recalled, 'so when they made clear their position on Diem, we sent a cable to Senator Mansfield, of the Foreign Relations Committee, who was abroad, asking him what he thought of Diem as Premier. Mansfield was an old friend of Diem's and we knew what the answer would be in advance, of course, but it stunned the French. While they then dropped their open campaign to dump Diem, it became apparent that they were still maneuvering behind the scenes toward the same objective, and we realized that while we still had to work with the French in Vietnam, we would have to adopt a more independent position.' " Shaplen obviously refers to the situation prevailing in August 1954. Washington's concern was caused mainly by Buu Hoi's statement on his arrival in Saigon (Aug. 17). Nothing in the French files or sources confirms Shaplen's interpretation of French policy, but Shaplen casts an interesting light on the importance of Kenneth Young's task force in the framing of American policy at this time.

[22] The official text of the letter was published in *Department of State Bulletin* No. 803 (Washington), November 15, 1954, p. 735, and quoted in many American works.

ment. Because the Franco-American negotiations about Vietnam had been secret, Mendès-France found himself in an embarrassing position; he was forced to feign surprise. On October 25, La Chambre, who was just back from Indochina, summoned the United States Ambassador, Douglas Dillon, and repeated his protest against what he described as Washington's unilateral move. Dillon then showed the minister a telegram from the new under-secretary of state, Herbert Hoover, Jr., pointing out that the whole subject had been discussed with the French Government ever since August and that no objection had been raised.

From that moment on, the French Government was in difficulty with French public opinion. Both the right and the left began to accuse it of giving in too easily to American pressures and machinations. Its embarrassment became even greater when, on November 3, Washington appointed General Lawton Collins (a former Army Chief of Staff) as U.S. special representative to Saigon in charge of coordinating American aid.[23]

[23] As special representative, Collins held the rank of ambassador. White House Press Release, November 3, 1954. *Department of State Bulletin No. 804* (Washington), November 22, 1954, p. 777.

26

THE SAINTENY MISSION

In October, 1954, an event of major importance took place in Indochina: the legitimate government of Vietnam returned to Hanoi.[1]

In accordance with the armistice, the "Hanoi perimeter" was the first area to be evacuated by the French Union forces in Tonkin. The Franco–Bao-Daist forces withdrew punctually during the evening of October 10. On October 11, the People's Army of Vietnam made its entry into the city of Hanoi, which was handed over to it quietly and with restraint by a French military delegation. On the following day, the Government of the Republic repossessed the historical capital of the country, which it had been forced to abandon some eight years earlier.

Almost immediately, it received an important mark of international recognition. Prime Minister Nehru of India, accompanied

[1] The question of its legitimacy is explored in Philippe Devillers, "De la légitimité du pouvoir au Vietnam," *Le Monde* (Paris), August 3, 1968. On the transfer of Hanoi to the D.R.V., see Wilfred Burchett, *Au Nord du 17° Parallèle* (Hanoi, 1955), chap. v; Robert Shaplen, *The Lost Revolution* (New York, 1965), p. 98; and Donald Lancaster, *The Emancipation of French Indochina* (Oxford, 1961), pp. 362–64, 367–68.

by his daughter Indira, visited Hanoi on October 17. Nehru was on his way to Peking and made a point of stopping in Vietnam. Neutralist India had been eager to see Vietnam free of all colonial domination, and now Nehru wanted to learn more about its future intentions.

The completely trouble-free evacuation of Hanoi, carried out with perfect correctness within the prescribed time limits, and the establishment of the International Control Commission there, suggested that the terms of the Geneva armistice could be put into effect without friction. This, in turn, should permit some normalization of relations between France and the Democratic Republic of Vietnam before the further difficulties raised by the political agreements were tackled.

In Paris, it had seemed for a moment as though the Mendès-France government wanted to make a fresh start in Franco-Vietnamese relations. The subject was mentioned in general terms during the last stage of the Geneva conference, and Mendès-France lost no time in making a startling move. On August 7, he announced the appointment as "Delegate-General of the French Republic in North Vietnam" of Governor Jean Sainteny, who had negotiated and signed the agreements of March 6, 1946, between France and the Ho Chi Minh government.

General Ely rushed to Paris; his immediate and uncompromising opposition to any policy designed to even out the balance between North and South Vietnam succeeded in restricting the scope of the mission from the start.[2] Ely accepted Sainteny's visit only with the understanding that the Sainteny mission was being undertaken for the protection and defense of French interests and would be devoid of any genuinely political character. But, although he got a warm welcome from Diem when he stopped in Saigon on his way to Hanoi, his preliminary visit, from mid-August to early September, convinced Sainteny that it was essential to

[2] Paul Ely, *L'Indochine dans la tourmente* (Paris, 1964), p. 235. However, while Ely was in Paris, Ho Chi Minh stated (on August 13) "We are grateful to the French people who fought with success to bring the war in Indochina to an end. Peace has been restored. We would like now to strengthen the bonds of friendship between our two peoples." Quoted by Mai Van Bo, Delegate-General of the D.R.V. in Paris, Dec. 17, 1968.

move boldly toward a *rapprochement* with the Democratic Republic of Vietnam.

On his return from Hanoi, Sainteny wrote unhesitatingly (in a note dated September 16) that the game then being played in the South could lead only to a "setback and perhaps a new conflict." He urged that France put its money on an improvement of relations with the North, adding that this should be done in agreement with the Americans and in the common interest. He asserted that betting on the North, however uncertain and risky this might be, was the only wager at all likely to succeed. He thought that the Democratic Republic might well find it profitable to move closer to France, if only to consolidate its independence, and he felt that this might enable France to conduct a "realistic policy of coexistence" in Asia. Sainteny concluded with a warning against wishful thinking: the D.R.V. leaders would never give up the struggle for a united Vietnam. Therefore, any attempt to turn Cochin China into a sort of South Korea would lead only to a new conflict and would nullify all efforts to achieve improved relations.

The Sainteny mission naturally aroused the suspicions of every "Atlantically minded" French diplomat, official, and soldier. As we have seen, Ely had declared it unacceptable as it was originally presented. He managed to limit its scope during his conversation with Mendès-France on August 14 and continued to do so during his stay in Paris from August 13 to 23 and after his return to Saigon (for example, in an interview with Agence France-Presse on August 31). Both in private and in his messages to the government he repeatedly emphasized its dangers, described it as unethical, and maintained that it was arousing the suspicions of Diem and the Americans.[3]

Cheysson, Mendès-France's chief adviser on Indochina, supported Ely as usual and repeated his warnings about the dangers involved. On September 17, he advised Mendès-France that the idea should definitely not be mentioned to the Americans during the Washington conference at the end of that month. To do so, said Cheysson, would strengthen the doubts already prevalent in certain American circles about the French Government's commit-

[3] *Ibid.*, pp. 238–48.

ment to the Western alliance and would persuaded these Americans that the French planned to concentrate their efforts in North Vietnam. Cheysson recommended that La Chambre refer to the Sainteny mission only in passing and should repeat that its task was merely to represent and defend French interests before the "*de facto* authorities of North Vietnam." As it turned out, La Chambre was able to avoid the question of French policy in North Vietnam completely.

Sainteny was back at his post the day before the Vietnamese Government returned to Hanoi, and he had his first conversation with President Ho Chi Minh on October 18, immediately after Nehru's visit. It was an extremely cordial meeting, during which the Vietnamese President made a point of avoiding anything that might recall the struggle of the previous eight years. As Sainteny reported three days later, Ho Chi Minh wanted to pick up the dialogue where it had been interrupted in 1946 and felt no bitterness about the life-and-death struggle that was ended at last. Sainteny's report continued, "Democratic Vietnam asserts that it is ready to talk, to negotiate, to keep a very acceptable position open for us, in other words to respect the Geneva agreements and to 'play the game.' "

Sainteny did not think that the Democratic Republic was moving toward "sovietization," in the sense of unconditional subordination to Moscow. It was certainly Communist, but, according to him, it wished to retain its independence. It was, therefore, the duty of France to support it in this independent policy, particularly by obtaining for it the contacts it needed in the West. He admitted that this gave the French no more than small grounds for hope, that the road was thick with obstacles, and that infinite patience would be needed, but he emphasized that—in contrast with the situation in the South—there was only this one way of avoiding total eviction. Sainteny concluded that, if this card was to be played, his mission to Hanoi must be officially and unequivocally defined.

Sainteny's position in the Vietnamese capital was unusual. There was as yet no official letter from Paris describing the object of his mission and no document of accreditation to the D.R.V., but the

Ho Chi Minh government openly treated him as a friend and a sort of dean of the diplomatic corps. Because he had arrived in the capital before any other diplomat, he even took precedence over the Chinese and Soviet ambassadors. During Nehru's visit to Hanoi, after the diplomatic dinner given by the Indians (at which the French delegate was seated facing Nehru, and on the right of his daughter Indira), Sainteny had a two-hour talk with Nehru, who expressed stimulating views on the future of Indochina.

Alexander Lavrishchev, the Soviet ambassador, arrived on October 29; he and his colleagues at the Soviet embassy did not seem in the least inclined to oppose French political activity in Hanoi or a friendly normalization of Franco-Vietminh relations. It is true that the Soviet officials spoke little or no French and, therefore, could not be as effective as Sainteny and his staff in a country where French was the only widespread foreign language.[4]

But since mid-August Ely, Cheysson, and some other influential Frenchmen had persuaded Mendès-France not to attempt a genuine improvement of relations with the D.R.V. Their arguments mixed international morality with generous quantities of naïveté and a vast ignorance of the real resilience of American policy.[5] As Ely had demanded, the Sainteny mission was already scheduled for demotion to the consular role of defending French economic and cultural interests in the northern zone.

October went by. The tripartite discussions in Paris, the new "Atlantic and European" orientation of Mendès-France, Eisenhower's letter to Diem, and, finally, the appointment of General

4 On one occasion, when a Soviet diplomat apologized for his inability to improvise a speech in French, President Ho Chi Minh exclaimed, "How very odd, not to know French!" On these first weeks of the Sainteny mission, see Georges Chaffard, *Indochine. Dix ans d'independance* (Paris, 1964), pp. 118–21.

5 General Ely stated his position in a note dated September 8, 1954; he repeats the argument in his book: "Even if nationalist Vietnam had only one chance in ten of winning the elections, we had to bet on that single chance. I considered that even a political defeat in Asia, which we would share equally with the United States on this occasion—since our aim was necessarily to keep them with us to the fullest possible extent—would be less serious for our country than to give up or give in and thus shake our fundamental alliance at a moment when the rejection of EDC in Europe restricted our freedom of action in Asia even further." Ely, *op. cit.*, p. 245.

Collins as the White House's "special representative" in Saigon soon made it clear to Hanoi that France, contrary to what seemed likely in Geneva, was failing to draw the consequences of seven years of mistakes and illusions, even though thousands had died to pay for them. The fact that Paris was allowing the Sainteny mission to remain in an equivocal position was a very discouraging sign.

Militant statements by members of the Diem government, the renewal of police repression in the South, and the massive exodus of French businessmen from the North quickly aroused disappointment, coolness, and bitterness in Hanoi. During a conversation at the beginning of November with General de Beaufort, the head of the French liaison mission with the International Control Commission, Pham Van Dong spoke (as had General Giap a little earlier) of his uneasiness about the situation in the South. He said, in effect: we had hoped to come to an agreement with you, but now we doubt whether this will be possible, because you will not be allowed to do so. You will be forced to withdraw everything from here, down to the last franc and the last man. Dong insisted on the need to reach an agreement reasonably soon about the details of the elections, the way in which they would be supervised, and the way in which they would be followed by a solution in accordance with the Geneva agreements.

In fact, the leaders in Hanoi saw the situation clearly. In October, Ho Chi Minh told the head of the International Control Commission (Manilal Desai of India) that he hoped the Commission would succeed in forcing the French to comply with the provisions of the Geneva agreements. But by October, the French Government was too deeply involved in collaboration with the United States to conduct an independent policy in Vietnam. Mendès-France was anxious to be "forgiven" for the foundering of the European Defense Community, and this drove him to fall increasingly into line with American policies in Asia.[6] The start

[6] La Chambre later recalled that throughout the Franco-American conference in Washington, he had been guided by the directive he received from Mendès-France: "In Southeast Asia it is the American who is the leader of the coalition." See also Ely, *op. cit.*, pp. 246–49.

of the Algerian war, early in November, 1954, was to accentuate this trend even more and leave France financially dependent on Washington for several years longer.

General de Beaufort reported to Paris that Hanoi was honestly worried by American activities in the South and was disturbed by persistent rumors, emanating from Vietnamese officials in Saigon, that the elections agreed to at Geneva would be suppressed so as to preserve the status quo. Moreover, the French Government's coolness left Hanoi little hope of establishing the contacts and reciprocal arrangements they had confidently expected as a result of the exchange of letters between Mendès-France and Dong in Geneva. But de Beaufort noted that although Hanoi was growing cautious, it still appeared to be hesitating about the path that it should take. Its desire for peace seemed sincere, but it would soon have to make a choice. Hanoi urgently needed technicians and a variety of products. If France did not supply them, Hanoi would be driven to negotiate with Moscow and Peking.

In concluding this report (which was written at the beginning of November), de Beaufort pointed out that the D.R.V.'s wish for peace would certainly not lead it to abandon reunification, which had been one of its chief war aims and "which it can be sure of achieving if we respect the agreements." No one could yet predict what Hanoi would do if the Geneva agreements were not carried out.

Dong discussed the situation in the South with Sainteny on November 12. He asked to see an article that Buu Hoi had published in *L'Express* in Paris on November 6.[7] Dong indicated that his government hoped to work out the unification of the country in agreement with moderate leaders who could restore order in the South and establish real democracy there. He added that many people in the South were already committed to the resistance movement and were longing for the Vietminh to take over, even though they were not Communists themselves. Only certain members of the middle class remained opposed to the Vietminh, said

[7] For an analysis of this article, see Ellen J. Hammer, *The Struggle for Indochina, 1940–1955* (Stanford, 1966), p. 353.

Dong, because they wished to preserve a regime that encouraged all kinds of illicit deals.

During Sainteny's conversations with Dong on November 12 and 24 and with Ho on November 24, both Vietnamese leaders expressed concern about the attitude of representatives of French business concerns in the North. The majority had left Hanoi for Haiphong, and many were even getting ready to leave for the South. Sainteny stressed that the vagueness of the D.R.V.'s guarantees and the likelihood of severe currency restrictions had done a great deal to cause this flight. He suggested an immediate agreement that would define the conditions for French economic activities in the North.[8]

The economic agreement was soon negotiated and prepared, but Sainteny could not sign it until he had official accreditation. Therefore, he was sent a letter, dated December 8, from Mendès-France to Ho. The letter informed Ho that, in accordance with the exchange of letters in Geneva on July 21, 1954 (between Mendès-France and Dong),[9] concerning "the operation of French commercial undertakings and cultural establishments in North Vietnam . . . M. Sainteny has been appointed Delegate-General of the French Government to Your Excellency." The letter specified that the purpose of the Sainteny mission was "to provide for the implementation of the arrangements set out in the exchange of letters of July 21." This caused very sharp disappointment in Hanoi. But although all the illusions of the D.R.V. leaders had now vanished, they put a good face on the matter. Ho told Sainteny "I am happy that France has sent an ambassador, and that this ambassador is you. M. Sainteny, when do you think I will be able to send an ambassador to Paris?" Thus began a long and obscure diplomatic struggle.

The agreement signed in Hanoi on December 11 gave some

[8] Dong said to Sainteny on November 12: "But who has told you that we are a *Communist* regime? Such a regime would not wish, as we do, to encourage capitalist enterprises."

[9] The full text of these letters is in Chaffard, *op. cit.*, pp. 115–16. French interests in North Vietnam were analyzed in "Les investissements privés dans le Nord Vietnam," Pierre Chauleur, *Le Monde* (Paris), August 1, 1954.

guarantees to French firms that would stay in the North after the evacuation of Haiphong. In particular, it stated that firms would be given reasonable advance warning of any nationalization plans so as to provide for discussion about fair compensation. The principal firms involved were the Hong Gay coal mines, the Haiphong cement works, and the cotton mill at Nam Dinh. The economic agreement was supplemented by cultural agreements of fairly limited scope.

The reactions in French business circles was unfavorable. Yet the Vietnam correspondent of *The Times* (London) remarked that it was difficult to see what more Hanoi could have conceded in a document that was only intended to provide a framework for the activities of those Frenchmen who chose to remain in the North.[10] Phan Anh, the Vietnamese minister for economic affairs, told the Agence France-Presse correspondent that the agreement made it possible to contemplate practical cooperation between his country and purely capitalist French concerns. "We can cooperate with any branch of French industry on a basis of equality and mutual interest within the legal framework of the Democratic Republic."[11]

But it was already too late. The French and Americans in the South had reached the point of no return during the crucial weeks of November and December, 1954.

[10] *The Times* (London), December 15, 1954. According to the British correspondent, French business circles were afraid that D.R.V. taxation would be raised so high that profits would be nullified, or very nearly so. The guarantees covering the supervision of manpower, the transfer of profits, freedom of exports, and pricing were also regarded as inadequate. In addition, many French firms were afraid of being blacklisted in America.

[11] Out of 6,500 French residents in Hanoi before the Geneva agreements were signed, only 114 were left in the Vietnamese capital by December, according to a statement made in the French National Assembly on December 17, 1954, by M. Massot, a radical representative.

27

TRANSFERS OF POWER

The arrival of General Lawton Collins as U.S. special representative heralded a new stage in South Vietnam. Every sign indicated that Washington had made up its mind to do whatever was necessary to consolidate the Diem regime and break up the factions and dissident elements that still seemed to be impeding his actions. As soon as Eisenhower's letter was delivered, the Diem clan—who made the most of it—complained to the Americans, the press, and above all to Colonel Lansdale that they were doing their utmost but were unable to operate efficiently. They claimed that they were being neutralized by the army, which was loyal to Hinh, and by the police, who were controlled by Le Van Vien. Hinh and Vien were supported by many Frenchmen in the administrative service and the Expeditionary Corps,[1] and by Bao Dai and several Vietnamese politicians as well. The Diemists pointed out that Hinh was a French citizen and, by inclination, was likely to be more French than Vietnamese, while Vien and his Binh Xuyen were mixed up in gambling and prostitution rackets. The result

1 During the tripartite conference in Paris in October, the Americans protested about the support the French gave to Diem's opponents.

was a new campaign by the American press, which accused the French of supporting an unscrupulous military clique in Saigon in order to maintain their outdated colonial domination. This stung Mendès-France's supporters to the quick and caused concern among the "Atlantic" diplomats and soldiers.

General Collins arrived in Saigon on November 8, a mere five days after his appointment. He stated as he emerged from his aircraft that he had come without any preconceived ideas, but that he was convinced of the crucial political and economic importance of Vietnam to Southeast Asia and the Free World. Next day, Collins went to Dalat to visit Ely, who was an old friend of his. Collins told Ely that he had come to Vietnam for only a brief stay, but that he held very wide powers. He explained that he had been given authority, without exception, over all American services operating in Vietnam for any reason. This was an obvious reference to the CIA, which Ely believed was slipping from Ambassador Heath's control. Collins went on to make it clear that his mission was to give Diem the fullest support.[2]

In fact, Ely himself was beginning to have serious misgivings about American intentions. In his report of November 6, he pointed to the dangerous discrepancy between the two countries' attitudes toward the 1956 elections.

> The French Government's view, as I see it, is that, while supporting the state of Vietnam unreservedly, Paris does not intend to rescue it from a confrontation at the polls, but simply plans to enable it to face such a confrontation under the most favorable conditions. The intention is to enable it to negotiate the reunification of the country with its opponent in a way that will take account of local circumstances and the actual situation revealed by the voting, even if the state of Vietnam does not secure a nationwide majority.
>
> I fear that Washington, on the other hand, is repelled by the idea of general elections, if it is not determinedly hostile to them. Our American contacts . . . will not make any firm statements about the general elections. The American correspondents, who do not need to be as reticent, say that such elections are out of the ques-

[2] Paul Ely, *L'Indochine dans la tourmente* (Paris, 1964), pp. 299–300.

> tion. Finally, Diem and the members of the government are telling everyone that the elections will not take place.
>
> This interpretation . . . sheds a curious light on the American Government's special addiction to Diem. He is the only Vietnamese politician who would absolutely never enter into contact with the Vietminh under any circumstances, and he is the one for whom constant American pressures of various kinds are being exerted on Bao Dai. This accounts for the diverse activities of the American agencies: the recruitment of a militarized police, the proposed training of the Vietnamese Army, the posting of Vietnamese officers to "psychological warfare" courses in Manila and Bangkok, and the arming of dissident guerrilla fighters under Bacut and Trinh Minh The. Finally, this alone accounts for both the Eisenhower letter to Diem and the assignment of General Collins. . . .
>
> We and our American friends may decide together to play "power politics" in this country; we must not allow ourselves to be drawn into such a situation by failing to define our aims. The dangers which this would involve are both obvious and numerous.

However, the ambiguity about the elections was not the most pressing problem; it appeared that Washington's first move would be an attempt to break the solidarity between the French and Vietnamese armed forces. It is not yet possible to judge whether the strange coincidences that now occurred were intended as a preparation for the forthcoming Franco-American financial and military talks, or as a means of "conditioning" General Collins to support the Vietnamese Army in its existing state. Whatever the case, wholly unexpected information about the intensification of the Communist threat in Vietnam burst into the open simultaneously in Saigon, Paris, and London at that very moment.

On November 6, *L'Express* published an article by Buu Hoi that was liberal, anti-Diemist, and anti-Communist and seemed to reflect a British rather than an American way of thinking. On November 8, Eden made a statement in the House of Commons about the growing military strength of North Vietnam. On the same day, "French sources" reported that the situation in Vietnam was becoming critical, and that the Vietminh, with Chinese help, was making a tremendous effort to reorganize and Communize Tonkin. According to these reports, the North Vietnamese had begun to carry out a plan to double the size of their army; they would soon have three heavy divisions, one of them armored; and they were receiving massive quantities of Chinese equipment, transported across the border in violation of the armistice and despite the presence (at a distance, to be sure) of the International Control Commission's observers.[3] American correspondents pointed out that, according to the French, nationalist Vietnam could only be saved by energetic Franco-American cooperation. With Collins on the scene, it would finally be possible to get things done properly, provided that the Americans recognized the "experience" of the French and the value of their forces on the spot. The French and British press repeated these items of "information" and these assertions. The former minister for the Associated States, Frédéric-Dupont, took up the story in the French National Assembly on November 10, and insisted on the urgency of giving the Expeditionary Corps the means of countering the Communist threat, "so that our friends will not be abandoned."

Dulles seems to have been alone—except for the International Control Commission[4]—in not taking this information too seriously. He probably surmised the source and the purpose of the rumors. In his testimony before the House Foreign Affairs Committee on November 11, he emphasized that the situation in South Vietnam was far from satisfactory, but he seemed to think that the "external" threat had been warded off by the Manila Pact. The threat of internal subversion seemed infinitely more serious to him. "South Vietnam," he said, "must be given a strong government supported by effective police and security forces." Dulles was clearly not allowing himself to be deflected from his purpose by the Anglo-French maneuvers.[5]

[3] *The New York Times,* November 9, 1954.

[4] The Control Commission immediately reacted with skepticism to the existence of these "Chinese supplies." It pointed out that the rumors had originated in certain agencies in Saigon and expressed surprise that it had not been asked to investigate sooner. See B. S. N. Murti, *Vietnam Divided: The Unfinished Struggle* (New York, 1964), p. 54.

[5] In Paris, on the afternoon of November 11, a formal message from the State Department was delivered to Mendès-France. This message concerned Buu Hoi, whose article in *L'Express* was still being discussed in the French press. The State Department said that American policy toward Vietnam

It was obvious that the Vietnamese Army—solidly grouped around Hinh, well equipped, and supported by both the French and the Binh Xuyen's police—could carry out a coup at any moment, overthrow Diem (who could still muster only very little support), eliminate the pro-American faction, and install a regime of its own choosing. The Vietnamese military leaders and some of their French advisers were putting strong pressures on Hinh to do just this. Ely, on the other hand, did everything he could to urge restraint.[6] He was, as we have seen, a convinced supporter of Franco-American solidarity and knew that such a coup would create a serious crisis in the relations between Paris and Washington. Therefore, he argued against the use of force, still hoping that diplomacy could win the Americans over to a policy of joint action that would safeguard French interests. This earned him the hostility and even the contempt of several Vietnamese leaders, who could not see how this vaunted "Franco-American solidarity" coincided with the true interests of Vietnam, and who saw very clearly what Colonel Lansdale was up to.

In any case, General Collins immediately set out to "ward off the military threat." He had a long conversation with General Hinh on November 11, but failed to obtain anything from him. On the following day, November 12, probably as a result of combined Franco-American pressure,[7] Bao Dai summoned Hinh to France. This news was broadcast in Saigon by the Army radio, to the accompaniment of renewed and vigorous criticism of Diem; then, Hinh indicated that he would leave for France the following week and would probably be away for two or three weeks.

---

would have to be reconsidered if Buu Hoi, or anyone sharing his views, was appointed to head the Vietnamese Government or took over important responsibilities in the state of Vietnam. The message said that such an event could cause grave reactions in Congress. The State Department felt it necessary to point this out since Mendès-France was due to visit Washington within a few days.

[6] Ely, *op. cit.*, p. 291.

[7] See *The New York Times*, November 15, 1954. Shaplen reports that "When Bao Dai realized that the Americans meant business with their threat to cut off aid unless Hinh stopped his plotting or would-be plotting, he ordered him to go to France, where he has remained ever since." Robert Shaplen, *The Lost Revolution* (New York, 1965), p. 119.

But on that same day, American sources stated that although General Collins was there to coordinate American aid, his special concern was to make sure that the Vietnamese Army was ready to fight if need be. Before buckling down to this task, however, he had to be certain that the army supported Diem. But Diem, it seemed, could not trust the army.

After the conversation between Collins and Hinh, all American sources, both official and unofficial, made it very clear that, if the existing situation were not quickly ended, the termination of American aid to Vietnam could be expected. In Washington, Stassen pointed out that the continuation of aid would depend on the report that General Collins was due to make.

The argument was obviously very telling. It was plain to the Vietnamese Army that France would no longer give generous aid to Vietnam (particularly now that the Algerian revolt had begun), that it seemed to be losing interest in Asia, that the money it spent in Vietnam came from America in any case, and that everything—pay, equipment, and the rest—would depend hereafter on American aid. If this were withdrawn, a Communist victory would become inevitable. Those who held the purse strings must therefore be allowed to have their way.

This was also, officially, the reason for Bao Dai's acquiescence. Given the threat of Communism, so he later explained, he could not expose nationalist Vietnam to the possible loss of American aid, which was absolutely vital to its survival. It was whispered, however, that this official reason was not the only one, and that American emissaries had made it easier for the former emperor to "understand"—thereby also ensuring his silence on the subject in the future.

To remove all possible doubt, Collins unreservedly pledged the complete support of the United States for the Diem government on November 17. He said that he had come to take whatever steps were necessary to preserve the country from Communism and that the present government was capable of waging an effective fight against Communism. Collins emphasized that he had indeed been sent to organize and coordinate American aid, but that this aid would go only to Diem, the head of the only legitimate government and the sole legal authority in the country, and that this aid would be substantial enough to make salvation of the country possible. He therefore hoped that all groups in Vietnam would rally round Diem to create a national union against Communism. The United States was prepared to begin training a modern Vietnamese Army and had already prepared the necessary plans to do so.[8]

This statement made it plain to Hinh that he had no choice but to obey Bao Dai and comply with his summons. He handed over his post to General Nguyen Van Vy on November 19, and left Saigon forever. But his departure did not solve the problem of the army, which had been deeply humiliated by this affair.

In the meantime, Washington had officially announced on November 11, that American aid would be allocated directly to the Associated States after January 1, 1955, and would no longer be channeled through France, provided that agencies qualified to receive it were set up by that date—in other words, provided genuine independence had been established and the necessary transfers of authority carried out.

Ely had several long conversations with Collins during this period. He pointed out that, although France agreed to the formation of a smaller but more effective Vietnamese Army which could relieve the Expeditionary Corps, it feared that this might provoke reactions from Hanoi. Collins replied that the American Government did not believe the Vietminh would resume hostilities. In any case, the Manila Pact, when ratified, would provide a guarantee—by the United States, in particular—that would cure the enemy of any aggressive ideas. He added that Washington appreciated the cover provided by the Expeditionary Corps and hoped that it would be kept in position until the 1956 elections. When Ely sought to discover exactly what guarantees the United States would offer in case of Vietminh aggression, Collins told him that Congress would certainly refuse to make any commitments involving the intervention of ground forces, whatever the circumstances.

[8] *The New York Times*, November 18, 1954.

During these conversations, Collins handed Ely a draft agreement on American participation in the training of the Vietnamese forces. To put it plainly, this plan meant the gradual replacement of French instructors by American officers. These would be made available by substituting American army instructors for supporting personnel (drivers, cooks, etc.) within MAAG itself.[9] Ely commented that this was more or less in accordance with the Geneva agreements. However, Ely did not accept the plan and alerted Paris immediately. He emphasized that, if the proposed agreement were adopted, it would result in the eviction of French officers in favor of Americans and would soon end French influence in Vietnamese military affairs. In addition, Collins was planning to send several hundred Vietnamese officers every year for training in the United States. These moves would quickly affect France's position in cultural matters as well, Ely said. They would also slow down the training of Vietnamese officers and hinder cooperation between the Vietnamese Army and the Expeditionary Corps.

In spite of his disagreement with Ely, Collins publicly emphasized the need to improve the Vietnamese Army and announced that an American military mission had been formed to train it. It would soon be going to work and would introduce special methods that had proved their value in Korea, Greece, and Turkey. Collins added that this mission would operate under General Ely's control, although the details of the program had not yet been worked out by the French General Staff and the American Government. French and American training methods would be brought into step, but the aim was the rapid creation of a completely autonomous Vietnamese Army.[10]

These statements provided clear evidence of the Pentagon's wish to reduce French military responsibilities in Vietnam. It really looked as though the Eisenhower Administration wanted to

[9] According to Ely, at the time of the cease fire, MAAG comprised "225 officers, 60 enlisted men, and a number of civilians, working in administrative or supervisory positions. In 1954, there were 1,200 French officers and 5,000 NCO's attached to the three national armies. Ely, *op. cit.*, p. 271.

[10] *The New York Times*, November 18, 1954.

create an irreversible situation before the impending visit of Mendès-France to Washington.

When Mendès-France arrived in Washington on the evening of November 17, he already knew about the Collins statement. The purposes of his short visit, according to the French, were to strengthen Franco-American relations and to create an even closer understanding between the two governments on the great problems of foreign policy. The session on Indochina took up the afternoon of November 18. A *New York Times* correspondent summed up the course of the meeting as follows:

> Premier Mendès-France appealed to the United States today for greater financial help in holding South Vietnam against Communism. In a meeting at the State Department this afternoon the French Premier laid down his government's estimate of the grave problems in Indochina. At the same time he indicated that continued U.S.-French cooperation would safeguard the countries not now under Communist control, informants said.[11]

As he was to tell the Foreign Affairs Committee of the French National Assembly at the beginning of December, Mendès-France had been reluctant to discuss financial questions and American aid with his hosts, because he did not want to confuse the issues and thereby run the risk of throwing French policy off its course.[12] Therefore, these questions were not dealt with in the negotiations, and the Americans merely promised to hasten their answers to the questions Faure had asked in September.

The discussion dealt entirely with political and military problems. Mendès-France told Dulles on the very evening of his arrival that he felt that Collins's statements were very dangerous indeed. On November 18, he emphasized that the Vietminh could be expected to react vigorously if it became apparent that the Americans proposed to maintain partition by force. He pointed out that the Vietminh might even resume hostilities. Mendès-France added that Collins's public statements were already being interpreted as

[11] "Further U.S. Help to Vietnam Urged by Mendès-France. Premier Tells Dulles and Other Key Officials More Funds Are Needed to Stop Reds," by Walter H. Waggoner. *The New York Times*, November 19, 1954.

[12] *Le Monde* (Paris), December 4, 1954.

evidence that the Pentagon wished to replace the French with Americans in Vietnam, and that such suspicions were bound to cause difficulties in France. Neither the French public nor the Vietminh could remain indifferent if France were evicted from Indochina, and the United States would earn the resulting hostility of both parties.

Once again, Mendès-France told Dulles that they must reach agreement not only about long-term aims but also about present policy. The French Government was willing to acknowledge American leadership in Asia, but a lessening of French influence in Indochina seemed absolutely against their common interest. Therefore, it was vital that neither side should take an initiative without the prior agreement of the other.

Dulles agreed that cooperation was absolutely essential and that all jockeying for influence over questions of prestige should be avoided. He again declared that there was no wish on America's part to infringe the armistice, let alone cause a resumption of hostilities. He even agreed that the responsibilities of France in Vietnam were greater than those of America. He played down Collins's statements and again stressed the need for cooperation.

Arrangements were then agreed upon for the joint working parties that had been specified in the protocol of September 29, following the earlier Franco-American meeting. It was also agreed that common instructions would be sent to Collins and Ely. Nonetheless, it was clear throughout the talks that Dulles was determined to preserve Collins's freedom of action.

The military problem was then studied in order to assess the threat which, according to the French, had obviously been intensified by Collins's statements. In view of the information then becoming available,[13] it was agreed that caution was necessary. Dulles repeated that there was certainly no question of eliminating France but, given the general situation—an obvious refer-

[13] The reported strengthening of the D.R.V. formed the background to these conversations. It was the main subject of James Reston's article in *The New York Times* of November 20, under the headline: "New Red Divisions in Indochina Stir U.S.-French Alarm: Mr. Mendès-France Agreed With U.S. Officials to Build Military Strength in South Vietnam."

ence to Algeria and the Aurès rising—the French might suddenly wish to withdraw their troops, and, because of that possibility, an effective Vietnamese Army was urgently needed. This led to a discussion of the plan submitted by Collins to Ely. Mendès-France felt that the proposed reduction of the Vietnamese Army's strength to 90,000 men was too drastic. Who would defend Vietnam against an act of aggression, he asked, if France withdrew and the national army was cut back?

Dulles replied that, in his opinion, the Vietnamese forces were not intended for the defense of South Vietnam against external aggression; their sole purpose was to preserve public order and suppress any attempts of subversion. There could be no question of raising funds sufficient to enable the Vietnamese Army to oppose a Vietminh attack that might well be supported by China. Only the Manila Pact could provide the requisite deterrent against such an act of aggression. This was why Dulles believed that such a reduction of the Vietnamese forces did not involve any real risk.

The talks then moved on to the political situation in South Vietnam. It was agreed that the political vacuum there must be remedied as quickly as possible and that a detailed program of reforms should be put to Diem and followed up by regular inspection of its results. Once again, Dulles did not hide his belief that Diem was not the ideal man, but he still thought that Diem's nationalism and anti-Communism justified the decision to keep him in power. In this connection, Dulles confirmed that he was still opposed to Bao Dai's return to Vietnam. In conclusion, he agreed that Ely and Collins should develop a program of reforms and should set up joint working parties for this purpose.

The joint communiqué, published on November 20, at the end of Mendès-France's visit, reaffirmed the identity of French and American views and the determination on both sides to conduct a common policy in complete cooperation.[14] The last French barriers were about to be demolished.

[14] The complete text is in *Department of State Bulletin No. 804* (Washington), November 22, 1954. "The only way the situation could be remedied, according to American opinion, was to take over the defense of South Vietnam from the French." Murti, *op. cit.*, p. 52.

When he arrived in Paris, General Hinh made no secret of his intention to ask Bao Dai for the dismissal of Diem and the formation of a new government of national union capable of carrying out the necessary reforms.[15] On November 29, however, Bao Dai relieved Hinh of his duties as Army Chief of Staff—for "indiscipline"—thus ridding Diem and the Americans of the main obstacle to their plans.[16] A few days later, Bao Dai agreed to a compromise that also suited them very well: on December 8, at Diem's request, he appointed General Le Van Ty, a fifty-year-old southerner, as chief of staff. At the same time, General Nguyen Van Vy was appointed inspector general of the army. Diem still carried no authority whatsoever with the army and had needed Bao Dai's help in order to impose a new command on it.

Le Van Ty was known as a moderate who favored Diem. In order to gain acceptance from his subordinates, and probably because he did not wish to appear—or to be—a mere tool in Diem's hands, Ty adopted a neutral attitude and laid down conditions for the President.[17] He also came to an agreement with General Nguyen Van Vy and informed Diem that he would accept the post only if Vy were given extensive powers and allowed to exercise genuine influence in the army.[18] Diem accepted these terms under American pressure, and the two generals took up their posts on December 13. As the correspondent of *The New York Times* pointed out, the army had, in fact, successfully preserved its autonomy. It appeared to have renounced any attempt to interfere in

[15] See *Le Monde* (Paris) and *The New York Times*, November 24, 1954.

[16] *The Times* (London) and *The New York Times*, November 30, 1954. The text of the communiqué issued by Bao Dai's office was published in *L'Information* (Paris), November 30, 1954. For further details on the crisis, see Georges Chaffard, *Indochine. Dix Ans d'Independence* (Paris, 1964), pp. 60–61.

[17] Agence France-Presse, December 10, 1954.

[18] Ely noted that the Americans had been annoyed by the change from Vy to Ty. It is safe to infer from this that Vy retained extensive powers at the request of the Americans. Scigliano, referring to *The New York Times* of December 5, 1954, reports that Diem opposed Vy, Collins's candidate, because Vy was "insufficiently submissive." Collins, on the other hand, "apparently feared that army morale would suffer if Diem's choice, Ty, were given the post."

politics, but it had succeeded in establishing its right to be left alone by the President.[19]

That same day, Representative James P. Richards (Democrat, South Carolina), who was due to become chairman of the House Foreign Affairs Committee in the new Congress, returned from a tour of Asia and stated that, "Vietnam will be lost to Communism unless the French get out 100 per cent—militarily, economically, and politically." He said that the people of Vietnam would no longer follow French military leadership and the task of building up an anti-Communist force must be assumed by the United States, which did not mean sending troops. The Vietnamese had lost all confidence in the French administration. As things stood now, he said, the Communists were certain to win the 1956 election. They were now infiltrating from the north and building up Communist strength in violation of the armistice.[20]

But on December 13, after many weeks of negotiations, Collins and Ely secretly signed the agreement that defined the terms of Franco-American cooperation in the training of the new Vietnamese Army. What were the provisions of this agreement, whose imminent conclusion the American press had been announcing for a long time?

First, there was to be a large-scale demobilization of the Vietnamese Army, which was to be cut back from 270,000 to 90,000 men. France was to grant it complete autonomy by July 1, 1955, at the latest. On January 1, 1955, Lieutenant General John O'Daniel, Chief of MAAG, was to take over full responsibility for assisting "the government of Vietnam" in the organization and training of its armed forces, "under supreme authority of the French commander in chief" (i.e., General Ely). Both American and French personnel would be attached to the Vietnamese armed forces as advisers and instructors, but all of them would come under the direction of the Chief of MAAG.

However, there was an essential proviso. Article 5 of the agreement specified that the Chief of MAAG would acknowledge "the

19 *The New York Times*, December 14, 1954.

20 *The New York Times*, December 14, 1954, and *The Times* (London), December 15, 1954.

superior authority of the French Commander in Chief" (Ely), especially with regard to "the strategic concept governing the employment of the French and Vietnamese armed forces in case of either external aggression or internal subversive activities, in accordance with the agreements in force." An annex to the document specified that the phrase "internal subversive activities" meant "subversive activities of a military nature conducted by the Vietminh within Vietnam." Thus the agreement linked the French and Americans in the action to be taken as a result of the Geneva agreements. But in practical terms, it meant that France was giving way to the United States.

The agreement was secret, but it immediately led to a further demonstration of American power. On December 16, as Ely was leaving for Paris, O'Daniel declared that South Vietnam could still be saved from Communism. It was, he said, a matter of courage, stubbornness, and perseverance. The stakes were too high to allow for defeatism. "We are willing to stand by our friends, even though they may be down."[21]

European observers were surprised and disturbed. Robert Guillain of *Le Monde* drew attention to the "recklessness" of Diem, "a dedicated pro-American who does not hesitate to install American advisers backstage in the Palais Norodom,[22] or even to allow them to appear at his side on the stage itself. Meanwhile, the Americans guilelessly push themselves forward. O'Daniel went off in person to make a fearful scene with General Hinh and demand his resignation." Guillain added: "The Americans have intervened in Vietnam, now supposedly at last independent, with a brazenness that the French would never have dared to show."[23]

The *Times* correspondent reported:

> In the South, French policy has become subordinate to American policy, and in so doing bears no relationship to the negotiations which are being conducted in the North. It is all horribly like 1946 and, unless the French are seized soon with the need to coordinate

[21] *The New York Times*, December 17, 1954.

[22] Lansdale had in fact been given an office near that of the President, as had a new "adviser," Wesley R. Fishel.

[23] *Le Monde* (Paris), December 3, 1954.

short and long term policies, one can see an equally critical situation developing.[24]

A senior French official assigned to Saigon included the following devastating passage in his report dated November 24: "Our vacillation has deprived us of all our best tactical support in Saigon. Now we have lost the confidence of the Vietnamese Army, while the Americans—whom we tried to 'involve' but who have made mere onlookers of us instead—have bought the allegiance of the two main sects and then of Bao Dai."

Franco-American "cooperation" began as a game of trickery and ended in a rout. Ely and his staff had planned a gradual reduction of the Expeditionary Corps from 150,000 men on January 1, 1955, to 100,000 men on January 1, 1956. This plan depended on America's willingness to continue its financial support, which had amounted to $400 million in 1954. On November 22, however, Douglas Dillon, the United States ambassador in Paris, warned the French Government that Washington would only be able to allocate $100 million for the support of the French forces in Vietnam in 1955.

This would naturally force France to liquidate its military commitments in Vietnam much more quickly, and thus make room for the Americans and their Vietnamese agents. French documents show that some French officials in Paris concluded that the United States no longer believed the South could be saved, that it had started a withdrawal, and that the French should take the opportunity to get out as well. Yet some intermediate solution had to be found between Ely's plans and the wholesale evacuation of the French Expeditionary Corps; some French forces had to be kept in Indochina to provide for the safety of French residents during the danger period.

Meanwhile, the main outlines of the new American plan rapidly emerged, and the extremely well-informed weekly *U.S. News and World Report*[25] gave an exact description of it. The plan included the following points:

[24] *The Times* (London), December 15, 1954.
[25] *U.S. News and World Report*, December 10, 1954, pp. 24–26.

1. The Vietnamese Army was to be cut back from 270,000 to 90,000 men.

2. The French were to be encouraged to go away quickly; French forces were to be reduced from 150,000 men in December, 1954, to 30,000 men in December, 1955, and concentrated around Saigon.

3. American aid to the French forces were therefore to be reduced from $385 million in 1954, to $100 million in 1955. The Vietnamese Army would receive $200 million (instead of the $385 million granted to the Associated States in 1954), while economic aid to southern Indochina would be increased from $25 million to $100 million.

The magazine said that the State Department sought only to prevent Communist infiltration south of the 17th Parallel and estimated that the South Vietnamese forces would be sufficient for this police assignment. The French would continue to be responsible for the training of the national forces but would use new methods and accept American supervision. Aid would go directly to the Associated States as of January 1, 1955. From this, *U.S. News and World Report* concluded that "the United States has relieved France of responsibility for an Indochina policy."[26]

In the face of this continual erosion of French positions, the Mendès-France government adopted a post of moderate optimism. The rightists had been attacking it more and more vigorously; they accused it of yielding too much to Ho Chi Minh in July, and too much to the Americans since then. Now the government began to be the target of increasing criticism from the left, which had spared it so far. But Mendès-France was undaunted. He accepted a wide-ranging parliamentary debate on the budget of the Ministry for the Associated States, in order to prepare for his talks about Southeast Asia with Dulles and Eden, which were to be held in Paris on December 18.

[26] This weekly also reported that French officials saw the joint instructions to Ely and Collins (sent by Mendès-France and Dulles after the November talks in Washington) as meaning that Mendès-France had gotten rid of Indochina. In addition, Mendès-France was reported to have said in Washington that he regarded the Far East as essentially an American sphere of influence. *Le Monde* and *L'Information* (Paris), December 9, 1954.

Predictably, Mendès-France was attacked for his Indochina policy by his opponents in the MRP and by the moderates, who could not forgive him for the Geneva agreements or the defeat of the European Defense Community. The Communists on the opposite side of the Assembly attacked in their turn. Then Bidault once again indicted the Geneva agreements in a way which showed that, if he had not learned anything, he had already forgotten a great deal. Letourneau criticized "the meddling Americans who, in their incorrigible guilelessness, believed that once the French Army leaves, Vietnamese independence will burst forth for all to see."[27] A speech by the Socialist leader Christian Pineau attracted some attention. The Christian Democrats (MRP) and the Socialists (SFIO), who had jointly steered the colonial war to the brink of disaster, were now side by side again, denouncing "the reversal of alliances" that they feared Ho and Sainteny were arranging in Hanoi.

On the right, disenchantment was expressed even among the Gaullist Social Republicans. Their spokesman, M. J. P. Palewski, exclaimed: "No government in Indochina has ever been loathed as much as that of Diem. Alas! It is supported by our allies."[28]

Mendès-France stood his ground: "The Geneva agreements are our charter. We are honoring them. We will see to it that they are honored." In his view, the Manila Pact was the logical complement to the Geneva agreements and served to maintain a balance in Southeast Asia. It was strictly defensive by nature and offered no threat of any sort. By means of the Manila Pact, France had secured for the Associated States the legal safeguard that the United States had not given in Geneva. Mendès-France announced that he would soon submit the Manila Pact to parliament for ratification.

He indicated that he wanted to align his policies more closely

[27] For this debate, see *Débats parlementaires, Assemblée Nationale,* Nos. 124, 125, and 126, December 17, 18, and 19, 1954, pp. 6504–21, 6526–28, 6540–60, 6566, 6616–38.

[28] In April, 1954, General de Gaulle met Sainteny, who had sent the General a copy of his book (*Histoire d'une paix manquée*), and said to him in obvious reference to the events of 1946, "Well, Sainteny, you will eventually be right after all."

with those of the British, and that, for this reason, France would ask for membership in the Colombo group. He also dealt with the problem of relations between France and the United States. He asserted that he wished to confine American influence in Indochina within the framework of the Geneva agreements and pointed out that "common aims" had emerged in the course of the Paris and Washington talks. Of course, each nation retained its freedom of judgment, but preliminary consultations would take place before any decisions were made, and local action would be coordinated. Mendès-France emphasized that, in any case, Dulles had given a clear assurance that the United States was in no way trying to weaken France or replace its influence. He continued:

> We were determined to leave sufficient troops in the Far East to ensure the safety of Vietnam, but the government of that country felt that it was sufficiently safeguarded by the Manila Pact. It also considers that the Vietnamese Army is capable of maintaining order. We were therefore withdrawing those French forces that are not essential for the protection of our citizens. The people can thus be certain that our soldiers will not be involved in any new and horrible Asian war.

Mendès-France won his fight; the budget of the Ministry of the Associated States was passed with a large majority.

The French, the Americans, and the British met once again in Paris, on December 18, to discuss Southeast Asia, and Vietnam in particular. Mendès-France, Dulles, and Eden all noted and deplored the fact that Diem still refused to accept the reform program worked out by the Franco-American committee.[29] All those present stressed the obstinacy and ineffectiveness of the Vietnamese President, but, as no replacement could be found for him, the Americans urged that the experiment should be carried to its conclusion. Dulles summed up a long tripartite discussion about alternative candidates, in which the names of Nguyen Van

[29] There was, in particular, a working group of Vietnamese, French, and American agricultural specialists that was preparing the ordinance on agrarian reform. See Price Gittinger, "Agrarian Reform," in Richard W. Lindholm (ed.), *Vietnam: The First Five Years* (East Lansing, 1959), p. 200.

Tam, Phan Huy Quat, and the late Nguyen Huu Tri were mentioned, by saying: "So the ideal Vietnamese President is either dead or not yet born!"[30] His actual conclusion was that Diem should be supported for the foreseeable future, while a very discreet search was made for an alternative possibility.

The Ely-Collins agreement was also discussed. It had been accepted in Washington, and the American embassy had so informed the French Government on December 17. Mendès-France, however, had raised some objections to it and told Dulles about them on December 18. To avoid upsetting the agreement, they decided (after lengthy discussions) to exchange letters of clarification.[31]

On December 23, an article by Homer Bigart in the *New York Herald Tribune* outlined the conclusions that Washington was thought to have reached as a result of the latest talks in Paris.

1. The Diem government would be firmly supported against all factions.

[30] For an account of this Paris conference of December 18, 1954, see Pierre Rouanet, *Mendès-France au pouvoir* (Paris, 1965), pp. 485–93.

[31] In January, 1955, an official French letter guaranteed that the Vietnamese Army would become independent of the French Army on July 1, 1955. Another agreed that the French instructors in the Vietnamese Army would be subordinate to the Chief of MAAG, who would act, in turn, under the authority of the French Commander in Chief. The United States confirmed that the training of the Vietnamese Army would be carried out in conformity with existing agreements; that the establishment of MAAG would remain at the level of July 20, 1954; that the introduction of replacements would be phased; and that there would be Franco-American consultation throughout. Edgar Faure replied on behalf of France on February 11. The "Franco-American mission for the training and organization of the Vietnamese Army" was set up in February, 1955 (Ely, *op. cit.*, p. 27), after the agreement signed on February 10, 1955, between General Agostini (France) and General Le Van Ty (Vietnam) on the transfer of the Armed Forces Command from France to Vietnam. Chaffard, *op. cit.*, p. 61. "A Training Relations Instruction Mission (TRIM) was established, headed by General John O'Daniel . . . O'Daniel had a French chief of staff and an American deputy chief of staff, and each of the four divisions—Army, Navy, Air Force, and National Security—had alternate American chiefs and French deputies. The National Security division, which was the only one actually advising the Vietnamese on operations, was headed by Lansdale, and this was how the Americans began advising and training the Vietnamese forces." Shaplen, *op. cit.*, p. 119.

2. The Vietnamese Army would be reorganized "on the pattern of the Philippine forces which, under the direction of President Magsaysay" had crushed the Huk revolt (Lansdale's hand showed clearly here).
3. A genuinely national Vietnamese Army would be set up and its complete autonomy would be assured by the replacement of its French officers.
4. The Diem government would be asked to convoke a National Assembly as soon as possible, in order to work out a constitution on which a democratic regime could be based. This would make it possible to deprive Bao Dai, the absentee head of state, of his powers.
5. Congress would be asked to allocate $300 million in direct aid to South Vietnam in 1955.

According to Bigart, the plan for the reorganization of the Vietnamese Army on the Philippine model was already well advanced. The army was to be given police tasks rather than a defense role. It would, thus, collaborate with the peasants and work to convert Vietminh supporters rather than to suppress them. Its chief task would be to help establish a functioning administration in the countryside—an administration capable of helping the peasants build roads, bridges, and schools. Bigart also said that the American plan provided for pilot projects in the Vietnamese villages. In conclusion, he reported that the Americans had weighed the qualities and shortcomings of President Diem and had decided that there was no other, better qualified leader in sight.[32]

By December 22, Admiral Radford, who had taken part in the Paris talks (as had General Ely), had already reached Saigon. He told Collins that the game had at last been won. Two days later, on December 24, Cardinal Spellman of New York arrived in Saigon to spend Christmas with the Catholic refugees. He had made Diem's acquaintance a year or two earlier and had given him encouragement and support; in addition, he was a good friend of Diem's brother, Monsignor Ngo Dinh Thuc, with whom he had studied at the *Collegium Augustinum* in Rome.

[32] Quoted by *L'Information* (Paris), December 24, 1954.

Saigon was also talking about the creation of a school of administration, to train officials "emancipated from the colonial burden." The official feeling seemed to be that the school could best be established by Michigan State College—the very institution to which Professor Wesley R. Fishel belonged.[33]

American aid went directly to South Vietnam from January 1 on. The transfers of French sovereignty were carried out on January 1, 1955, as agreed, after a quadripartite conference in Paris had virtually dissolved the Indochina customs and currency union. The Exchange Office, in particular, was transferred to the Diem government, thereby enabling it to receive dollars directly. "Nationalist" Vietnam was now free to enter into the American "prosperity sphere." Diem did not hesitate to say that the Paris agreement had established "the true independence" of his country.[34]

[33] *The New York Times,* December 17, 1954.
[34] *L'Information* (Paris), January 7, 1955.

28

THE CREATION OF A DICTATOR

The American intervention in favor of Diem did not go unopposed. We have seen how Hinh and the army tried to resist Diem, and how they were forced to yield when the French and Bao Dai ceased to support them. The police, and the Binh Xuyen sect that controlled them, were totally uncommunicative. It was clear that Diem would have more trouble with the sects; in Paris, on December 18, General Ely described their deep hostility toward Diem. The puritanical Catholic mandarin, for many years, had heartily detested the sects in return. In fact, the army had already launched an operation in western Cochin China against Ba Cut, a well-known Hoa Hao dissenter, by early December, 1954.

But although Diem had more or less shrugged off the threat of a Vietminh attack by the end of August, the Americans and most of the right-wing nationalists still regarded it as the greatest danger.

In accordance with the terms of the armistice, the "Franco–Baodaist" government had gradually resumed control of the villages evacuated by the Vietminh forces.[1] This "resumption of

[1] According to a Saigon spokesman, Tran Van Lam, the number of villages under government control rose from 682 before the cease-fire at the beginning

authority," initially carried out by the Baodaist army, had caused some incidents of violence.[2] Yet, the resistance movement's instructions to the peasants concerning the arrival of the Baodaist troops and administrators were by no means provocative. They amounted to the three traditional rules "see nothing, say nothing, and know nothing." The peasants were advised not to clash head-on with the Baodaists but to "comply with their demands without complaining, except in certain well-defined cases (arrests, collection of taxes for previous years, seizure by landowners of land that had been distributed to the peasants, etc.), . . . listen without protest to nationalist propaganda, and, in general, put up with the new regime, avoiding open clashes." But the peasants were to act as though the Baodaist regime did not exist. The village UBKC's (committees of resistance and administration) would be converted into "Committees for the Defense of Peace," and would in fact continue to administer the population. Legal disputes would still be brought before the former Vietminh courts, re-named "Committees for the Defense of the Peasants' Interests." Even the sick would continue to go to the Vietminh doctor. The best Vietminh cadres were to remain in the South in any case, except for those who were too well known to avoid arrest. A slogan embodied the mood of the moment: "To go north is glorious, but to remain is heroic."[3]

Yet the Geneva agreements did not forbid political activity of any kind on either side of the 17th Parallel. As a political organization, the Vietminh was therefore fully entitled to retain all its cadres in the South. "Democratic liberties" were guaranteed under Article 14 of the armistice, and reprisals were forbidden.

---

of August to 1,162 at the end of December. *Le Monde* (Paris), December 31, 1954. Tran Van Lam was Diem's first delegate to the southern region of Vietnam. Robert Scigliano, *South Vietnam: Nation Under Stress* (Boston, 1963), p. 67.

[2] For further details, see B. S. N. Murti, *Vietnam Divided: The Unfinished Struggle* (New York, 1964), pp. 64–65. For an account of the Cho-Duoc incident in Quang Nam province in September, 1954, see Nguyen Huu Tho's interview in Wilfred Burchett, *Vietnam: Inside Story of the Guerrilla War* (New York, 1965), chap. ii.

[3] Max Clos, *Le Monde* (Paris), December 12, 1954.

Nevertheless, police repression began in rural areas, in central Vietnam as well as to the south, as soon as the troops took possession of villages.[4] The big landowners also returned, repossessed the land they had abandoned during the fighting, and, with the help of the armed forces, evicted the peasants who had moved in. As a result, the agrarian problem became pressing,[5] and an atmosphere of tension and insecurity affected several provinces. The London *Times* correspondent wrote that neither the government nor the army seemed to have "any clear policy in attempting to re-establish control over villages evacuated by the Vietminh leaders." They did take some precautions, but "such dubious measures have not provided sufficient assurances for the government officials sent to take over, who retreat to the larger towns for the night."[6]

The repression launched in the countryside was already causing far-reaching political repercussions. The Vietminh radio (The Voice of Vietnam) said on about December 15, that the operations in the Long Xuyen area against Ba Cut and his Hoa Hao dissidents were merely the prelude to a decisive action against the Cao Dai and the Binh Xuyen. The Vietminh radio (which also broadcast the appeals of Cao Trieu Phat, a Cao Dai leader who had gone north) accused the Americans and Diem of planning to take advantage of the cut in the size of the national army to purge Hinh's supporters from it. In Saigon, it was reported that Vietminh agents in the provinces were reported to be establishing increasingly close contacts with minor rebel leaders in the sects and the national army.[7]

It appeared that Diem's regime did not even balk at premedi-

[4] Pham Thieu, Vice President of the Nam Bo Executive Committee, told Max Clos the correspondent of *Le Monde*, "Every day hundreds of our compatriots are arrested or assassinated by the police or the army because of the views they hold. But the Geneva agreements stipulate that a democratic regime should be set up in each zone." *Le Monde* (Paris), December 16, 1954.

[5] Tillman Durdin, *The New York Times*, November 15, 1954.

[6] *The Times* (London), December 15, 1954.

[7] *Le Monde* (Paris), December 17, 1954. For the political aspects of the operation against Ba Cut, see Georges Chaffard, *Indochine: Dix ans d'indépendance* (Paris, 1964), pp. 64–65.

tated murder to eliminate its opponents, and these methods aroused reactions as far away as Paris. At the Assembly of the French Union on December 3, a Radical member, Jacques Raphaël-Leygues (who had been sent to Vietnam some weeks earlier by the French Government on a fact-finding mission), asked some sharp questions: "Why support the present government of the South? Should we be supporting murder committees—for who actually arranged for the execution of Governor Nguyen Van An at Qui Nhon? And that of the former mayor of Hanoi? And that of the officers who would not join a movement in support of President Diem?"[8]

The heavy hand of repression had also fallen on the capital, and one might well have asked whether peace had really returned. Article 14 of the Geneva agreements was being openly flouted. The London *Times* correspondent wrote: "The impulse towards political expression has been stifled by press censorship[9] and arrests. The political silence that one feels in Saigon is not the silence of apathy."[10]

The persistent government-inspired rumors that the 1956 elections would not be held, together with the arrival in Saigon of General Collins and American military personnel, provoked misgivings, protests, and even public gatherings. The suppression of a demonstration against Collins's arrival created the case of the "Movement for the Defense of Peace." This movement was launched in Saigon in April, 1954, at the start of the Geneva conference, and organized a demonstration in Saigon, near the central market, as early as August 1. It then opened its doors—as it was allowed to do under the agreements—to members of the resistance who had fought for the Vietminh. The leaders of the movement were mostly non-Communist professionals and intellectuals—Catholics, Buddhists, and members of the Cao Dai and Binh

[8] *Le Monde* (Paris), December 4, 1954.

[9] In mid-December, for example, publication of the most important Saigon periodical *Dien-Tra Phong-Su* (*Inquiries and Reports*) classified by Agence France-Presse as "pro-Geneva," was suspended for three months. *Le Monde* (Paris), December 17, 1954.

[10] *The Times* (London), December 17, 1954.

Xuyen sects—and a number of them were people of considerable standing in Saigon. The president was Tran Kim Quan. Among its vice-presidents were Thich Hue Quang, a Buddhist leader, and Nguyen Huu Tho, a lawyer. This "Movement for the Defense of Peace" was not linked with the Communist-dominated "World Council for Peace." Its main aims were to mobilize public opinion in support of the Geneva agreements and to see to it that they were carried out, especially by preparing for the 1956 elections.

The Diem government decided that the movement was "subversive" and Vietminh-inspired. On the day after the November 11 demonstration, and in violation of the Geneva agreements, it ordered the arrest of twenty-six of the movement's principal leaders including all eight members of the executive committee. Among the latter were the Buddhist priest Thich Hue Quang, Nguyen Huu Tho, another lawyer, Trinh Dinh Thao (former Minister of Justice in the Tran Trong Kim Government),[11] Luu Van Lang (an engineer), Nguyen Van Vi (a banker), Pham Huy Thong (a philosopher), and Nguyen Van Duong (a professor). Four of the eight were released a few days later, owing to the intervention of Foreign Minister Tran Van Do (whose father-in-law, Luu Van Lang, was one of the four men released), but the political police relentlessly pursued their efforts to prove that the movement had ties with the Vietminh.

The twenty-two men who remained in custody were threatened with legal proceedings for starting a movement without official permission—although there was no legal requirement for such permission—and for circulating documents which had not been

[11] At the beginning of 1968, Trinh Dinh Thao was elected president of the "Alliance of National, Democratic, and Peace-loving Forces of South Vietnam," formed after the Tet offensive. Nguyen Huu Tho has been president of the National Liberation Front of the South since 1961. On the beginnings of the movement and the August 1 demonstration, see *Le Monde* (Paris), August 3, 1954; Max Clos, "Le gouvernment Diem est impuissant," *Le Monde* (Paris), August 10, 1954, and Chaffard, *op. cit.*, p. 40. On the "Movement for the Defense of Peace," see also Murti, *op. cit.*, p. 66; Nguyen Huu Tho's interview in Burchett, *op. cit.*, chap. II;, and Nguyen Huu Tho's speech to the first congress of the NLF in March, 1962, *Documents du Front National de Liberation du Sud Vietnam* (Hanoi, 1965), I, 38–9.

submitted for censorship. As a result, there was a further marked increase in tension.[12] Hanoi protested to the International Control Commission about the repeated infringements of democratic liberties in the South. On December 18, in Paris, Mendès-France reminded Dulles of the need to avoid feeding the Vietminh propaganda machine with such flagrant violations of the Geneva agreements. Dulles was not in the least interested in this view of things. He replied that there was no sense in being defensive; it was far better to criticize the lack of freedom in the other zone and the infringements of the agreements by Hanoi.

Events in the South left little room for doubt among those who had taken part in the resistance and the War of National Liberation during the previous eight years. Max Clos recorded their disillusionment and bitterness at the beginning of December, 1954, during a visit to the Vietminh zone. Pham Thieu, Vice President of the Nam Bo Executive Committee, told him:

> The Americans want to start the war again. We know that their goal, and Diem's, is to prevent, at all costs, the 1956 elections which will give us certain victory.[13] We feel nothing but hatred for those who would consider plunging the Vietnamese people into another fratricidal war. The French consistently break the agreements. They do so principally by supporting the Diem government, which is oppressing the people. We signed the agreements with the French, not with Diem's government. The French are responsible for seeing to it that these agreements are implemented. Their duty

[12] D. Bloodworth, "Saigon Trial Endangers Ceasefire," *The Observer* (London), December 5, 1954.

[13] Some Western journalists in Saigon had excellent sources and a clear view of the situation. Robert Guillain of *Le Monde* wrote at the time: "American policy in Saigon . . . seeks to make the division of Indochina final. . . . The design which shows everywhere, even though it is never officially admitted because it completely contradicts the terms of the Geneva armistice, is to prevent the elections due to be held in July, 1956. In fact, it is a matter of not allowing the two stumps of Vietnam to be joined together again and, as in the Korea of Syngman Rhee, of turning the southern half of the country into a bastion of anti-Communism. . . . For this policy to be practicable, it would obviously be necessary to bring about a solution by force, as quickly as possible, and, at the very latest, by the prescribed deadline." *Le Monde* (Paris), December 4, 1954.

> is to stop Diem from carrying out his policies; by failing in this, they break the agreements they signed. Why has Mendès-France abandoned the policy of cooperating with us that he initiated in Geneva? What we cannot understand is the blindness of the French, who allow the Americans to take over and do not realize that, by the same token, they themselves are being completely ousted from Vietnam. But we are not worried; nothing can stop the wheels of history, and victory will be ours in the end, even if this means another war.[14]

During the same visit to the Vietminh zone, Clos also talked to some peasants. One of them told him: "My two sons died in the war. Now peace has returned, and the war must never start again. Those who want to start it again are criminals. Why don't the French stop the Americans from going on with their policy of aggression?"[15]

Hanoi had watched this gradual elimination of French influence in the South with growing anxiety.[16] At an informal dinner on November 24, Ho and Dong anxiously questioned Sainteny about the nature of the decisions made in Washington the week before. His hosts expressed their fear at seeing France hand over its positions in Indochina to the United States. The Vietnamese leaders had had a moment of hope in November, when some French politicians visited Hanoi. René Capitant, a former Gaullist deputy, assured them that, with a few exceptions, the Mendès-France cabinet genuinely wished for peaceful coexistence, and should be encouraged in this spirit.[17]

Hanoi, however, had lost no time in reacting through diplomatic channels. As early as October 22, 1954, the D.R.V. Government had made it clear that, in its view, the Manila Pact "constitutes

[14] *Le Monde* (Paris), December 16, 1954.

[15] *Le Monde* (Paris), December 9, 1954.

[16] The Vietnamese were not alone in being surprised. During the same period, the London *Times* correspondent in Indochina emphasized the dynamic nature of Sainteny's views "in contrast to the self-effacing attitude of the French here [in Saigon] in allowing the Americans to take the lead." *The Times* (London), December 15, 1954.

[17] D. Bloodworth, "An Uneasy Triangle in Indochina," *The Observer* (London), November 28, 1954.

a flagrant violation of the Geneva Agreement; an encroachment upon the independence and sovereignty of Vietnam, Laos, and Cambodia, and a threat to the security and peace of Southeast Asia."[18] Shortly afterward, the case of the American consulate in Hanoi revealed to the Republic's leaders the scope of American ambitions.

By the end of September, Washington had made it clear that it meant to keep its consulate in Hanoi after the Vietminh authorities returned there. The D.R.V. indicated that it saw no reason why the American and British consulates should not stay in the capital, provided that Washington and London asked for accreditation to the republican government. This D.R.V. note got curt replies from Washington and London, which claimed that accreditation was unnecessary, since it had already been obtained from the only legal government of Vietnam—the Saigon government. Hanoi was in Vietnam, and the Americans and British pointed out that, under Article 6 of the Final Declaration, Vietnam was one single country and the 17th Parallel was not to be regarded as a frontier.[19] Hanoi considered this reply very "arrogant" and cordoned off the American consulate, which, after being helped and supplied for several weeks by Sainteny's office, finally had to be shut down in November.

Hanoi concluded from this incident that Washington was intent on reunification. By accepting the Saigon government as the only legal government in Vietnam and asserting the unity of Vietnam as defined by Article 6 of the Geneva Declaration, Washington was preparing to "roll back" the Vietminh. It was the policy of "reconquest" that Dulles had described to the French during the Geneva conference, and that Chauvel and Sainteny had mentioned in several notes. It was clear that henceforth America would deal with Vietnam as it did with Germany and Korea,

[18] B. S. N. Murti, *op. cit.*, p. 50. Murti adds that, in a speech before the Indian Parliament on September 29, 1954, Nehru had said: "The whole approach of this Manila Treaty is not only a wrong approach, but a dangerous one from the point of view of any Asian country."

[19] *The New York Times,* October 29, 1954. See also Murti, *op. cit.*, pp. 173–74.

where Bonn and Seoul had a "mission" to achieve unification in the interests of the "Free World."

Thereafter, the issues were clear. Giap wrote to the International Control Commission on December 5, and Dong wrote to the co-chairmen of the Geneva conference (Eden and Molotov) on December 8. Both Vietnamese condemned the presence in the South of the Collins mission as the "first manifestation of the aggressive aims of the Manila Pact." The notes specifically denounced America's intention to train and equip the South Vietnamese armed forces. It protested against the *de facto* inclusion of the Associated States in SEATO, an organization designed to "consolidate American influence in Southeast Asia and turn Indochina into a colony and an American base."[20]

These misgivings were aggravated by Ngo Dinh Diem's rigid and doctrinaire attitude. He rejected coexistence even in its most basic form: at the end of November he turned down Hanoi's proposals for the re-establishment of normal postal communications between the North and the South.[21] Yet Hanoi looked on the re-establishment of economic relations with the South as being even more important than the attempted improvement of relations with France. Phan Anh, the D.R.V. minister of economic affairs, protested: "South Vietnam and North Vietnam are integral parts of Vietnam. According to the Geneva agreements, the demarcation line, which is only a military and temporary line, cannot in any way form an obstacle to exchanges across the Parallel from either side."[22]

Faced with the limitations and ambiguous nature of the Sainteny mission,[23] even Hanoi began to show signs of impatience. On December 30, 1954, Dong outlined his government's policy

[20] Murti, *op. cit.*, p. 50, and *L'Information* (Paris), December 9, 1954.

[21] D. Bloodworth, *The Observer* (London), November 28, 1954.

[22] *Le Monde* (Paris), December 17, 1954.

[23] On December 3, Raphaël-Leygues said at the Assembly of the French Union: "M. Sainteny deserves our confidence even though the government sends him out every eight years when the situation has been compromised. . . . M. Sainteny is accustomed to being used as an alibi and a hostage. But he knows that he can do no good whatsoever if France and the West fail to do what they have to do in the South." *Le Monde* (Paris), December 4, 1954.

to some Western journalists in Hanoi. "I believe in peaceful co-existence in Asia," said the Vietnamese Prime Minister. He re-affirmed Vietnam's friendship with France and his hope that economic relations between the two countries would be established without delay. Dong said that he was pleased with the results achieved in this area during the three months of negotiations with Sainteny, but regretted that the delegate-general had not been backed more wholeheartedly by his government, "which would have made it possible to obtain even better results." He added: "The People's Government genuinely wants to establish economic relations with France, for reasons that are both political and economic. This is in our interest and that of France as well. It does not prevent the establishment of relations with other friendly countries, such as China, but we are used to working with the French and we can continue to do so on a basis of equality and reciprocity."

Dong deplored the fact that the Mendès-France government had not continued the policy initiated at Geneva, a policy "which produced excellent results." He continued:

> France must choose between Washington and Hanoi, and only the latter choice will enable it to maintain its political and economic position in the Pacific area. Yet France is moving towards Washington. It went to Manila to sign a pact of aggression. France is of two minds, but a policy must have firm foundations. One cannot do a juggling act forever. . . . No doubt there are obstacles to the establishment of relations between our two countries, but they are not insurmountable if sincere efforts are made to overcome them. We need friends, and we want to regard the French as friends. It is in the interest of France to come to an understanding with us.

Dong was asked about the rumors that Saigon was preparing to announce its refusal to proceed with the 1956 elections. He replied: "That would be a very serious decision, but it is you—the French—who carry the responsibility, because it is with you that we signed the Geneva agreements, and it is up to you to make sure that they are respected." Then, raising his voice, he declared:

> Vietnam will be united one way or the other, with France or against it.[24] But if France tries to stand in the way, it will be beaten, because there is no stopping the course of history. The Saigon government, however, cannot refuse to hold these elections, because it would thereby show itself up as an unpopular regime. The Vietnamese people demand elections so that their voice may be heard, and the elections will take place. We do not exclude any single Vietnamese, because we need the help of all in order to rebuild the country. Our only enemies are those who combat unity and peace.[25]

In his New Year message to the Vietnamese people, Ho Chi Minh stated once again that Vietnam still wished to establish economic and cultural relations with France, based on the principles of equality and mutual advantage. He emphasized that Vietnam could not remain divided:

> We must establish close relations between the North and the South, and help our Southern compatriots in their struggle to secure democratic liberties in accordance with the Geneva agreements. We must stimulate economic and cultural contacts and foster communications between our compatriots in the North and in the South. These tasks must be undertaken in order to make it easier to hold free general elections and to unify the country. We are willing to join with every individual and every group intent on peace, unification, independence, and democracy.[26]

In an interview granted to the correspondent of *The Observer*, Ho also denied that separate elections would be arranged in the Democratic Republic before the general elections of 1956, which should be "universal, free, democratic, and secret."[27]

[24] In the article quoted earlier, Guillain also said: "The first principle of our policy should be to back unity in Vietnam, and not division. . . . The second principle should be to ensure that unity is achieved not against us, but with us." *Le Monde* (Paris), December 4, 1954. The London *Times* correspondent said: "Any long-term policy must look towards the elections" and, "Some of the short-term threats have been staved off; none of the long-term problems have even been seen fully in their context." *The Times* (London), December 15 and 17, 1954.

[25] Max Clos, *Le Monde* (Paris), January 3, 1955.

[26] *L'Information* (Paris), January 4, 1955.

[27] *The Observer* (London), January 2, 1955.

But at the end of December, Paris demonstrated once again that Atlantic solidarity took precedence over all other considerations, in Southeast Asia as in Germany (which had just been admitted to NATO). When France transferred its sovereignty to Diem on January 1, 1955, Hanoi finally became convinced that the Mendès-France government was locked into the patterns of its predecessors.

On January 22, 1955, Ely sent Paris disturbing reports from very reliable sources: both Russia and China were insisting to the leaders in Hanoi that they could expect nothing more from the Geneva agreements; the Russians were being particularly adamant on this point. The French Union army command would undoubtedly continue to observe the military clauses, they said, but the political clauses outlined in Article 14 and spelled out in the final declaration would be deliberately disregarded by the Saigon government, with American encouragement. Moscow and Peking pointed out that France would be in no position to counter this trend. According to the Russians and the Chinese, the only solution for Hanoi was to rely entirely on its two great allies, since, from now on, only global politics could create the circumstances in which Vietnam could be unified.[28]

A frontier between two worlds was being built across the heart of Vietnam.

28 On Chinese aid in December, 1954, see Donald Lancaster, *The Emancipation of French Indochina* (London, 1961), pp. 369–70.

29

FULL CIRCLE

It had taken the Fourth French Republic less than a year to rid itself of its war in Vietnam, and to shrug off its entire Indochinese burden. Only 310 days after the Berlin conference decision to negotiate (February 18, 1954), the French were handing over the Exchange Office in Saigon (December 31, 1954). Those few months had seen Dien Bien Phu, the Geneva conference and the armistice, the installation of Ngo Dinh Diem, and Washington's takeover in the South. They had also seen the declaration of the Five Principles of Peaceful Coexistence in New Delhi in June, the Guatemala affair, the entry of West Germany into NATO, and the start of the Algerian War. It had been a fateful year indeed.

The inflexibility of the international "system of blocs" showed up most clearly, and in its most cynical form, in Vietnam. The people and the government of Vietnam had tried to escape from the grinding wheels, and, at one moment, thanks to Mendès-France, they thought that they might succeed. But, since 1945, the Communists had led the Vietnamese people's century-long struggle to escape from white colonial domination, and, thus, they were opposed by all the forces in the world that opposed Stalin and the Kremlin's policy. The identification was both crude and meaningless, but the Vietnamese people's aspirations toward independence, unity, and democracy were condemned as mere ruses and disguises to cover the Machiavellian plots of Communist conspirators, simply because they were stated by Ho Chi Minh.

In fact, the French colonial power had begun as early as 1920 to label as "Communists" all those who disputed their absolute supremacy. The French succeeded in making the Communist Party of Indochina into the leading Vietnamese nationalist party, and the most popular one by far, precisely because they constantly identified "Communism" with "opposition to the colonial government." The final outcome of this short-sighted policy was Dien Bien Phu.

But rather than switch policies and see Vietnam in its true colors at long last, the French establishment chose to hand on the torch and "sell" its war, its bitterness, and its resentments to the United States, its powerful ally. The deal was made by leaders who did not know Indochina,[1] and by diplomats and soldiers who had been involved for years in both the conflict and the deadlock.

These men thought that they had good reason to be pleased: the Vietminh—the "League for the Independence of Vietnam"—would not triumph. America was now in the front line. These Frenchmen had succeeded in involving the Americans, who, with their proverbial stubbornness, would cling indefinitely to the barrier of the 17th Parallel that had been drawn across the living body of Vietnam. The views and feelings of the Vietnamese people, the fact that Hanoi had declared itself willing to cooperate with France and had proved that it was ready to follow an independent policy—all went for nothing. What mattered to these men was the need to keep the Atlantic alliance together and to

[1] Ely writes that General Salan "was of particular assistance to me at the early stages because of his wide experience with a country which I hardly knew and in which I had first traveled at the time of the Pleven mission" (i.e., in February, 1954). Paul Ely, *L'Indochine dans la tourmente* (Paris, 1964), p. 296.

maintain the strategic positions of the whites in Asia—positions that might be jeopardized, so it was claimed, by the "military neutrality" of Indochina. In the opinion of the French Commissioner in Indochina, it was better to lose with the United States than to win alone.[2]

The tragedy was that, for all intents and purposes, the United States had neither knowledge of nor practical experience with Vietnam. There were no more than skeletal American diplomatic missions in Vietnam until 1954. Books in English about Vietnam were few and far between.[3] Neither the academics nor the general public had any notion of the country's history and its real problems. But when a few French politicians, diplomats, and generals mentioned "the threat of Communism" in 1949, Indochina was swept into the plans of the "global strategists." Mao Tse-tung's victory in China, the Korean War, and McCarthyism did the rest.

Washington came to believe that it could pattern its action in Vietnam on the "Korean model." To the Pentagon, Indochina's history began in 1953–54. Everything before that could be explained by deftly combining the perennial principles of anti-colonialism with the French version of recent events. Thereafter, the escalation could proceed with relentless logic.

The Americans seemed unaware that, for the last quarter of a century, the French had labeled all their serious opponents as "Communists." But unaware or not, the Americans based their *entire* policy in Vietnam on anti-Communism. The Americans also did not seem to know that, ever since 1885, the French had consistently imposed on the Vietnamese people puppet kings, dim ministers, and civil servants whom the people either despised or thought nothing of. These American neophytes, who had never (with perhaps two dozen exceptions) established any real contacts

[2] Ely, *op. cit.*, p. 245.

[3] Among the few books that could then have provided a better understanding of Vietnam, three are worthy of special mention: Ellen J. Hammer, *The Struggle for Indochina* (Stanford, 1954); Joseph Starobin, *Eyewitness in Indochina* (New York, 1954); and Virginia Thompson, *French Indochina*, (New York, 1937).

with the Vietminh leaders, never doubted that Diem was "genuinely nationalist" and "representative." Yet this was a man, living on a reputation established by a flash in the pan in 1933, who had done no more since then than demonstrate his personal integrity, stubbornness, and sectarianism. In fact, it was the Americans, not the Vietnamese, who decided that Diem should continue to lead South Vietnam after September, 1954,[4] just as the French had decided upon Dong Khanh, in 1885; Dr. Nguyen Van Thinh, in 1946; and Bao Dai, in 1948. The Americans were ignorant of history, but not the Vietnamese—they knew it only too well.

This profound and disturbing ignorance among American politicians and strategists led to an unconscious imitation of the French colonial way; it soon became even more strikingly evident. The Americans thought they were counteracting "international Communism," as they had in Germany or Korea. But by trying to turn the 17th Parallel into a new "Dong Hoi Wall" against Hanoi, the historic capital, the Americans in fact merely revived the southern separatism of 1946. Unwittingly, they re-created and "modernized" it by providing a Catholic mandarin president from central Vietnam and a flood of supporters (mostly Catholic) from the North.

Thus, nine years after the arrival of the British in Saigon (September, 1945), things were back where they had started. Between Admiral Mountbatten and the successors of Douglas MacArthur, there had been a French interlude. But now it was "full circle," and America was stepping into France's boots. Once more, the South was turned into the colonial base for a policy of "pacifica-

[4] B. S. N. Murti, the Indian diplomat who was a member of the International Control Commission at the time, put this well:

> In addition to Diem's nationalist background and personal integrity, it was the American influence which removed General Hinh, and it was the American dollar aid which enabled Diem to divide and defeat the sects, and it was again the Americans who displaced the French in South Vietnam and kept the field clear for Diem. The promise of substantial dollar aid to South Vietnam gave the Americans such influence that in September, 1954, it was the United States, not the Vietnamese people, who decided that Ngo Dinh Diem would continue to be the President of South Vietnam. Murti, *Vietnam Divided: The Unfinished Struggle* (New York, 1964), p. 145.

tion and democracy," while the North, the bastion of national resistance, sought to negotiate rather than resume the conflict which may already have seemed inevitable. Would Vietnam ever cease to be the plaything and the prey of the great powers? In truth, as the London *Times* correspondent put it so lucidly, it was "all horribly like 1946."

BIBLIOGRAPHY

Adams, Sherman. *First-Hand Report*. New York: Harper & Row, 1961.

Azeau, Henri. *Ho Chi Minh, dernièr chance?* Paris: Flammarion, 1968.

Bach-Thai, Jean. *Le Viet-Minh face à la France et aux nationalistes vietnamiens*. Paris: Thèse I.E.P., 1955.

Bator, Victor. *Vietnam, A Diplomatic Tragedy*. New York: Oceana, 1965.

Bauchar, René. (pseudonym of Jean Charbonneau). *Rafales sur l'Indochine*. Paris: Fournier, 1946.

Beal, John R. *John Foster Dulles: 1888–1959*. New York: Harper & Row, 1959.

Blanchet, André. *Au pays des ballila jaunes: Relations d'un correspondant de guerre en Indochine*. Saint-Etienne, France: Editions Dorian, 1947.

Blanchet, M. T. *La naissance de l'État associé du Viêtnam*. Paris: Genin, 1954.

Bodard, Lucien. *La Guerre d'Indochine*. 3 vols. Paris: Gallimard, 1963–67.

Bromberger, Serge. "Face au communisme asiatique," *Le Figaro* (Paris), June 4–12, 1959.

Burchett, Wilfred. *En remontant le Mékong*. Hanoi: Editions Fleuve Rouge, 1957.

———. *North of the 17th Parallel*. Hanoi: Editions Fleuve Rouge, 1955.

———. *Vietnam: Inside Story of the Guerrilla War*. New York: International Publishers, 1966.

BUTTINGER, JOSEPH. *Vietnam: A Dragon Embattled*. 2 vols. New York: Frederick A. Praeger, 1967.

CALAMANDREI, FRANCO. *Guerra e pace nel Viet-Nam*. Florence: Parenti, 1956.

CATROUX, GEORGES. *Deux actes du drame indochinois*. Paris: Librairie Plon, 1959.

CHAFFARD, GEORGES. *Indochine: Dix ans d'indépendance*. Paris: Calmann-Levy, 1964.

———. *Les carnets secrets de la décolonisation*. Paris: n.p., n.d.

CHESNEAUX, JEAN. *Contribution à l'histoire de la nation vietnamienne*. Paris: Editions Sociales, 1955.

COLE, ALLAN B. (ed.). *Conflict in Indo-China and International Repercussions: A Documentary History, 1945–1955*. Ithaca, N.Y.: Cornell University Press, 1956.

Contribution á l'histoire de Dien Bien Phu. Hanoi: n.p., 1965.

COURTADE, PIERRE. *La Rivière Noire*. Paris: Editions français réunis, n.d.

DABEZIES, PIERRE. *Forces politiques au Viet-Nam*. Mimeographed, n.p., n.d. [1957?].

DECOUX, JEAN. *A la barre de l'Indochine: Histoire de mon gouvernement général, 1940–1945*. Paris: Librairie Plon, 1952.

DEVILLERS, PHILIPPE. *Histoire du Viêt-Nam de 1940 à 1952*. Paris: Editions du Seuil, 1952.

———. *Le Viet-Nam contemporain*. Paris: Centre d'Etudes de Politique étrangère, 1950.

———. "Problemes du Sud Viêt-Nam." *Paris-Normandie*. February 26 and 28 and March 2 and 5, 1957.

———. "Vietnamese Nationalism and French Policies," in WILLIAM L. HOLLAND (ed.), *Asian Nationalism and the West*. New York: Macmillan, 1953.

DINFREVILLE, JACQUES. *L'opération Indochine*. Paris: Editions Internationales, 1953.

Documents du Front National de Liberation du Sud Vietnam. Vol. I. Hanoi: Foreign Languages Publishing House, 1965.

DONOVAN, ROBERT J. *Eisenhower: The Inside Story*. New York: Harper & Row, 1956.

EDEN, ANTHONY. *Full Circle: Memoirs of Sir Anthony Eden*. Boston: Cassell, 1960.

EISENHOWER, DWIGHT D. *Mandate for Change, 1953–1956*. New York: Doubleday, 1963.

———. *Public Papers of the Presidents of the United States: 1954*. Washington, D.C.: Government Printing Office, 1955.

ELGEY, GEORGETTE. *Histoire de la IVe République*. 2 vols. Paris: Fayard, 1965, 1968.

ELY, PAUL. *L'Indochine dans la tourmente*. Paris: Librairie Plon, 1964.

"Les Etats associés d'Indochine." *Ecrits de Paris*, November, 1952.

Etudes Vietnamiennes. Hanoi: n.p., n.d.

FALL, BERNARD. *Hell in a Very Small Place*. New York: Lippincott, 1966.

———. *Le Gouvernement et l'économie de la République démocratique du Viêt-Nam*. Paris: Colin, 1960.

———. *Street Without Joy: Insurgency in Indochina*. Harrisburg, Pa.: Stackpole, 1961.

———. *The International Position of South Viet-Nam, 1954–58*. New York: Institute of Pacific Relations, 1958.

———. *The Two Viet-Nams: A Political and Military Analysis*. 2d rev. ed. New York: Frederick A. Praeger, 1967.

———. *The Viet-Minh Regime*. Ithaca, N.Y.: Cornell University Southeast Asia Program and the Institute of Pacific Relations, 1956.

FAUVET, JACQUES. *La IVe République*. Paris: Fayard, 1959.

FIGUÈRES, LÉO. *Je reviens du Viêt-Nam libre*. Paris: n.p., 1950.

FISHEL, WESLEY R. (ed.). *Problems of Freedom: South Vietnam Since Independence*. Chicago: Free Press of Glencoe, 1961.

FONDETTES, PIERRE DE. *Solution pour l'Indochine*. Paris: Julliard, 1952.

FOREIGN OFFICE. *Reports of the International Commission for Supervision and Control of Armistice in Viet-Nam, Cambodia and Laos*. London: H.M.S.O., n.d.

FRÉDÉRIC-DUPONT. *Mission de la France en Asie*. Paris. Editions France-Empire, 1956.

GAUDEL, ANDRÉ. *L'Indochine française en face du Japon*. Paris: Susse, 1947.

GRAUWIN, PAUL. *Doctor at Dien Bien Phu*. New York: John Day, 1955.

GREENE, GRAHAM. *The Quiet American*. New York: The Viking Press, 1956.

GUILLAIN, ROBERT. *La fin des illusions: Notes d'Indochine, Fevrier–Juillet 1954*. Paris: Centre d'Etudes de Politique étrangère, 1954.

GUIRAUD, GEORGES-H. *Aux frontières de l'enfer*. Monaco: Regain, 1956.

GURTOV, MELVIN. *The First Vietnam Crisis: Chinese Communist Strategy and United States Involvement, 1953–1954*. New York: Columbia University Press, 1967.

HAMMER, ELLEN J. *The Struggle for Indochina*. Stanford, Calif.: Stanford University Press, 1954.

———. *The Struggle for Indochina Continues.* Stanford, Calif.: Stanford University Press, 1955.

HERTRICH, JEAN-MICHEL. *Doc-Lap! L'indépendance ou la mort.* Paris: Vigneau, 1946.

HERZ, MARTIN F. *A Short History of Cambodia: From the Days of Angkor to the Present.* New York: Frederick A. Praeger, 1958.

HO CHI MINH. *Selected Works.* 3 vols. Hanoi: Foreign Languages Publishing House, 1960, 1961.

HOUGRON, JEAN. *La nuit indochinoise.* 6 vols. Paris: Domat-Del Duca, 1950–58.

ISOART, PIERRE. *Le phénomène national viêtnamien: De l'indépendance unitaire à l'indépendance fractionée.* Paris: Librairie Générale de Droit et de Jurisprudence, 1961.

KAHIN, GEORGE M. and LEWIS, JOHN W. *The United States in Vietnam.* New York: Dial Press, 1967.

LACOUTURE, JEAN. *Ho Chi Minh.* New York: Random House, 1968.

LANCASTER, DONALD. *The Emancipation of French Indochina.* New York: Oxford University Press, 1961.

LANIEL, JOSEPH. *Le drame indochinois: De Dien-Bien-Phù au pari de Genève.* Paris: Librairie Plon, 1957.

LE BOURGEOIS, JACQUES. *Saigon sans la France: Des Japonais au Viêt-Minh.* Paris: Librairie Plon, 1949.

LEROY, COL. JEAN. *Un homme dans la rizière.* Paris: Editions de Paris, 1955.

LINDHOLM, RICHARD W. (ed.). *Viet-nam, the First Five Years: An International Symposium.* East Lansing: Michigan State University Press, 1959.

MARTIN, FRANÇOISE. *Heures tragiques au Tonkin: 9 mars 1945–18 mars 1946.* Paris: Berger-Levraut, 1948.

MEEKER, ODEN. *The Little World of Laos.* New York: Charles Scribner's Sons, 1959.

MENDE, TIBOR. "Les deux Viêt-Nam." *Esprit,* June, 1957.

MURTI, B. S. N. *Vietnam Divided: The Unfinished Struggle.* New York: Asia Publishing House, 1964.

MUS, PAUL. *Le Vietnam chez lui.* Paris: Centre d'Etudes de Politique Etrangère, 1946.

———. *Viêt-Nam: Sociologie d'une guerre.* Paris: Editions du Seuil, 1952.

NAVARRE, HENRI. *Agonie de l'Indochine, 1953–1954.* Paris: Librairie Plon, 1956.

NAVILLE, PIERRE. *La guerre du Viêt-Nam.* Paris: Editions de Minuit, 1949.

NGO TON DAT. "The Geneva Partition of Vietnam and the Question of Reunification During the First Two Years." Unpublished Ph.D. dissertation, Cornell University, 1963.

NGÔ VAN CHIEU. *Journal d'un combattant Viêt-Minh.* Paris: Editions du Seuil, 1955.

NGUYEN TIEN LANG. *Les chemins de la révolte.* Paris: Amiot-Dument, 1953.

O'BALLANCE, EDGAR. *The Indo-China War 1945–54: A Study in Guerrilla Warfare.* London: Faber & Faber, 1964.

PAGNIEZ, YVONNE. *Choses vues au Viêtnam: Naissance d'une nation.* Paris: La Palatine, 1954.

PAILLAT, CLAUDE. *Dossier secret de l'Indochine.* Paris: Presse de la Cité, 1964.

PIREY, P. DE. *Opération Gâchis.* Paris: La Table Ronde, 1953.

RIDGWAY, MATTHEW B., and MARTIN, H. H. *Soldier: Memoirs of Matthew B. Ridgway.* New York: Harper & Row, 1956.

ROCOLLE, PIERRE. *Pourquoi Dien Bien Phu?* Paris: Flammarion, 1968.

ROUANET, PIERRE. *Mendès-France au pouvoir.* Paris: R. Laffont, 1965.

ROY, JULES. *La bataille dans la rizière.* Paris: Gallimard, 1953.

———. *The Battle of Dienbienphu.* New York: Harper & Row, 1965.

SABATTIER, G. *Le destin de l'Indochine: Souvenir et documents, 1941–1951.* Paris: Librairie Plon, 1952.

SAINTENY, JEAN. *Histoire d'une paix manquée.* Paris: Amiot Dumont, 1953.

SAUREL, L. *La guerre d'Indochine.* Paris: Rouff, 1966.

SAVANI, ANTOINE M. *Visage et images du Sud Viêt-Nam.* Saigon: Imprimerie Française d'Outre-Mer, 1955.

SCIGLIANO, ROBERT. *South Vietnam: Nation Under Stress.* Boston: Houghton Mifflin, 1963.

SHAPLEN, ROBERT. *The Lost Revolution.* New York: Harper & Row, 1965.

STAROBIN, JOSEPH R. *Eyewitness in Indochina.* New York: Cameron & Kahn, 1954.

STEINBERG, DAVID J., *et al.* Cambodia. New York: Taplinger, 1959.

TOURNAIRE, HÉLÈNE. *Le Livre Jaune du Viêt-Nam.* Paris: n.p., 1966.

TOURNOUX, JEAN-RAYMOND. Secrets d'etat. Paris: Librairie Plon, 1960.

"Viet-Nam," *Les Temps Modernes,* Nos. 93–94 (August–September, 1953).

VO NGUYEN GIAP. *Dien Bien Phu.* Hanoi: Foreign Languages Publishing House, 1954.

WARNER, DENIS. *The Last Confucian.* New York: Macmillan, 1963.

WISE, DAVID, and ROSS, THOMAS B. *The Invisible Government.* New York: Random House, 1964.

INDEX

Abrams, General Creighton, viii
Acheson, Dean, vii
Adenauer, Konrad, 104
Algerian War, 30, 358
Allen, Denis, 129
An Khe, 302
Anderson, Robert B., 80*n.*
Anglo-American seven points, 266, 267, 274, 291, 307, 341
Annam: Central, 37; South, 7
ANZUS, 326
Armistice commission, 263
Associated States, 18*n.*, 33, 34, 35, 42, 47
Attlee, Clement, 323
"August Revolution," 7
Auriol, Vincent, 43
Australia, 326

Ba Cut, 382, 384
Baeyens, Jacques, 130, 157
Bai Vien, 338
Bao Dai, 5, 6, 13, 14, 16, 19, 26, 32, 34*n.*, 36, 41, 49, 86*n.*, 110*n.*, 114, 115, 116, 127, 133, 134, 224, 247, 264, 307, 331, 332, 337, 338, 339, 345, 347, 350, 361, 365, 366, 372, 382, 397
Bator, Victor, 39*n.*
Baudet, Philippe, 247, 323
Beaufort, General de, 357, 358
Bergasse, Henri, 311
Bidault, Georges, 123, 124, 129, 130, 131, 133, 134, 136, 137, 139, 140, 144, 146, 150, 152, 153, 154, 155, 160, 164, 166–67, 168, 184, 186, 189, 190, 196, 201, 203, 204, 205, 207, 208, 209, 214, 215, 225, 229, 230, 235, 238, 240, 241, 242, 245, 250, 251, 295, 307, 312, 317, 377
Binh Xuyen, 20, 338, 339, 345, 348, 361, 365, 382, 384, 385–86
Blanc, General, 64, 244, 245
Blum, Léon, 14
Bollaert, Emile, 15
Bolovens Plateau, 51, 261
Bonnet, Henri, 82, 95, 188, 191, 192, 215, 221, 222, 267, 346
Boris, Georges, 247
Brebisson, Colonel Michel de, 126, 130, 201, 202, 230, 232, 233, 234, 247, 261, 292, 308
Brohon, Colonel, 76, 288
Bui Chu, 235, 262, 303, 335
Bullitt, William C., 323
Buu Hoi, 32, 337, 347, 358, 363

Buu Loc, Prince, 49, 127, 213, 214, 223, 227, 307, 345

Cabanier, Admiral, 43, 44
Caldara, General, 92
Cambodia, 5, 35, 36, 51, 109, 113, 127, 134, 138, 139, 143, 153, 159, 160, 165, 167, 202, 203, 205, 236, 237, 239, 249, 253, 267–68, 276, 278, 286, 289, 291, 292, 293, 296, 297, 298, 299, 302, 305, 306, 322
Canada, 263
Cao Bang, 24
Cao Dai, 336, 338, 339, 345, 384, 385
Cao Trieu Phat, 384
Caodaists, 20, 224
Capitant, René, 388
Carney, Admiral, 218, 219
Casey, Richard, 208
Castries, General de, 63, 69, 90, 147, 148
Catroux, General, 45*n.*
Chauvel, Jean, 124, 130, 131, 137, 230, 233, 235, 237, 239, 240, 245, 247, 252, 255, 256, 257, 258, 259, 260, 263, 265, 277, 285–86, 307, 313, 320–21, 322*n.*, 323, 389
Chen Yun, 67
Chevigné, 61, 63, 76*n.*, 176
Cheysson, Claude, 130, 137, 207, 247, 323, 332, 338, 354–55, 356
China, civil war in, 22
"China lobby," 111
Chinese People's Republic, 23, 26–27, 32, 36, 39, 122, 184; aid to Vietminh from, 65, 74, 102, 103
Chou En-lai, 122, 123, 124, 125, 153, 161, 202, 205, 238, 239, 240, 245, 249, 252, 253, 254, 255, 263, 269, 275, 278, 280, 284, 290–91, 292, 293, 295, 308, 330
Christiaens, Louis, 91
Churchill, Winston, 35, 85, 86, 87, 97, 98, 197, 219, 238, 240, 263, 266
Civilian internees, 304
Clark, General Mark, 216
Clements, Earle C., 80*n.*
Cochin China, 5, 7, 8, 10, 14, 15, 37, 38
Cogny, General, 63, 172, 180*n.*, 183
Collins, General Lawton, 351, 356–57, 361, 362, 364, 365, 366, 367, 368, 373
Colonial Route 9, 285, 292, 304
Committee for the Defense of the North, 334
Committee for National Defense, 43, 181
Connell, Arthur J., 216
"Containment Policy," 323
Coty, René, 115, 243
Crépin, General, 76*n.*, 312

Da Nang, 281
Dai Viet, 224
Daladier, Edouard, 108
Dang Xuan Khu, 11
D'Argenlieu, Admiral Thierry, 10, 12*n.*, 13
Daridan, Jean, 79, 345
Debré, Michel, 19*n.*, 105
Dejean, Maurice, 44, 61, 69, 72, 90, 92*n.*, 135*n.*, 185, 264, 280, 345
Delteil, General, 126, 131, 232, 233, 234, 235, 247, 260, 261, 299, 300*n.*, 303, 308
Demarcation line, 275–83, 286, 287, 292, 293, 308–9
Democratic Republic of Vietnam (D.R.V.), 3, 7–8, 10, 12, 27, 45, 354, 355
Desai, Manilal, 357
Diem, Ngo Dinh, *see* Ngo Dinh Diem
Dien Bien Phu, vii, 4, 39*n.*, 44, 45, 51, 52, 62, 69, 70, 71, 72, 76, 90, 136; fall of, 147, 171
Dillon, C. Douglas, 77, 104, 191, 194, 210, 212, 214, 215, 220, 221, 270, 271, 351, 375
Dong Hoi, 268
Dong Khanh, 397
Donovan, General William J., 211, 224
Dronne, Raymond, 312
D.R.V., *see* Democratic Republic of Vietnam
Duclos, Jacques, 105
Dulles, John Foster, vii–viii, 39, 54, 55, 56, 57, 72, 77, 78, 79, 80, 81,

82, 83, 84, 86, 87, 88, 91, 93, 103, 113, 114, 123, 127, 140, 141 142, 143, 159*n.*, 186, 187, 188, 189, 192, 193, 198, 212, 213, 220*n.*, 221, 222, 223, 224, 231, 238, 242, 266, 270, 271, 272, 273, 274, 289, 292, 295, 306, 308, 322, 323, 325, 332, 340, 341, 348, 349, 350, 364, 370–71, 376, 378, 387

EDC, *see* European Defense Community
Eden, Anthony, 54, 58, 86, 87, 95, 96, 97, 123, 129, 134, 144, 151, 154, 157, 158, 159, 160, 167, 196, 197, 202, 203, 204, 208, 238, 247, 248, 263, 266, 271, 272, 275, 280, 284, 286, 287, 290, 292, 293, 296, 309, 313, 348, 363, 376, 378
18th Parallel, 138, 140, 180, 256, 257, 260, 276, 279, 281, 308
Eisenhower, Dwight D., 48, 54, 72, 79, 80, 83, 98*n.*, 99, 130, 142, 143, 186, 194*n.*, 197, 198, 217, 221, 222, 226*n.*, 231, 238, 240, 242, 248, 263, 313, 341, 348, 349, 356, 361
Elections, date of, 286, 293, 303, 309–11
Ely, General Paul, 62, 63, 64, 68, 72, 73, 74, 76*n.*, 77, 175, 178, 179, 181, 185, 195, 235, 244, 247, 255, 256, 258, 262, 263, 288, 290, 293*n.*, 299, 307, 323, 339, 340, 343, 345, 347, 353*n.*, 356, 362, 365, 367, 368, 373, 374, 375, 382
Etter, Philipp, 252
European Defense Community (EDC), 48, 104–5, 325*n.*, 357, 377

Faifo, 261
Falaize, Pierre, 133
Faure, Edgar, 36, 229, 275, 340
Fay, General, 62, 64, 244
Ferguson, Homer, 89*n.*
"Final declaration," 302, 303
Fishel, Wesley R., 381
Fleurant, Colonel, 232
Four Power conference (1954), 54–59, 104
Fourçade, Jacques, 311
14th Parallel, 279, 293, 308
France, 136, 140, 208; army of, 19–20, 28–29, 33; Communists in government of, 12–13; and confederation plan, 10; and D.R.V. nationalists, 11; and European Defense Community, 48, 104–5; long-term victory hopes of, 30; and North Africa, 23; political-settlement hopes in, 41; political strife in, 16; war aims of, 4–5
Franco-Vietnamese agreement (March, 6, 1946), 8
Franco-Vietnamese Military High Committee, 214
Frédéric-Dupont, 130, 229, 230, 235, 237, 245, 250, 307, 364
French Expeditionary Corps, 20, 23, 28, 30, 33, 34, 64, 175, 176, 177, 181, 182, 184, 219, 245, 278, 302, 307, 310, 340, 342–43, 346, 361, 364, 367, 375
French High Commission, 337
French Union, 10, 36, 41, 42, 44
Front for National Safety, 223

Gandhi, Shrimati Indira, 353, 356
Gaucher, Colonel, 69
Gaulle, Charles de, 7, 14*n.*, 377*n.*
Gavini, 76
Giang River, 308
Giap, Vo Nguyen, *see* Vo Nguyen Giap
Great Britain, 48, 108–10, 128, 196, 208, 325, 326
Gros, Professor, 131
Guerrilla warfare, 17, 20
Guillaume, General, 244, 245
Guillermaz, Jacques, 130
Gurtov, Melvin, 81*n.*

Ha Van Lau, Colonel, 126, 201, 202, 230, 232, 233, 235, 237, 259, 260, 261, 262, 308
Haiphong, 139, 235, 236, 245, 256, 257, 285
Hanoi, 139, 245, 302, 352, 353
Harding, Field-Marshal, 219
Harriman, Averell, 334*n.*

Heath, Donald R., 133, 263, 280, 345, 350, 362
Ho Chi Minh, vii, 3, 8, 10, 11, 12, 14, 23, 26, 32, 43, 45, 46, 47, 48, 263, 318, 355, 356*n.*, 357, 388, 392
Ho Thong Minh, 339
Hoa Binh, 31
Hoa Hao, 20, 224, 336, 338, 339, 345, 384
Hoang Co Binh, 334
Hoang Minh Giam, 11
Hoang Quoc Viet, 11, 307
Hoang Van Hoan, 126, 159, 206, 249
Hoi An, 261
Hoover, Herbert, Jr., 351
Hue, 269, 281, 285
Humphrey, George, 218

India, 110, 167, 168, 263, 304, 325
Indochinese Communist Party, 13, 26
Indochinese Federation, 18*n.*
Indonesia, 325
International Control Commission, 304, 310, 318, 336, 353, 364

Jacquet, Marc, 47, 61, 76*n.*, 130, 176, 182*n.*, 229
Jacquinot, Louis, 137
Japanese in Indochina, 5
Johnson, Lyndon B., 80*n.*
Johnson, U. Alexis, 127, 263, 280, 284
Joint Commission, 304, 305
Juin, Marshal Alphonse-Pierre, 18, 29*n.*, 34, 185, 302

Keyes, Roger, 80*n.*
Khmer High Command, 36
Khmer Issarak, 153, 167, 202, 236, 278, 306
Khrushchev, Nikita, 106
Kim Il Sung, 23*n.*
Knowland, William F., 80, 81, 111, 195
Koenig, General, 182*n.*, 228
Korea, 23*n.*, 122; armistice negotiations in, 31, 32, 34–35, 40
Krishna Menon, V. K., 168, 205, 208, 284
Kuomintang, 22

La Chambre, Guy, 247, 255, 257, 307, 320, 324, 340, 343, 345, 346, 348, 351, 357*n.*
Laloy, Jean, 130, 247
Land-reform program, Democratic Republic of Vietnam, 27
Lang Son, 24, 38
Laniel, Joseph, 14, 35, 42, 43, 48, 56, 76*n.*, 77, 85, 94, 97, 100, 101, 104, 145, 146, 172, 176, 183*n.*, 184, 191, 195, 210, 214, 227, 229, 230
Lansdale, Colonel Edward G., 211, 212, 224, 333*n.*, 339, 361, 365
Lao Dong, 27, 46, 320
Laos, 32, 38, 44, 51, 61, 109, 113, 127, 134, 137, 139, 143, 153, 159, 160, 165, 167, 202, 203, 205, 211, 236, 237, 239, 249, 253, 261, 267, 268, 276, 278, 286, 289, 291, 292, 293, 299, 302, 304–5, 306
Lattre de Tassigny, General Jean de, vii, 5, 27, 28, 29, 31, 34*n.*
Lavrishchev, Alexander, 356
Le Quang Luat, 334
Le Van Kim, Colonel, 232
Le Van Ty, 372
Le Van Vien, 338, 339, 347, 361
Leclerc, General Philippe, 3, 8, 9, 13, 19, 312
Letourneau, Jean, 31, 32, 311, 377
Li Chen Hou, 84
Lien Viet, 320
Lignon, Léon, 9
Lippmann, Walter, 140
Liu Shao-chi, 23
Lloyd, Selwyn, 196
Löfgren, Sven, 45, 46, 47
Luang Prabang, 32, 33, 52, 63, 305
Luu Van Lang, 386

MAAG, 349, 368, 373–74
McArthur, Douglas, Jr., 270, 322*n.*
McCarthy, Joseph, 334*n.*
McCormack, John, 80*n.*
Magsaysay, Ramon, 211
Mahaxay Plateau, 50
Mai Van Bo, 353*n.*
Makins, Roger, 89, 110, 197
Malaya, 109

Malenkov, Georgi, 40, 106
Manila Pact, 317–28, 329, 330, 337, 346, 364, 367, 371, 377, 388–89
Mansfield, Mike, 53, 195, 347
Mao Khe, 27
Mao Tse-tung, 22, 252
Margerie, 130, 245
Marie, André, 35
Martin, Joseph P., 80*n.*
Massigli, René, 96, 97
Mayer, Daniel, 145, 186*n.*
Mayer, René, 33*n.*, 247
Mehta, Gaganrihari, 168
Mekong River, 33, 36, 50
Mendès-France, Pierre, 24–25, 29, 43, 48, 108, 228, 236, 238, 240, 241, 242, 243, 267, 268, 269, 270, 271, 272, 273, 274, 275, 276, 278, 279, 280, 281, 284–94, 295–300, 303, 307, 308, 309, 311, 323, 324, 330, 331, 332, 338, 343*n.*, 347, 348, 350, 351, 353, 357, 369, 370, 371, 376, 377, 378, 379, 387
Milliken, Eugene D., 80*n.*
Mitterand, François, 227
Moc Chau, 174
Moi Plateaus, 11*n.*
Molotov, Vyacheslav, 54, 55, 57, 123, 125, 128, 131, 133, 135, 153, 154, 155, 164, 165, 166, 167, 168, 169, 200, 201, 202, 203, 204, 205, 209, 225, 226, 227, 237, 239, 249, 252, 263, 275, 276, 278, 284, 286, 287, 290, 292, 293, 295, 296, 298–99, 308
Mons, Jean, 245
Montagnard Plateaus, 11*n.*
Morocco, 30, 42
Moutet, Marius, 10, 13*n.*
Mouvement Républicain Populaire (MRP), 14, 15, 43
Movement for the Defense of Peace, 385–86
MRP, *see* Mouvement Républicain Populaire
Muong Phalane, 51
Muong Phine, 51
Muong Soi, 52
Murphy, Robert, 188
Na Phao, 50
Na San, 39
Nam Dinh, 360
Nam Il, General, 122, 140
National Defense Committee, 18, 38, 61, 175, 178, 262
National Security Council, 143, 218, 341, 348
Nationalists, Vietnamese, 208
Navarre, General Henri, viii, 4, 10*n.*, 29*n.*, 33*n.*, 34, 36, 37, 38, 40, 43, 44, 45, 49, 50, 51, 52, 53, 59*n.*, 60, 61, 62, 65, 69, 70, 71, 72, 90, 94*n.*, 138, 139, 171, 172, 174*n.*, 176, 177, 178, 180, 181, 185, 308*n.*
Navarre Plan, 65, 72
Nehru, Jawaharlal, 66–67, 137, 144, 168, 352–53, 356
New York Herald Tribune, 140
New Zealand, 326
Nghia Lo, 32
Nghiem Van Tri, 34*n.*
Ngo Dinh Diem, 13, 15, 127, 224, 248, 249, 257, 280, 307, 332, 333, 334, 336, 337, 338, 339, 342, 343, 344, 345, 349, 365, 366, 371, 378, 379, 381, 382–93, 397
Ngo Dinh Nhu, 211, 223, 257
Ngo Dinh Thuc, 380
Nguyen Huu Tho, vii, 386
Nguyen Huu Tri, 379
Nguyen Quoc Dinh, 115, 212–13
Nguyen Van An, 385
Nguyen Van Chi, 32
Nguyen Van Duong, 386
Nguyen Van Hinh, 34, 337, 338, 339, 347, 348, 349, 361, 365, 367, 372, 382
Nguyen Van Tam, 41, 49, 378–79
Nguyen Van Thinh, 397
Nguyen Van Vi, 386
Nguyen Van Vy, General, 181, 338, 367, 372
Nguyen Van Xuan, 339
Nhiek Tioulong, General, 300*n.*
Ninh Binh, 27
Ninh Giang, 174
Nixon, Richard M., 53, 92, 193, 197, 242
Nomy, Admiral, 76*n.*, 245

Norodom Palace, 337
North Africa, 31, 42; French forces in, 23, 29
North Korea, 23*n*.
North Koreans, 122
North Vietnam, *see* Democratic Republic of Vietnam

O'Daniel, General John, 73, 373, 374
Offroy, Raymond, 130, 137
Operation Atlante, 60, 62, 71–89, 91, 92, 97, 302
Operation Auvergne, 262
Operation Castor, 44
Operation Mouette, 39, 44
Operation Vulture, vii, 83, 128, 130, 245

Pak Sane, 38
Pakistan, 326
Pakse, 51, 173
Palewski, M. J. P., 377
Panmunjom, 32, 34
Parodi, Alexandre, 212, 255, 307
Partition, 207, 224, 250, 259, 303–4
Partridge, General Earle E., 92
Pathet Lao, 153, 167, 202, 236, 253, 261, 291, 293, 306
Paul-Bancour, Jean, 131
Pearson, Lester, 208
Pélissié, General, 178
People's National Front, 320
Pham Anh, 281
Pham Huy Thong, 386
Pham Ngoc Thach, 5, 30*n*.
Pham Thieu, 384*n*., 387
Pham Van Dong, 11, 124, 125, 126, 154, 155, 156, 172, 202, 206, 207, 209, 213, 233, 237, 249, 250, 254, 255, 259, 260, 272, 281, 282, 289, 290, 292, 293, 295, 298, 308, 357, 358–59, 388, 390, 391
Phan Anh, 5, 11, 126, 360, 390
Phan Huy Quat, 211, 224
Phat Diem, 175, 235, 262, 303, 335
Phnom Penh, 305
Phong Saly, 306
Phu Ly, 174, 175
Pignon, Léon, 12*n*.
Pinay, Antoine, 32
Pineau, Christian, 377
Plain of Jars, 33, 52
Plas, Bernard de, 41
Pleven, René, 36, 43, 48, 60–70, 76, 105, 114*n*., 176, 177, 227
Poland, 263
Porte d'Annam, 38, 235, 308
Priest, J. Percy, 80*n*.
Prisoners of war, 304

Queuille, Henri, 29
Qui Nhon, 261

Radford, Admiral Arthur W., 39, 53, 68, 72, 74, 75, 78, 80, 81, 91, 92, 97, 193, 197, 216, 220*n*., 380
Raphaël-Leygues, Jacques, 33, 385, 390*n*.
Rassemblement du Peuple Français (RPF), 14, 34
Reading, Lord, 129
Red River delta, 27, 31, 32, 33, 38, 39, 44, 63, 64, 171, 172, 235, 268, 289
Repiton, Colonel, 312
Repiton-Preneuf, Colonel, 9, 13
Revers, General, 16, 22
Reynaud, Paul, 35, 36, 48, 55, 76*n*., 103, 114*n*., 137, 144, 158*n*., 177, 213
Rhee, Syngman, 220*n*., 323
Richards, James P., 373
Ridgway, General Matthew, 193, 217
Robertson, Walter S., 103, 111, 127, 297
"Roll Back," 323
Roux, Jacques, 130
RPF, *see* Rassemblement du Peuple, Français
Rusk, Dean, viii
Russell, Richard B., 80*n*.

Sainteny, Jean, 8, 9, 320, 352–60, 377*n*., 389
Salan, General Raoul, 8, 33, 36, 39*n*., 178, 182*n*., 195, 262
Sam Sary, 154, 296, 297, 298, 306
Samneua, 33, 306
Sarraut, Albert, 288, 308
Savary, Alain, 48–49

Schumann, Maurice, 12*n.*, 76*n.*, 77, 191, 194
SEATO, 326, 327–28, 390
Section Française de l'International Ouvrière (SFIO), 14
Security Council (U.N.), 211
Seno, 50, 52
"Seven Anglo-American Points," 266, 267, 274, 291, 307, 341
17th Parallel, 268, 293, 304, 308, 395, 397
SFIO, *see* Section Française de l'International Ouvrière
Sihanouk, Norodom, 5
16th Parallel, 138, 140, 250, 281, 285, 292, 293, 308
Smith, Alexander, 89*n.*
Smith, Walter Bedell, 95, 98, 127, 134, 154, 157, 167, 168*n.*, 190, 197, 203, 204, 214, 220, 238, 239, 247, 248, 269, 273, 288, 297, 303, 322, 344, 345, 346
Social Republicans, 145
Soustelle, Jacques, 228, 231*n.*
South East Asia Treaty Organization (SEATO), 326, 327–28, 390
South Vietnam, 127, 133, 134, 322, 324, 325, 332, 364
Southeast Asia pact, 321–22
Soviet Union, 23, 104, 133
Spellman, Francis Cardinal, 380
Stennis, John, 54

Ta Quang Buu, 5, 126, 232, 233, 235, 236, 237, 250, 259, 260, 261, 262, 299, 300*n.*, 303, 308
Tchepone, 51
Tep Phan, 284, 303
Thai area, 32, 38
Thai Binh, 175
Thailand, 109, 113, 211
Thakhek, 50
Thanh Hoa, 44
Thich Hue Quang, 386
13th Parallel, 260, 279, 308
Tonkin, 19, 28, 29, 33, 63, 139, 235, 278, 302
Tourane, 281
Tran Chan Thanh, 110*n.*, 115*n.*
Tran Cong Tuong, 126
Tran Huy Lieu, 11
Tran Kim Quan, 386
Tran Kim Tuyen, 334
Tran Trong Kim, 5
Tran Van Chuong, 5, 333
Tran Van Do, 127, 249, 280, 282, 288, 299, 303, 386
Tran Van Huu, 282
Tran Van Lam, 382*n.*
Trevelyan, Humphrey, 129
Trinh Dinh Thao, 386
Trinh Van Binh, 11
Trung Gia, 304, 318
Truong, Chinh, 27, 307
Tu Ve, 11
Tuan Giao, 51
Tunisia, 30, 42
Tuy Hoa, 60
Twining, General Nathan, 193, 217

"Unilateral declaration," 302, 303
Union of Soviet Socialist Republics 23, 104, 133
Unions des Republicains et d'Action Sociale (URAS), 145*n.*
United Nations, 211
United States, 42, 48, 52–54, 73–89, 108, 111–14, 208, 220, 321–22, 361–81
United States Consulate, Hanoi, 389
United States Military Group (MAAG), 349
URAS, 145*n.*

Valluy, General, 11, 17, 19, 219, 220
Vietminh, 7, 8, 17, 24, 31, 33, 44, 45*n.*, 47, 49, 50, 51, 52, 63, 65, 66, 76, 90, 95, 125, 126, 132, 133, 146, 155, 168, 207, 259–65, 278, 301, 307, 309, 363, 383; Chinese aid to, 65, 74, 102, 103
Vietnam, 166, 307; effects of war in, 23; *see also* Democratic Republic of Vietnam; South Vietnam
Vietnam Liberation Front, 7; *see also* Vietminh
Vietnamese, nationalist, 208
Vietnamese National Army, 23, 30, 34*n.*, 37, 64, 65, 347, 363, 365, 366, 367, 368, 371, 373, 376

Vietnamese People's Army (VPA), 4
Vinh Yen, 27
Vinogradov, Sergei, 106
Vo Nguyen Giap, 4, 8, 12, 24, 27, 33, 38, 44, 46, 47, 51, 90, 147, 148, 175, 182, 307, 318, 357, 390
VPA, *see* Vietnamese People's Army
Vu Hong Khanh, 8

Wan Waithayakon, 159
Wang Ping-nan, 130
Wiley, Alexander, 111*n*.
Willoughby, General, 216
Wilson, Charles E., 53, 190*n*., 193, 218, 219, 226*n*.

Yenan, 23*n*.

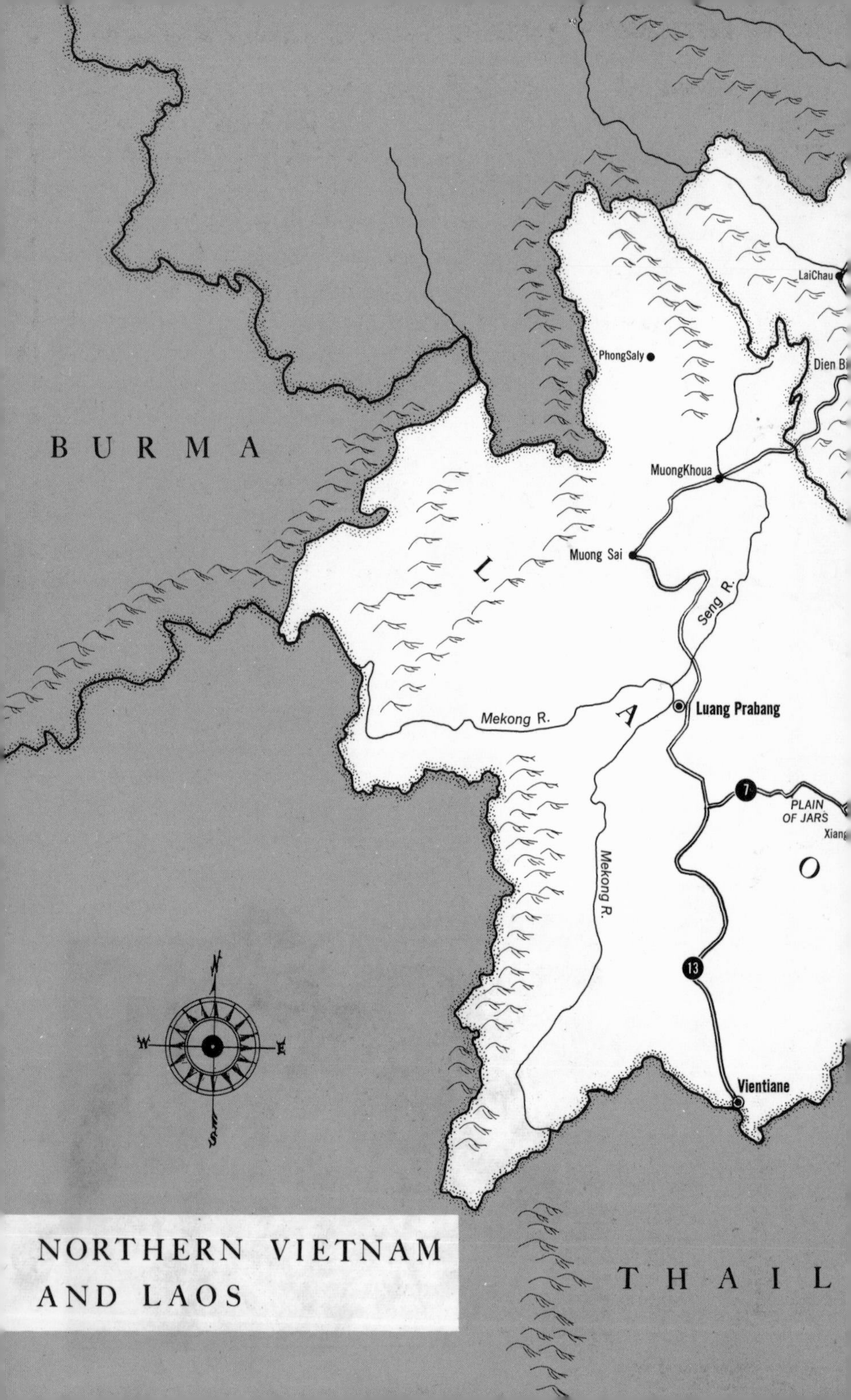

NORTHERN VIETNAM AND LAOS